Research as Transformative Learning for Sustainable Futures

Bold Visions in Educational Research

Series Editors

Kenneth Tobin (*The Graduate Center, City University of New York, USA*)
Carolyne Ali-Khan (*College of Education & Human Services, University of North Florida, USA*)

Co-founding Editor

Joe Kincheloe (with Kenneth Tobin)

Editorial Board

Daniel L. Dinsmore (*University of North Florida, USA*)
Barry Down (*School of Education, Murdoch University, Australia*)
Gene Fellner (*College of Staten Island, City University of New York, USA*)
L. Earle Reybold (*College of Education and Human Development, George Mason University, USA*)
Stephen Ritchie (*School of Education, Murdoch University, Australia*)

VOLUME 64

The titles published in this series are listed at *brill.com/bver*

Research as Transformative Learning for Sustainable Futures

Glocal Voices and Visions

Edited by

Peter Charles Taylor and Bal Chandra Luitel

BRILL
SENSE

LEIDEN | BOSTON

All chapters in this book have undergone peer review.

Library of Congress Cataloging-in-Publication Data

Names: Taylor, Peter Charles, editor. | Luitel, Bal Chandra, editor.
Title: Research as transformative learning for sustainable futures : glocal voices and visions / edited by Peter Charles Taylor and Bal Chandra Luitel.
Description: Leiden ; Boston : Brill Sense, [2019] | Series: Bold visions in educational research ; volume 64 | Includes bibliographical references.index.
Identifiers: LCCN 2018061026 (print) | LCCN 2019005473 (ebook) | ISBN 9789004393349 (ebook) | ISBN 9789004393332 (hardback : alk. paper) | ISBN 9789004393325 (pbk. : alk. paper)
Subjects: LCSH: Transformative learning. | Education and globalization. | Educational change. | Sustainability.
Classification: LCC LC1100 (ebook) | LCC LC1100 .R47 2019 (print) | DDC 370.11/5--dc23
LC record available at https://lccn.loc.gov/2018061026

ISSN 1879-4262
ISBN 978-90-04-39332-5 (paperback)
ISBN 978-90-04-39333-2 (hardback)
ISBN 978-90-04-39334-9 (e-book)

Copyright 2019 by Koninklijke Brill NV, Leiden, The Netherlands.
Koninklijke Brill NV incorporates the imprints Brill, Brill Hes & De Graaf, Brill Nijhoff, Brill Rodopi, Brill Sense, Hotei Publishing, mentis Verlag, Verlag Ferdinand Schöningh and Wilhelm Fink Verlag.
All rights reserved. No part of this publication may be reproduced, translated, stored in a retrieval system, or transmitted in any form or by any means, electronic, mechanical, photocopying, recording or otherwise, without prior written permission from the publisher.
Authorization to photocopy items for internal or personal use is granted by Koninklijke Brill NV provided that the appropriate fees are paid directly to The Copyright Clearance Center, 222 Rosewood Drive, Suite 910, Danvers, MA 01923, USA. Fees are subject to change.

This book is printed on acid-free paper and produced in a sustainable manner.

THE EARTH CHARTER

We stand at a critical moment in Earth's history, a time when humanity must choose its future. As the world becomes increasingly interdependent and fragile, the future at once holds great peril and great promise. To move forward we must recognize that in the midst of a magnificent diversity of cultures and life forms we are one human family and one Earth community with a common destiny. We must join together to bring forth a sustainable global society founded on respect for nature, universal human rights, economic justice, and a culture of peace. Towards this end, it is imperative that we, the peoples of Earth, declare our responsibility to one another, to the greater community of life, and to future generations.

http://earthcharter.org/discover/the-earth-charter/

CONTENTS

Preface ix

Acknowledgements xi

List of Figures and Tables xiii

1. Introduction: Research as Transformative Learning for Sustainable Futures 1
   Bal Chandra Luitel and Peter Charles Taylor

Part 1: Teaching & Learning Transformative Research

2. Journeying towards a Multi-Paradigmatic Transformative Research Program: An East-West Symbiosis 19
   Bal Chandra Luitel

3. Teaching and Learning Transformative Research: Complexity, Challenge and Change 39
   Peter Charles Taylor and Milton Norman Medina

Part 2: Contemplating Transformative Research Methods

4. Letter to Professor Auguste Comte: A Counter Narrative to Positivism 61
   Suresh Gautam

5. An Integral Perspective on Research: Methodological and Theoretical Journey of a Teacher Educator 75
   Binod Prasad Pant

6. Transforming Saudi Educators' Professional Practices: Critical Auto/Ethnography, an Islamic Perspective 89
   Naif Mastoor Alsulami

7. Contemplating My Autoethnography: From Idiosyncracy to Retrospection 109
   Shashidhar Belbase

Part 3: Transforming Culturally Situated Selves

8. Excavating My Cultural Identity: Promoting Local Culture and Stability in a Post/Colonial Era 129
   Alberto Felisberto Cupane

CONTENTS

9. Cultural-Self Knowing: Transforming Self and Others 147
   Sadruddin Bahadur Qutoshi

10. Where Do I Come From? What Am I? Where Am I Going? How the Grandson of a Mahayana Buddhism Priest Became a Science Educator 161
    Hisashi Otsuji

11. Being Animated by a Transformative Soul: Ethical Responsibility in Mathematics Education 173
    Mangaratua M. Simanjorang

12. Exorcising Satan from the Science Classroom: Ending the Hereditary Syndrome of Science Teaching in Malawi 187
    Doris Pilirani Mtemang'ombe

Part 4: Envisioning Transformative Pedagogies

13. A Reflective Journey within Five Ways of Transformative Knowing: Indonesia, Islam, International 207
    Neni Mariana

14. Facilitating Culturally De/Contextualised Mathematics Education: An Arts-Based Ethnodrama 225
    Indra Mani Shrestha

15. Unshackling from Cultural Hegemony via Third Spacing Pedagogy: Learning to Think Indigenously 239
    Indra Mani Rai (Yamphu)

16. Envisioning Creative Learning in Science Teacher Education: Currere, Emancipation and Creativity 251
    Siti Shamsiah Sani

Part 5: Sustaining Transformative Pedagogies

17. Returning Home: Key Challenges Facing a Transformative Educator 265
    Yuli Rahmawati

18. Transcending Boundaries: Enacting a Transformative Philosophy of Professional Practice 279
    Nalini Chitanand

19. Viewing Curriculum as Possibilities for Freedom: An Ndo'Nkodo of My Research Path 301
    Emilia Afonso Nhalevilo

Name Index 321

Subject Index 329

PREFACE

In this book we illustrate how prospective educational leaders from universities in Asian, African, Middle Eastern and South Pacific nations embraced multiple research paradigms to design and conduct transformative research inquiries in which they reconceptualised their philosophies of professional practice. By engaging in arts-based critical auto/ethnographic inquiries these university teacher educators gained critical understandings of the deep complexity of their culturally-framed professional lives. We learn how they struggled to overcome ingrained positivist epistemologies, how they undertook emergent inquiries armed with transgressive theoretical idea (l)s, how they used literary genres (e.g., poetry, ethnodrama) and visual imagery to foster critical reflexivity and imaginative thinking, and how they drew on faith-based traditions (Islam, Hinduism, Buddhism, Christianity) to expose the hegemony of the neo-colonial Western modern worldview and envision alternative philosophies of practice for promoting the cultural diversity of their respective countries.

Introduction
In the opening chapter, we map the rationale and scope of the book: from the problem of diminishing cultural diversity due to the hegemony of the Western modern worldview, to how research as transformative learning can enable educational leaders to develop culturally inclusive philosophies of professional practice.

Part 1: Teaching and Learning Transformative Research
In these chapters we explain our development and teaching of research as transformative learning, and include the voice of an initially resistant student.

Part 2: Contemplating Transformative Research Methods
Chapter authors discuss how they designed multi-paradigm methodologies for undertaking research as transformative learning in their diverse cultural contexts.

Part 3: Transforming Culturally Situated Selves
Chapter authors portray their deep engagement in research as transformative learning as they excavated and reconceptualised their culturally situated lives and professional practices.

Part 4: Envisioning Transformative Pedagogies
Chapter authors present a range of culturally responsive pedagogies as key outcomes of their research inquiries.

Part 5: Sustaining Transformative Pedagogies
Our book concludes with chapter authors discussing their strategies to gain traction for transformative pedagogies in their teacher education programs.

ACKNOWLEDGEMENTS

In their roles as 'sub editors' of this book, Binod Prasad Pant and Suresh Gautam, faculty members of the School of Education, Kathmandu University, Nepal, provided valuable assistance in reviewing draft chapters and compiling the Name Index.

In her role as production coordinator for Brill Sense, Jolanda Karada enabled us to readily navigate the complex requirements of formatting and cover design.

As inaugural members of the International Transformative Educational Research Network (ITERN), our chapter authors' contributions signify exemplary professional leadership in teacher education programs across Asia, Africa and the Pacific. Their ongoing endeavours lie at the heart of an intergenerational struggle to ensure young people develop the essential capabilities, courage and commitment to live and work sustainably in a rapidly globalising world.

FIGURES AND TABLES

FIGURES

3.1.	Research paradigm emergence	44
7.1.	Anjila's play with lego models	113
9.1.	Multi-paradigmatic research design space	151
11.1.	Integrative ethics based on awareness, respect and critical thinking	180
11.2.	Drawing hands, by M. C. Escher	182
13.1.	The cycle of five ways of transformative knowing	211
13.2.	3I mathematics	221
16.1.	Integration of curriculum as agenda for social reconstruction, emancipatory interest, and creative learning	258
16.2.	Outline of the activity for the scientific investigation theme	260
18.1.	Strategies for uncovering assumptions	293

TABLES

8.1.	Triadic form of dialectical thinking	132
8.2.	Essentialism and nonessentialism	136
8.3.	Essentialism, nonessentialism and non/essentialism	140

BAL CHANDRA LUITEL AND PETER CHARLES TAYLOR

1. INTRODUCTION: RESEARCH AS TRANSFORMATIVE LEARNING FOR SUSTAINABLE FUTURES

We instinctively know, with no need for explanation, that maintaining a connection with the unique character of our historic and natural environment, with the language, the music, the arts and the literature, which accompanied us throughout our life, is fundamental for our spiritual wellbeing and for providing a sense of who we are. There is an intrinsic value of culture to a society, irrespective of its place in the human development index, which is apparent to everyone and which makes it a development outcome in itself. (UNESCO, n.d.a)

Internal transformation requires an integration of those thought-currents of the East and West that are now heading for the rise of planetary worldview, a world centric consciousness, and a global conscience for taking side with life, with righteousness, with compassion, with human dignity. (Beg, 2000, p. 24)

Welcome to the future of education, fueled by a transformative perspective on how research as transformative learning can help prepare future generations to resolve the global sustainability crises of our rapidly changing world!

EDUCATION AND WORLDVIEW

The world is undergoing rapid modernization as we enter the *fourth industrial revolution,* characterized by emerging digital technologies, artificial intelligence, DNA mapping, robotics, nanotechnologies, 3D printing, biotechnologies, and the internet of things (Infosys, 2016). Beginning in the 16th century, a much slower process of modernization occurred as European powers invaded, colonized and subjugated indigenous and local civilizations in Africa, Asia, Australasia and the Americas. Today, the digital era of high speed communications is accelerating the global reach of modernity.

Loss of Cultural Diversity

Although nearly all major political powers withdrew from their overseas territories during the 20th century, the colonial project did not necessarily leave with them. It morphed into subtle forms of *neo-colonialism* (Nkrumah, 1966) which govern

© KONINKLIJKE BRILL NV, LEIDEN, 2019 | DOI:10.1163/9789004393349_001 the social, political and economic policies and practices of many newly *independent* nations, as well as those that were never directly occupied (such as Nepal) but were subject to "economic, cultural and (to varying degrees) political penetration" (Loomba, 2005, p. 12) by their colonised neighbours (e.g., British India). Cultural studies researchers warn that neo-colonialism devalues indigenous knowledge systems (Aikenhead & Michell, 2011) and "renders the cultural identity and experiences of the Other invisible" (Mutua & Swadener, 2004, p. 209). During the 20th century, and continuing today, a major vector of neo-colonialism has been the Western education export industry and its international benchmarking systems, such as TIMMS and PISA.

For any nation of non-Western heritage, buying into a global one-size-fits-all education system can be a Faustian bargain. On the one hand, modern education is designed to produce a highly skilled workforce essential for improving a nation's infrastructure, social services, and material standard of living. On the other hand, the absence of local cultural capital in imported curricula contributes to loss of cultural and linguistic diversity, especially in monolingual English-speaking international schools.

Linguistic extinction has been recognised as the major contributor to the loss of humanity's *library* of indigenous wisdom, as evidenced in The Index of Linguistic Diversity (Harmon & Loh, 2010), and thus to a breakdown in the spiritual link between humans and Nature (Nadarajah, 2014). The importance of the interrelationship between language, culture and the natural environment (i.e., *biocultural diversity*) has been documented by UNESCO, The World Wide Fund for Nature, and Terralingua.

> In the language of ecology, the strongest ecosystems are those that are the most diverse. That is, diversity is directly related to stability; variety is important for long-term survival. Our success on this planet has been due to an ability to adapt to different kinds of environment over thousands of years (atmospheric as well as cultural). Such ability is born out of diversity. Thus language and cultural diversity maximises chances of human success and adaptability. (Skutnabb-Kanga, Maffi, & Harmon, 2003, p. 10)

Along with anthropogenic climate change, loss of ecosystems and biodiversity, industrial pollution of our air, soil, rivers and oceans (especially by highly invasive plastic waste), unfettered economic growth (Jackson, 2009), proliferation of nuclear weapons, militant religious fundamentalism, highly divisive politics, ultra-nationalism and chauvinistic elitism, we are facing unparalleled crises at a global level that are seriously challenging the future of life on our planet; causing us to rethink what it means to be human (Baldwin, 2017).

Education for Sustainable Development

As the Doomsday Clock – now set at two minutes to midnight – signals impending global catastrophe (Bulletin of Atomic Scientists, 2018), and as governments struggle to unite in a coherent international effort to respond meaningfully, the role of education has become paramount in helping to resolve arguably the greatest ethical challenge of modern times: *sustainable development*.

For decades, UNESCO (n.d.b) has been urging the world to reverse these destructive global trends by embracing *education for sustainable development*, based on the United Nations' three pillars of sustainability: society, environment and economy (ECOSOC, 2018). However, UNESCO (n.d.c) recognises that although "placing culture at the heart of our strategies is both the condition for enabling sustainable development, and a powerful driving factor for its achievement", much remains to be achieved in integrating cultural identities and values into sustainable development policies and practices, including education for sustainable development.

Education for sustainable development is not a simple process of inculcating new knowledge and skills; rather, it involves transforming the learner's habituated ways of knowing, acting and valuing (Fien, 2003). Ervin Laszlo (2008) argues that fostering heightened consciousness based on an ethic of planetary stewardship should be the goal of education for sustainable development. It makes good sense, therefore, that curricula and pedagogies that aim to facilitate education for sustainable development need to integrate disciplinary knowledge and skills, values education, and citizenship education (Settelmaier, 2009; Taylor, Taylor, & Chow, 2013).

The premise of this book is that education for sustainable development is essential to help resolve our proliferating global crises, especially the worldwide decline in cultural diversity, which is the main focus of our chapter authors. Our holistic notion of sustainability aligns with Paolo Freire's view that a socially just, equitable, Nature-friendly, and conscientization-driven planetary system is needed if we are to ameliorate the global crises faced by humanity (Ferreira, 2017).

Education's Economic Imperative

However, Western science and mathematics education (now being widely incorporated with engineering and technology disciplines as STEM education) is too narrowly focused on the goal of (sustainable?) economic development; thereby, turning a blind eye to the equally important sustainable development pillars: the natural environment and the culturally diverse social world.

As teacher educators with backgrounds in science and mathematics education, we believe that education (and STEM education, in particular) can and should help to provide a sustainable development pathway through the ongoing chaos, complexity and confusion by preparing young people; not only to be job-ready for the *gig economy* but, equally importantly, to be socially aware and responsible citizens capable of thinking globally and acting locally, willing to exercise their democratic rights to make the world a better place for all sentient and non-sentient beings, as heralded by The Earth Charter (2001).

However, the task is far from easy because science and mathematics education remains highly resilient to fundamental change. During the latter part of the 20th century, powerful theories drawn from sociology and psychology (e.g., constructivism) were imported to address major shortcomings in teaching and learning practices (Taylor, 2015a). The result was to marginally reform science and mathematics education to be more *student-centred*; overall, more *punctuated equilibrium* than revolutionary change. The prevailing science and mathematics education paradigm, which frames the transmission of objective theoretical knowledge and confirmatory problem-solving skills, has largely resisted recent calls by visionary curriculum reformers to develop students' *transdisciplinary capabilities* – critical reflection, ethical understanding, empathic communication, creative thinking, communicative competence, collaborative decision-making, intercultural awareness – that are part and parcel of education for participating in the new digital economy and for living sustainably (ACARA, 2016; Gonski et al., 2018).

For example, Australian government-funded STEM education initiatives overlook sustainability in favor of harnessing innovative digital technologies to develop young people's information and technology capability (Birmingham, 2018). This is serving a largely economic imperative; a necessary course of action but one that is wholly insufficient.

Western Modern Worldview

A major reason for the resilience of the established science and mathematics education paradigm is its historical embeddedness in the powerful *Western modern worldview* that arose in Europe during the Enlightenment, or Age of Reason (Carroll, 2004), and which fueled European colonialism. This universalist worldview holds that Nature is subordinate to the so-called triumph of human reason (i.e., anthropocentrism) and that each of material/spirit, object/subject and fact/value are incommensurable dichotomies (i.e., *dualism*) (Christians, 2005). Culture studies researchers (e.g., Abrams, Taylor, & Guo, 2013) argue that the fundamental premises of the Western modern worldview severely constrain the possibility of reconceptualising modern STEM education policy and practice, including educational research:

- an ontology of *materialism* that regards mind-independent matter as the only reality in the world, and is blind to spirituality, values, aesthetics, ethics, and emotionality.
- an epistemology of *positivism* that drives a wedge of objectivity between the observer and the supposedly mechanical universe.
- a *neo-colonial* and essentialist predisposition of deficit thinking about the cultural capital of the culturally different (e.g., Eastern, indigenous) other.
- a strategic alliance with the economic growth imperatives of *capitalism* to produce a social elite of scientists and researchers, industry and military leaders, engineers and doctors, and STEM teachers, amongst others.

These grand narrative premises are grounded in historic Eurocentric notions of society, the culturally reproductive function of schooling, and philosophically insufficient empiricist views of the nature of science. They have long acted in concert, mostly at a subliminal level, to shape normative Western science and mathematics education policy and practice, including the positivist epistemology of educational research (Denzin & Lincoln, 2000; Taylor, 2011). Globalization of the Western science and mathematics education paradigm has contributed to eliminating cultural difference worldwide, thereby threatening the sustainability of non-Western worldviews (Ladson-Billings, 2000).

The basic premises of the Western modern worldview – unemotional objectivity, material reality, value-neutral facts – are at odds with Eastern and indigenous wisdom traditions in which an aesthetic, intuitive, spiritual relationship connects humans and Nature (i.e., *nondualism*), giving rise to moral and ethical values that govern sustainable development practices (Chakrabarti, 2004; Cheon, 2018; Nadarajah, 2014). This nondual perspective resonates strongly with the ethicist, Christian Becker (2012), who argues that "Sustainability ethics requires at its basis a certain concept of the human being as an emotional, rational, creative, communicative, and fundamentally relational being" (p. 80).

Thus, for sustainable development (economic, cultural, and environmental) to be successful, education systems worldwide need to: (i) deconstruct the hegemony of the Western modern worldview; (ii) explore *bridges* between Western and Eastern (and indigenous) worldviews (Aikenhead & Michell, 2011; Beg, 2005); and (iii) enrich STEM with the Arts (i.e., STEAM) to develop students' transdisciplinary capabilities (Taylor, 2018).

In teacher education we need to embrace the worldviews of all students as we strive to prepare 21st century educators who can develop and implement culturally inclusive policies and practices that facilitate sustainable development of local cultural capital and the natural environment, while also serving the economic development needs of their respective nations (UNESCO, 2005). This book provides a model of transformative professional development for achieving this goal.

TRANSFORMATIVE LEARNING

Resolving global sustainable development challenges requires future citizens who can act ethically, critically and imaginatively in conceiving, developing and implementing visions for a sustainable planet. To produce such competent and ethically astute citizens we need to radically restructure education systems in accordance with the metaphor of *education as cultural reconstruction*. A paradigm shift is required that reconceptualises the purpose of education as addressing both global and local perspectives: a *glocalized* education (Robertson, 1995). In our endeavor to achieve this goal, we have developed an approach to postgraduate professional development that engages participants in the experience of transformative learning to develop transdisciplinary capabilities (Luitel, 2018; Taylor, 2013).

Transformative learning has its roots in the scholarly work of Jack Mezirow (1991) who drew on philosophers such as John Dewey and Jurgen Habermas to reveal how our perspectives are subject to epistemic, sociocultural and psychological constraints that restrict the way we make sense of our experience of the world. Recognising that we have limited ability to participate fully as creative, communicative and self-determining agents in the processes of democracy, Mezirow and colleagues have articulated theories of transformative learning that enable us to develop our innate potential and become more fully human (Taylor, Cranton, & Associates, 2012) by expanding conscious awareness of our situatedness in the world in order to understand deeply who we are and who we might yet become, as individuals and as social beings:

> …experiencing a deep, structural shift in the basic premises of thought, feelings, and actions. It is a shift of consciousness that dramatically and permanently alters our way of being in the world. Such a shift involves our understanding of ourselves and our self-locations; our relationships with other humans and with the natural world; our understanding of relations of power in interlocking structures of class, race, and gender; our body-awareness; our visions of alternative approaches to living; our sense of possibilities for social justice and peace and personal joy. (Morrell & O'Connor, 2002, p. xvii)

Transformative learning involves using cognitive, emotional, social and spiritual *tools* to reconceptualise and reshape this relationship. Heightened consciousness can be attained by developing higher-order abilities: critical awareness and critical self-reflection, ethical and political astuteness, empathy and compassion, and visionary and altruistic perspectives (Taylor, 2015b). These higher-order abilities are essential for future community leaders to resolve complex ethical dilemmas arising from competing interests associated with issues of sustainable development (Taylor, Taylor, & Chow, 2013).

East-West Reconciliation

The literature of Western and Eastern wisdom traditions supports our embrace of transformative learning (McLaren & Kincheloe, 2007; Shivanand, 2018). As the Sufi scholar, Moazziz Ali Beg (2005), argues: "To achieve unity between men, we must cultivate unity within ourselves: to enact a unity, we must have a vision of it before our eyes" (p. 217). Since time immemorial, we have been evolving in many ways. The Upanishads mention that we can change ourselves to come out of the conditions and conditionalities of birth-death cycles. We do not just change ourselves; rather we have the capacity to change others. For millennia, the Guru-disciple relationship has been presented as a model for enabling liberation from the illusions of day-to-day conditionalities. Transformative processes are impactful on our thinking and actions as the shift in thinking is likely to be demonstrated in our daily actions. Because the change may be very subtle, we need to develop a heightened consciousness in order to perceive it. However, the transformative process is not linear, easily predictable, and one-size-fits-all; rather, it is a multi-pronged, multi-dimensional and multi-paradigmatic process.

INTRODUCTION

All chapter authors of this book engaged in transformative learning under the influence of the poignant question of Parker Palmer (1998): *who is the self that teaches?* This question focused their research inquiries, enabling them to examine contradictions, dilemmas and paradoxes embedded in their thinking and actions, beliefs and advocacy, and personal and professional values. By addressing this question, one can deepen self-understanding as an educational practitioner and develop a vision for an empowering, agentic and inclusive education system that is meaning-centred, life-affirming, and inclusive of practices arising from wide-ranging cultural lifeworlds. In their inquiries these practitioner researchers heeded the transformative call of Mahatma Gandhi: *be the change you want to see in the world*. This defining feature renders the primacy of the practitioner researcher's identity reconstruction as a social change agent (Kincheloe & Pinar, 1991).

In designing their research studies, these practitioner researchers created a mix of contemporary research paradigms and methods, such as auto/ethnography, narrative inquiry, arts-based research, self-study, critical inquiry, and philosophical inquiry. Their hybrid epistemic inquiries drew on their faith-based wisdom traditions – Muslim, Hindu, Kiranti (Rai), Buddhist, Christian – to bring their cultural capital into the foreground of their inquiries, enabling them to contest the hegemony of the Western modern worldview and envision culturally contextualised education policies and practices better suited to their diverse national aspirations. These exemplars of culturally-embedded research inquiries are likely to enable researchers who hold a diverse range of worldviews to see their own cultural ways of knowing to be as legitimate as the mainstream epistemologies developed in Western universities.

TRANSFORMATIVE RESEARCH

Our transformative research approach engages educational practitioners in research *as* a transformative learning experience *for* the purpose of transforming their professional practices, and thus the lives of future generations.

This *activist* approach draws on resistance education research (McLaren, 2005), critical reflective inquiry (Freire, Freire, & Macedo, 1998), arts-based critical inquiry (Barone & Eisner, 2006), critical autoethnography (Ellis, 2004), mindful inquiry (Bentz & Shapiro, 1998) and philosophical inquiry (Greene, 1997). Research as transformative professional development enables practitioners to deconstruct the hegemonic grip of the Western modern worldview on their everyday practices as a basis for envisioning culturally inclusive education systems. In the opening chapters we explain how, as educational practitioners, we have come to understand the unique power of transformative research to revitalize education at this critical moment in history as a paradigm shift transforms societies around the world.

As Thomas Kuhn (1962) famously explained, a paradigm shift is a revolutionary social act that disrupts the status quo and involves critical scrutiny of existing norms (i.e., frames of reference that give rise to our basic assumptions). Such was the case with the transformation of perspective and practice from the mechanistic worldview of Isaac Newton to Albert Einstein's relativistic worldview. This radical shift occurred because of intractable problems inherent in the prevailing Newtonian paradigm, giving rise to ontologically counterintuitive paradigms such as relativity and quantum theory (Omnès, 1999; Rae, 2004). These new paradigms have opened up a discourse between Eastern (e.g., Buddhist and Vedantic) and Western scholars, especially in relation to the nature of human consciousness, with exciting commonalities being discovered (e.g., Ricard & Thuan, 2001).

Multi-Paradigm Research

In the field of educational research, a transdisciplinary paradigm shift has been underway since the 1980s due to perceived limitations of the prevailing positivist paradigm. New research paradigms – *interpretivism, criticalism, postmodernism,* and *integralism* – have offered new epistemologies of practice (i.e., ways of knowing, being, valuing and acting) for researchers (Taylor & Medina, 2013). This transdisciplinary perspective, which "starts with the logic of everyday actions rather than with traditional scientific disciplines" (Werlen, 2015, p. 11), has democratized research by placing it in the hands of practitioner researchers, empowering them as social activists and change agents. Following the *vision-logic* of philosopher Ken Wilber (2007), transformative research adopts an integral perspective that enables researchers to design multi-paradigmatic inquiries aimed, ultimately, at transforming educational policy and practice (Taylor, Taylor, & Luitel, 2012).

Taking the ethical view of *beneficence*, we argue that educational research as transformative professional development contributes to achieving sustainable development in four ways.

- Practitioner researchers are enabled to become lifelong learners who reflect critically on their societal roles as citizens, teachers, teacher educators, and social activists so as to address global crises through their engagement in educational processes.
- Through various scholarly approaches embedded in research as transformative professional development, practitioners are prepared to take educational action (e.g., developing curricula, implementing pedagogies, initiating structural change) in their personal and professional contexts.
- Because of our mentoring focus on critical thinking (i.e., what are the shortcomings of our educational processes?) and creative thinking (i.e., what can be done to overcome these shortcomings?), transformative practitioners do not invest in being cynical or unduly skeptical; rather, they generate culturally contextualized solutions to the pressing problems faced by humanity.
- One of the major outcomes of research as/for transformative professional development is to develop practitioners capable of looking into and reassessing their own culturally-situated ethical standpoints through critical reflective practice.

INTRODUCTION

Over the past 35 years working in graduate centres in Australian and Asian universities, we have taught transformative research courses and mentored hundreds of students undertaking transformative research studies. We have been fortunate that our students – professional school teachers and university teacher educators – have brought with them distinctive worldviews from Nepal, Indonesia, Thailand, Japan, Singapore, Pakistan, Mozambique, South Africa, Malawi, Saudi Arabia, and the Philippines. As chapter authors of this book, these professional educators share their unique experiences of designing transformative research studies to examine their deeply rooted beliefs and practices, transforming their culturally situated selves, envisioning transformative pedagogies, and endeavoring to sustain them on return to their home universities where they have been confronted by varying forms of normative resistance.

Pedagogical Challenges

Engaging postgraduate students in an epistemological paradigm shift, especially professional STEM educators, can be a challenging pedagogical task. Typically, at an early stage in their careers nearly all have been indoctrinated into the objectivist epistemology of the positivistic paradigm. As the default paradigm for postgraduate research, positivism does not provide space to raise the consciousness of researchers about the hegemonic nature of culturally disempowering educational processes or enable them to develop a vision of a culturally inclusive and agentic education system. The positivistic assumption of *determinism* influences researchers to respond with instrumental rationality to social environments, thereby restricting the nature and scope of their roles (Literat, 2016). Such a totalising perspective (or narrow methodological prescription) does not empower postgraduate researchers to exercise the free will necessary to reflect critically on their personal and professional experiences and to re-envision their future practices.

We have struggled long and hard to develop empowering teaching approaches that enable our postgraduate students to embrace the counterintuitive power of the newer research paradigms. See Chapters 2 and 3 on our experience of developing and implementing transformative teaching approaches. Here we present a brief overview of transformative research methods that we employ to engage our research students in transformative learning (For a fuller account see Taylor, Taylor, & Luitel, 2012; Taylor, 2014).

Ideology critique. To counter the hegemonic grip of positivism, we strive to enable our postgraduate research students to expose and critique the realist ontology's limited possibility for articulating their unfolding *selves* during the research process. As they come to understand how the epistemology of objectivism provides a disempowering notion of what counts as social reality and restricts them from developing a vision of *what is possible*, we engage them in critical self-reflection as a basis for knowing who they are going to become as transformative professionals.

Narrative writing. We invite our postgraduate researchers to exercise their free will by articulating their research problems through writing narratives of their lifeworlds. Such an ontology-driven activity is strengthened through exposure to multiple research paradigms that allow them to generate *thick descriptions* of their personal-professional practices (i.e., interpretivism), to develop their professional praxis through critical self-reflection (i.e., criticalism), and to utilise arts-based methods in making sense of and expressing their unfolding subjectivities (i.e., postmodernism) (Luitel & Taylor, 2011).

Cultivating cultural values. Because the (seemingly) value-neutral regime of the positivistic research paradigm is unhelpful for promoting research that aims to cultivate passion, feelings and vision, we enable our postgraduate researchers to develop their axiological standpoints as activist researchers. We encourage them to unpack how/why they find their professional identities to be in conflict with the core values they grew up with in their (e.g., Asian, African, Arabic) cultures that promote ecological well-being, symbiosis of materiality and spirituality, and learning by embodiment.

Arts-based logics and genres. The positivistic paradigm is enacted by means of the logics of proposition, deduction and analysis, and is enforced by the assumption that these are the only legitimate thinking and representational tools at our disposal, a key stumbling block for enabling practitioner researchers to unpack phenomena under study. The exclusive use of propositional logic enslaves researchers to narrowly expressed syllogisms, deductive logic serves to reproduce pre-existing theories and perspectives, while the logic of analysis employs divisive dualisms in making knowledge claims (Willis, 2007). In order to loosen the hegemonic grip of exclusionary logics and genres, we enable our postgraduate researchers to draw from the postmodern arts-based research paradigm to develop and employ dialectical, narrative, poetic and metaphorical logics and genres (Luitel & Taylor, 2013).

Dialectical logic. We value dialectical logic as a means for engaging productively (rather than eliminating) contradictions imbued in *either-or* dualistic logic in order to generate synergistic and complementary perspectives. Conceived as useful for addressing everyday contradictions, dialectical logic can be portrayed as the logic of *and*, meaning that sometimes opposing entities should be allowed to co-exist in our lived reality (Edwards, 2011).

Metaphorical logic. We employ metaphorical logic to enable practitioner researchers to engage in multi-schema envisioning, using elastic correspondence (cf. one-to-one correspondence theory of truth) between conflicting schemas to capture the complexity of a phenomenon or event. Metaphorical logic is used also to explore the meaning of concepts and ideas otherwise hidden in the narrowness of literalism. This logic offers a platform for thinking and acting through perspectival *as-thoughs* to minimise extreme essentialism embedded in the positivistic research tradition (Joanna, 2011).

INTRODUCTION

Poetic logic. Transformative research offers a space for poetic logic and genres as a basis for exploring nonreal, felt, mythical, perceptual, imagistic and atypical realities otherwise neglected by hypothetico-deductive logic, thereby disrupting the stereotypical view of research as producing *real* (i.e., not fictive), *clean* (i.e., not messy), and unequivocal texts (Faulkner, 2007). We have experienced how narrative logic and genres are important means for thinking through multiple dimensions of researchers' lifeworlds as they promote *post/reductionist* thinking that integrates place, people, action, and time in generating *diachronic* research texts. Embedded in the traditions of world cultures, diachronic vision enables practitioner researchers to make their narratives intelligible by mapping transpired moments of their unfolding inquiries across space and time.

Visual genres. We take visual genres as incorporating photographs, paintings, cartoons, collage and creative models, to name a few. We employ these genres to demonstrate the multi-vocal, embodied and nonlinear nature of knowledge claims. Such nonlinguistic genres permit researchers to represent particulars, peculiarities and extraordinariness otherwise distorted through the mediative process of linguistic textuality (Butler-Kisber, 2008).

Quality standards. Another major challenge lies in enabling researchers to identify quality standards for transformative research inquiries that explore the complex, dynamic, fluid and ever-changing lifeworlds of educational practitioners. Because the positivistic standards of validity and reliability are epistemologically irrelevant for judging the quality of the process and product of research as reconceptualising professional praxis, we facilitate our postgraduate researchers to address quality standards from multiple research paradigms, such as: incisiveness, illuminating, and verisimilitude in postmodernism; credibility and transferability in interpretivism; and pedagogical thoughtfulness, critical reflexivity, and ideology critique in criticalism, to name but a few (Taylor, 2014).

ENCOUNTERING RESISTANCE

Not surprisingly, when newly graduated transformative educators return to their workplaces and passionately endeavor to exercise their roles of change agents, they encounter resistance (and/or indifference) from their institutions, colleagues, and students. This has been our experience in breaking new ground in the postgraduate programs of our departments of teacher education. Reflecting on our collective experience, we have identified four major challenges that transformative educators are likely to encounter.

Cultural Mismatch

Graduates of transformative research programs are likely to encounter a cultural mismatch between what they have learned to become – transformed professionals committed to education for sustainable development – and what they experience on return to their teacher education programs. Institutional cultural practices are often expressed in the form of hierarchical and bureaucratic power relations. In many cases, resistance by management (i.e., elitism) dismisses the legitimacy of local wisdom traditions in favor of the imperatives of the Western modern worldview, an attitude known to postcolonial scholars as *comprador intelligentsia* (Fanon, 1986). Facing the prevailing attitude of business-as-usual, recently returned graduates can be blamed for being professionally unrealistic in their desire to promote education for sustainable development of local communities.

Epistemological Clash

The second challenge is epistemological. Transformative research graduates face resistance to their promotion of research as transformative learning because of the prevailing positivistic view of research as testing a priori hypotheses. Hostilities may develop as colleagues' state forcefully in research forums that research as transformative learning is not considered to be legitimate research. This view can be held by seemingly innovative researchers who favor qualitative research methods which, on close examination, often turn out to be framed (invisibly) by the post-positivist paradigm (Taylor, 2014). Likewise, *cryptopositivism* embedded (invisibly) in *mixed-methods* research makes it difficult for transformative researchers to promote epistemological debates and discussions (Kincheloe & Tobin, 2009). Because research funding regimes and institutional productivity demands are very much tied to the positivist language of *hypothesis testing, data analysis* and *research findings*, transformative researchers can encounter difficulties in participating in this dominant language game.

Pedagogical

The third challenge is pedagogical. Transformative research graduates are likely to teach research methods courses to postgraduate students who hold (tightly to) a fixed set of beliefs and habits about teaching and learning shaped by conventional didactic (i.e. teacher-centred) educational practices. So, attempts to introduce a pedagogical approach informed by transformative learning can meet student resistance. For example, inviting students to be critical of their personal-professional practices takes many to the edge of (and perhaps beyond) their established comfort zones. In attempting to transform resistant attitudes of conformist learners, transformative research graduates will be at risk of disillusioning (perhaps losing) some students. Because research as transformative learning demands a deep and prolonged engagement for both research student and mentor/supervisor, sustaining the student's prolonged commitment to complete the research at a high standard of self-evaluation, can be yet another challenge.

INTRODUCTION

Associational

The fourth major challenge is associational. Although transformative research graduates are keen to expand their professional networks, they may not find a compatible local peer group and so feel the need to compromise in accordance with their colleagues' normative agendas. Working in relative intellectual isolation they are less likely to communicate their ideas freely and may not be able to further develop their transformative teaching and research capabilities unless they take part in a broader network.

In the final part of this book, three experienced transformative educators explain how they developed strategies to deal with these and other challenges experienced in their universities in Mozambique, South Africa and Indonesia.

REFERENCES

Abrams, E., Taylor, P. C., & Guo, C. J. (2013). Contextualizing culturally relevant science and mathematics teaching for indigenous learning. *International Journal of Science and Mathematics Education, 11*(1), 1–21. Retrieved from http://link.springer.com/journal/10763/11/1/page/1

ACARA. (2016). *Australian curriculum: General capabilities*. Australian Curriculum Assessment and Reporting Authority. Retrieved from http://www.acara.edu.au/curriculum/general-capabilities

Aikenhead, G., & Michell, M. (2011). *Bridging cultures: Indigenous and scientific ways of knowing nature*. Toronto: Pearson Canada.

Baldwin, A. (2017). Climate change, migration, and the crisis of humanism. *Wiley Interdisciplinary Reviews: Climate Change, 8*(3), e460. doi:10.1002/wcc.460

Barone, T., & Eisner, E. (2006). Arts-based educational research. In J. L. Green, G. Camilli, & P. B. Elmore (Eds.), *Handbook of complementary methods in education research* (pp. 93–107). New York, NY: Lawrence Erlbaum Associates.

Becker, C. U. (2012). *Sustainability ethics and sustainability research*. Dordrecht: Springer.

Beg, M. A. (2005). *The ideological integration of East and West: An enquiry concerning world peace*. Daryaganj: Global Vision Publishing House.

Bentz, V. M., & Shapiro, J. J. (1998). *Mindful inquiry in social research*. Thousands Oaks, CA: Sage Publications.

Birmingham, S. (2018). *New initiative to enhance STEM leaders in our schools*. Retrieved from https://ministers.education.gov.au/birmingham/new-initiative-enhance-stem-leaders-our-schools

Bulletin of the Atomic Scientists. (2018). *The doomsday clock: A time of conflict, culture, and change*. Retrieved from https://thebulletin.org/doomsday-clock

Butler-Kisber, L. (2008). Collage as inquiry. In J. G. Knowles & A. L. Cole (Eds.), *Handbook of arts in qualitative research* (pp. 265–276). Thousand Oaks, CA: Sage Publications.

Carroll, J. (2004). *The wreck of Western culture: Humanism revisited*. Melbourne: Scribe Publications.

Chakrabarti, P. (2004). *Western science in modern India: Metropolitan methods, colonial practices*. New Delhi: Permanent Black.

Cheon, Y.-C. (2018). *Overviews of Western and Eastern worldviews*. Institute of Communication for Life. Retrieved from http://www.lifecommunication.org/2010/03/overviews-of-western-and-eastern.html

Christians, C. G. (2005). Ethics and politics in qualitative research. In N. K. Denzin & Y. S. Lincoln (Eds.) *The Sage handbook of qualitative research* (3rd ed., pp. 139–164). Thousand Oaks, CA: Sage Publications.

Denzin, N. K., & Lincoln, Y. S. (2000). Introduction: The discipline and practice of qualitative research. In N. K. Denzin & Y. S. Lincoln (Eds.), *Handbook of qualitative research* (2nd ed.). Thousand Oaks, CA: Sage Publications.

Earth Charter Commission. (2001). *The Earth Charter*. Retrieved from http://earthcharter.org/biblio-category/the-earth-charter/

ECOSOC. (2018). *Sustainable development*. United Nations Economic and Social Council. Retrieved from https://www.un.org/ecosoc/en/sustainable-development

Edwards, G. (2011). The past and future inside the present: Dialectical thinking and the transformation of teaching. *Journal for Critical Education Policy Studies, 9*(2), 43–59.

Ellis, C. (2004). *The ethnographic I: A methodological novel about autoethnography*. Walnut Creek, CA: AltaMira Press.

Fanon, F. (1986). *Black skin, White masks*. London: Pluto Press.

Faulkner, S. L. (2007). Concern with craft: Using ars poetica as criteria for reading research poetry. *Qualitative Inquiry, 13*(2), 218–234. doi:10.1177/1077800406295636

Ferreira, F. (2017). Critical sustainability studies: A holistic and visionary conception of socioecological conscientization. *Journal of Sustainability Education, 13*. Retrieved from http://www.susted.com/wordpress/wp-content/uploads/2017/2004/Felipe-JSE-March-2017-Future-Casting-Issue-PDF.pdf

Fien, J. (2003). Learning to care: Education and compassion. *Australian Journal of Environmental Education, 19*, 1–13.

Freire, P., Freire, A. M. A., & Macedo, D. P. (1998). *The Paulo Freire reader*. New York, NY: Continuum.

Gonski, D., Arcus, T., Boson, K., Gould, V., O'Brien, L., Perry, L.-A., & Roberts, M. (2018). *Through growth to achievement: Report of the review to achieve educational excellence in Australian schools*. Canberra: Commonwealth of Australia.

Greene, M. (1997). A philosopher looks at qualitative research. In R. M. Jaeger (Ed.), *Complementary methods for research in education* (Vol. 2, pp. 189–206). Washington, DC: AERA.

Harmon, D., & Loh, J. (2010). *The index of linguistic diversity: A new quantitative measure of trends in the status of the world's languages*. Honolulu, HI: University of Hawai'i Press. Retrieved from https://scholarspace.manoa.hawaii.edu/handle/10125/4474

Infosys. (2016). *Amplifying human potential: Education and skills for the fourth industrial revolution*. Retrieved from http://www.experienceinfosys.com/humanpotential

Jackson, T. (2009). *Prosperity without growth: Economics for a finite planet*. London: Earthscan.

Joanna, W. (2011). Re-thinking metaphor, experience and aesthetic awareness. *Kybernetes, 40*(7–8), 1196–1206.

Kincheloe, J. L., & Pinar, W. (1991). Introduction. In J. L. Kincheloe & W. Pinar (Eds.), *Curriculum as social psychoanalysis: The significance of place* (pp. 1–23). Albany, NY: SUNY Press.

Kincheloe, J. L., & Tobin, K. (2009). The much exaggerated death of positivism. *Cultural Studies of Science Education, 4*(3), 513–528.

Kuhn, T. (1962). *The structure of scientific revolutions*. Chicago, IL: University of Chicago Press.

Ladson-Billings, G. (2000). Racialized discourses and ethnic epistemologies. In N. K. Denzin & Y. S. Lincoln (Eds.), *The Sage handbook of qualitative research* (2nd ed., pp. 257–277). Thousand Oaks, CA: Sage Publications.

Laszlo, E. (2008). *Quantum shift in the global brain: How the new scientific reality can change us and our world*. Rochester, VT: Inner Traditions.

Literat, I. (2016). Interrogating participation across disciplinary boundaries: Lessons from political philosophy, cultural studies, art, and education. *New Media & Society, 18*(8), 1787–1803.

Loomba, A. (2005). *Colonialism/postcolonialism* (2nd ed.). London: Routledge.

Luitel, B. C. (2018). A mindful inquiry towards transformative curriculum vision for inclusive mathematics education. *Learning: Research and Practice, 4*(1) 78–90. doi:10.1080/23735082.2018.1428141

Luitel, B. C., & Taylor, P. C. (2011). Kincheloe's bricolage. In K. Hayes, S. R. Steinberg, & K. Tobin (Eds.), *Key works in critical pedagogy* (pp. 191–200). Dordrecht: Springer.

Luitel, B. C., & Taylor, P. C. (2013). Fractals of 'old' and 'new'logics: A post/modern proposal for transformative mathematics pedagogy. *Philosophy of Mathematics Education Journal, 27*, 1–31.

McLaren, P. (2005). Critical pedagogy in the age of neo-liberal globalization. In P. McLaren (Ed.), *Capitalists and conquerors: A critical pedagogy against empire* (pp. 19–74). Oxford: Rowman & Littlefield.

McLaren, P., & Kincheloe, J. L. (Eds.). (2007). *Critical pedagogy: Where are we now?* New York, NY: Peter Lang.

Mezirow, J. (1991). *Transformative dimensions of adult learning*. San Fransisco, CA: Jossey-Bass.

INTRODUCTION

Morrell, A., & O'Connor, M. A. (2002). Introduction. In E. V. O'Sullivan, A. Morrell, & M. A. O'Connor (Eds.), *Expanding the boundaries of transformative learning: Essays on theory and praxis* (p. xvii). New York, NY: Palgrave.

Mutua, K., & Swadener, B. B. (Eds.). (2004). *Decolonizing research in cross-cultural contexts: Critical personal narratives.* Albany, NY: SUNY Press.

Nadarajah, M. (2014). *Living pathways: Meditations on sustainable cultures and cosmologies in Asia.* Penang: Areca Books.

Nkrumah, K. (1966). *Neo-colonialism: The last stage of imperialism.* New York, NY: International Publishers.

Omnès, R. (1999). *Quantum philosophy: Understanding and interpreting contemporary science.* Princeton, NJ: Princeton University Press.

Palmer, P. J. (1998). *The courage to teach: Exploring the inner landscape of a teacher's life.* San Francisco, CA: Jossey-Bass.

Rae, A. I. M. (2004). *Quantum physics: Illusion or reality?* (2nd ed.). Cambridge: Cambridge University Press.

Ricard, M., & Thuan, T. X. (2001). *The quantum and the lotus: A journey to the frontiers where science and Buddhism meet.* New York, NY: Three Rivers Press.

Robertson, R. (1995). Glocalization: Time-space and homogenity-heterogenity. In M. Featherstone, S. Lash, & R. Robertson (Eds.), *Global modernities* (pp. 25–44). London: Sage Publications.

Settelmaier, E. (2009). *'Adding zest' to science education: Transforming the culture of science education through ethical dilemma story pedagogy.* Saarbrucken: Verlag Dr Muller.

Shivanand, A. (2018). *Every human being has a multi-dimensional existence.* Retrieved from https://www.youtube.com/watch?v=PvcVJQedkMw:ShivYogChannel

Skutnabb-Kanga, T., Maffi, L., & Harmon, D. (2003). *Sharing a world of difference: The earth's linguistic, cultural and biological diversity.* Paris: UNESCO. Retrieved from http://terralingua.org/sharing/

Taylor, E., Taylor, P. C., & Chow, M. L. (2013). Diverse, disengaged and reactive: A teacher's adaptation of ethical dilemma story pedagogy as a strategy to re-engage learners in education for sustainability. In N. Mansour & R. Wegerif (Eds.), *Science education for diversity: Theory and practice* (pp. 97–117). Dordrecht: Springer.

Taylor, E. W., Cranton, P., & Associates. (2012). *The handbook of transformative learning: Theory, research, and practice.* San Fransisco, CA: Jossey-Bass.

Taylor, P. C. (2011). Counter-storying the grand narrative of science (teacher) education: Towards culturally responsive teaching. *Cultural Studies of Science Education, 6*(4), 795–801.

Taylor, P. C. (2013). Research as transformative learning for meaning-centered professional development. In O. Kovbasyuk & P. Blessinger (Eds.), *Meaning-centred education: International perspectives and explorations in higher education* (pp. 168–185). New York, NY: Routledge.

Taylor, P. C. (2014). Contemporary qualitative research: Toward an integral research perspective. In N. G. Lederman & S. K. Abell (Eds.), *Handbook of research on science education* (Vol. 2, pp. 38–54). New York, NY: Routledge.

Taylor, P. C. (2015a). Constructivism. In R. Gunstone (Ed.), *Encyclopedia of science education* (pp. 218–224). Dordrecht: Springer.

Taylor, P. C. (2015b). Transformative science teacher education. In R. Gunstone (Ed.), *Encyclopedia of science education* (pp. 1079–1082). Dordrecht: Springer.

Taylor, P. C. (2018). *Enriching STEM with the arts to better prepare 21st century citizens.* Proceedings of the 5th International Conference for Science Educators and Teachers (ISET) 2017 (pp. 020002-1–020002-5), Phuket & Melville, NY.

Taylor, P. C., & Medina, M. N. D. (2013). Educational research paradigms: From positivism to multi-paradigmatic. *Journal for Meaning-Centered Education.* Retrieved from https://www.hetl.org/educational-research-paradigms-from-positivism-to-multiparadigmatic/

Taylor, P. C., Taylor, E., & Luitel, B. C. (2012). Multi-Paradigmatic transformative research as/for teacher education: An integral perspective. In K. Tobin, B. Fraser, & C. McRobbie (Eds.), *International handbook of science education* (pp. 373–387). Dordrecht: Springer.

UNESCO. (2005). *The 2005 convention on the protection and promotion of the diversity of cultural expressions*. Retrieved from https://en.unesco.org/creativity/sites/creativity/files/passeport-convention2005-web2.pdf

UNESCO. (n.d.a). *The contribution of culture to sustainable development*. Retrieved from http://www.unesco.org/new/en/culture/themes/culture-and-development/the-future-we-want-the-role-of-culture/the-contribution-of-culture/

UNESCO. (n.d.b). *Education for sustainable development*. Retrieved from https://en.unesco.org/themes/education-sustainable-development/what-is-esd

UNESCO. (n.d.c). *The future we want: The role of culture in sustainable development*. Retrieved from http://www.unesco.org/new/en/culture/themes/culture-and-development/the-future-we-want-the-role-of-culture/

Werlen, B. (2015). From local to global sustainability: Transdisciplinary integrated research in the digital age. In B. Werlen (Ed.), *Global sustainability: Cultural perspectives and challenges for transdisciplinary integrated research* (pp. 3–16). Heidelberg: Springer.

Wilber, K. (2007). *The integral vision: A very short introduction to the revolutionary integral approach to life, god, the universe, and everything*. Boston, MA: Shambhala.

Willis, J. (2007). *Foundations of qualitative research: Interpretive and critical approaches*. Thousand Oaks, CA: Sage Publications.

ABOUT THE AUTHORS

Bal Chandra Luitel. According to my parents, the Hindu priest of my naming ceremony in consultation with my father (who was an astrologer) chose my name as *Bal Chandra*, the English meaning of these Sanskrit words would be 'young moon'. These two words together with my family title, *Luitel*, which refers to a place in Western Nepal, have signified aspects of me since I started school. Currently, I work at Kathmandu University School of Education as Professor of Mathematics Education. My areas of expertise include transformative learning, cultural studies of mathematics education, integrated education and practitioner research.

Peter Charles Sinclair Taylor. I have been in academia since 1982, after practising as a science/maths teacher in secondary schools in Australia and the UK and an adult educator in an Indigenous community in Central Australia. For 3 decades I worked at the Science and Mathematics Education Centre, Curtin University, Western Australia. As a postgraduate supervisor/advisor/mentor of many teacher educators from universities in Asia, Africa and the South Pacific, I became deeply attuned to their rich cultural capital, and came to appreciate the pressing need for education systems worldwide to protect and nurture biocultural diversity. This abiding ethical commitment was the driving force behind developing the approach of research as transformative learning, the theme of this book.

PART 1

TEACHING & LEARNING TRANSFORMATIVE RESEARCH

BAL CHANDRA LUITEL

2. JOURNEYING TOWARDS A MULTI-PARADIGMATIC TRANSFORMATIVE RESEARCH PROGRAM

An East-West Symbiosis

*A sentence says more than
what it aims to convey
A word is more than
what it appears to be
An alphabet is more than
what it carries
A sound is more than
what it entails*

*If it was merely a sound,
no punctuation would be needed
If it was merely an alphabet,
cases would be meaningless
If it was merely a word
dictionary would not be popular
If it was merely a sentence
clarifications would be redundant*

(Luitel, 2009, p. 128)

Subscribing to the method of writing as inquiry, I review my journey of conceiving a multi-paradigmatic research design program that enables educational researchers to work as agents for transforming the pedagogical landscape of mathematics education from a culturally decontextualised discipline to an inclusive and empowering learning enterprise. I explore how concepts arising from Eastern Wisdom Traditions have enabled me to develop a multi-paradigmatic transformative research perspective suited to challenging the problem of culturally decontextualised mathematics education in Nepal.

The chapter begins with a discussion on use of auto/ethnography in my master's research project as a contestatory methodology to critique the culturally decontextualised mathematics education widespread in Nepali schools. In the process of this undertaking, I discuss my use of epistemic metaphors of research, such as constructing context-based meaning, challenging the status quo, and reconceptualising mathematics pedagogy. While these metaphors enabled me to challenge the conventional metaphor of *research as testing and proving*, the use of a diachronic narrative style demonstrated a radical shift in adapting a cutting-edge research methodology in the field of mathematics education – a discipline known for its conservative fervour in welcoming newer paradigms of research and practice.

Next, I discuss the continuation of a similar approach in my doctoral research in which I sought to answer the research question: "How can I envision mathematics teacher education in Nepal as an empowering and inclusive learning enterprise?" My doctoral research journey was guided by a host of concepts and ideas arising from Eastern Wisdom Traditions, such as Advaita Vedanta and Madhyamika Buddhism. Bringing this to light, I demonstrate interactivity, symbiosis and synergy among ideas developed in different historical moments, spatial contexts, cultural traditions and political processes. The contemporary idea of postmodernity can be connected with longstanding Eastern traditions of interpreting the same verse with differing meanings and perspectives. In the final section, I discuss how Lila-Rita dialectics, Mukti, and mysticism can contribute to enriching the nascent tradition of transformative educational research in Nepal and elsewhere.

CREATING A NEW SPACE

In 2003, I undertook a critical inquiry to examine my lived experience of culturally decontextualized mathematics education, a source of widespread underachievement in school mathematics education for many students in Nepal (Luitel, 2003). With the aim of developing a vision of inclusive mathematics pedagogy by critically reflecting on my experiences of exclusionary pedagogical practices, my master's research project was guided by four non-positivistic assumptions about research and practice in mathematics education: (a) that evidence can be both internal and external to the researcher, (b) that the language of mathematics education research can be personalised, (c) that research can demonstrate the personal-professional development of the researcher, and (d) that mathematics education research can be instrumental in creating a new vision of inclusivity via the use of non-positivistic ways of knowing as constructing, contesting and creating (Luitel, 2009).

Auto/Ethnography as Contestatory Methodology

The use of critical auto/ethnography as a research methodology enabled me to develop a better understanding of key disempowering features of culturally decontextualised mathematics education (e.g., exclusive emphasis on mathematics curriculum as subject matter, student as a means to another end, mathematics as a foreign subject, and teaching as controlling students) via my lived experience as a student, mathematics teacher and teacher educator. I used the symbolism of the slash ('/')

When?

When will they enter maths class?
The petals of marigold
The banquet of rhododendron
The collection of pippal (fig) tree leafs
The fractal of Bodhi tree
When will they enter in maths class?

When will they enter maths class?
The map of my village settlements
The matrix of my mother's work schedule
The method of my father's problem solving
The pattern of land distribution in my village
When will they enter in maths class?

When will they enter maths class?
The algebra of my family genealogy
The geometry of wicker baskets
The arithmetic of local harvests
The statistics of my village budget
When will they enter in maths class?

(Luitel, 2009, p. 135)

Sarcasm

How can you use your voice?
How can you go beyond pre-conceived device?

This is research. You are doing science.
Don't ever try to go away from your course.

Research is all about probing variables
A handful of them represents the whole system
This is the mantra. Attach to your database
Be a robot-like person as you play with numbers

Words are fuzzy and sentences are clumsy
Use numbers and equations for clarity
Avoid metaphors, similes and stanzas
Cut and dry should be your language

(Luitel, 2009, p. 173)

to represent the dialectical relationship between opposing attributes, notions and categories embedded in my practice as learner, teacher and teacher educator. Thus, the term *auto/ethnography* infers a dialectical relationship between autobiography (self) and ethnography (culture) (Roth, 2005). As a form of self-culture dialectics, this *insider* methodology enabled me to develop much-needed intellectual capital to act as a resistor who could challenge a number of status-quos embedded in the prevailing teacher-centric pedagogy, context insensitive curricula, and mathematics as a collection of muted symbols (Luitel & Taylor, 2005; Spry, 2001).

Contesting the positivistic notion of research language as an assemblage of *atma-free* texts, I developed my research report in a diachronic-narrative style, akin to an *atma-laden* style, that is, a representational approach that makes visible the unfolding research process over a period of time (Taylor, Luitel, Désautels, & Tobin, 2007). Based on the Vedic notion of *atma* – a corporeal body is needed to give life – *atma-free* texts refer to a dispassionate mode of representation prevalent in positivistic research traditions, whereas *atma-laden* texts refers to a personalised, passion-filled and reflective genre.

In this way, I subscribed to the poststructuralist notion of disrupting the canonical five-chapter structure of a research thesis, using the transgressive metaphor of *conscious writing as inquiry*. The idea of conscious writing facilitates the educational researcher to become critically reflective of the strengths and limitations of his/her practices as teacher and teacher educator. More so, a conscious form of writing is a way of connecting the authorial self with the present moment, thereby creating a dialogical space for readers to elicit thoughtfulness about their own pedagogical values and beliefs (Richardson & St Pierre, 2005). In so doing, I became aware of my strengths and limitations in different personal and professional roles as a student, mathematics teacher and teacher educator. Could this type of epistemic activity possibly offer better opportunities for professional development?

Metaphors at Hand

Having subscribed to the notion of *epistemological pluralism*, I employed a number of epistemic metaphors to facilitate my research inquiry: *research as de/constructing, research as reconceptualizing self,* and *research as semi-fictive imagining* (Luitel, 2007). These epistemic metaphors are associated with Kuhnian research paradigms (Denzin & Lincoln, 2003) and offer a more inclusive space than the space created by the positivistic metaphor of *research as proving hypotheses*.

Research as de/constructing. This metaphor, which is associated with the paradigm of Criticalism, enabled me, via heretical scholarly standpoints – critical mathematics education, contextualism, cultural studies – to critique the widespread phenomenon in Nepal of culturally decontextualised mathematics education. Critical mathematics education helped me critique the elitist metaphor of mathematics as a subject for a select few. I used the idea of contextualism as a strategic perspective to challenge the widespread emphasis of universalism as an excuse for blindly importing decontextualised prescriptions from international curriculum donor communities. Likewise, the cultural studies perspective enabled me to envision educational activities from within the framework of mythopoetic traditions of Nepali communities, such as folklore, storytelling and metaphors.

Research as reconceptualising self. This metaphor is associated with the paradigm of Interpretivism and gives rise to emergent knowing. Having this metaphor at my disposal, I realised the usefulness of a multi-epistemic inquiry in transforming my own actions as a controlling teacher (i.e., a major cultural means for maintaining culturally decontextualised mathematics education) towards a more participatory facilitator (i.e., a reform-oriented image of teacher who could help develop an inclusive and empowering mathematics education).

Research as semi-fictive imagining. This metaphor, which is associated with the paradigm of Postmodentism, helped me capture various subtleties associated with my experience of culturally decontextualised mathematics education (Clough, 2002). I represented multiple phenomena embedded in my experiences via a host of poetically oriented genres, such as reflective, storied letter-writing and poems (Cahnmann, 2003; Kearney, 1998).

Impacts and Effects

My research generated a range of responses from within the established community of educational researchers in Nepal. Given the prevailing context of the narrowly conceived view of *research as hypothesis testing* held by teacher educators and professors working in the field of teacher education, the idea of auto/ethnography was unsurprisingly perceived as a misfit research methodology for postgraduate researchers. For example, a senior colleague held the view that despite this research offering an engaging read it lacked precision and objectivity. Perhaps it was not a surprising comment in the context of the presumed hallmarks of the educational research tradition that he had practised thus far. Another prominent local scholar allowed that auto/ethnography could be used for advocacy and raising consciousness, but that it would not be readily called research.

Dismissal. These initial responses suggested that I was away from *real* research because my approach did not follow *the* appropriate method. The notion of real seemed to be guided by the narrowly conceived view of reality as an outcome of a one-to-one correspondence between our select mental schema (i.e., representations) and the objects and events in the world (Fumerton, 2005). These critics might also have regarded my research as an example of an infiltration by postmodernism, which was portrayed among traditionally-minded teacher educators and researchers as whimsical, ambiguous and morally dissolving. Possibly, these comments resulted from the widespread metaphor of *research as completing a jigsaw puzzle*, thereby discarding the researcher's imagination and creativity in generating knowledge claims. Perhaps, the worried critics witnessed the beginning of the dilapidation of their comfort zone that had been created by the invisible epistemology of positivism.

On the contrary, I could articulate the practical significance of my research for the field of mathematics teacher education which was ripe for transformation from a culturally dislocated activity to a culturally empowering enterprise. In this progression, I used my narratives in professional development sessions that I conducted in schools in the capital city of Nepal, and beyond. Following this course of action, my tone was more inclusive in terms of accepting the co-existence of different knowledge systems, such as local and global, objective and subjective, Western and Non-Western, to name but a few.

Critical appreciation. Nevertheless, use of a critical epistemic standpoint was deemed to be necessary by some teacher educators because it could be a way to challenge the status-quo of hitherto unexamined exclusionary practices in mathematics education, such as an undue emphasis on the nature of mathematics as a *culture-free* foreign subject, a hegemonic image of curriculum as an *assemblage of muted texts*, and a non-participative metaphor of *pedagogy as one-way traffic*. In a nutshell, the Chinese dictum, "opposition as the precondition to change" (i.e., "xiang-fan-xiang-yin") (Wong, 2006, p. 246) reflected my ongoing use of a critical social perspective. Besides, I also encountered a sense of resentment towards criticalism because of its historical propensity to criticise without offering visions of possibility (Polanyi, 1998). Because of the scope of my research project and the limitations in my consciousness about the possibilities of criticalism, I might have been more critical of the other side than paying attention to considering much-needed visions of possibility.

An eastern-western nexus. Interestingly, another set of supportive comments proffered a perspective that my narrative inquiry resonated with how knowledge claims are portrayed in Eastern Wisdom Traditions, which represent a range of traditions arising from diverse cultural-spiritual practices of the people in Nepal, such as Vedic, Buddhist, Kirati, and many other animistic traditions (Bajracharya & Brouwer, 1997; Koirala & Acharya, 2005; Pradhan, Shrestha, & Mission, 2005). In retrospect, I could have used this unique and culturally-embedded perspective to highlight a number of commonalities across the Eastern and Western Wisdom traditions, such as Nature-human symbiosis, synergistic thinking, imbued ecological sensibilities, and non-separation as a defining feature of human-nonhuman relationships.

Perhaps, this was one of many wake-up calls for me to be aware of the possibility of expanding the dimension of this newfound approach to inquiry. Having grown up in a Hindu familial context and multicultural social environment (i.e., a mix of Vedic, Buddhist and Animist), the education system under which I studied might have prevented me from fully realising the use of resources from my own cultural traditions in producing and disseminating knowledge claims. Perhaps, such propositions enabled me to embrace yet another empowering perspective that could enable me to think, express and act in a wholistic way!

DOCTORAL RESEARCH JOURNEY

With a view to improving further my practice as a mathematics education practitioner, with the initial research question: "How could I envision mathematics teacher education in Nepal as an empowering and inclusive learning enterprise?", I continued my doctoral research journey with two specific goals in mind: (a) to examine key features, assumptions and orientations of culturally decontextualised mathematics education, and (b) to construct visions of inclusive, empowering and meaning-centred mathematics education. From the outset, I employed a number of perspectives arising from the confluence of Eastern Wisdom Traditions and contemporary thinking in science and mathematics education.

Postformality

Associated with the writing of the integral philosopher Ken Wilber (2007), and arising from the Upanisadic notion of liberation as going beyond the conditioning of the mundane (Sri Aurobindo, 1970), postformality, as a radical shift from the formalist and bureaucratic way of thinking, expressing and acting, is an approach to making sense through non-canonical forms of logic such as dialectical, narrative, poetic and narrative, to name but a few. In this process, I came to realise that postformality would enable me to understand complexity, contradictions and non-linearity as important descriptors of being in the world of mathematics education (Gidley, 2007). My exploration of inclusive visions of mathematics pedagogy, mathematics teacher education programs, mathematics curricula and the nature of mathematics would not be possible through the logics and genres of linearity, causation and deduction; rather, my exploration would require a much more complex form of thinking and representation.

Undoing Dualism

Gradually, I came to realise that the mythopoetic traditions of the East explain the cosmos, the creation and the sentient world through the synergistic blending of otherwise contrasting attributes of categories of the human world and beyond. For example, the Vedic idea of Goddesses Kali and Saraswati, co-existing in moments of destruction and creation, helped me to understand the very nature of our being as dialectical rather than dualistic. Many other similar analogies enabled me to challenge dualistic antagonisms between different paradigms, thereby conceiving a multi-paradigmatic design space that would help me work through seemingly antagonistic, contradictory and incommensurable phenomena and notions (Deussen, 1973). In this course of action, my journey of conceiving a research design gave rise to four major perspectives: (a) that dualism tells a partial and misleading story of reality, (b) that there are always interactions among the so-called binary opposites of dualism, (c) that knowing is not independent of the consciousness of the knower, and (d) that the self is central to seeking knowledge and wisdom (Loy, 1997). Here, the idea of dualism is a tendency to classify concepts, statements and events according to binary opposites, as belonging to only one of two all-encompassing, mutually-exclusive categories with essential fixed meanings (Núñez, Edwards, & Filipe Matos, 1999).

Being Critical from Within and Without

Initially, I chose an ethical standpoint of *doing good* for many school students who would only have experienced the nature of mathematics as *a body of pure knowledge*, a dualistic view that depicts mathematics as exclusively abstract, algorithmic, symbolic and formal, thereby discarding another powerful view of the nature of mathematics as *an impure knowledge system* (i.e., mathematics associated with ethnic, communal, professional, occupational and trade groups). Unlike the Greek philosophical traditions in which reality is considered to be the first philosophy, an important feature of Vedic and Buddhist traditions is to regard ethics (e.g., doing and being good) as the first philosophy (Raju, 1973) which gives rise to ways of being and knowing.

Given these initial ethical perspectives, I started conceiving the contemporary paradigm of Criticalism to be a key aspect of the design space of my research. Indeed, I chose the paradigm not only to critique a number of disempowering structures and systems associated with and arising from culturally decontextualised mathematics education, but also to critique limitations associated with my own subjectivities developed over my lifetime and comprising un/consciously chosen ideologies, developed habits (of mind and body) and performed actions. Was the paradigm of Criticalism sufficient for me to continue this journey of transformative inquiry? Didn't I also need a paradigm that would better explain the unfolding nature of my inquiry into a culturally dislocated mathematics education?

Methodological Mixture

Developing a mix of auto/ethnography and philosophical inquiry as my methodology, I continued to examine a number of subtle and obvious features of mathematics education in Nepal (e.g., dualist-reductionist thinking, uni-dimensionality in conceiving the nature of mathematics, and undue emphasis on globalism), thereby constructing visions of inclusive mathematics education that enable learners to appreciate and use mathematical knowledge for their various roles as both current and future citizens (Luitel & Taylor, 2008).

I used the methodology of auto/ethnography to deepen my multi-perspectival understanding of different aspects of mathematics education that I experienced during my lifetime as a university student, mathematics teacher and teacher educator. In contrast to the conventional positivist metaphor of analysis, auto/ethnography offered new ways of conceiving of, producing and processing *data*.

Following this, the act of envisioning was greatly facilitated by the method of philosophical inquiry, an approach to constructing a vision of "what could be and should be possible". My notion of philosophical inquiry was guided by Richard Rorty's (1999) *pragmatic philosophy* as an everyday activity of understanding and imagining the world in which we live. Likewise, the Upanishadic notion of *philosophy as vision* (Johnson, 1971) embedded in the lifeworld of each human-seer equally contributed to my conceptualisation of philosophical inquiry as *practitioner research* methodology.

Blending Narada with Interpretivism

Let me introduce a Vedic sage, Narada, who is considered to be a messenger sage in Vedic (and some Buddhist) traditions, who would travel through different realms of beings (i.e., divine, humans, demons) and *pass* messages from one to the other. He would travel not only to share the message but also to interpret it according to the context and mindset of the person involved in sharing the message (Chinmayananda, 2013). As a wandering sage, Narada's message sharing process could be regarded as an emergent method of interpretive inquiry.

Taking Narada's approach as a metaphor, I commenced with the present-day paradigm of Interpretivism to portray the ever-unfolding nature of my inquiry as unpacking complexities and subtleties embedded in the practice of culturally decontextualised mathematics education. More so, this paradigm enabled me to offer context-based interpretations of phenomena, issues and problems under consideration via narratives of my experience (Taylor, 2013).

During the process of narrative construction, I felt the need for yet another paradigm that would enable me to use multiple modes of expression and thinking to illuminate many hidden and obvious features of culturally decontextualised mathematics education in Nepal.

Postmodernism Meets Vedic-Buddhist Pluri-Textuality

In the next detour, I came to realise through various Vedic and Buddhist texts that a person, category or phenomenon is expressed by many names to portray the many facets it involves. Giving multiple names to sages, yogis and gods is commonplace in Vedic literature. Similarly, the idea that sages interpret the truth in many possible ways suggests pluri-textuality being a key feature of Vedic and Buddhist traditions, which appears to represent one of many conditions of knowledge generation in postmodernity. Rather than prescribing one particular method for seeking liberation, the Gita epitomises different pathways (e.g., devotion, karma, knowledge) to wisdom and liberation (Muller, 1955). Composed as a dialogue between Krishna (the realised Master) and Arjuna (the great archer) with a host of metaphors woven in the polysemous verses, the Gita is epitomised as a Vedic philosophical text that expounds virtues, values and duties required for humans to fulfill both mundane and pluralistic liberatory goals of human life.

Allowing this, I aligned myself with *constructive postmodernism* (Shea, 1998) because of its emphasis on developing and employing newer heuristics to construct visions of inclusive mathematics education. The *deconstructive* version of postmodernism (through its emphasis on excessive deconstructionism and moral relativism) was not very useful for me in developing an inclusive alternative to culturally decontextualised mathematics education.

So, as there are multiple ways of interpreting truths and seeking wisdom in Vedic-Buddhist traditions, the contemporary paradigm of Postmodernism enabled me to employ multiple logics and genres to challenge unhelpful dualisms (e.g., algorithmic mathematics versus informal mathematics, mathematical content versus mathematics pedagogy, globalism versus contextualism) and unexamined reductionism (e.g., reducing teaching *to* tests, pedagogy *to* lecturing, mathematics *to* muted symbols) embedded in mathematics education in Nepal. Out of many possible logics and genres, I chose narrative, poetic, metaphorical, dialectical and non-linguistic textual forms (Taylor, Taylor, & Luitel, 2012) to (a) portray the multi-faceted nature of culturally decontextualised mathematics education, and (b) construct visions of inclusive and meaning-centric mathematics education.

Narrative logics and genres enabled me to tell otherwise untold stories of my experiences of culturally dislocated mathematics education, whereas poetic logics and genres enabled me to express ineffability associated with my visions. The use of metaphorical logic assisted me to overcome the narrowness of literalism whilst portraying issues about the nature of mathematics, pedagogy and curriculum.

With the realisation that visual approaches to thinking and expression have an important role in clarifying otherwise very complex and abstract ideas under consideration, I used various forms of non-linguistic genres (e.g., photographs, cartoons, creative drawings, montages) to illuminate different forms of exclusionary practices associated with culturally decontextualised mathematics education in Nepal. Such forms of thinking and expression could also be useful to generate pedagogical thoughtfulness among the readers of my research texts.

Neti-Neti and Co-Dependent Arising

Likewise, I used different forms of dialectical thinking, such as Advaitin *neti-neti* and Madhyamika *co-dependent arising*, to name but a few. According to Advaitin literature, the world of humans comprises antagonistic attributes with a propensity to subscribe to one aspect of those attributes, the act of which may lead to darkness (Nikhilananda, 2008). The Advaitin neti-neti version of dialectical thinking enabled me to visualise an in-between space for an inclusive mathematics education, as the term neti-neti refers to the in-between space by its repeated use in worldly categories

The Moment I Speak To You

The moment I speak to you
I am not merely releasing words
I am not merely uttering sounds
I am not merely mimicking sentences
I am not merely vibrating my lips
The moment I speak to you

The moment I speak to you
I am sharing my vantage points
I am drawing my picture of reality
I am thinking of possible payoffs
I am refreshing my beliefs
The moment I speak to you

The moment I speak to you
I am calculating how much I owe you
I am wondering how I can pay you
I am undecidedly wandering
I am asking: Why are thoughts meandering?
The moment I speak to you

The moment I speak to you
I am telling a story of the day
I am disrupting your way
I am going far away and then
I am coming to my inn
The moment I speak to you

The moment I speak to you
I am longing for my presence
I am making claims of my sense
I am bespeaking complicities
I am requesting a space
The moment I speak to you

(Luitel, 2009, p. 269)

One and Many

Don't show me this monochrome again
I say to the photographer with passion
Please bring images of different effects
I say, the monochrome is not enough

Why don't you like the realistic image?
The photographer says,
You have a surprising craze
Rejecting what is real, true and exact
What are you trying to achieve?

How do you know your image is real?
I question, why don't you think of multiple?
Your exactness can be bounded
Your truth can be misguided
Come on, construct multicoloured image-icon
Not just one from one, but many out of one

Colourful images are inspirational
Don't worry about real, unreal and nonreal
I am happy with all of them
But be aware I need a great deal of collection

The photographer begins to listen
As if he is going to be educated soon
I say, strict boundaries have no charm
Just like being restricted inside a locked room

I stress further, images signify possibilities
They embody normal, abnormal and otherwise
My friend, use as many pixels as you can
I encourage, use as many effects as you can
Employ multiple lenses to capture dimensions
Apply colour combinations for imaginations

Finally, the photographer nods
I continue with my proddings
The world is colourful and so are our beings
Allow images to sprout freely from your lenses
Remember many is the essence of one
And one is a basis for and gives rise to many.

(Luitel, 2009, p. 288)

such as *pure* and *impure* mathematics. The term refers to an English equivalent translation "not this not that", thereby indicating the limitations of dualistic categories. Taking neti-neti as a referent, I argued that neither mathematics as a pure body of knowledge nor mathematics as an impure knowledge system is inclusive; thereby enabling me to explore a *hybrid space* that does not preclude both forms of mathematics. I have demonstrated the use of such neti-neti and other dialectics in a recently published paper (Luitel, 2013).

Whilst applying the notion of co-dependent arising from worldly categories, Madhyamika Buddhism enabled me to visualise the nonessentialist nature of *pure* and *impure* categories associated with opposing views of the nature of mathematics; for the category of pure gives rise to impure, and vice-versa. Such a Madhyamika dialectics gives rise to impermanence and fluidity associated with worldly categories, including these two. The idea of co-dependent arising is attributed to Nagarjuna (a second century Madhyamika Buddhist sage) who said that worldly concepts are empty because of their presupposing opposite nature. Madhyamika dialectics refers to the non-essentialist view of the nature of worldly ideas, things or any categories (Nagarjuna, Bhattacharya, Johnston, & Kunst, 1990). Such a dialectics has been the basis for me conceiving a multi-dimensional view of the nature of mathematics as *an im/pure knowledge system* (i.e., a symbiosis of pure and impure categories embedded in the nature of mathematics) to expand the scope of mathematics education as a much more inclusive learning enterprise (Luitel, 2013).

CHALLENGES AND OPPORTUNITIES

Immediately after completing my doctoral research I returned to my university in Nepal and began to implement my newfound vision of research and practice in the context of postgraduate teacher education programs. I began to teach a research methodology course to postgraduate students, some of whom would be undertaking multi-paradigmatic research as/for transformative professional development (see chapters by Sadruddin Qutoshi, Suresh Gautam, Binod Pant, Indra Mani Shrestha, Indra Mani Rai) to fulfil the partial requirements of their study. Of course, teaching research methodology and supervising postgraduate students with multi-paradigmatic sensibilities has been a challenging (and rewarding) task for me (and my colleagues) because of the prevailing narrowness in the way educational research is being taught, understood and valued in many universities.

Comprador Intelligentsia Attitude

One of many challenges arises from what we may call the *comprador intelligentsia* attitude towards intellectual capital being invested in non-positivistic and non-Western Wisdom traditions (Roy, 2017). A comprador intelligentsia un/wittingly celebrates the (colonial) master('s) narratives, thereby rejecting narratives associated with his or her own people. Such an attitude takes refuge in many unhelpful dualisms (e.g., quantitative is superior to qualitative, Western is better than Eastern, local is less useful than global) and thinks exclusively through reductionist logics, as if there are no other ways of making sense of reality. An exclusive emphasis on reductionist logics does not enable researchers and practitioners to think beyond the propositional nature of language (cut-and-dried, third-person writing style), a hypothetico-deductive approach (*a priori* view of categories and concepts) to legitimating select knowledge systems, and the narrowly conceived notion of analysis as privileging one form of value judgement over others.

Crypto-Positivism

Another challenge to conceiving a multi-paradigmatic research discourse and practice among postgraduate students arises from forms of crypto-positivism that promote seemingly epistemology-free *mixed methods* (Kincheloe & Tobin, 2009). The misconception that mixing methods and data is a default option to increasing the credibility of research promotes intellectual passivity among graduate students in designing their research (Flick, 2017). I argue that transformative educational researchers need to be intellectually active in conceiving and implementing their research designs so that they can fully realise the potentiality of their inquiries for transforming their professional roles from promoters of culturally decontextualised mathematics education to *change agents* who work for the development of inclusive mathematics education. Of course, the importance of any particular method, epistemology, tradition or paradigm should not be denied. Privileging one over many other possibilities does not help researchers make informed choice about their research.

Discourse on Transformative Education Research on the Rise

Despite these challenges, my colleagues and I have been engaging in adapting a discourse and practice of change-seeking research in Nepal through the *Transformative Education Research Group* at Kathmandu University, which organised its first conference in 2016 (Luitel, Gautam, Pant, Wagle, & Pangeni, 2018). An important outcome of such a discourse is to provide postgraduate students with multiple possibilities of doing their master's and doctoral research. As most of our students are in-service teachers and teacher educators they are eager to undertake meaningful research projects so that they can immediately apply the research in their professional contexts.

In such research projects, postgraduate students reflect critically on their experiences of encountering difficulties in applying empowering, creative and inclusive pedagogical approaches in their teaching contexts, thereby stimulating development of visions for possibilities through a host of theoretical referents, such as radical constructivism, advaita Vedanta, Sufi mysticism, and transformative learning. The following list comprises exemplary MPhil and PhD research topics that were undertaken through multi-paradigmatic research designs and recently completed at Kathmandu University.

PhD topics:

- A journey towards peaceful living: An educational practitioner's muse (Thakur, 2017)
- Creating my living educational theory: A journey towards transformative teacher education in Pakistan (Qutoshi, 2016)

- Urban youth and their everyday life in Kathmandu: Arts-based narrative inquiry (Gautam, 2017)

MPhil topics:

- From hopelessness to hope at academics: A self-reflective inquiry on conditioning of learning emotions (Wagle, 2016)
- Journeying into motherly mathematics education: A muse towards transformation (Poudel, 2016)
- Pondering my beliefs and practices on mathematics, pedagogy, curriculum and assessment (Pant, 2015)
- You are not intelligent enough to learn Mathematics! A journey towards un/intelligence (Thapa, 2016)

CONTINUING THE JOURNEY

As of now, my colleagues and I have continued to conceive of enabling epistemic referents arising from the Eastern Wisdom Traditions – the mystical nature of language and logics, self-inquiry, Lila-Rita dialectics, and Mukti – to enrich further the nascent multi-paradigmatic transformative educational research tradition.

The Mystical Nature of Language and Logics

In an attempt to transform the hearts and minds of mathematics education, genres and their associated logics have a very important role to play. As per the Vedic and Buddhist traditions, language (e.g., spoken, written, read, heard, felt, dreamt, and many more) is regarded as having great power via a range of logics and expressions, to represent human consciousness than is possible by use of literal-propositional expressions and reductionist thinking alone (Yaden et al., 2016). The mystics of all traditions use poetry and songs, images and metaphors, parables and stories to demonstrate ways of being in the world (Sri Aurobindo, 1998). Unlike the prevailing *conduit* view of language, which presents language merely as a channel for communicating ideas and which is independent of consciousness, the mystical traditions have demonstrated that: (a) poetry and songs are useful means for expression and thinking to get closer to the unknown, (b) images and metaphors enable us to express and make sense of many unknown facets of the world around us, and (c) parables and stories help us to express a connection between the past and present.

Self-Inquiry

The idea of self-inquiry entails the process of identifying one's own limitations, possibly arising from egotistic thinking, thereby radically shifting one's consciousness from an ignorant-exclusionary person to a wise-inclusive person (Maharshi, 1997).

For example, a mathematics teacher may say: "I am transmitting adequate mathematics, but it is the student who needs to study well". Another mathematics teacher may say, "It is not my duty to work for restructuring the field of mathematics education". These standpoints illustrate how egoism often takes away all forms of altruistic vision about everything and anything. By contrast, the ontological and epistemological positions of self-inquiry are based in *nondualism*, a perspective of non-separation of self from the world and cosmos, of knower from the known, of being from becoming. Self-inquiry can profoundly resolve the ongoing debate of "evocative versus analytical autoethnography" (or of the methods embedded in such unhelpful dualisms) (Anderson, 2006; Ellis & Bochner, 2006) because such a dualistic classification is unhelpful for researchers who aim at developing inclusive visions for their practices.

Lila-Rita Dialectics

The idea of lila-rita dialectics can be another powerful notion arising from Vedic traditions. An empowering referent for carrying out research for reconceptualising the field of mathematics education, from the perspective of inclusion and empowerment (Panikkar, 1977). The idea of lila can be equated with play, chaos and disorderliness, whereas rita represents the order developed out of a series of lilas (Coomaraswamy, 1941). Unpredictable *lila-plays* (in the form of dance and playful acts of gods with humans) are commonplace in the world of humans and beyond. Again, rita is not separate from lila, nor is it a given structure for lila to occur. Rather, rita develops out of lila. Symbolically, the water in the ocean at the sub/atomic level can be seen playfully performing lila. Such lila-play creates an apparent order at the surface of the ocean (Mahony, 1998). Mathematics education researchers can use lila as a referent for emergent epistemic activities, whereas rita can explain the order that is developed out of several forms of their personal and professional lilas.

Mukti as Epistemic Possibility

Foundation?

Aftermath of a big quake
Person 1 asks,
Was the foundation not strong enough?
Person 2 says,
Foundation was too strong and rigid!
Person 3 opines,
A flexible foundation could minimize the damage

(Luitel, 2009, p. 343)

BAL CHANDRA LUITEL

As of now, I have conceived the notion of Mukti as another metaphor for representing the process and outcome of transformative educational research (Warrier, 1981). This Sanskrit term can be translated into English as "liberation from all conditionings". An important dimension associated with Mukti is to understand ourselves better so that we can live and act in the world in more meaningful, justifiable and inclusive ways. An important aspect associated with the metaphor of Mukti could be to help mathematics education researchers to continuously examine their own beliefs, values and conditionings, thereby preparing for better pedagogic actions needed to liberate many students from the harmful experience of exclusionary practices of mathematics education. This process requires the researcher to act as a meaning maker, change agent and multi-dimensional thinker. More so, the idea of Mukti as an epistemic metaphor enables researchers to pay attention to their conditionings that could impede their ideal ways of being in the world. The idea that the human body is transitory and thus needs to serve others selflessly is likely to promote an ethics of responsibility towards others.

FINAL REMARKS

Postformality has been a key source of my own reconceptualization of an empowering multi-paradigmatic research design space, within which I have integrated opposing views, ideas, frameworks and methods. A major challenge in conceiving an educational research program that rests upon the notion of multiple paradigms and supervising students with such a sensibility is that it cannot be guided or oriented solely by the exclusionary logics of proposition, deduction and analysis. Rather, inclusive logics are needed to enable researchers to make sense of the potentially complex (complementary, iterative, mutually pre-supposing, opposing, etc.) relationships between seemingly incompatible paradigms. More so, the regime of simplistic scientific writing (*sans* allegories, metaphors and playfulness) has been a major stumbling block for conceptualising mathematics education practitioners' lifeworlds which are naturally full of lila-plays. Let us envisage that more educational researchers will realise the possibility of employing multi-dimensional ways of valuing, knowing and being in their research.

REFERENCES

Anderson, L. (2006). Analytic autoethnography. *Journal of Contemporary Ethnography, 35*(4), 373–395.
Bajracharya, H., & Brouwer, W. (1997). A narrative approach to science teaching in Nepal. *International Journal of Science Education, 19*(4), 429–446.
Cahnmann, M. (2003). The craft, practice, and possibility of poetry in educational research. *Educational Researcher, 32*(3), 29–36. doi:10.3102/0013189x032003029
Chinmayananda, S. (2013). *Narada Bhakti Sutra*. Mumbai: Central Chinmaya Mission Trust.
Clough, P. (2002). *Narratives and fictions in educational research*. Buckingham: Open University Press.
Denzin, N., & Lincoln, Y. (2003). Introduction: The discipline and practice of qualitative research. In N. Denzin & Y. Lincoln (Eds.), *The landscape of qualitative research: Theories and issues* (pp. 1–46). Thousand Oaks, CA: Sage Publications.

Deussen, P. (1973). *The system of the Vedanta: According to Badarayana's Brahma-Sutras and Cankara's commentary thereon set forth as a compendium of the dogmatics of Brahmanism*. New York, NY: Dover.

Ellis, C., & Bochner, A. P. (2006). Analyzing analytic autoethnography: An autopsy. *Journal of Contemporary Ethnography, 35*(4), 429–449. doi:10.1177/0891241606286979

Flick, U. (2017). Mantras and myths: The disenchantment of mixed-methods research and revisiting triangulation as a perspective. *Qualitative Inquiry, 23*(1), 46–57.

Fumerton, R. (2005). Foundationalist theories of epistemic justification. In E. N. Zalta (Ed.), *Stanford encyclopaedia of philosophy*. Retrieved from http://plato.stanford.edu/

Gautam, S. (2017). *Urban youth and their everyday life in Kathmandu: Arts-based narrative Inquiry* (Unpublished PhD thesis). Kathmandu University, Dhulikhel, Kavre.

Gidley, J. M. (2007). The evolution of consciousness as a planetary imperative: An integration of integral views. *Integral Review: A Transdisciplinary and Transcultural Journal for New Thought, Research and Praxis, 5,* 4–226.

Johnson, C. (1971). *Vedanta: An anthology of Hindu scripture: Commentary and poetry*. New York, NY: Harper & Row.

Kearney, R. (1998). *Poetics of imagining: Modern and postmodern*. New York, NY: Fordham University Press.

Kincheloe, J. L., & Tobin, K. (2009). The much exaggerated death of positivism. *Cultural Studies of Science Education, 4*(3), 513–528.

Koirala, B. N., & Acharya, S. (2005). *Girls in science and technology education: A study on access and performance of girls in Nepal*. Kathmandu: UNESCO.

Loy, D. (1997). *Nonduality: A study in comparative philosophy*. Atlantic Highlands, NJ: Humanities Press.

Luitel, B. C. (2003). *Narrative explorations of Nepali mathematics curriculum landscapes: An epic journey* (Unpublished MSc Project). Curtin University of Technology, Perth.

Luitel, B. C. (2007). Storying, critical reflexivity, and imagination. In P. C. Taylor & J. Wallace (Eds.), *Contemporary qualitative research: Exemplars for science and mathematics educators* (pp. 217–228). Dordrecht: Springer.

Luitel, B. C. (2009). *Culture, worldview and transformative philosophy of mathematics education in Nepal: A cultural-philosophical inquiry* (Unpublished PhD thesis). Curtin University, Perth. Retrieved from https://espace.curtin.edu.au/handle/20.500.11937/682

Luitel, B. C. (2013). Mathematics as an im/pure knowledge system: Symbiosis, (w)holism and synergy in mathematics education. *International Journal of Science and Mathematics Education, 11*(1), 65–87. doi:10.1007/s10763-012-9366-8

Luitel, B. C., Gautam, S., Pant, B. P., Wagle, S. K., & Pangeni, S. K. (2018). *Second international conference on transformative education research and sustainable development*. Retrieved from http://tersd2018.kusoed.edu.np

Luitel, B. C., & Taylor, P. C. (2005, April). *Overcoming culturally dislocated curricula in a transitional society: An autoethnographic journey towards pragmatic wisdom*. Paper presented at the the annual meeting of the American Educational Research Association (AERA), Montreal, Canada.

Luitel, B. C., & Taylor, P. C. (2008, January). *Globalization, ecological consciousness and curriculum as montage: A vision for culturally contextualized mathematics education*. Paper presented at the Southern African Association for Research in Mathematics Science and Technology Education, Maseru, Lesotho.

Maharshi, R. (1997). Self-enquiry. In A. Osborne (Ed.), *The collected works of Ramana Maharshi* (pp. 17–38). York Beach, ME: Samuel Weiser.

Mahony, W. K. (1998). *The artful universe: An introduction to the Vedic religious imagination*. New York, NY: State University of New York Press.

Muller, F. M. (1955). *The sacred books of the East*. New Delhi: Motilal Banarsidass.

Nagarjuna, A., Bhattacharya, K., Johnston, E. H., & Kunst, A. (1990). *The dialectical method of Nagarjuna: Vigrahavyavartani* (3rd ed.). New Delhi: Motilal Banarsidass.

Nikhilananda, S. (2008). *The Upanishads-Svetasvatara, Prasna, and Mandukya with Gaudapada's Karika*. New York, NY: Pomona Press.

Núñez, R. E., Edwards, L. D., & Filipe Matos, J. (1999). Embodied cognition as grounding for situatedness and context in mathematics education. *Educational Studies in Mathematics, 39*(1), 45–65.

Panikkar, R. (1977). *The Vedic experience: Mantramanjari: An anthology of the Vedas for modern man and contemporary celebration*. Berkeley, CA: University of California Press.
Pant, B. P. (2015). *Pondering on my beliefs and practices on mathematics, pedagogy, curriculum and assessment* (Unpublished MPhil dissertation). Kathmandu University, Dhulikhel, Kavre.
Polanyi, M. (1998). *Personal knowledge: Towards a post-critical philosophy*. London: Routledge.
Poudel, A. B. (2016). *Journeying into motherly mathematics education: A muse towards transformation* (Unpublished MPhil dissertation). Kathmandu University, Dhulikhel, Kavre.
Pradhan, R., Shrestha, A., & Mission, N. R. (2005). *Ethnic and caste diversity: Implications for development* (Working paper series No. 4). Kathmandu: Asian Development Bank, Nepal Resident Mission.
Qutoshi, S. B. (2016). *Creating living educational theory: A journey towards transformative teacher education in Pakistan* (Unpublished PhD thesis). Kathmandu University, Dhulikhel, Kavre. Retrieved from http://www.actionresearch.net/living/living.shtml
Raju, P. T. (1973). *Idealistic thought of India: Vedanta and Buddhism in the light of Western idealism*. New York, NY: Johnson Reprint.
Richardson, L., & St Pierre, E. (2005). Writing: A method of inquiry. In N. Denzin & Y. Lincoln (Eds.), *The Sage handbook of qualitative research* (3rd ed., pp. 959–578). Thousand Oaks, CA: Sage Publications.
Rorty, R. (1999). *Philosophy and social hope*. London: Penguin.
Roth, W.-M. (Ed.). (2005). *Auto/biography and auto/ethnography: Praxis of research method*. Rotterdam, The Netherlands: Sense Publishers.
Roy, K. (2017). *Rethinking curriculum in times of shifting educational context*. Cham: Palgrave Macmillan.
Shea, C. M. (1998). Critical and constructive postmodernism: The transformative power of holistic education. In H. S. Shapiro & D. E. Purpel (Eds.), *Critical social issues in American education: Transformation in a postmodern world* (pp. 337–354). Mahwah, NJ: Lawrence Erlbaum Associates.
Spry, T. (2001). Performing autoethnography: An embedded methodological praxis. *Qualitative Inquiry, 7*(6), 706–732.
Sri Aurobindo. (1970). *Sri Aurobindo collected works* (Vol. 22, set. ed.). Pondicherry: Sri Aurobindo Ashram.
Sri Aurobindo. (1998). *Supramental manifestation and other writings* (2nd ed.). Twin Lakes, WI: Lotus Press.
Taylor, P. C. (2013). Research as transformative learning for meaning-centered professional development. In O. Kovbasyuk & P. Blessinger (Eds.), *Meaning-centred education: International perspectives and explorations in higher education* (pp. 168–185). New York, NY: Routledge.
Taylor, P. C., Luitel, B. C., Désautels, J., & Tobin, K. (2007). Contextualism and/or decontextualism, painting rich cultural pictures, and ethics of co-authorship. *Cultural Studies of Science Education, 2*(3), 639–655.
Taylor, P. C., Taylor, E., & Luitel, B. C. (2012). Multi-Paradigmatic transformative research as/for teacher education: An integral perspective. In K. Tobin, B. Fraser, & C. McRobbie (Eds.), *International handbook of science education* (pp. 373–387). Dordrecht: Springer.
Thakur, R. (2017). *A journey towards peaceful living: An educational practitioner's muse* (Unpublished PhD thesis). Kathmandu University, Dhulikhel, Kavre.
Thapa, A. (2016). *You are not intelligent enough to learn mathematics! A journey towards un/intelligence* (Unpublished MPhil dissertation). Kathmandu University, Dhulikhel, Kavre.
Wagle, S. K. (2016). *From hopelessness to hope at academics: A self-reflective inquiry on conditioning of learning emotions*. (Unpublished MPhil dissertation). Kathmandu University, Dhulikhel, Kavre.
Warrier, A. G. K. (1981). *The concept of Mukti in Advaita Vedanta*. Madras: University of Madras.
Wilber, K. (2007). *The integral vision: A very short introduction to the revolutionary integral approach to life, God, the universe, and everything*. Boston, MA: Shambhala.
Wong, W. C. (2006). Understanding dialectical thinking from a cultural-historical perspective. *Philosophical Psychology, 19*(2), 239–260.
Yaden, D. B., Eichstaedt, J. C., Schwartz, H. A., Kern, M. L., Le Nguyen, K. D., Wintering, N. A., & Newberg, A. B. (2016). The language of ineffability: Linguistic analysis of mystical experiences. *Psychology of Religion and Spirituality, 8*(3), 244–252.

ABOUT THE AUTHOR

According to my parents, the Hindu priest of my naming ceremony in consultation with my father (who was an astrologer) chose my name as *Bal Chandra*, the English meaning of these Sanskrit words would be 'young moon'. These two words together with my family title, *Luitel*, which refers to a place in Western Nepal, have signified aspects of me since I started school. Currently, I work at Kathmandu University School of Education as Professor of Mathematics Education. My areas of expertise include transformative learning, cultural studies of mathematics education, integrated education and practitioner research.

PETER CHARLES TAYLOR AND MILTON NORMAN MEDINA

3. TEACHING AND LEARNING TRANSFORMATIVE RESEARCH

Complexity, Challenge and Change

THE EARTH CHARTER – CHALLENGES AHEAD

The choice is ours: form a global partnership to care for Earth and one another or risk the destruction of ourselves and the diversity of life. Fundamental changes are needed in our values, institutions, and ways of living. We must realize that when basic needs have been met, human development is primarily about being more, not having more. We have the knowledge and technology to provide for all and to reduce our impacts on the environment. The emergence of a global civil society is creating new opportunities to build a democratic and humane world. Our environmental, economic, political, social, and spiritual challenges are interconnected, and together we can forge inclusive solutions. (Earth Charter Commission, 2001)

We are living at a time of great historical change that is both inspiring and ethically troubling. The digital age is ushering in unparalleled technological innovations for improving the material quality of our lives. On the other hand, our carbon-based market economy is polluting the atmosphere, oceans and food chains around the world. Geologists have identified the arrival of a new geological epoch – the Anthropocene – characterised by the unprecedented impact of the human footprint on the planet's natural systems (Crutzen & Stoermer, 2001). We have kick-started highly destructive firestorms, super hurricanes, devastating floods, and potentially genocidal sea-level rise. Despite the recent end of the European colonial era, loss of cultural identity, especially indigenous knowledge systems (Aikenhead & Michell, 2011), continues apace due in no small way to the neo-colonial discourse of modernity (Semali & Kincheloe, 1999; Smith, 2012) embedded, like a Trojan horse, in our international education export industry.

These global crises are negatively impacting young people worldwide, contributing to their sense of social alienation (Taylor, 2018), which is widening fractures in the fabric of our rapidly globalising and violence-prone societies. Ervin Laszlo (2008), a social systems theorist, argues that to break through cycles of social chaos, destruction and despair we need to develop a planetary consciousness. However, raising the consciousness of young people involves much more than imparting objective knowledge about the world; it involves developing the whole person – intellectually, emotionally, morally, spiritually. If we want young people to participate in making the world a better place – inclusive, fair, equitable, socially just, peaceable – we need to help them develop self-transcendence motivation (Maslow, 1971), that is, a commitment to directing compassion, humility and empathy towards other people, other species and Nature.

Education that raises consciousness in this way has been a focus of adult education since Jack Mezirow (1991) published his seminal scholarly work on transformative learning. Transformative learning involves expanding conscious awareness of our social and cultural situatedness, coming to understand deeply who we are and who we might yet become as individuals and social beings (Morrell & O'Connor, 2002). Transformative learning involves developing higher-order capabilities such as critical self-reflection, ethical and political astuteness, empathy and compassion, and visionary and altruistic thinking.

For nearly three decades, transformative learning has been the focus of the first author's (Peter's) teaching and research in an Australian graduate school of science and mathematics education (Taylor, 2013). In 2009, the second author (Milton), a science educator working in Philippines' higher education, enrolled in a Master of Science Education program and completed a research project under Peter's mentorship.

> Peter: I endeavour to engage students (professional educators) in research as/for transformative learning; to develop higher-order abilities for designing teacher education and research programs in their home universities aimed at promoting cultural and environmental sustainable development. My transformative teaching is not without anxiety, for both teacher and students.

> Milton: I experienced great dissonance when first encountering research as transformative learning, and again later when I endeavoured to establish a transformative educational research program in my college in The Philippines. But the journey has proven to be very well worthwhile.

Our purpose in co-writing this chapter is to illustrate some of the complex challenges and changes we have experienced firsthand as teachers and learners of transformative educational research. Drawing on arts-based research methods (Barone & Eisner, 2012), we present narrative, poetic and critically reflective portrayals of some of our trials, tribulations and triumphs. We hope that you, our reader, will come to appreciate the value of research as transformative learning for producing a new generation of educational practitioners – teachers, teacher educators, researchers – who are highly motivated and capable of engaging young people in learning to live and work sustainably in their rapidly globalising communities.

TEACHING TRANSFORMATIVE RESEARCH – PETER

> Again, I tell you, it is easier for a camel to go through the eye of a needle than for a rich man to enter the kingdom of God. (Matthew, pp. 19, 23–36)

Day One (For the 25th Time)

It is the beginning of semester as I walk into the master's research project class for my first encounter with this new group of overseas students. I'm feeling anxious about the pedagogical challenge ahead. That I've been teaching this course for over two decades doesn't make it any easier. It must be ever so for an actor on the opening night. Who amongst these novice researchers will accept my invitation to engage in transformative learning, who will resist, and how strongly? How difficult will it be to *sell* transformative educational research to science and mathematics teacher educators, ambassador-academics from overseas universities, their nations' future educational leaders? Experience tells me that most are likely to be deeply invested in an objectivist epistemology, widely recognised as the royal road to an academic career. How readily will I be able to dissolve their resistance to crossing research paradigm borders and coax them to explore (reflectively, critically, imaginatively) and to represent (narratively, poetically, visually) their subjectivities, and to accept these qualitative methods as legitimate educational research? I contemplate the challenge of the pedagogical pathway ahead.

Contemplating Liberation

For many, research has but one hue,
the Western modern worldly view.

But

… if objectivity denotes what's real,
how can we really hope to deal
with complex truths and how we feel?

…if neutrality is our holy stand,
how can we possibly draw by hand
an ethical line in shifting sand?

…if nothing but numbers validly measure,
how can we ever hope to treasure
poetic truth, love and pleasure?

…if certainty is our endless crave,
how can we be so bold and brave
to risk a vision, a world to save?

So, let us

…expose the iron boundaries, masked
by wolves in sheep's clothes, tasked
to pull the wool over questions asked.

...realise cold reason stills warm hearts at source,
power, control and Truth, of course,
mask the peril of the Trojan horse.

...free the serf, the bonded slave,
to no longer serve as naïve prey,
lest we become in time as they.

...expand our minds, not to conquer,
self-serve, or worship silvered coffer,
wary what Faustian bargains proffer.

...reset our moral compass on,
deeper human interests beckon
needing newer ways to reckon.

...envision a bright utopic age,
artful images dance the page,
a rainbow worldview, beyond the cage.

While preparing the data projector, I reflect on the untapped potential before me, and am buoyed by the success stories of years gone by, stories that portray rich lived experiences of engaging in research as transformative learning by teacher educators from China (Song & Taylor, 2005), Mozambique (Afonso & Taylor, 2009), Nepal (Luitel & Taylor, 2007), Indonesia (Rahmawati & Taylor, 2017), Malaysia (Yusuf, Taylor, & Damanhuri, 2017). Amongst others, their voices can be heard in chapters throughout this book speaking about their vision as agents of transformative change in their places of professional work. But despite these success stories I am careful not to be complacent when first engaging students in research as transformative learning, an experience that is likely to seem deeply counter-intuitive, if not heretical.

The tension I feel is due, in no small part, to the realisation that I need to cater to all students, including those who remain committed to positivistic research, whether by informed choice or blind prejudice; the latter is rare but does happen. On the one hand, a key goal of my transformative pedagogy is to enable students to deconstruct the hegemony of positivism; to open the prison door and explore a landscape of undreamt of possibilities; to flourish in the freedom of a creative research design space in which their subjectivities are liberated.

On the other hand, I also advocate an integral research perspective that values pluralism: from positivism to postmodernism (Taylor, Taylor, & Luitel, 2012). Different epistemologies provide us with the means to produce and represent different types of knowledge; and thus, in designing a study the researcher needs to be mindful of his/her epistemic, moral and aesthetic purposes. It is ironic that the goals of counter-hegemony and inclusiveness can be perceived by students to be in conflict. Initially, it can be difficult to differentiate between deconstructing the hegemony of a dominant ideology and rejecting it *in toto*; it is the former that I advocate, not the latter. Nevertheless, committed positivists tend to conflate the two and can be defensive about their cherished scientific method being under perceived attack.

As I stand before the class I'm keenly aware of this potential dilemma, and am on edge about how to take the students to the creative edge of, what Lev Vygotsky (1978) referred to as, their *zones of proximal development*, where cognitive uncertainty is accompanied by emotional dissonance, if not turmoil. An ethic of care is needed. A source of tension is that I'm never satisfied with my teaching, and constantly seek better ways to engage students in modes of transformative learning – cultural self-knowing, relational knowing, critical knowing, visionary and ethical knowing, knowing in action – that are associated with contemporary qualitative research paradigms (Taylor, 2015). It is important for research students to develop these higher-order abilities through practical experience, rather than learning about them simply in left-brain theoretical terms.

Each semester as I prepare for this class I reflect on crucial pedagogical questions: How should I start my teaching? Should I present a 'big picture' view of the field of contemporary educational research, or does this pose a formidable learning challenge when students face a deluge of new philosophical theories and concepts, such as *paradigm, epistemology, ontology* and *axiology*; especially for those from non-English-speaking-backgrounds? Should I commence with the paradigm of greatest familiarity, notably positivism, or does this prioritising tend to reinforce its hegemony? Should I rather begin by deconstructing its hegemony by situating students in the critical paradigm and have them practice ideology critique, or does this set up an unhelpful antinomy that reinforces a sense of incommensurability between research paradigms? Should I start by engaging students in writing narratively about their research goals and aspirations, encouraging them to value their subjectivities, or does this seem too *fluffy* to hard-nosed objectivists? Should I first engage them non-rationally (imaginatively, altruistically, aesthetically) by reading poetry or stories written by previous research students, or is this likely to be experienced as *weird*? Over the years, I have tried all these starting points, and I recycle and recombine them in response to students' reactions and end-of-unit evaluations.

So, today, I greet the class and ask for introductions. I'm pleasantly surprised that the majority speak excellent English. Given their language proficiency I'm buoyed by my plan to begin by revealing their assumptions about the nature of research, making explicit their taken-for-granted epistemic values! I direct them to write narratively about the purpose of educational research and the governing standards that ensure quality. A predictable whole-class discussion ensues in which students' responses generally are indicative of a commitment to the positivist research paradigm, with reference to the scientific method and the gold standards of objectivity, reliability and validity.

With the intention to evoke their curiosity and disturb their complacency, I read out several poems written by previous students that constituted data texts of their qualitative research inquiries. I explain that these poems serve a legitimate function as both the process and product of contemporary qualitative research.

With the aid of a big picture diagram that depicts the emergence of research paradigms (see Figure 3.1), I explain that poetry is a way of knowing, feeling and expressing that is situated within the arts-based research paradigm of postmodernism (Prendergast, Leggo, & Sameshima, 2009), along with other literary and non-literary genres and modes of reasoning, such as metaphorical and dialectical thinking. This map portrays a succession of research paradigms – positivism, interpretivism, criticalism, postmodernism, integralism – that have crossed disciplinary borders and found their way into educational research during the past 30 years. And this onion-like holonic spectrum (Koestler, 1967) is expanding as newer layers are continually added, enabling us to produce ever new understandings of self and other. I try to reassure that this obscure big picture map is akin to observing a mountain range from a satellite in geosynchronous orbit, and that as the semester progresses we will descend to the peaks and river valleys and explore on foot the details of the rich and varying landscape. I refer to the concept of metaphor and briefly unpack its significance as an important arts-based mode of reasoning. "But for now", I coax, "please have the courage to suspend your disbelief in new ideas, and seek not to understand deeply in the first few weeks".

In preparation for the second class, I allocate a reading on research paradigms (Willis, 2007). My plan for the next few weeks is to alternate between theoretical explanations of successive research paradigms and engaging the students in *possibility thinking* by reading extracts of studies conducted by previous students – to alternate between theory and practice. While doing this, they are to commence writing narratively (and increasingly reflectively) about the professional contexts they are bringing to their research, outlining the personal and professional significance

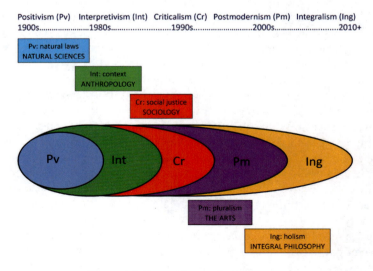

Figure 3.1. Research paradigm emergence

of their intended studies. This writing constitutes the background section of their emergent research proposals, which is the assessment goal for the semester.

The Path Ahead

A few weeks pass, and students begin presenting tentative research questions to the class. Milton Medina refers to his *re-entry action plan*, which his sponsor required him to design before his departure for Australia to ensure that his research will be of practical relevance to The Philippines. Milton outlines a classic instructional development and evaluation project based on a positivistic research approach. At this point, the newer research paradigms he has encountered in the past few weeks seem (not surprisingly) to have been like water off a duck's back. I gently challenge his sense of research purpose and his epistemological assumptions, and I invite him to consider bringing his subjectivity into the foreground of his research, in the form of narratives of his lived experience.

Like many students, once given permission to pass thru the positivist paradigm door into a landscape of infinite creative research design possibilities, Milton accepts the challenge. For the remainder of the semester he designs an auto/ethnographic study (Ellis, 1997) to find answers to the following emergent research questions.

- How did my past teaching and learning experiences (as an undergraduate researcher, a postgraduate researcher in The Philippines, a teacher, and a practising researcher) influence my thoughts of being a positivist?
- Why do I need to understand and consider other research worldviews?
- What are the current perspectives of my co-faculties towards educational research?
- What could be done to influence conceptually transforming myself and my colleagues to embrace multi-paradigmatic educational research?

During second semester, Milton conducts his *research as writing inquiry*, reflecting self-consciously, critically and imaginatively on the experience of engaging in research as transformative learning, all the while writing in a narrative voice about his unique learning journey. Later, we write a journal article for beginning research students on contemporary research paradigms (Taylor & Medina, 2013).

What follows is Milton's portrayal of his encounter with research as transformative learning. Drawing on his Master's dissertation (Medina, 2009), Milton recounts the struggle to shed his traditional epistemological baggage in order to *pass thru the eye of a needle*, and the profound but conflicted impact of research as transformative learning on his professional practice as a university teacher and researcher in The Philippines.

LEARNING TRANSFORMATIVE RESEARCH

Like many of you, I [Milton] want to contribute to the transformation of science education in my country. In writing this chapter, I draw on my personal experiences as a benchmark of the transformative change that I want to experience with my co-educators and students. It is my contention that this transformation can be achieved only through proper mentoring and inspired leadership.

My story starts years ago when I was given the opportunity to undertake a Master of Science Education degree in a prestigious Australian university that specialised in postgraduate professional development of science and mathematics teachers. This opportunity not only allowed me to enjoy what Australia could offer, but also changed my perspective on education, particularly educational research. The experience transformed me as a science educator, as a continuing learner, as a beginning researcher, and as a person. If you can imagine your first time going outside your country, it would surely be a unique experience, with excitement perhaps beyond measure.

Research as Poetry!?

I arrive in Perth in early January, in the height of the summer season, and it's my first time to experience a very long day–the sun sets at 9pm–indeed, a chaotic-confusing circadian rhythm. The first two months are enjoyable and I'm longing to take time out to travel to different cities and other states. The orientation period soon ends and I must face what I have been sent for. I am very excited to attend my first day of the two-semester research project class. While waiting for our professor to arrive, I practise my English by trying to communicate with my foreign classmates: getting to know their backgrounds, professions and life stories; trying to fit-in and understand each other's cultures.

A few minutes pass and someone enters our lecture room: a tall White man carrying a truckload of books. We become quiet. The professor breaks the silence by allowing us to introduce ourselves, stating which country we come from and the purpose of our study. The task is not difficult for me because all Filipino scholars have developed a re-entry action plan that serves as our guide. After this sharing, our professor starts talking about research paradigms and shows us excerpts from the work of previous scholars. I am quite confused because this is a research class but what he shows us is POETRY! Though I am amazed at the stories he shares, I am annoyed because my mind keeps telling me that "these are not research, these are poetry". Indeed, the first day of class is a mixture of both excitement and discouragement. I have been sent for a scholarship to develop my capability to design and produce instructional materials for college science, not to learn how to write POETRY.

Our professor directs us to write down our research goals and aspirations, but I don't know how to start or where to begin; all I do is start writing, and for the first time I write something about my life. But I hate writing! Maybe when I was a child I was fond of writing diaries. But now it seems I have no choice in this *poetry class*, so I continue writing. Amazingly, it is in writing that I find the answer to one of my life-long questions: *"Why do I not like research? What is in research that I hate it so very much?"* The following are extracts from my Master's dissertation (Medina, 2009).

TEACHING AND LEARNING TRANSFORMATIVE RESEARCH

FIRST ENCOUNTER

All of us have our own first encounter; it could be so exciting or so depressing. When I first encountered the word *research* [as an undergraduate student] it only meant one thing for me…a scientific method consisting of logical ways to solve problems which should start with a problem, develop a hypothesis, literature review, methodology, results and interpretations, and then a generalization… doing research was to follow a concrete, inflexible design which apparently has been done also by famous scientists working in the laboratory…This first encounter became the foundation of my ideology about research.

SECOND ENCOUNTER

At the University of North-Eastern Philippines I am studying for a Master of Arts degree in Science Teaching, majoring in Biology. "Good day sir, is this the Research Methods class?" I ask a late fifties gentleman seated at the centre table of the room. "Yes, you're doing the Research Methods for the Masters course?", he replies. He is Dr Positivist from the College of Engineering and a visiting professor of the College of Education. "Yes sir", I reply. A few minutes pass and my classmates are all seated, then he stands and says, "I'm sure there is no need for this class to define what research is because I know you know very well what it is all about", he speaks with authority as an opening salvo. "But what I am interested to teach everybody in this course is the what, why and how of statistics", he continues. As I was expecting, the first day of the class is the heaviest time of the semester for I get to know the high expectations of the lecturers in every subject. "Next meeting we will discuss validity and reliability of educational research, so I encourage you to start reading about it", Dr Positivist says. While packing-up my backpack my mind is puzzled, "What is validity? Reliability?"

The following Saturday in Dr Positivist's Research Methods class: "From now on start choosing your thesis adviser from your college and sit down with him/her for your possible title", says Dr Positivist. "Ok, let's discuss statistics in educational research". And so, another day ends in Dr Positivist's class.

The same struggle continues. The ghost of my baccalaureate research practice keeps haunting me. Thinking again of a possible problem and going through thick literature, writing a methodology in the past tense, findings, conclusion, and recommendations. It is just a cycle of events, as though living in a wheel but at a different level. With a strong background in natural science, I start thinking about what possible experiment could I / would I do as educational research in the human context. It is just a cycle, a cycle of pain, yet I cannot do anything about it. Is there a life other than this practice? Could there be something more beautiful, meaningful, or life-changing?

I attend Dr Positivist's office. "Sir, I plan to include the values of my respondents on biotechnology", I say to Dr Positivist. "No, do not include that question because we cannot quantify that in your research. Try to think of questions which are specific, measurable, attainable, reliable, and time bounded (SMART). They are all we need to justify your research claims", Dr Positivist replies. "Yes, perhaps you're right, Sir, I only have one year for my research so it must be SMART. Ok, I will think about it, Sir". It seems like Dr Positivist is not convinced with my proposed questions, I sigh.

Another time in Dr Positivist's office: "Sir, I have no longer included the values of my respondents. I will be using two groups, one will be experimental which will utilize a modelling approach of teaching and the other would be a control group which will be using a conventional lecture method". Then I smile at him hoping that my opinion will be accepted. "Good! This study is very feasible, and has the assurance of good validity and reliability", says Dr Positivist. "You can go to Dr Statistics for the computation of your experimental results, including the validity of your questionnaires. It will cost you 3,000 pesos. You can also ask Prof Reliability for the reliability of your test questionnaires. I know you two are friends so maybe you can ask for a discount! Lastly, to Dr Grammar for your grammar check which I think the cost is usually 3,000 pesos as a standard payment", Dr Positivist happily adds. "This is great, Sir, so I can now start my research", I leave Dr Positivist's office with huge relief.

Six months later during my thesis defence nobody questions my study. My panel comprises the Doctors I paid for my statistics, grammar and reliability tests. Who then would question my research?

A few months pass and I am awarded my degree and am now a certified Master of Arts. But what did I master?

RESISTANCE: WHAT'S WRONG WITH MY OLD THINKING?

Studying the unknown involves leaving the familiar. Leaving is a prerequisite to transcending self and society. (Alsop, 2002, p. 1)

Back to the Future in Australia

Being armed with a positivist worldview, my life is stressful as I'm bothered by daily threats of academic transformation. My resistance to understand and adopt paradigm shifts is like a Van-der-Waal's tension between the same electronic charges. I firmly hold to the notion that every problem should be solved by the scientific method and explained by numbers. Every scientific truth can only be achieved by carefully following the scientific method embedded with internal/external validity assurances.

"Oh God, have I enrolled in the correct subject? Do I need this? Is this a theology class? I have an obligation and I need to do something for my re-entry action plan", I say to myself during the first day of the Master's research project class. The first week is horrible, as I cannot relate to what my teacher is saying in class; after class I come away with lots of doubts and questions.

I share with another professor about being sceptical of auto/ethnographic studies after attending the research presentation of a PhD student. "I doubt how can such research process bring about transformation? Is it just navel gazing stuff? I know every research has limitations, but do these new research paradigms have the capacity to address the urgency of various educational problems?", I ask. But she calmly replies, "Ok, every research has limitations, but that is not the question. The question is what can be done to address its limitations?". The professor is patient and tells me to read more about auto/ethnography. She refers me to different resource materials. So, I continue reading but my readings seem to only prolong my doubts.

UNEXPECTED CHANGE

We meet the new environment with enthusiasm, experience the widening of our horizon as empowering, and explore aspects of our identity that were buried at home. We fall in love at first sight. (Alsop, 2002, p. 4)

As the weeks pass, I start to realize that there is life aside from experimental research. I brainstorm and uncover these questions: "Why is it so hard for most of us to produce research? Why is it that research in our country is as though for an aristocratic world only? What is wrong with our ideologies in educational research?" These emergent research questions help to unveil my past painful and exhausting experiences of educational research, using an auto/ethnographic methodology that changes my perspective towards research forever.

As I reflect critically on where I have come from, as far as my research experiences are concerned, I say to myself, "What have I done before?", and the tears in my eyes start to flow as my conscience shakes my heart while I think about the animals – *biological specimens* – that I have killed when conducting experimental research. A feeling of self-pity grows as I realize that research is expensive; research has become a business in my country. Scientific research is sometimes heartless! Yes, I need to transform and examine critically the different schemes of my past experiences that have built up the hegemony of my positivist thinking. I reflect on what our professor said in this week's class about single paradigm (positivist) research: "You're building a house where you treat all the materials as nails because you only have a hammer". Let me revise this, "I'm doing an experiment where I treat all my respondents as mice, by living in the dogma of positivism".

At the same time my auto/ethnographic inquiry brings to the surface my deeply sedimented values, and I feel energised by the realisation that there are life's questions which cannot be measured by numbers or proven by statistics. I recollect the following experience.

> One time, I was invited to a forum with stakeholders and Congress to present the data of our biodiversity research on one of the Protected Areas in Mindanao. During the forum, I presented several endemic and threatened species that are struggling to thrive in the area which urgently needs protection and conservation. I emphasised their role in the ecosystem and the long-term benefits for the local communities. The area is not only rich with biodiversity but also with gold, copper and other high value ores. Hence, people illegally mining the area are having a detrimental effect on biodiversity's survival. A representative of the mining group presented some figures saying, "During the height of the availability of the ores in the area, miners could gain 7,000,000 Php (~1.4 million US dollars) from gold ores alone. This excludes copper and other mineral ores. This money obtained from mining generates income for local villagers, puts food on their table, and they could send their children to school".
>
> Later, I was asked by a Congressman (a policy maker), "Sir, what is the value of biodiversity in the area? Is this equitable to what miners are taking?" I kept silent for a few minutes and said to the congressman, "It is true that miners are taking plenty of money from the mineral ores, but I think we need to consider the future of our generations. I believe that life is more precious than gold, our biodiversity is more precious than the mineral ores. The destruction of our environment cannot be paid by money, and often we realize its importance when we have no more freely available potable water, our rivers are polluted with mercury or cyanide, and our children are dying of infections and contamination. It is true we can gain millions from the mining, but what good is our money yet we compromise the life of our future generations?" Then, a moment of silence.

As I continue my journey in this inquiry, I realize that there should be diversity in the ways in which knowledge is produced and we must respect the emerging epistemologies and methodologies (Kincheloe & Tobin, 2009) for everyone to have freedom to design research that addresses his/her unique inquiry. I realise that what I have done previously is to treat positivist research as an end to all educational problems (Guba & Lincoln, 1989) – the gold standard of research practice in the higher institutions in my country – often doing research only for our own technical benefit (Grundy, 1987). I open my eyes to the realisation that there are concepts in educational research that cannot be explained meaningfully by the positivist paradigm. There is life aside from experimental research and there are diverse ways we can address the complex problems we face in our society. More often than not, we make better decisions about crucial problems in our society from our experiences and values as a person, rather than relying only on statistics.

My professional role now, as I reconceptualise it, is to help my own students to understand that there is more than one research paradigm, that there are other quality standards equally powerful to those of positivism and that they must be observed carefully in order to ensure that alternative research is conducted at a high level of quality. Like a prisoner set free, I commit myself to working on projects in local communities in Mindanao, empowering them to engage in biodiversity research and conservation. I feel the potential freedom of conducting meaningful research projects that benefit local communities.

A NEW BEGINNING AND NEW CHALLENGES

I return to my college in The Philippines, so fired up that I cannot wait to change the hegemony and injustices of positivism that have been controlling our institutions for more than half a century. Guided by my new transformative research understandings, I start making small steps towards the transformation of our institution's research culture.

Prescribing Transformative Research

Although the minimum qualification for managing a college research office is a doctorate, I boldly volunteer for the role because I believe that I need the office for my plans to work out. Thankfully, the new President shows faith in me and gives me the opportunity to manage the college research program as Director of Research. It's quite a relief, but a scary challenge.

One of my first actions is to redesign the College Research Handbook. The revised Handbook showcases new policies for doing research in the College, with added elements of new research paradigms for faculty and students to choose from that suit the ontology and epistemology of their individual inquiries. I establish the Transformative Education Research Group (TERG) for the College, aiming to enhance its research capability and culture. The program presents a monthly seminar for students and faculty on the importance of research in the institution, gradually introducing new research paradigms.

After a year of implementing the TERG surprisingly none of the faculty show signs of interest in adopting new research paradigms. But perhaps this is quite a short time for major change to occur? A professor from Australia visits the College and presents a seminar on action research, emphasising how it can help teachers, students and the entire college. This is strong support for me as the new Director of Research. After the visit, I have renewed hope that it will encourage teachers to start conducting research as part of their professional practice. But I am wrong.

Two years pass and no-one from the faculty has submitted a research proposal to my office. Several factors could account for this: heavy workloads, lack of capability in doing research, or lack of interest. A faculty member tells me, "We are doing research! When I send my students to the library to answer their assignments that is already research. What more do you want? What more do you expect?". These questions puzzle me and trouble my aspirations for establishing a culture of research as part of our professional practice, which seems increasingly impossible.

So, I start thinking all over again: "Who among the college community has an open heart to accept change?" Then I realise that there is one piece in the puzzle that I have forgotten: my Biology students, who are beginning teachers.

Co-Generating Transformative Research

This year, my Biology students and I take up the challenge to conduct a massive biodiversity survey at Mainit Hot Springs Protected Landscape, an important biodiversity "hot spot" in Compostela Valley (Maglana, Medina, Nabayra, & Cabras, 2016). Some of my co-faculty doubt that we can do this because, firstly, we do not seem to have the capability for biodiversity research as experts are thought to be found only in large universities in our country. And, secondly, the area is massive (1,775 hectares) and unsafe, especially for students, as it contains an old gold mining site. But despite these odds I see this as a valuable opportunity, not only for the school but for the students – future science teachers.

To resolve the first crisis, I collaborate with my former professor at Central Mindanao University as well as friends from the International Union for Conservation of Nature and the University of the Philippines to guide us on the project. This is an excellent opportunity for us to work hand-in-hand with scientists in the field, and for learning to flourish for all of us, even though not formally taught inside the four walls of the classroom. Students are assigned to study particular species and evaluate their ecological status. During fieldwork, a Biology student says to me:

> How I wish that politicians will see the destruction of the park, so that they will know that gold is not worthy in exchange for biodiversity!

I am surprised when I hear these words from the student. Then I realise that what we have done so far is not just biodiversity research, but also involves developing the ethical standards, judgement making and moral values of the students. Suddenly I understand deeply for the first time the statement by Professor Patrick Awuah, the transformative educator and co-founder of Ashesi University in Ghana: "Our society must be very intentional in educating its leaders". For me, this sentiment is what transformative research is really all about. Awuah continues: "All we need to do is to give them the skills, involve our students in their education, and discuss with them social issues that our society is facing, and then magic will happen" (Awuah, 2007).

We are in the field and, after analysing our captured species of bats and birds, I take a quiet moment to sit by myself and reflect on my undergraduate years, saying to myself, "I have not experienced this before. My Biology education was just full of memorising facts and repeating back to our professor. Now I understand what it means to be an educator". I admit that there are times when I wanted to give up and go back to my old nature, into *just teaching,* like most teachers do: teaching inside the four walls of the classroom. But what now gives me great hope is seeing my students starting to develop their passion for doing biodiversity research with a strong emphasis on ethics and moral values. After a little while a student comes to me and says, "Sir, I have seen my future now!". I pause for a moment and deeply understand what he means. I recall my past experience as an undergraduate biology student when I didn't know where to go after graduation because I had not been trained like this young man. This is indeed a heart-warming experience, sitting here in the mountain range of Sitio New Bohol, Mindanao.

I believe that my college has now taken the first step towards transformation of its research culture. I understand that transformative research is not only about introducing new research paradigms, or compiling research work from teachers, or getting funding from research agencies, or telling stories, or writing poetry. Transformative research is about giving our students the opportunity to develop in themselves skills, right judgment, ethics and good moral values, and enabling them to have the ability to face their future. As Professor Ken Robinson (2006), the inspiring public speaker on transforming education, observed recently about our young people: "We may not see their future but they will. Our role as educators is to help them make something out of it". Transformative research is about touching lives: touching the lives of students and at the same time students' lives touching ours. And it is my contention that the manner in which we properly mentor and inspire our students will make all the difference.

THE HEART OF TRANSFORMATIVE EDUCATION

I believe that transformative education goes beyond formal education (i.e., learning in the university) and that everyone is capable of a paradigm shift. Transformative education is more than a subject or style of teaching. It is about changing the paradigms of our students, giving them hope and a sense of purpose.

I met Neil two years ago during our biodiversity research study at Mt Candalaga in Maragusan, Compostela Valley. He is a mountaineer who recently fell in love with Odonata studies – an insect order that I have been studying for the past years. To me, he was a spoiled brat with no plans for his life, he slept everywhere in the city at night since he didn't want to go home and stay with his broken family. Without having a purpose in life he had learned to believe that life was just *come what may.*

In one of my biodiversity expeditions I took him along as a field assistant. One night in the forest we shared our life's experiences, learned from each other, opened up our life stories, and I learned that he is an avid mountaineer. So, I suggested to him the possibility of being my research assistant, and he gladly accepted. After a series of fieldworks, Neil transformed into a person of social worth. He has come to realise that all people, whether they have undergone formal or informal education, can do something better with their lives, especially helping to save our natural environment. In his words:

> Before I have been climbing several mountains around Mindanao, it was fun especially with my friends. When we reached the summit, we stayed there for a day or two partying, but it was just a climb. I did not know that there was more to being a mountaineer. I did not know that even a lone mountaineer can do great things for saving our environment. I know that I have not finished

school, I even do not have a stable job, but the things I do today [as research assistant] – doing the right thing for our country – is something that I can be proud of to my daughter and family.

Now he leads the fieldwork in Compostela Valley Province, training young students with the basic protocols of biological fieldwork, encouraging them that they can do greater things for our Mother Earth. My heart fills with gratitude and satisfaction seeing the transformation of Neil from a street kid to a conservationist.

I believe that our society needs not only brilliant minds but also people with a passionate heart willing to do the right thing (Amorado, 2011). I am more than happy now that biodiversity has been included in the curriculum of the Bachelor of Science in Biology degree program at the University of Mindanao, where I now work. I am hopeful that this course will encourage more students to participate in biodiversity research for the benefit of both Filipinos and humanity at large, while giving them hope and a sense of purpose of what it means to be a true biologist, a steward of humanity and of our Mother Earth.

FROM WRITING TO PRACTICE

I didn't fully understand transformative education until I returned to the Philippines and continued doing the things I really love: undertaking fieldwork, educating students, and being part of conserving and preserving Philippine biodiversity. In the process, I have come to realise that my earlier understanding was rather mediocre. As I now contemplate my actions I realise that transformative education has a deeper meaning; it is about changing my whole paradigm as a person, as a teacher and teacher educator, as a beginning researcher, and that the poetic style of writing shared by Peter in 2009 was just an instrument for opening myself to the diverse realities of life.

I am happy now that many of my students and co-faculty are embracing the idea of taking part in biodiversity research in Mindanao, not only as a formal course or institutional requirement but as their social responsibility in helping to restore the balance of our unique and fragile ecosystem. This is giving them a much deeper sense of purpose, and is awakening their moral obligation as citizens of our country and of our planet as a whole.

Indeed, *from writing to practice* depicts the cycle of my engagement in research as transformative learning: from learning to write, understanding and accepting the change of paradigm of the *I*, practicing transformation *for* others, and then learning again to write (as in this chapter).

CODA

Milton

When I remember my first few days in Peter's research project class, especially my attitude of "This is POETRY!", I cannot help laughing as I now see the wonderful transformation that I experienced. It was, indeed, writing an auto/ethnography that unlocked my life's question of "Why do I hate research?", leading me to deconstruct the mystery of my anti-research attitude. This mode of writing as inquiry enabled me to adopt critical reflective thinking to challenge my own assumptions and empowered me with creative means to represent and reconceptualise my lived experiences. Ultimately, engaging in research as transformative learning has empowered me to empower others.

Peter

My conviction is to prepare teachers and teacher educators with a heartfelt moral conscience and higher-order capabilities to engage future generations of students in education for sustainable development. My commitment is fortified by Parker Palmer's (2010) call for teachers to have the courage to nurture their students' minds, hearts and spirit.

Stories like Milton's inspire me, in my role as a teacher of transformative educational research, to accept the inevitable anxiety of pushing against the momentum of history that privileges positivistic research. There is much of great personal and social significance to be gained from engaging in research as transformative learning – for our professional selves, our students, and the world at large.

Rather than remaining fixated with an arid world of numbers so favoured by quantitative research purists, research as transformative learning impels us to search inwards while contemplating the world around us, to encounter the richness of lived experience at our fingertips, and to invite others to open their hearts and minds to the infinite possibilities of our rapidly developing worlds. We only need to look inward to encounter our infinite potential to develop more fully as human beings. In the words of William Blake's (1863) epic poem, Auguries of Innocence:

> To see a world in a grain of sand
> And a heaven in a wild flower
> Hold infinity in the palm of your hand
> And eternity in an hour

REFERENCES

Afonso, E. Z. (2006). *Developing a culturally inclusive philosophy of science teacher education in Mozambique* (Doctoral thesis). Curtin University of Technology, Bentley, WA. Retrieved from https://catalogue.curtin.edu.au/primo-explore/fulldisplay?docid=CUR_ALMA2193975520001951&context=L&vid=CUR_ALMA&search_scope=CurtinBlended&tab=default_tab&lang=en_US

Afonso, E. Z., & Taylor, P. (2009). Critical autoethnographic inquiry for culture-sensitive professional development. *Reflective Practice, 10*(2), 1–12.

Aikenhead, G., & Michell, H. (2011). *Bridging cultures: Indigenous and scientific ways of knowing nature*. Ontario, CA: Pearson.

Alsop, C. K. (2002). Home and away: Self-reflexive auto-/ethnography. *Forum: Qualitative Social Research, 3*(2), 10. Retrieved from http://www.qualitative-research.net/index.php/fqs/article/view/823

Amorado, R. V. (2011). *Kakistocracy: Rule of the unprincipled, unethical, and unqualified.* Davao City: Research and Publication Office, Ateneo de Davao University, Philippines.

Awuah, P. (2007). *How to educate leaders: Liberal arts.* Retrieved from http://www.ted.com/talks/patrick_awuah_on_educating_leaders

Barone, T., & Eisner, E. W. (2012). *Arts based research.* Thousand Oaks, CA: Sage Publications.

Blake, W. (1863). *Auguries of innocence.* Retrieved from https://www.poetryfoundation.org/poems/43650/auguries-of-innocence

Crutzen, P. J., & Stoermer, E. (2000, May). The anthropocene. *Global Change Newsletter, 41,* 17–18.

Earth Charter Commission. (2001). *The Earth Charter.* Retrieved from http://earthcharter.org/bibliocategory/the-earth-charter/

Ellis, C. (1997). Evocative autoethnography: Writing emotionally about our lives. In W. G. Tierney & Y. S. Lincoln (Eds.), *Representation and the text: Re-framing the narrative voice* (pp. 115–139). Albany, NY: State University of New York Press.

Grundy, S. (1987). *Curriculum: Product or praxis?* New York, NY: The Falmer Press.

Guba, E. G., & Lincoln, Y. S. (1989). *Fourth generation evaluation.* London & New Delhi: Sage Publications.

Kincheloe, J., & Tobin, K. (2009). The much exaggerated death of positivism. *Cultural Studies of Science Education Journal, 4*(3), 513–528.

Koestler, A. (1967). *The ghost in the machine.* Last Century Media.

Laszlo, E. (2008). *Quantum shift in the global brain: How the new scientific reality can change us and our world.* Rochester, VT: Inner Traditions.

Luitel, B. C., & Taylor, P. C. (2007). The Shanai, the pseudosphere and other imaginings: Envisioning a culturally contextualised mathematics education. *Cultural Studies of Science Education, 2*(3), 621–638.

Maglana, W. P., Medina, M. N. D., Nabayra, E. S., & Cabras, A. A. (2016). *Mainit Hot Springs protected landscape: Requiem for a watershed, Reclaiming a lost heritage.* Davao City: NabunturanBalik-Kinyaiahan Foundation.

Maslow, A. H. (1971). *The farther reaches of human nature.* New York, NY: Viking Press.

Matthew. (n.d.). *The gospel according to Matthew.* The New Testament. Retrieved from http://en.wikipedia.org/wiki/Eye_of_a_needle

Medina, M. (2009). *Transforming the old thinking: Understanding and adopting new conceptual world views for educational research* (Masters dissertation). Science and Mathematics Education Centre, Curtin University, Bentley, Western Australia.

Mezirow, J. (1991). *Transformative dimensions of adult learning.* San Fransisco, CA: Jossey-Bass.

Morrell, A., & O'Connor, M. A. (2002). Introduction. In E. V. O'Sullivan, A. Morrell, & M. A. O'Connor (Eds.), *Expanding the boundaries of transformative learning: Essays on theory and praxis* (pp. xv–xx). New York, NY: Palgrave.

Palmer, P. J., Zajonc, A., & Scribner, M. (2010). *The heart of higher education: A call to renewal: Transforming the academy through collegial conversations.* San Fransisco, CA: Jossey-Bass.

Prendergast, M., Leggo, C., & Sameshima, P. (Eds.). (2009). *Poetic inquiry: Vibrant voices in the social sciences.* Rotterdam, The Netherlands: Sense Publishers.

Rahmawati, Y., & Taylor, P. C. (2017). The fish becomes aware of the water in which it swims: Revealing the power of culture in her chemistry teaching identity. *Cultural Studies of Science Education, 13*(2), 525–537. Retrieved from http://link.springer.com/journal/11422

Robinson, K. (2006). *How schools kill creativity.* Retrieved from http://www.ted.com/talks/ken_robinson_says_schools_kill_creativity

Semali, L. M., & Kincheloe, J. L. (Eds.). (1999). *What is indigenous knowledge? Voices from the academy.* New York, NY: Falmer Press.

Smith, L. T. (2012). *Decolonising methodologies: Research and indigenous peoples* (2nd ed.). London & New York, NY: Zed Books.

Song, J., & Taylor, P. C. (2005). Pure blue sky: A soulful autoethnography of chemistry teaching in China. *Reflective Practice, 6*(1), 141–163.

Taylor, E. L. (2018). Reaching out to the disaffected: Mindfulness and art therapy for building resilience to violent extremism. *Learning: Research and Practice, 4*(1), 39–51.

Taylor, P. C. (2013). Research as transformative learning for meaning-centred professional development. In O. Kovbasyuk & P. Blessinger (Eds.), *Meaning-centered education: International perspectives and explorations in higher education* (pp. 168–185). New York, NY: Routledge.

Taylor, P. C. (2015). Transformative science teacher education. In R. Gunstone (Ed.), *Encyclopedia of science education* (pp. 981–983). Dordrecht: Springer.

Taylor, P. C., & Medina, M. N. D. (2013). Educational research paradigms: From positivism to multi-paradigmatic. *Journal for Meaning-Centered Education, 1*(2). Retrieved from https://www.researchgate.net/publication/264196558_Educational_research_paradigms_From_positivism_to_multiparadigmatic

Taylor, P. C., Taylor, E., & Luitel, B. C. (2012). Multi-paradigmatic transformative research as/for teacher education: An integral perspective. In B. J. Fraser, K. G. Tobin, & C. J. McRobbie (Eds.), *Second international handbook of science education* (pp. 373–387). Dordrecht: Springer.

Vygotsky, L. (1978). *Mind in society: The development of higher psychological processes.* Cambridge, MA: Harvard University Press.

Willis, J. W. (2007). *Foundations of qualitative research: Interpretive and critical approaches.* Thousand Oaks, CA: Sage Publications.

Yusuf, L., Taylor, P. C., & Damanhuri, M. I. M. (2017). Designing critical pedagogy for counteracting the hegemonic culture of the traditional chemistry classroom: An auto/ethnographic account. *Issues in Educational Research, 27*(1), 168–184. Retrieved from http://www.iier.org.au/iier

ABOUT THE AUTHORS

Milton Norman D. Medina is my name. I was born in Montevista Compostela Valley, Philippines. I hold a Master of Science in Science Education from Curtin University, Western Australia, and am currently completing my PhD in Biology, majoring in Systematics, at Central Mindanao University, Bukidnon, Philippines. I am the Director of the Institute for Biodiversity and Environment at the University of Mindanao, Davao City, Philippines. My research interests include taxonomy of the genus *Hoya* (Apocynaceae), order Coleoptera, tropical ecology and conservation, and transformative science education for engaging local communities in sustainable development of the rich natural heritage of the Philippines.

Peter Charles Sinclair Taylor. I have been in academia since 1982, after practising as a science/maths teacher in secondary schools in Australia and the UK and an adult educator in an Indigenous community in Central Australia. For 3 decades I worked at the Science and Mathematics Education Centre, Curtin University, Western Australia. As a postgraduate supervisor/advisor/mentor of many teacher educators from universities in Asia, Africa and the South Pacific, I became deeply attuned to their rich cultural capital, and came to appreciate the pressing need for education systems worldwide to protect and nurture biocultural diversity. This abiding ethical commitment was the driving force behind developing the approach of research as transformative learning, the theme of this book.

PART 2

CONTEMPLATING TRANSFORMATIVE RESEARCH METHODS

SURESH GAUTAM

4. LETTER TO PROFESSOR AUGUSTE COMTE

A Counter Narrative to Positivism

It is one of the chilly days of September 2011. I am standing in a conference hall at Kathmandu University in front of academicians, researchers and professors to present my Master of Philosophy (MPhil) dissertation – *"Literacy Sucks!" Voice of Tharu Women* (Gautam, 2011). The group of academicians and researchers is standing by to offer their comments on my dissertation to help make it a world class thesis, although they do not seem to be so sure about the world they represent. Most of the people in the hall are desperately waiting to know the 'findings' of my research. The Dean of the School briefly addresses the academic community and requests me to present my dissertation. I start telling the stories from my dissertation of Tharu women and their literacy practices.

The Tharu people are an ethnic group living in the inner Terai of Nepal. I conducted ethnographic field work in one of the villages of Dang District in the Mid-Western Development Region, my home village. I have observed these Tharu women since my childhood days. They were working as bonded laborers in the community.

I share that contemporary literacy practices neither recognize the cultural practices of Tharu culture nor prepare them to conduct their lives. As soon as I complete my presentation, the floor opens for a question and answer session.

"Is this *a* research?", a voice asks.
"How can he claim *truth*?", another voice questions.
"Are narratives and vignettes sufficient for you to claim *truth*?", probes another voice.
"Can you see the methodology, there is no trace of validity and reliability!", shouts the next voice.
"How can you derive *the* conclusion?", implores another voice.
"The findings are not related to any variables", asserts yet another voice.
"Can it be research without generalization?"
"Sampling…". "Test…". "Prove…".

The hall echoes with such voices that question me along Comtian lines of thought. I sense that the expectations behind these voices are clearly aligned with positivism. They are searching for the validity and reliability of my research, as clichés of positivism. Clearly, they cannot accept alternative ways of thinking, doing and researching. At that moment, I am standing like a culprit in front of advocates in the court of positivism.

This event illustrates how much social science research has been impressed by the positivism of Professor Auguste Comte, the so-called founder of positivism who rejected theological and metaphysical explanations of the sociology of his time. During my MPhil and subsequent doctoral studies, I experienced such situations in a host of academic forums, both in Nepal and abroad.

On completion of my MPhil in 2012 I enrolled in a PhD program in the same university. I was fortunate to have the opportunity to facilitate research courses in the university as a teaching assistant and lecturer with professors who cultivated the seed of creative ways of doing research in my soul/mind.

In 2009, in my initial days as a higher education student, I would say that I was a perfect positivist who believed that research *must* be objective and value free. During those days I was a new Nepali Comte in the university. Gradually, however, the Comte inside me realized that positivism was not sufficient to present the social complexities of where I was living. It took me a couple of years to cultivate the seed of humanist research that values the human world and sociocultural contexts.

Moreover, in 2015 when I started working as a lecturer in the university, I had the opportunity to facilitate research courses and to supervise MEd and MPhil dissertations. During supervision of my students' research I struggled to deconstruct their ways of thinking, expression and representation of ideas. I would find my earlier image of Nepali Comte among them, deeply rooted in their minds/souls. Motivated by a desire to contest the dominance of positivism, I decided to write a letter to Comte. In doing so, I wanted to challenge "single-paradigm" thinking in educational and social science research, and to create a counter narrative that legitimates the practice of transformative educational research in higher education.

The hegemony of the positivist research paradigm has ruled Nepali higher education for a century, perhaps imported from British India. As a university facilitator of graduate students, it is my experience that research in higher education in Nepal has taken positivism for granted as a "mainstream" practice. By and large, higher education in Nepal follows Comtian positivism in terms of thinking and researching. In this chapter, I question the ideals of positivism, arguing that positivism is not sufficient to deal with the chaos and complexities of contemporary social realities. However, I do not deny the legitimacy of positivism in social science research which offers a path to understanding society in a scientific way. Rather, my main concern is that the Comtian perspective is not helpful for creating sustainable research practices that acknowledge the rich diversity of local knowledge heritages. Thus, I believe that positivism fails to promote an epistemic ecology of research and practice.

Philosophically speaking, Comte's positivism arose from "positive philosophy" and became popular in the early days of the social sciences. In early Greek civilization Aristotle mentioned that truth is located in the world of action and that it is observable. However, I do not really know how much of present-day Aristotelian ideas are free from the distortion of 2000 years of subjugation by Christian theosophy. Moreover, the history of (Western) knowledge was dominated by scientific revolutionaries such as Copernicus, Kepler and Galileo (Roberts & Westad, 2013) who up-turned the "apple cart" of what constitutes legitimate knowledge claims in the West. People started feeling proud when claiming: "Look! Our society and human relations can be studied like science". Such a notion has been reflected in Nepali higher education where science has gained popularity in all social science disciplines, including psychology, history, political science and education.

As a contemporary transformative thinker, educationist and researcher, I have experienced the considerable challenge of engaging my students in promoting local cultural thinking and representation of local cosmologies and belief systems. I have observed that research and teaching practices are constrained in three ways. First, the positivist creed of a one-size-fits-all pedagogical approach is dominant. Second, students take positivism for granted in their thinking and practice. Third, university teachers are not prepared to engage in culture-specific thinking. This dominant positivist mindset makes it very difficult to address socio-cultural complexities. To counter positivist hegemony, I endeavor to enable my students to reconceptualize the positivist ideals that frame their thinking and research practice, especially objectivity, validity and reliability.

In this chapter, I draw on the "arts-based postmodernist" research paradigm (Taylor, Taylor, & Luitel, 2013) and employ a "letter writing" genre to address Professor August Comte, the so-called father of modern sociology who was largely responsible for incorporating the "scientific turn" into the social sciences. The letter writing genre is an artistic endeavor to examine everyday research practices in imaginative ways, drawing attention to the cruelties and contradictions inscribed in today's neoliberal society (Foster, 2016). Neoliberal thoughts mainly follow the agenda of the corporate world of social transformation (Birch, 2017) which aims to increase university business models. Written in a personalized manner, my letter challenges the hegemony of positivism, seeking alternatives to its unidimensionality. As Simon O'Sullivan (2010) argues, the arts help to affirm the method of the letter writing genre. In this regard, the letter writing genre is, like Foster's (2016) notion of "acrobatics", "intended to evoke ambiguities, a sense of being in the margins and balancing the acts as aspects of the research experience" (p. 14). I use this method to illustrate a personal, subjective and creative representation of the reflexive self, in accordance with O'Sullivan (2010) who identifies self-reflexivity as a *"transformative act* that has an impact on the researcher and researched" (p. 22).

In this regard, I present Comte with an argument that challenges his legacy of thinking and representation. My argument is structured according to five research roles that I imagine adopting as a transformative researcher: an anti-positivist, a reflective agent, a revolutionary actor, an artist, and an ecologist. From each vantage point my letter to Comte invites him to reflect critically on the efficacy of his espoused positivism.

IF I WERE AN ANTI-POSITIVIST

Dear Professor Comte, it was 1822 – you may still remember the year (perhaps it was our pre-incarnated life) – when you published your positive philosophy in an article entitled *Plan of the Scientific Operations Necessary for Reorganizing Society* (Comte, 1975).

Some of our colleagues (of the East and West) argue that you did a marvelous job by bringing the "hard core sciences" into the landscape of the social sciences. They refer to your ardent statement about replacing theological and metaphysical approaches by positive approaches because the former hindered sociology (social sciences) from being a physics-like discipline. Whether you replaced metaphysics by physics or you simply introduced a new form of metaphysics is another matter. I do not rule out that someone needed to challenge the prevailing "clergy-approach" to social research which was encapsulated in the grandiose doctrine of the Judeo-Christian worldview.

Perhaps it is appropriate for me to quote Theodore Adorno's (1999) method of "quicksilver", which means to critique the source concept by pinpointing its contradictory manifestations. Adopting this approach, I aim to critique your version of positivism by analyzing the key ideas of validity and reliability.

Reliability

Your view of reliability as consistency has been the basis for promoting staticity in the research enterprise. Well, a certain degree of staticity may be needed but how can you prescribe social researchers to be static in their research designs whilst a large part of the social world is always dynamic? I argue that your notion of reliability needs revising to address the dynamic interplay between knowledge, knowing and knower. It usually takes me a year to convince my students that the knower (researcher) can rigorously understand their own knowing process. The moral of my argument lies in the very nature of knowledge that is partly intangible and implicit and partly tangible and explicit. More so, can knowing always be tied to finding universal rules and values? Can knowing always be equated with 'number crunching'?

I am also very much concerned about your intention of making the researcher invisible! Perhaps, your initial interest in proposing a positive philosophy was to challenge contemporary aristocratic, elitist and inhuman practices of knowledge generation. Your proposition of reliability as stability could be a source of the status quo in which research designs became unresponsive to time and place and serve to reproduce the same template, over and over again.

Validity

Dear Professor Comte, I draw your attention to the notion of validity which students in higher education in Nepal attempt to maintain in any research they conduct. On a day in December 2013 in the corner of the cafeteria, faculties of the university were discussing ways of enhancing the creativity of their students. I proposed, "Let's make our students write stories!". Immediately, two students from the MPhil program in English Education joined the discussion. They voiced skepticism about using personal stories in their research. Their silent eyes were searching for validity in the research methods. Culturally, Nepali students are very reluctant to present a counter argument against their teacher.

Initially, my students want to search single-mindedly for validity through your positivist paradigm which proposes that validity should be judged on the basis of two conditions: (a) whether the research has a strong causality, and (b) whether it is generalisable to the population under study. Reflecting on my experience, the first condition has not been useful for exploring new possibilities, because the notion of a causal relationship has been the basis for curtailing creative thinking in research. I also argue that the second condition for fulfilling validity is not useful most of the time because undue emphasis is given to the notion of the static nature of social reality. Do you think that social reality is always static? Do causal relationships necessarily remain static? Can there be anything apart from a causal relationship?

Empirical Observations

Perhaps, a number of historic forces might have pushed you to create a positive sociology based upon empirical observations that are used to generate and test abstract laws of human organization (Turner, 2001). By the way, what do you mean by "empirical observation"? Does your notion of empirical observation consider the human body as an external object, or is there space in your philosophy for internal observation? Do you think that your extensive efforts of equating social science with pure science are justifiable in the case of describing unrecognized philosophies of the other that are manifested in the everyday lives of human beings?

You might not have expected that a person from *the third world* would challenge your "golden paradigm" of positivist research. The golden paradigm is a systematic process in which numerical data are used to test *a priori* theories. The golden paradigm was the outcome of your positivism which claims that human relationships should be studied in a rational and scientific way. Are you sure that you lived a rational and scientific life?

I wish to inform you that in this chapter I am not going to design an alternative "grand narrative", like yours, to challenge your positivistic ideas. Indeed, I might be somewhat unscientific and irrational while challenging the golden paradigm.

Myths

Dear Professor Comte, you seem to have dedicated your life to making social theories that avoid perpetuating *cultural myths*. However, cultural myths provide useful explanations for social realities, especially in the making of teachers (Britzman, 1986), and their usefulness depends on the hermeneutics of the people. I disagree that there is no logic or continuity in myths or that it is difficult to generalize myths, as Levi-Strauss (1955) says. I feel that your grand narrative of social reality is unduly linear and that you try to justify a linear sense of reality via the simple relationship of cause and effect between two or more variables. I suspect this was an outcome of "modernism" in Germany and that your orientation might reflect the European Enlightenment claims to truth and reality. Your paradigm has been a license to produce a particular culture, but your golden paradigm of research itself has become a present-day cultural myth. I argue that your research paradigm is full of myths about numbers, certainties, language, reality and people.

When you treated the social sciences as positivistic it produced many aftershocks in history of research and knowledge. Higher education in Nepal has been experiencing these aftershocks until now. Many of our social scientists remain at your epicenter, portraying social reality only in scientific ways. In this regard, these academicians are enthralled by "the myth of number". It is estimated that 80 percent of graduate students and institutions in Nepal focus exclusively on numerical values in their research. Thesis supervisors and professors in Nepali higher education have become less creative and soulful as a result. They run after the numbers. They even try to quantify our laughter, tears, emotions and perceptions.

Let me talk about another myth of your paradigm. The *myth of language*. Academicians in my country are still afraid of using the first-person pronoun, "I", in their writings and representations. Instead, they prefer to use the term "the researcher". They write in seemingly value-free language. How can the language be value free and neutral? Your notion of using language in this way does not help to foster the creative and subjective ability to illuminate the non/essence and indeterminacy of social realities, such as can be illustrated with performativity, subjectivity, agency and the position of the researcher (Barad, 2003). Positivist language hardly represents the indeterminacy of social complexities and chaos.

Well, another myth in your paradigm could be the *objective nature of reality*. Many research practitioners in my university share that they come up with "real" stories/observations, even in ethnographic and narrative inquiries. The idea of a real story is derived from your *naïve realism*. They believe that reality is empirical and observable. Can they observe your numbers which erect the whole of reality in your paradigm? Do they see the existence of reality through numbers? Is only your numerology real? Then what about the cosmologies of the Nepali people? How could the local cosmology be framed? The cultural heritage of Nepali students is so rich, denying the objective nature of reality that you proposed.

Dear Professor Comte, I am still working within the dominant positivistic era of research practice in the Nepali higher education system. Doubting your paradigm of positivity makes me a *punk researcher* who questions naïve realism. Many Comtes were born and died in the history of Nepali higher education research. And many Comtes have demonstrated their positivity in the universities of Nepal. Your myths of positivism are reflected in the logics, genres, structure, and conclusions of their dissertations, theses and publications.

Thesis Structure

Students in Nepali social science research mostly use a *positivist structure* while writing their dissertations. They introduce the main research problem, hypothesis and research questions in the first chapter. They separate the second chapter as the literature review. The third chapter is for the research methodology, and in the next two or three chapters they analyze their data, which they sometimes link with extant theories. They never forget to make recommendations in the final chapter. With this structure I believe they are unduly bureaucratizing positivist research.

It feels very strange for us to be assimilated into your positivistic social scientific approach while exploring the lived realities and experiences of majorities/minorities, nationalities/indigenes, men/women, Brahmins/Dalits, and elites/subalterns. How could such a research tradition contribute to the professional development of researchers, given that the positivist research paradigm excludes reflective, local, cultural and cosmological ways of knowing, including those of the researcher.

IF I WAS A REFLECTIVE AGENT

Dear Professor Comte, during my MPhil research I practiced being a reflective agent. In doing so, I learnt to use my imagination to create an intersubjective research space for understanding multiple social realities. Professor, we (you, me and others) generate meaning through social interactions which enables us to understand the social complexities of our everyday lives. A small group of social researchers in Nepal call themselves "ethnographers", "phenomenologists" and "grounded theorists". They engage in reflective thinking by means of evocative and sensuous arts-based forms of inquiry (Bagley, 2009). Unlike positivist researchers, they are "interpretivists" whose prolonged field engagement enables them to capture cyclic variability and patterns of change in human sensibility (Humphreys & Watson, 2009). In the journey of unpacking multiple realities, we may face methodological and ethical challenges in studying such issues. Our academic community is engaging increasingly with ways of generating knowledge from social interactions. Does this mean that the social world is not as objectively real as you claim?

I became a reflective agent to better engage as a teacher with my postgraduate students, especially in the classroom. This new capability provided me with a deeper understanding of teaching and learning interactions. However, I continue to experience difficulties in orienting novice research practitioners as epistemic relativists (rather than objectivists), in three ways: (a) my students struggle to unlearn objectivism, (b) they struggle to internalize a constructivist epistemology, and (c) they experience challenges when trying to represent relativism in their research. It takes a long time to convince them that research methods are situated in particular institutional and socio-culturally determined communities (Every, 1998 as cited in Willis & Jost, 2007).

Gradually I, along with my students, overcome our epistemic anxiety through a transferable research process. In this regard, we position ourselves as reflective thinkers whereby we no longer see the separate existence of an external world independent of the human mind. We learn gradually to understand the culturally different other by learning to "stand in their shoes", "look through their eyes" and "feel their pleasure or pain" (Taylor & Medina, 2011).

Dear Professor Comte, our discussion in the university classroom ranges from science to humanity, from rationalism to empiricism. In this regard, we experience the epistemology of your paradigm as rather dry because the horizon of contemporary research has expanded to include studies of human perceptions and aspirations. We are able to sense our lives as being a colorful mosaic, and we have colorful perceptions, attitudes, consciousness and experiences too. Our experiences are not as static as you have described. We appreciate your "position to lead to a general doctrine of positivism which held that all genuine knowledge is based on sense experiences and can only be advanced by means of observation and experiment" (Cohen, Manion, & Morrison, 2000, p. 8). For us, however, it is neither fair nor reasonable to emphasise only the externality of human beings.

Higher education research practice in Nepal is gradually moving towards conducting more interpretive forms of research. Although my students are not easily convinced to engage in reflective inquiries (because they are predisposed to validating with numbers), over time they come to understand that numbers cannot serve the interest of exploring the intersubjective research space. Gradually, they shift their realist ontology to a relativist ontology, in accordance with Haverkamp and Young (2007) who argued that "[g]rounded in relativist ontology, it posits multiple, equally valid social realities" (p. 268). We (my students and I) try to derive meaning through interactions with persons, theories and methods, which is best described as "co-constructed".

Here, I refer to two giants of qualitative research –Norman Denzin and Yvonne Lincoln (2005) – who have explained that interpretive inquiry takes place in natural settings with the aim of understanding a particular group of people by focusing on their meaning-making process. Is this a neutral science as you claim? Being a reflective research practitioner, I elicit subjective ways of knowing that draw on my intuition and emotions, as John Dirkx (2001) argued, so that my research practice becomes soulful and engaging. In doing so, research practitioners sense that they are common people who can conduct research in their everyday lives. Moreover, using this approach has transformed me into a more relational person who can inquire co-constructively into research issues, as advocated by Kenneth Gergen (2011). When our research practice is guided by story-telling and arts-based research it gradually brings profound change in our ways of thinking, valuing and being.

IF I WAS A REVOLUTIONARY ACTOR

Dear Professor Comte, I appreciate your effort and reasoning (of course, from a White man's perspective) to render the social sciences a so-called pure science that operates through knowing as proving pre-existing conjectures (i.e., hypothetico-deductive reasoning, objective epistemology, naïve realist ontology). Nowadays, however, my students are conducting research on how issues such as social injustice and exclusion have shaped the formation of their identities, a research approach that requires an epistemology beyond pure science. Their research involves multiple ways of knowing arising from their felt, lived, embodied and experiential realisms. In Patti Lather's (1997) terms, this is science as a "contested site". Let me give the example of a colleague's research on the identity of *Yamphu* – an indigenous group in Kathmandu (Rai, 2017). The research rejected the White man's perspective to argue that identities are negotiated in fragmented social realities. In doing so, the researcher illuminated *Yamphu* people's identities in terms of their gender, caste and ethnic minority status in a contested urban space.

Gradually, research practitioners in higher education in Nepal have sensed that the positivistic paradigm is detached from the principle of living together in which pre-existing hierarchies, arising both from within and imported from the outside world, are dismantled. Like me, you believe that society is dynamic and shaped by imagination, as you mentioned that society has "dialectical facets of structures" (Ritzer & Goodman, 2004). In effect, however, a positivistic methodology does the opposite: it predisposes researchers to apply dualistic logic in making sense of the world around them. We think that your positive science pays insufficient attention to resolving the dualism of 'objectivism vs subjectivism'.

I do not reject the whole structure of positivistic consciousness; instead, my aim is to curtail your exclusionary logic because it does not enable our research students to engage in the multiple dialogues of life. By engaging in multiple dialogues, students experience research as a revolutionary act wherein they come to recognize the voices of multiple selves; the voices of their participants and of themselves. The act of eliciting the voices of voiceless people during the research process helps to liberate our students from being 'armchair researchers'.

Now, you are possibly asking, "Who is doing this type of research? Are they magicians? Are they healers? Are they political agents?" Professor Comte, we do, in fact, attempt to be healers and magicians who can recognise and resolve existing social injustices and slavery in our society. In doing so, our research students intend to perform socially engaged activities where they serve as advocates of social justice in local communities, such as the Tharu and Yamphu. In stark contrast, the objective voice of your positivism would not allow us to assert an authorial voice for stimulating public debate and reforming public policy. However, our research students aspire to be political agents and magicians who critique and transform the status quo.

Through the lens of a 'revolutionist' perspective, our students become aware of the historical realism of existing social, political, economic and cultural values. They learn that war, injustice, oppression, exploitation and resistance do not exist like some theological or metaphysical truth. In our university, the recent trend in social research is to embrace a holistic view of social realities. This approach enables us to adopt a critical social perspective to engage in advocacy for the purpose of transforming the human condition. As revolutionary agents, students become critically aware of their situatedness in conducting research. They come to understand that social realities are a by-product of history and, in doing so, they become aware of the power relations practiced in everyday life. This critical engagement enables them to become dialogic and dialectical during the research process. This critical perspective leads our research students to adopting transformative research practices.

IF I WAS AN ARTIST

Dear Professor Comte, I experimented with arts-based, narrative inquiry during my recent doctoral research to investigate and portray the everyday life of urban youth with the sense of understanding their emotive, affective and imaginative experiences of living and being in the city (Gautam, 2017). I employed non-linguistic logics and genres as methods of researching and representation. The humanities and social sciences were dominated for much of the 20th century by linguistic paradigms. In this regard, the "pictorial turn", as Christopher Pinney (2006) argued, counters linguistic colonialism with its use of visual logics and genres. Gradually, Nepali academicians are becoming familiar with such alternative forms of discourse.

I am pleased to share a saying by the famous artist, Pablo Picasso, who believed that everything we can imagine is real. Perhaps, you imagined positivism as real, but reality might not be as straightforward as you suppose. Reality can be expressed via paintings and pictures, music and mandalas, poems and portraits, *tudals* and tapestries. Now, it is time to understand our life and society poetically and lyrically, as full of pain and pleasure, intoxication and ecstasy.

Alternative logics make research socially and culturally inclusive, but we know that artful research sometimes can be passionately misleading, and thus it can be difficult to create a demarcation line between facts and fictions. Such discourse-laden research challenges the modern Western worldview with poetic, dialogic, dialectical, and narrative logics (Saldana, 2015) that cast new light on social realities. In particular, we use playful, ironic and metaphorical language in our postmodern research. Hearing this, you might laugh, Dear Professor Comte.

IF I WAS AN ECOLOGIST

Dear Professor Comte, as we reflect on the history of research paradigms I find that people are becoming increasingly skeptical towards your positivism. They have started thinking spiritually (Saldana, 2015) and ecologically, with a strong sense of coexistence and living together. Epistemic ecology promotes wellbeing and living together peacefully. Lorraine Code (2006) believes that epistemic ecology helps to develop ecological thinking that inspires socially responsible transformation for sustainable coexistence. In this context, theological interpretations of society are partly helping to understand coexistence principles of communities. It is quite likely that thinking spiritually is compatible with the historic theological assumptions that you critiqued. However, peoples across the world are subscribing to various spiritual traditions that shape their worldviews. Possibly the philosophy (and paradigm) of "integralism" is fostering a renaissance that is bridging cultural, humanistic and technocratic worldviews. Ken Wilber (1999) unpacks the notion of integralism as wisdom tradition which recognizes the plural ways of knowing across the cultures to cultivate the higher order of consciousness. The notion of integralism was later introduced by Peter Charles Taylor, Elizabeth Taylor, and Bal Chandra Luitel (2013) as a research paradigm thereby recognising all research traditions and creating new research approaches which are not only sensitive to human beings but also to ecology.

Increasingly, students in Nepali universities no longer wish to frame their research with the positivistic paradigm, and instead are using other paradigms as methodological referents. To promote ecological thinking, they are embracing artistic thinking and genres such as narrative, poetic, and performative arts-based research (Bochner & Ellis, 2003). Epistemic ecology recognizes knowledge that is generated in diverse societies and geographies, valuing the interrelationship between humans, nature and the environment for sustainable research practices (Code, 2006). By and large, however, Nepali higher education still promotes scientific research methods that are mandated by the governing neoliberal ideology. In stark contrast, the *ecological turn* has cultivated ethical and dialectical modes of thinking, being and valuing that we are using to foster wellbeing and co-existence in local communities.

RE-ORIENTATION: A TRANSFORMATIVE PRACTITIONER

Dear Comte, if you visit the library in our university you will see that very little recent educational research has adhered to your positivism. Rather, you will see mostly ethnographic, phenomenological, narrative and arts-based research. This is how people in the so-called third world are using the notion of research in academia to contribute directly to transforming our society and local communities. I have positioned myself as an educator, a researcher and a practitioner who is attempting to transform ways of thinking and researching in order to address social complexities. As a research community we are endeavoring to bring Eastern and Western wisdom traditions together to articulate and enrich our transformative research space.

REFERENCES

Adorno, T. W. (1999). Conclusion: Contemporary Christian music and the contemporary Christian life. In J. R. Howard & J. M. Streck (Eds.), *Apostles of rock: The splintered world of contemporary Christian music* (pp. 185–220). Lexington, KY: University Press of Kentucky.

Bagley, C. (2009). Shifting boundaries in ethnographic methodology. *Ethnography and Education, 4*(3), 251–254.

Barad, K. (2003). Posthumanist performativity: Toward an understanding of how matter comes to matter. *Signs: Journal of Women in Culture and Society, 28*(3), 801–831.

Birch, K. (2017). *A research agenda for neoliberalism*. Cheltenham: Edward Elgar.

Bochner, A. P., & Ellis, C. (2003). An introduction to the arts and narrative research: Art as inquiry. *Qualitative Inquiry, 9*(4), 506–514.

Britzman, D. (1986). Cultural myths in the making of a teacher: Biography and social structure in teacher education. *Harvard Educational Review, 56*(4), 442–457.
Code, L. (2006). *Ecological thinking: The politics of epistemic location.* Oxford: Oxford University Press.
Cohen, L., Manion, L., & Morrison, K. (2000). *Research methods in education* (5th ed.). London: Routledge.
Comte, A. (1975). Plan of the scientific operations necessary for reorganizing society. In G. Lenzer (Ed.), *Auguste Comte and positivism: The essential writings* (pp. 9–69). New York, NY: Harper Torchbooks. (Original work published in 1822)
Denzin, N. K., & Lincoln, Y. S. (2005). Epilogue: The eighth and ninth moments of qualitative research in/and the fractured future. In N. K. Denzin & Y. S. Lincoln (Eds.), *The Sage handbook of qualitative research* (3rd ed., pp. 1115–1126). Thousand Oaks, CA: Sage Publications.
Denzin, N. K., & Lincoln, Y. S. (2005). Introduction: The discipline and practice of qualitative research. In N. K. Denzin & Y. S. Lincoln (Eds.), *The Sage handbook of qualitative research* (3rd ed., pp. 1–32). Thousand Oaks, CA: Sage Publications.
Dirkx, J. M. (2001). Images, transformative learning and the work of soul. *Adult Learning, 12*(3), 15–16.
Foster, V. (2016). *Collaborative arts based research for social justice.* New York, NY: Routledge.
Gautam, S. (2011). *"Literacy sucks!": Voice of Tharu women* (Masters dissertation). School of Education Kathmandu University, Nepal.
Gautam, S. (2017). *Urban youth and their everyday life: Arts-based narrative inquiry* (Doctoral dissertation). School of Education, Kathmandu University, Nepal.
Gergen, K. J. (2011). Relational being: A brief introduction. *Journal of Constructivist Psychology, 24*(4), 280–282.
Haverkamp, B. E., & Young, R. A. (2007). Paradigms, purpose, and the role of the literature: Formulating a rationale for qualitative investigations. *The Counseling Psychologist, 35*(2), 265–294.
Humphreys, M., & Watson, T. J. (2009). Ethnographic practices: From 'writing-up ethnographic research' to 'writing ethnography'. In S. Ybema, D. Yanow, H. Wels, & F. Kamsteeg (Eds.), *Organizational ethnography: Studying the complexities of everyday life* (pp. 40–55). London: Sage Publications.
Lather, P. (1997). Creating a multilayered text: Women, AIDS and angels. In W. G. Tierney & Y. S. Lincoln (Eds.), *Representation and the text: Reframing the narrative voice* (pp. 233–258). New York, NY: State University of New York.
Levi-Strauss, C. (1955). The structural study of myth. *The Journal of American Folklore, 68*(270), 428–444.
O'Sullivan, S. (2010). From aesthetics to the abstract machine: Deleuze, Guattari, and contemporary art practice. In S. Zepke & S. O'Sullivan (Eds.), *Deleuze and contemporary art* (pp. 189–207). Edinburgh: Edinburgh University Press.
Pinney, C. (2006). Four types of visual culture. In C. Tilley, W. Keane, & P. Spyer (Eds.), *Handbook of material culture* (pp. 131–144). London: Sage Publications.
Rai, I. M. (2017). *Identity paradoxes of Kirat migrants in urban context: An auto/ethnographic inquiry* (Doctoral dissertation). School of Education, Kathmandu University, Nepal.
Ritzer, G., & Goodman, D. J. (2004). *Sociological theory.* Boston, MA: McGraw Hill.
Roberts, J. M., & Westad, O. A. (2013). *The history of the world.* Oxford: Oxford University Press.
Saldana, J. (2015). *Thinking qualitatively: Methods of mind.* New York, NY: Sage Publications.
Taylor, P. C., & Medina, M. N. D. (2013). Educational research paradigms: From positivism to multiparadigmatic. *The Journal of Meaning-Centered Education, 1*(2), 1–13.
Taylor, P. C., Taylor, E., & Luitel, B. C. (2012). Multi-paradigmatic transformative research as/for teacher education: An integral perspective. In B. J. Fraser, K. G. Tobin, & C. J. McRobbie (Eds.), *Second international handbook of science education* (pp. 373–387). Dordrecht: Springer.
Turner, J. H. (2001). The origins of positivism: The contributions of Auguste Compte and Herbert Spencer. In G. Ritzer & B. Smart (Eds), *Handbook of social theory.* London: Sage Publications.
Wilber, K. (1999). *The collected works of Ken Wilber* (Vol. 3). Boston, MA: Shambhala.
Willis, J. W., & Jost, M. (2007). *Foundations of qualitative research: Interpretive and critical approaches.* London: Sage Publications.

ABOUT THE AUTHOR

People call me **Suresh Gautam**. I was born in a village of Dang District in the Mid-Western Region which is located in Province 5 of the Federal Republic Nepal. I hold a PhD degree in Education from Kathmandu University, School of Education, Nepal, specializing in Development Studies. At present I am a facilitator, educator and researcher working at Kathmandu University's School of Education, Hattiban. My research interests include: urban youth, youth culture, adult learning, lifelong learning, inclusive pedagogy, transformative research, sociology of education.

BINOD PRASAD PANT

5. AN INTEGRAL PERSPECTIVE ON RESEARCH

Methodological and Theoretical Journey of a Teacher Educator

The use of a particular research methodology and theoretical orientation is always a challenging task for research students. It was 2012 when I enrolled in a Master of Philosophy (MPhil) research degree in Kathmandu University, Nepal. At that time, I was thinking about research from the dualistic perspective of quantitative versus qualitative research. As I progressed in my studies, I realized that such categories are too simplistic and can be better understood at the "data" level (Wooda & Welcha, 2010). I decided that this dichotomous way of knowing would not govern my research. Thereby, I chose an "integral" perspective for my MPhil research where two or more worldviews are used in a single study. I came to realize that my deep-seated belief about the nature and role of theory as an overall controlling framework was unduly restrictive. As a practitioner in the field of teacher education, I grew to realise that theory can be used as a perspective that is potentially helpful to argue from a particular viewpoint. Thus, for my research study I applied several theoretical perspectives within a multi-paradigmatic research design (Taylor, Taylor, & Luitel, 2012). In this chapter, I discuss my journey of using this integral perspective, especially how this approach helped me to rationalize my research agenda in a more vivid way.

WHERE I GREW UP

After I completed my School Leaving Examination in 1998 I started teaching mathematics in one of the primary schools of Kavre, my hometown district in rural Nepal. At the time, teaching mathematics was thought to be no more than solving mathematical problems. (Don't worry, I'm not going to discuss teaching mathematics in detail in this chapter!) Deep-seated beliefs towards the "absolutist" nature of mathematics (Lerman, 1990) and an overemphasis on the view of mathematics as a "pure subject" (Luitel, 2013) shaped my teaching to be teacher-centered. During the initial days of my teaching career I was busy identifying better tricks, tips and techniques to enable my students to solve mathematical problems and produce good results in the national examination. Later, I learned that I had been engaged in, what Paolo Freire (1993) called, "banking pedagogy". As a teacher I understood my role as depositing lots of "money" in the "bank", and I tried my best to have maximum "transactions" with my "clients". I was also heavily guided by the "technical interest" as discussed by Jurgen Habermas (1972). The purpose of the technical interest is to reproduce the law-like patterns of mathematical knowledge focusing on memorization of facts and formulas. The role of a "technical" teacher is to control and manage the classroom environment, with a focus on hypothetico-deductive logic serving the agenda of empirical-analytical science. I realize that such a notion of teaching mathematics is still dominant in many parts of my country.

Joining Kathmandu University for my MPhil study in 2012 became a turning point in my professional life. The classroom discourse and the practices of transformative education challenged my beliefs about the nature of mathematics, curricula, pedagogy and assessment. During the coursework, I wrote my narratives as a student and as a teacher, and I critically assessed the empowering and disempowering factors that had shaped me as a mathematics teacher. I reflected critically on my long journey of teaching and learning mathematics. I thought that my unfolding narratives would be a milestone for improving my professional practice for the rest of my career, and that the verisimilitude of these narratives might make my readers thoughtful about their own teaching approaches by reflecting on their perceptions and practices regarding mathematics and its pedagogy. In this context, I decided that "autoethnography" would be the best methodology for my research study.

BEYOND QUANTITATIVE VERSUS QUALITATIVE RESEARCH

Earlier in 2007/2008 when I was struggling to explore my research agenda and develop an appropriate methodology for my Master of Education (MEd) dissertation, I interacted frequently with friends and teachers, trying to get useful suggestions for the question: "Where do you stand: quantitative or qualitative?". This was a frequently raised question during that period. My friends and I made great effort in our discussions to prove our particular approaches to be superior or inferior. Normally, friends with a statistics background, including myself, argued from the perspective of quantitative research, mentioning that it has power to generalize the results. During that time, I was guided by the notion that the use of statistics is the only way to prove or disprove knowledge of social reality, and I was very much interested in playing with numerical data. Collecting a large chunk of data, inserting them into mathematical software, deriving tables and charts, testing hypotheses, claiming single knowledge as the absolute truth, and sharing the findings among scholars was a very interesting trajectory for me as a researcher. I spent a lot of time going through such research projects and memorizing the findings as ultimate truths. In many cases, I was guided by those findings as a classroom teacher and teacher educator. In the early days of teaching I was not in the position to challenge the knowledge obtained from such research. Perhaps, an over trust in numerical data had played a key role in shaping my beliefs. On the other hand, friends having the background of anthropology and sociology used to argue in favor of in-depth investigation of a phenomenon in which generalization is not the main goal of social science. But I completed my MEd degree believing in the idea that research cannot be done outside the framework of statistics.

A few years later during my MPhil, as I studied courses on research methodology, I had many opportunities to interact with various research traditions in education. One of the vital instances that made me thoughtful about alternative research traditions was my reading of an article by Peter Taylor and Milton Medina (2011). I came to understand that my established belief in educational research was guided by the *post/positivist paradigm*. The construct of *paradigm* is explicitly discussed in the paper as a comprehensive belief system, worldview, or framework that guides research and practice in a field (Willis, 2007). The convincing part of the paper was the bountiful effort to justify the essence and uses of each research paradigm, with sufficient examples under distinct sets of quality standards. "No research paradigm is superior, but each has a specific purpose in providing a distinct means of producing unique knowledge" (Taylor & Medina, 2011, p. 1) was the eye-opening sentence for me that helped me to think from the perspective of paradigm dialogue rather than paradigm war.

My efforts to make particular research approaches superior or inferior at the beginning of my research journey slowly became a meaningless activity. I realized that the methodological criticisms of both sides of the quantitative versus qualitative debate were not being used in a productive manner, as mentioned by Udo Kelle and Nils Buchholtz (2015) who argued that, "the criticism of the other side is not taken seriously as an inducement to deal with the weaknesses of one's own approach but answered in a *tit for tat* way by pointing to the shortcomings of the other side" (p. 322). I came to realize that *mono-method* study was not helpful for exploring the complexities of the issues of teacher education.

In the course of time, out of many journal articles written by great scholars, the article by Norman Denzin (2013), *The Death of Data*, gave me a lot of insights regarding uses of data in research. He began the article with the sentence, "Data died a long time ago, but few noticed" (p. 1). Denzin writes, "the reader is asked to imagine a world without data, a world without method, a world without hegemonic politics of evidences, a world where no one counts, a world without end" (p. 1). During my MPhil journey, my thesis supervisor encouraged me to think *out of the box*. "Do not be slaves of particular theories and research paradigms. We are practitioners. We need to apply theories as referents, not as an ultimate framework", he asserted repeatedly. It helped me to emerge from my narrowly conceived understanding of research traditions and issues.

As a student of mathematics education, I was planning to study the beliefs of mathematics teachers towards the nature of mathematics, mathematics curricula, assessment and their pedagogical practices. One of the initial objectives of my MPhil research was to unpack how teachers' beliefs affect their classroom teaching. For this, I chose ethnography as my methodology and started to develop a research proposal.

During the time of materializing the proposal, I encountered various research theses and dissertations (e.g., Belbase, 2006; Afonso, 2007; Cupane, 2008; Luitel, 2009) that made me thoughtful about (re)searching my own professional experience, giving sense to those events, and critically assessing my own assumptions and strategies for a better future. I thought that my stories could be the best mirror to represent the state of teachers' beliefs and practices in Nepalese context. At that time, I had more than ten years of teaching experience in various educational institutions, from primary school to university. The beliefs I held regarding mathematics, teaching and learning, curricula, evaluation and assessment practices were undergoing a drastic change, and the practices I employed as a teacher and as a teacher educator were likewise being impacted. I believed that examining my personal-political and professional narratives would help to improve my professional practice, and that my MPhil dissertation (Pant, 2015) might be a useful document for others working in the field of teaching and research. One of the emergent purposes of this study, therefore, was to understand and reconstruct new meanings of my own beliefs and practices about various aspects of my subject (i.e., mathematics) and the teaching and learning issues of my field.

MULTI-PARADIGMATIC RESEARCH AND AUTOETHNOGRAPHY

In 2013, I was struggling to make better sense of the research approach that I was aiming to employ in my MPhil research study. How can I choose a particular research agenda under a specific paradigm? How can I set paradigmatic considerations? These difficult questions always stoked my mind at the time of developing my research theme. As I mentioned earlier, though Taylor and Medina (2011) gave helpful insights into contemporary research paradigms, I could not fit myself within a specific paradigm. Then, I read the article: *Multi-Paradigmatic Transformative Research as/ for Teacher Education: An Integral Perspective* (Taylor, Taylor, & Luitel, 2012). This helped me to make sense of multiple paradigm research within a single study. The interaction of various ways of knowing (or epistemologies) became very fruitful for me in understanding how to use multiple research paradigms in my study.

As a student of mathematics education, at the beginning of my teaching career I was guided by the classical hypothetico-deductive logic of the post/positivist research paradigm, which comprises powerful but restrictive logics, namely, propositional, deductive and analytical. Later, as a researcher, alternative forms of logic played significant roles in my thinking:

- *dialectical logic* allows the transformative researcher to hold contradictions together in creative tension (Luitel, 2009);
- *metaphorical logic* promotes open and embodied inquiry for exploring multiple facets of knowledge and knowing (Lakoff & Johnson, 1999); and
- *narrative logic* enables transformative researchers to contextualize their knowledge claims within their personal, professional and cultural contexts (Clandinin & Connelly, 2000).

These radical new ways of thinking directed me to create spaces for using multiple paradigms in my study.

Interpretivism

During my study I recalled my experiences as a mathematics teacher. At the same time I engaged with other mathematics teachers in informal interviews and discussions. This helped me to reflect on my own ways of teaching which I could not measure in numbers. I was learning to generate meaning from my practices and the practices of other teachers. During this time I sensed that narrative accounts of my ways of interacting and learning give a much better understanding than presenting dead numbers in a bar diagram. During fieldwork this became an inseparable part of my stand within the interpretative paradigm. This paradigm is shaped by the philosophy of social constructivism (Guba & Lincoln, 2005) which promotes engaging in *inter-subjectivity* so as to understand a social phenomenon through the lived experience of the actors. This way of knowing enabled me to make sense of my own professional narratives together with the perspectives of fellow teachers, school leaders and other stakeholders. Through the interpretive paradigm lens, I observed different approaches to solving mathematical problems in specific and generic ways.

Criticalism

While interpreting the teaching and learning activities of mathematics teachers and myself, I posed questions about my/others' existing beliefs and practices. The teaching approaches that I used to think of as ideal became problematic. In this way, the paradigm of criticalism was very fruitful in my study. It was employed for ideology critique to understand how power imbalances serve as key sources of social injustice within normative social structures, especially in terms of reproducing habituated behaviors of teachers and students. This perspective can help us to create emancipatory learning environments in which students develop a critical consciousness of their daily activities and become aware of the various governing forces behind such activities (Taylor, 2008). The critical paradigm promotes the notion of social justice in order to create a world that is fairer, more equitable, more inclusive and more harmonious. I hope that the voices raised for changing classroom teaching, assessment practices, and curriculum (re)form using dialogical forms of writing will engage my readers in reflecting critically on their own beliefs and assumptions about normative social values and practices. In doing so, my readers might engage in *pedagogical thoughtfulness*, as mentioned by Max van Manen (1991).

Postmodernism

In addition to the interpretive and critical paradigms, I was trying to use various genres (such as stories, poems, letters) to capture my professional narratives and the anecdotes of other teachers. In order to legitimate this approach, I referred to the postmodern paradigm which employs arts-based research methods to engage, empower and envision readers, as well as the researcher. At the beginning, I was overwhelmed by this approach and tried to capture meaningful and relevant events with a range of genres. Although I did not feel that I could fully represent what I was thinking/feeling, I hope that I have done justice to this paradigm by aligning with Denzin and Lincoln's (2000) notion that the postmodern paradigm allows researchers to comprise their personal-professional responsibility and emotionality in multi-voiced dialogical texts. While doing so, the researcher makes an attempt to know something without claiming to know everything. With the help of performative and non-linguistic genres, I tried to produce narratives with orientated, strong, rich and deep textual representations.

Autoethnography

It was not easy for me to preserve the epistemic integrity of research methods drawn from each of these paradigms. To maintain epistemic integrity, I employed the overarching method of autoethnography that connects the autobiographical and personal to the cultural, social and political (Ellis & Adams, 2014). I presented my memoirs related to my personal and professional experiences as a teacher and teacher educator. These personal narratives are a way of connecting the personal to cultural practices by reflecting on the role of one's own self as a participant in an ongoing social and cultural practice (Reed-Danahay, 1997). As an autoethnographer, I wanted to explore the work of *I* and to focus on the experiences of the other, which Carolyn Ellis (2017) pointed out is one of the main concerns of the autoethnographer. I believe that unfolding my experiences in this study fulfilled the purpose of autoethnographic inquiry: "writing autoethnography and experimenting with textual fragmentation and formatting might enable us to extend our understandings of personal emotions/feelings which is primarily underlined in personal experiences" (Das & Mullick, 2015, p. 265). Elements of self-critical awareness were evoked in writing and reflecting on my narratives as I deconstructed, reconceptualized and envisioned transforming classroom practices in teaching and learning mathematics. This created the foundations for a critical autoethnography.

So, my MPhil research was a progressive journey of choosing a research approach, starting from a quantitative perspective, slowly moving to the tradition of ethnography, and finally landing in the multi-paradigmatic research design space where I chose autoethnography as a rich approach for my study. In this regard, I agree with the thoughts of Sadruddin Qutoshi (2015) who argued recently that autoethnography is one of the most suitable spaces for transformative researchers to serve the agenda of envisioning a transformative teacher education. Throughout this study, I engaged in critical reflection about the meaning of my past, present and possible future experiences. These personal reflections allowed me to envisage better images of mathematics, pedagogy, curriculum and assessment that I want to employ and that may be a mirror for changes and improvement in my professional career.

AN INTEGRAL PERSPECTIVE ON RESEARCH

MY THEORETICAL REFERENTS: LENSES TO VIEW THE WORLD

While conducting multi-paradigmatic research in the thread of autoethnography, I encountered several theoretical approaches. In this regard, many questions hovered in my mind: Why do we need theories in research? Does a theory orient us in our research process or provide a complete framework to be followed? Such questions created very tacit difficulties for me while selecting theories and using them in my research. Perhaps, my research supervisor invested a long period to convince me to use theories as "referents" in such research, not as a cage to put all research processes inside.

Perhaps, because long-seated beliefs about certain theories resided in my mind I needed great effort to become aware of my beloved and potentially invisible theories (such as: learning takes place through stimulus-response bonding, mind is separate from the body, curriculum is designed and given by the experts). As a student, teacher and teacher educator, I realized that theories are important to view the world through various lenses (in my case, the nature of mathematics, pedagogical practices, curriculum and assessment strategies). But, at the same time, the experiences gained through practices in a professional context should not be underestimated. In conventional research theories are treated as a complete framework, having a major role from the beginning to the end, that is, from identifying the research purpose to drawing conclusions.

In my study, I used several theories to interpret and critique teaching and learning activities of self and other. Theories helped me to analyze my narratives, akin to what Ken Tobin and Deborah Tippins (1993) advocated as employing theories as *referents*. For me, theories did not override ideas and context. Rather, I took theories as possible ways of understanding social phenomena with conceptual and critically reflexive sensibilities. The conceptual dimension of theories enabled me to identify and make sense of teachers' beliefs and underlying assumptions, which helped me to interpret various teaching and learning approaches in the mathematics classroom. Likewise, theories such as *living theory methodology* (Whitehead, 1989, 2008), *transformative learning theory* (Mezirow, 1991) and *knowledge constitutive interests* (Habermas, 1972) enabled me to deconstruct the hegemony of grand narratives (such as mathematics is an absolutist subject, teaching mathematics is for developing procedural understanding, curriculum as a fixed set of contents, assessment is testing the memories – facts and formulas – of the students). These theories provided me with enough space to deconstruct the hegemony of such grand narratives, and to make sense of my own experience in cultivating the possibility of culminating my own theory, which is also discussed as *small t* theories by Bal Chandra Luitel (2009).

Living Theory Methodology

As a teacher and teacher educator, I have been seeking better alternatives in my professional context, believing that there is always enough space to improve. Living theory methodology provided me with the grounds to ask questions of the kind, *How do I improve what I am doing?* Whitehead (2008) explained, "A living theory is an explanation produced by an individual for their educational influence in their own learning, in the learning of others and in the learning of the social formation in which they live and work" (p. 104). Throughout my MPhil research, I presented my stories offering sufficient explanation aimed at demonstrating my lived experiences. While doing so, the stories I told were those of myself in company with others who were also telling their stories (McNiff, 2013). I tried my best to show the significance of "I as a living contradiction", which is considered to be a necessary component in living theory methodology.

Transformative Learning Theory

I had space to be critically reflexive while applying transformative learning theory which is rooted in the 1990's work of Jack Mezirow in the area of adult education. Regarding how we make sense of our experiences with the world from subjective perspectives, Mezirow drew on the ideas of well-known philosophers such as John Dewey and Jurgen Habermas. I was frequently trying to make sense of my various professional episodes by reflecting critically on the presuppositions underpinning my/our values and beliefs. During the time of presenting and analyzing my narratives, I attempted to elicit critical awareness in relation to my own past, present and possible future, being aware of the world in which I live. The focus of transformative learning is on expanding conscious awareness of our situatedness in the world or, to put it more simply, in our understanding of who we are and who we might yet become, both as individuals and social beings (Morrell & O'Connor, 2002). I grew up in a traditional village life-style, a non-Western society and a less-affluent country with the embodiment of postcolonial thoughts. In this context, transformative learning helped in preparing me to become a critical self-reflective citizen who contests taken-for-granted social norms and makes ethical judgments toward equity, justice and democratic practices, especially in the field of mathematics teaching and learning.

Knowledge-Constitutive Interests

Habermasian knowledge-constitutive interests (1972) was another theoretical referent I employed in my research. The notion of *interest*, according to Habermas, is different from the common notion of interest that shows a desire or an inclination towards some activity to gain pleasure. The notion of interest here describes a human ability to pursue goodness or wellbeing through knowledge and reasoning. Three knowledge-constitutive interests – *technical, practical, emancipatory* – are rooted in human existence and expressed in particular types of inquiry.

The technical interest is a view that knowledge exists somehow apart from people *out there* and can be discovered. It aims for the prediction of social phenomena based on normative-analytic science, assuming that control of the natural environment is necessary with a hypothetico-deductive model of logic. I realized that many of our actions as mathematics teachers were guided by the technical interest, thereby focusing exclusively on knowledge transmission approaches in mathematics teaching as ultimate facts. At that moment, as a teacher educator, neither was I aiming to reproduce the best ways of teaching and learning approaches nor was I looking for ultimate knowledge in the field of mathematics teaching and learning. I believe that teaching and learning approaches are always revisable by examining our existing beliefs and practices. So, the notion of the technical interest is not helpful for me.

The focus of the practical interest is towards contextual understanding through a meaning-making process by interacting with learners (Grundy, 1987). I used the practical interest to generate communicative knowledge derived from a consensus amongst myself, others, and the social norms of the mathematics education community in which I live.

For Habermas, emancipation means independence from all that is outside the individual. For this, critical self-reflection is the pathway towards liberation from dogmatic dependence. The notion of the emancipatory interest provided me with the grounds to challenge *taken-for-granted* assumptions about teaching, learning and assessment (e.g., the bell-shaped normal curve). I experienced being in the process of transforming towards a critically conscious mathematics educator with self-directed responsibilities and awareness. The emancipatory interest thus enabled me to develop a counter-hegemonic vision of teaching and learning mathematics. In this way, I used the emancipatory interest to develop awareness of *false consciousness*, which is a new form of hegemony, of the various episodes of my life as a student, a teacher and teacher educator.

I came to realize that over-reliance on any one of the three knowledge-constitutive interests does not function well in our classroom teaching and professional life; as a practitioner, achieving a balance is essential. I agree with Norma Presmeg's (2014) articulation that *instruction* (a behaviorist emphasis) and *construction* (pupils' active involvement) can mutually constitute each other in a fine-tuning of awareness. She explained this connection through the metaphor of dance in the knowledge generation process. The good part of taking Habermasian knowledge interests as a referent in my study is that it helped me realize that the use of a sole approach is not enough; wise choice is required while applying those theories in particular contexts.

ME AT PRESENT

At present, I am working as a university faculty in the field of teacher education. The purpose of my MPhil research was not simply to complete the requirement to receive the degree, but primarily was aimed at improving my own professional practice by examining the deep-seated beliefs underpinning my day-to-day practice. During the study I engaged as a critical reflective practitioner. Although it is very difficult to share the explicit changes that occurred in my professional life due the nature of the research, there are some significant changes that I feel are worth sharing.

I created ample opportunities to reflect critically on my own beliefs and practices as a mathematics teacher and teacher educator. While doing so, I gathered both local and global perspectives and examined my thoughts through both lenses. These incidents prepared me as a critically aware teacher educator in terms of understanding and describing various perspectives of mathematics education. I trust that my dissertation provides engaging narratives for my readers (teachers, teacher educators, researchers) to understand how to take steps towards improving their professional lives.

As a teacher educator, I believe that developing new ways of thinking is an essential skill that needs to be fostered. The journey I took during the research enabled me to develop new and valuable thinking skills. Although there are no straightforward and ready-made approaches to solving the professional problems of teacher education (such as pedagogy, curriculum, and assessment), I began to perceive things differently and tried to come up with alternatives that might address my professional challenges.

As a mathematics teacher I spent a lot of time considering that respect should be given by juniors to seniors and by *less talented students* to *more talented students*. I am now taking the notion of respect as an important phenomenon, but from a different perspective. I believe that everyone should respect each other. Respect of ideas and perspectives is more important than respect given automatically to elders. This is one of the ways of ensuring inclusiveness in teaching and learning.

A major aspect of the neo-colonial project is the Western education export industry and international benchmarking in education systems. These practices have maintained the *official knowledge* production agendas of education systems worldwide. The modern education system produces highly skilled professionals in the field of developing infrastructure and social services. My argument is that these are essential but not sufficient. It seems that not enough care for local *cultural capital* is being given in our curricula and teaching and learning approaches. In this context, transformative education may orient us towards culturally sustainable and inclusive practices in teacher education.

Due to the reductionist agenda of modern education (Kauffman, 2007), our learning and meaning-making have witnessed local and global anxiety regarding the lack of strength and potentiality of research enterprises. With the realization that the linear and fragmented approach to education and research is unlikely to address present complexities, the transformative educational research perspective is enabling us to design research that questions assumptions that are culturally and uncritically embedded in social systems. In such an approach, critical observation of lived experiences is vital for the personal/professional development of the researcher and the researched. Transformative educational research aims to produce graduates with higher-order abilities who are not only critical but also creative, innovative and socially responsible.

Transformative educational research is a dynamic process of meaning-making that has evolved with historic paradigm shifts in ways of thinking and acting (Molz & Gidley, 2008). This shift in worldview calls for subjective truths that are contextual in nature (Snow, 1993). Likewise, the philosophical transition from modernism to postmodernism challenges linear hierarchies and seeks new and useful possibilities in ways of doing things. For this, I believe that transformative educational research provides many new opportunities to prepare 21st century teachers and teacher educators with higher-order abilities so that they can develop transformative curricula, teaching approaches, and community development programs that promote sustainable development.

MY FINAL THOUGHTS

The journey I walked during my research was very meaningful from the perspective of realizing better approaches. As a mathematics teacher, writing was not an easy task for me; as Dwayne Custer (2014) mentioned, it is not an easy task to relate to whom we were in the past and understand how that translates into our identity today, but it is worth the effort in order to reap the rewards of reflexivity and introspection. Another problem I faced was how vulnerable I needed to be while writing my own stories. My supervisor always suggested that I engage in the writing process. For me, being engaged means bringing the right amount of vulnerability into my writing, as mentioned by Brené Brown (2012) who declared that in writing stories of oneself, "We need to feel trust to be vulnerable and we need to be vulnerable in order to trust" (p. 46). I believe that unfolding my experiences while crafting my research path can give insights to other researchers who have been carrying out similar studies in their fields.

The dilemma of choosing a research methodology, realizing the usefulness of a multi-paradigmatic research perspective, using autoethnography as a research approach, employing narrative as a method of developing my stories, and taking theories as referents were major turning points in my research. These key events helped me to transform not only my mind but also my heart as a teacher educator. My practices as a novice teacher educator have dramatically changed to now being a more responsive and critical teacher educator. I have realised that every educational researcher has walked their own path in the past. So, they should craft their own ways at present, believing that better alternatives can be perceived as they progress in the future. For this, educational researchers should not be the slaves of any established theories as they can restrict possibilities to cultivate "small t" theory that can be more powerful and useful as a homegrown theory.

REFERENCES

Afonso, E. Z. (2007). *Developing a culturally inclusive philosophy of science teacher education in Mozambique* (Unpublished doctoral thesis). Curtin University of Technology, Perth, Australia.

Belbase, S. (2006). *My journey of learning and teaching mathematics from traditionalism to constructivism: A portrayal of pedagogic metamorphosis* (Unpublished MPhil dissertation). School of Education, Kathmandu University, Nepal.

Brown, B. (2012). *Daring greatly: How the courage to be vulnerable transforms the way we live, love, parent, and lead.* New York, NY: Gotham Books.

Clandinin, D. J., & Connelly, F. M. (2000). *Narrative inquiry: Experience and story in qualitative research*. New York, NY: Jossey-Bass.

Cupane, A. F. (2007). *Towards a culture-sensitive pedagogy of physics teacher education in Mozambique* (Unpublished doctoral thesis). Science and Mathematics Education Centre, Curtin University, Perth, Australia.

Custer, D. (2014). Autoethnography as a transformative research method. *The Qualitative Report, 19*(21), 1–13. Retrieved from http://www.nova.edu/ssss/QR/QR19/custer21.pdf

Das, K., & Mullick, P. D. (2015). Autoethnography: An introduction to the art of representing the author's voice and experience in social research. *International Journal of Applied Research, 1*(7), 265–267.

Denzin, N. K. (2013). The death of data? *Cultural Studies ↔ Critical Methodologies, 20*(10), 1–4.

Denzin, N. K., & Lincoln, Y. S. (2000). *Handbook of qualitative research*. London: Sage Publications.

Denzin, N. K., & Lincoln, Y. S. (2011). Introduction: The discipline and practice of qualitative research. In N. K. Denzin & Y. S. Lincoln (Eds.), *Sage handbook of qualitative research* (4th ed., pp. 1–20). Thousand Oaks, CA: Sage Publications.

Ellis, C. (2017). Manifesting compassionate autoethnographic research. *International Review of Qualitative Research, 10*(1), 54–61.

Ellis, C., & Adams, T. E. (2014). The purposes, practices, and principles of autoethnographic research. In L. Patricia (Ed.), *The Oxford handbook of qualitative research* (pp. 254–276). New York, NY: Oxford University Press.

Freire, P. (1993). *Pedagogy of the oppressed*. New York, NY: Continuum.

Grundy, S. (1987). *Curriculum: Product or praxis?* London: Falmer Press.

Guba, E. G., & Lincoln, Y. S. (2005). Paradigmatic controversies, contradictions, and emerging confluences. In N. K. Denzin & Y. S. Lincoln (Eds.), *The Sage handbook of qualitative research* (3rd ed., pp. 191–215). Thousand Oaks, CA: Sage Publications.

Habermas, J. (1972). *Knowledge and human interests*. London: Heinemann Educational.

Kauffman, S. A. (2007). Beyond reductionism: Reinventing the sacred. *Zygon, 42*(4), 903–914.

Kelle, U., & Buchholtz, N. (2015). The combination of qualitative and quantitative research methods in mathematics education: A "mixed methods" study on the development of the professional knowledge of teachers. In S. Bikner-Ahsbahs, C. Knipping, & N. Presmeg (Eds.), *Approaches to qualitative research in mathematics education: Examples of methodology and methods* (pp. 321–361). Dordrecht: Springer.

Lakoff, G., & Johnson, M. (1980). *Metaphors we live by*. Chicago, IL: The University of Chicago Press.

Lerman, S. (1990). Alternative perspectives of the nature of mathematics and their influence on the teaching of mathematics. *British Educational Research Journal, 16*(1), 53–61.

Luitel, B. C. (2009). *Culture, worldview and transformative philosophy of mathematics education in Nepal: A cultural-philosophical inquiry* (Unpublished doctoral thesis). Science and Mathematics Education Centre, Curtin University, Perth, Australia.

McNiff, J. (2013). My story is my living educational theory. In D. J. Clandinin (Ed.), *Handbook of narrative inquiry: Mapping a methodology*. Thousand Oaks, CA: Sage Publications.

Mezirow, J. (1991). *Transformative dimensions of adult learning*. San Francisco, CA: Jossey Bass.

Molz, M., & Gidley, J. (2008). A transversal dialogue on integral education and planetary consciousness. *Integral Review: A Transdisciplinary and Transcultural Journal for New Thought, Research and Praxis, 4*(1), 47–70. Retrieved from https://epubs.scu.edu.au/ccyp_pubs/23

Morrell, A., & O'Connor, M. A. (2002). Introduction. In E. V. O'Sullivan, A. Morrell, & M. A. O'Connor (Eds.), *Expanding the boundaries of transformative learning: Essays on theory and praxis* (p. xvii). New York, NY: Palgrave.

Pant, B. P. (2015). *Pondering on my beliefs and practices on mathematics, pedagogy, curriculum and assessment* (Unpublished MPhil dissertation). School of Education, Kathmandu University, Nepal.

Presmeg, N. (2014). A dance of instruction with construction in mathematics education. In U. Kortenkamp, B. Brandt, C. Benz, G. Krummheuer, S. Ladel, & R. Vogel (Eds.), *Early mathematics learning* (pp. 9–17). New York, NY: Springer.

Qutoshi, S. B. (2015). Auto/ethnography: A transformative research paradigm. *Dhaulagiri Journal of Sociology and Anthropology, 9*, 161–190.

Reed-Danahay, D. E. (Ed.). (1997). *Auto/ethnography: Rewriting the self and the social (Explorations in anthropology)*. Oxford: Berg.
Snow, C. P. (1993). *Two cultures and the scientific revolution*. London: Cambridge University Press.
Taylor, P. C. (2008). Multi-paradigmatic research design spaces for cultural studies researchers embodying postcolonial theorizing. *Culture Studies of Science Education, 4*, 1–8.
Taylor, P. C., & Medina, M. (2011). Educational research paradigms: From positivism to pluralism. *College Research Journal, 1*(1), 1–16.
Taylor, P. C., Taylor, E. L., & Luitel, B. C. (2012). Multi-paradigmatic transformative research as/for teacher education: An integral perspective. In B. J. Fraser, K. G. Tobin, & C. J. McRobbie (Eds.), *Second international handbook of science education* (pp. 373–387). Dordrecht: Springer.
Tobin, K., & Tippins, D. (1993). Constructivism as a referent for teaching and learning. In K. Tobin (Ed.), *The practice of constructivism in science education* (pp. 3–21). Washington, DC: AAAS Press.
Van Manen, M. (1991). *Researching lived experience: Human science for an action sensitive pedagogy*. New York, NY: The State University of New York.
Whitehead, J. (1989). Creating a living educational theory from questions of the kind, 'How do I improve my practice?'. *Cambridge Journal of Education, 19*, 41–52.
Whitehead, J. (2008). Using a living theory methodology in improving practice and generating educational knowledge in living theories. *Educational Journal of Living Theories, 1*(1), 103–126.
Willis, J. (2007). *Foundations of qualitative research: Interpretive and critical approaches*. Thousand Oaks, CA: Sage Publications.
Wood, M., & Welch, C. (2010). Are 'qualitative' and 'quantitative' useful terms for describing research? *Methodological Innovations Online, 5*(1), 56–71.

ABOUT THE AUTHOR

Binod Prasad Pant is my name. I am working as an Assistant Professor of Mathematics Education at Kathmandu University, Nepal. I have been teaching masters courses and supervising masters dissertations and research projects. I am also a subject committee member of Science, Technology, Engineering, Arts and Mathematics (STEAM) Education in the School of Education. I have been working with a number of Nepali teachers and teacher educators who examine their lived experiences as students, teachers and teacher educators. I speak and write about pedagogical innovations, mathematics teachers' beliefs and practices, child friendly classrooms, authentic assessment. I am interested in transformative educational research and research studies on reflective practice.

NAIF MASTOOR ALSULAMI

6. TRANSFORMING SAUDI EDUCATORS' PROFESSIONAL PRACTICES

Critical Auto/Ethnography, an Islamic Perspective

Tell them such stories; perhaps they may reflect.
(Holy Qur'an, 7:176)

Prospective mathematics teachers in Saudi Arabia learn about innovative student-centred teaching approaches during their undergraduate study with the aim of improving their professional practice when they enter the educational field as teachers. Having said that, I as a former mathematics teacher noticed that many of them, including myself, were not interested in practicing what we learned during our pre-service teacher education. We were typically following the conventional teacher-centred approach and our students were mostly involved in the same traditional passive way of learning. It was clear to me that there is a huge gap between what teacher education programs provide and what mathematics teachers (after graduation) do in their classrooms. To investigate this issue, I needed an approach that enabled me to immerse deeply and reflect critically on my past experiences in order to envision possibilities for my future professional practice.

In my doctoral study (Alsulami, 2014), I found that mathematics teachers and their students are part of what I call the hegemonic classroom culture where the metaphor of "education as banking" (Freire, 2005) is dominant. Students do not learn to think for themselves, they depend on their teachers for knowledge. Besides, teachers are largely unaware of the traditional classroom culture they are involved in; they simply follow the everyday teaching practice they experienced as students. The ultimate goal of my inquiry was to transform the academic culture of mathematics education in Saudi Arabia. My educational experiences in the mathematics classroom played a core role in interpreting, criticising and visualising a transformative mathematics education for this purpose.

Yet, as a Saudi researcher who wants to conduct research that aims to achieve this goal and to investigate this kind of matter and answer related questions – How do I discern the culture of the mathematics classroom? How do I understand my role as a teacher and students' roles as learners? What are my beliefs towards teaching and learning mathematics and my previous learning experiences in the culture of mathematics education? - do I have to ignore my personal educational experiences to conduct such a study? More so, to what extent do Saudi scholars have to conduct their research only in an objective way – an approach that does not promote a transformative teaching and learning culture? To what extent can we look for an alternative research approach that enables us to become aware of and transform our professional practices?

Drawing on my doctoral research, I now promote the adoption of transformative research approaches for Saudi mathematics researchers to enable them to transform their professional practices. In this chapter, I shall demonstrate *critical auto/ethnography* as a transformative research methodology that draws on multiple research paradigms. And, I shall use present tense in my writing to illustrate authentic *writing as inquiry* that puts my story in its time. Critical auto/ethnography engaged me in critical reflexivity to transform my (and perhaps others') professional practices. The approach is unconventional in that it is based on myself as a researcher, my personal lived experiences, and the culture of Saudi mathematics education. Critical auto/ethnography enabled me, as a novice educational researcher, to be involved firsthand in the process of transformative learning, enabling me to generate new levels and forms of meaning and understanding, which in turn transformed my perspectives and actions (Krauss, 2005), and provided me with new lenses for envisioning the future of Saudi mathematics education culture.

Critical auto/ethnographic research seems to be very suitable for and compatible with Saudi Arabia, an Islamic country. A basic law of the Saudi government, Article 7 in Chapter 2 states: "Government in the Kingdom of Saudi Arabia derives its authority from the Book of God and the Sunna of the Prophet (PBUH[1]), which are the ultimate sources of reference for this Law and the other Laws of the State". Critical auto/ethnography allows me to draw on The Holy Qur'an and the Sunna of the Prophet (PBUH), and use them as a source of references to support some of my points. Not only this, but I also found that my use of critical auto/ethnography is inspired by The Holy Qur'an, in two ways.

First, from an Islamic view, it is bad practice to instruct people while you do not follow your own instructions. Allah (SWT) said in The Qur'an: "O you who believe, why do you say what you do not do? It is most hateful to Allah for you to say what you do not do" (Holy Qur'an, 61:2–3). The most helpless one to reform others is s/he who is unable to reform him/herself. In another Surah, Allah said: "Do you order righteousness for the people and forget yourselves while you recite the Scripture? Then will you not reason?" (Holy Qur'an, 2:44). Critical auto/ethnography does not just allow me to "preach", but importantly allows me to write this chapter critically using my own voice. Simply, I am practicing what I am advocating. I am using the way of writing that critical auto/ethnography endorses. Hence, you will find this chapter involves poetry and fictive dialogue that I use to convey the meanings that I want to convey.

Second, this transformative research approach enables me to tell stories and experiences – of mine and others. The Holy Qur'an consists of many stories; and there is a chapter in it named, "The Stories". Allah said in The Qur'an to the Prophet: "Tell them such stories; perhaps they may reflect" (Holy Qur'an, 7:176). Allah indicates that "stories" are a good tool that might stimulate people to reflect and think. This, to me, gives significant legitimacy to the knowledge this chapter contributes.

WHAT AM I DOING?

It could be any time during my doctoral study when I talk to my Saudi colleagues about the methodology of my research. Many times, I have been asked questions such as:

Ahmed: "Is what you are doing considered research?"

Ali: "Should it be called research?"

Saud: "Is what you have been doing *really* research?"

These questions imply that what I am doing is not research nor is it considered to be real research – from the questioner's point of view, of course. More so, these questions are often asked in a way that suggests scepticism, doubt, and even hostility or taunting. So, it would not have been helpful for me to respond directly and simply to these questions by exclaiming: "YES, it is! What I have been conducting is definitely considered real research". I believe that the best way to answer these questions is by identifying what I mean by research.

"In answer to your questions", I respond, "I would say that for many researchers their research should be objective, value free and involve looking for absolute truths (or Truths). However, what if I claim that human knowledge cannot be independent of the human mind? What if I do not believe in absolute truth? What if I believe that all truths are "contingent on the describing activities of human beings" (Ellis & Bochner, 2000, p. 746)? Does this mean that I cannot conduct research? In other words, am I unable to conduct research unless I accept an unquestionable Truth that needs to be discovered? I wonder: should I follow only one ideology and opinion in conducting research? Or should I follow what I think is valuable and appropriate for me and my inquiry? Basically, and simply, what if I embrace an alternative epistemology?"

Ahmed, Ali and Saud look to each other and offer no responses to my questions.

"But we as Muslims believe in Truth", Ali says after a while.

"Yes, you are right", I respond. "As a Muslim, I do not believe in absolute truth unless it has been mentioned in The Holy Qur'an by Allah or has been revealed to The Prophet Muhammad (PBUH). Imam Malik, a great Muslim scholar, said "everyone's talk is takeable and rejectable except who is in this grave" (he was pointing to The Prophet's grave in Medina). In The Qur'an we are commanded to think, meditate and reflect on everything around us, including ourselves. Moreover, The Qur'an questions those who believe in something just because they have found their parents following that belief, without meditating on themselves and the world around them. This leads me to question why we need to follow (blindly) conventional ideas about how to conduct research that have been established many years ago? We might choose to follow them but, as suggested in The Qur'an, only after careful consideration. From another aspect, my research is not about religious matters or questions. My research is about educational matters and we know better about our life in education, just as The Prophet said to his companions commenting on their cultivating palm trees, "You know best the affairs of your worldly life". He (PBUH) also said in another narration, "I am only a human being like you. If I tell you to do something with regard to religion, then follow it, but if I tell you to do something based on personal opinion, then [realise] that I am only human being". So, there is no conflict between what you said about Muslims needing to believe in Truth and what I do".

What About Me?!!
I want to see the world through my own eyes…not thru those of others
I want to hear voices with my own ears…not with those of others
I want to smell a smell with my own nose…not with that of others
I want to say a word with my own tongue…not with that of others
I want to understand an idea with my own mind…not with that of others
I want to do my research my own way which respects my values and beliefs

"Therefore, I began asking myself", I continue, "why can I not adopt, foster or cultivate an alternative epistemology of research practice that provides me with opportunities and means to transform my professional practice? I need to assert that with the hegemony of using only one perspective (whatever that may be), and without the possibility of choosing and using alternative epistemologies, the hope for development and transformation in Saudi mathematics education might have no place, the prospect of creativity might disappear, and the inspiration of Islamic values would not be allowed to appear".

Saud: "Excuse me Naif, I do not want to interrupt you but what are you looking for in your research?"

Ali: "Yea, that's a good question".

WHAT CAN I SAY I AM LOOKING FOR?

"For those who are looking for Truth", I reply to Saud and Ali, "critical auto/ethnographic research is not compatible with the epistemology they have chosen to follow. I believe that no one knows the Truth except Allah. The transformative research methodology I have designed does not require me to look for Truth. Rather, it enables me to build a new understanding of my learning and teaching experiences and to make meaning out of certain educational aspects of my life lived in the context of an academic mathematics education culture in Saudi Arabia. My aim is to transform that context and my professional practice, and to foster a profound change in Saudi mathematics education by providing transformative professional development. Not surprisingly, this approach provides non-deterministic outcomes. It provides new contextually plausible and possible understandings".

Ahmed: "Naif!!" [Ahmed closes his eyes and says with head moving] "What are you talking about? Could you please be specific?"

Saud: "What is your research...I mean, what's your definition of research?"

Asking the Right Question!!

"What you are doing is not research", he says...
"I know your epistemology!! Do you know my epistemology??", I say...
"No, I don't", he says...
"You do not know my research, then", I say...
"What is your research then?", he says...
"This is the right question, detective!!!", I say.

WHAT IS MY RESEARCH?

"It is easy to rewrite the definition of my type of research", I respond, "based on what is written in books by respected authors. But I am not going to do so. This is not because I am unable or I am not allowed to do so. It is because I tend to deem that there is not a single research definition that can fit all kinds of research purposes and because research definitions have usually been written from the point of view of specific epistemologies, ideologies and perspectives. These research definitions have been seemingly composed by nobody and out of nowhere. They do not necessarily need to be compatible with mine, and might not help me or you to understand my research. Consequently, I need to define my research based on my own sense of purpose. Hence, I define my research in the following way".

"My research involves:

- transformative learning about my own professional practices,
- engaging myself in critical reflection about my past experiences,
- examining critically my personal and professional values and beliefs,
- reconceptualising my own professionalism,
- committing myself to transform mathematics education culture (by transforming pedagogical practices, the images of teachers' and student' roles, and of mathematics and curricula images) within my own institution,
- building contextual understanding and making meaning of my professional practice,
- engaging myself and others to rethink about some educational aspects,
- designing a creative research structure,
- using alternative paradigms, an alternative methodology, alternative epistemologies, alternative quality standards and new logics,
- subjective, not value free, constructive, emergent, contextualized, narrative stories,
- complex and dynamic investigative processes, and
- my not being isolated or static; reflecting on, interacting with, and responding to new constructive knowledge".

"The nature of my research is complex, multi-dimensional and non-objective, which are characteristics of a postmodern worldview, because the context of the Saudi education system is complex and dynamic. So, it is not a simple matter to provide a clear-cut definition of my research that enables me to say, "This is a clear outline of my research". The points related above are clues for you about what my research might be. My research is what I have been doing".

My Story and My Life

What is my story? What is my life?
Here is my story; here is my life...
This is my story; this is me, Naif.

My life is a story; my story is my life...
Saying my story; to know my life...
This is my story; this is me, Naif.

I wanna say my story; it is my life...
Forgetting my story; losing my life...
This is my story; this is me, Naif.
Do you wanna know about me?
Looking for my story; to get my life...
Ignoring my story; ignoring my life...
This is my story; this is me, Naif.

Ahmed: "Can you give us more details about your research?"

"Sure, I can", I say smiling. "In my inquiry, I am applying an alternative (non-standard) approach to research, employing unconventional methods of writing and structuring the thesis. Drawing on the Interpretivist (how the world is perceived), Criticalist (how the world should be), Postmodernist (how the world can be) and Integralist (how the world can blend various theories) paradigms of research, I create my research methodology which provides multiple methods, such as writing as inquiry and reflective writing, in order to both conduct and represent my inquiry".

Ahmed: "Paradigm?!!"

Ali: "Now, excuse me a minute!"

Saud: "Calm down Ali. What does Paradigm mean, Naif?"

WHAT DO I MEAN BY PARADIGM?

"Well, this is a really good question", I respond, "Because it clarifies the school of thought that I am following. A paradigm can be defined as a "comprehensive belief system, worldview, or framework that guides research and practice in a [particular] field" (Willis, 2007, p. 8). So, it is a worldview that guides me as a researcher and learner, and can be identified by its fundamental assumptions of ontology, epistemology and methodology (Guba & Lincoln, 1994). Ontology and epistemology are two major aspects of metaphysics (a branch of philosophy) and are essential aspects of a paradigm. Ontology is concerned with the nature of reality (or being or existence). It concerns what can exist or what is real. Epistemology is concerned with what we can know about reality and how we can justify our claims to know. Epistemology is about theories of knowledge".

Saud: "Ontology and epistemology?!! Can you explain a bit more what these terms mean?"

Ali: "How do they work in your research?"

Me: "Do not be in a hurry. More details of what I mean by ontology and epistemology in my methodology are discussed in the following section".

INTERPRETIVISM

I use three features of this research paradigm: (1) new research process, (2) alternative ontology and epistemology, and (3) new understanding of the issue under investigation.

First, this paradigm allows me to embrace an open-ended research design process that enables me to welcome emergent research questions, an emergent mode of inquiry and an emergent thesis structure (Taylor, 2008). I found this paradigm appropriate for replacing the hegemony of conventional research that was restricting my thinking and writing in conducting and constructing a research inquiry.

Interpretivism Metaphorically

Interpretivism is like a salad...
You have to put something on it to make it better,

Interpretivism is like a farm...
You can cultivate whatever you like,

Interpretivism is like a garden...
It is full of colours,

Interpretivism is yours...
You can construct it as you like,

Interpretivism is like a bird...
It keeps me flying,

Interpretivism is like a sweet...
It can't be bitter,

> Interpretivism is like going to heaven...
> You never want to return back,
>
> Interpretivism is like liberty...
> It doesn't like restrictions.

Second, I was troubled by the limitations of the conventional ontological and epistemological aspects of research (Ellis & Bochner, 2000) – such as a materialist ontology in which reality, including thought and feeling, can be explained only in the material or physical world, and empirical epistemology in which I can come to know about the world only through experiments (Willis, 2007). Then I found an appropriate ontology and epistemology in Interpretivism.

An ontological position concerns the nature or essence of the phenomenon being studied. My way of relating to people is different from considering how I relate to objects of natural science. The differences between objects in the social and natural sciences are respected in this paradigm (Bryman, 2001) in which people can give their meanings of phenomena, unlike natural science objects that cannot. The objective methods of the natural sciences do not help me so effectively to understand my educational problems.

My ontology in this methodology is that the current academic culture of mathematics education in Saudi Arabia is not external to me because I grew up within it; it is not imposed upon my consciousness nor is it entirely separate from me. Rather, it is a product of my consciousness. I live within it and within the process of fashioning it (Cohen, Manion, & Morrison, 2000). From a constructivist point of view, there is no reality for me other than what I construct in my own mind. Therefore, my apprehension of reality could be experienced in a different way from the consciousness of another person. Therefore, I could say that the realities seen via this methodology are multiple as they could be highlighted in varied ways. Different ontological positions can lead me to varied stances on the issue (Willis, 2007). Hence, my ontology articulates that the Saudi mathematics education culture is not a single objective reality produced seemingly by no-one and existing 'out there'. I state that from my own professional perspective I get to understand the academic culture of mathematics education in Saudi Arabia based upon a specific context as a result of my cognition of my learning and teaching experiences.

An epistemological position concerns the nature of knowledge and its forms and how it can be acquired. It could also concern the nature of the relationship between me as inquirer and what can be known. By the way, ontological and epistemological positions are interconnected in such a way that my view of either of them constrains my view of the other (Guba & Lincoln, 1994). So, when I conceive a situation under study as a product of my consciousness my claim is that the knowledge produced is not an objective claim. Knowledge does not suddenly live in my mind or come from someone else. Knowledge is built in my mind in a long, complex and complicated process of cognition. Therefore, I can say that I construct my knowledge based upon my understanding of my experiences.

My epistemology in this methodology sees knowledge as subjective, personal and based upon one's experience (Cohen et al., 2000). So, the quality and the viability of the research information I produce via this approach do not necessarily produce a slavish correspondence to the "objective reality" "out there" (Kincheloe & Tobin, 2009, p. 524). Consequently, the knowledge claimed by critical auto/ethnography seems to be softer, more subjective and related to one's experiences. From a constructivist point of view, knowledge is not considered universal, it is contextualized. From the same perspective, knowledge is not considered common or standard; it is unique and personally experienced.

Third, the paradigm of Interpretivism encourages me as a researcher to understand and reconstruct a new meaning of the academic culture of mathematics education in Saudi Arabia (Guba & Lincoln, 1994) by interpreting and reflecting upon my own learning and teaching experiences within that culture, based on the context of my own and my research participants' thoughts, beliefs, values and associated aspects of the culture. So, I would be able to generate a new contextual understanding for mathematics education in Saudi Arabia. When I generate my data, I do not want to test an *a priori* theory; instead, I want to construct a fresh understanding. In other words, rather than seeking out an absolute form of truth in my inquiry, I intend to try to generate new understandings of the context of Saudi mathematics education. Interpretivism allows me to provide substantial descriptive details which are imperative in providing for contextual understanding (Bryman, 2004).

Let Me Go

Interpretivism…freedom to gain…freedom to share
Interpretivism…freedom to reflect…freedom to know
Interpretivism…freedom to imagine…freedom to learn
Interpretivism…freedom from error…freedom to be creative
Interpretivism…freedom from the 'objective'…freedom to be subjective
Interpretivism…I want to be free…I'll say my view
Interpretivism…end to restriction…freedom of expression…
conclusion isn't expected…Truth is depression…

CRITICALISM

This research paradigm provides me with power that allows me and encourages me to do three things: to deconstruct, reconceptualise and transform the culture of mathematics education in Saudi Arabia.

First, Criticalism provides me with an essential power that helps me to deconstruct the hegemonic ideology of mathematics education in Saudi Arabia which could be the major reason for holding back transformative education in the mathematics classroom. I orient the power of this paradigm towards revealing assumptions of mathematics education that have been taken for granted. Deconstructing the hegemonic can be attempted through questioning (Cohen et al., 2000) and criticizing the status quo (Orlikowski & Baroudi, 1991) of Saudi mathematics education, the assumptions of teaching and learning ideologies, the assumptions of the prevailing image of mathematics, and by questioning the aspects of mathematics education that have been taken as unquestionable. To move towards transformative education the hegemonic culture of mathematics education in Saudi Arabia needs to be scrutinised and re-evaluated.

Second, Criticism (along with Interpretivism) allows me to take a further step after deconstruction to create a new vision of mathematics education. It allows me to reconceptualise the academic culture of mathematics education in Saudi Arabia based on alternative assumptions of mathematics education that respect a person's subjective knowledge, but without privileging it. This combination of research paradigms enables me to reconceptualise the culture of mathematics education through critical reflection. So, during the process of evaluating the classroom culture critical questions need to be asked to highlight any flaws and to lead me to generate a professional praxis (Taylor, Taylor, & Luitel, 2012) for transforming the mathematics education culture.

Third, following deconstructing and reconceptualising, Criticism allows me to take action and create change (Cohen et al., 2000). Criticism does not only provide me with the power to criticize the current culture of mathematics education in Saudi Arabia but it also enables me to look at ways of transforming that culture (Guba & Lincoln, 1994). A "critical turn" is necessary to emancipate myself – my thoughts, beliefs, consciousness, awareness – from the current academic culture, the artificial boundaries of mathematics education around me into which I have been enculturated. Thus, I would seek to rid myself of the hegemonic situation in conventional teaching and learning in mathematics education, and thus have my professional conceptions transformed. This research paradigm has the capacity to empower me to link my research to the ideal of mental emancipation that could free me from viewpoints that control and restrict me to follow a specific educational perspective that does not fit my own interests (Vinden, 1999). This emancipation seems to be a crucial point in transformation. Without this power, I might find it impossible to think creatively and critically, to understand subjectively and contextually, or to change and be transformed.

POSTMODERNISM

To identify Postmodernism from a literal perspective I can say that *post* means *after*; so Postmodernism means *after Modernism*. It includes what does not work well within Modernism. Postmodernism tends to react against certain principles and practices of established Modernism (Desmond, 2011). However, these statements may not have added anything to Postmodernism's meaning and at the same time do not clarify or identify the essence of Postmodernism. When I say *after Modernism* it intends to be something which is not compatible with Modernism's ideas. However, what comes after could be more elaborate or, on the other hand, could be more conservative.

Postmodernism seems to be controversial in its definition and its features. To the best of my knowledge, there is no single accepted definition of Postmodernism. Postmodernism does not and cannot provide complete answers to questions about its own meaning (St. Pierre, 2000), simply because any attempt to define it would violate its premise "that no definite terms, boundaries or absolute truths exist" (allaboutphilosophy.org). So, when I attempt to state a clear literal meaning of it, I – at the same time – compromise its very essence, as it entirely rejects such objective truth. It refuses classifications and dualistic doctrines (e.g., right or wrong). It advocates pluralism. It dissolves restrictive definitions. However, a proper explanation of how Postmodernism fits my inquiry was characterised by Jean-François Lyotard, one of its leading theorists, as *incredulity towards metanarratives* (Meynell, 1999).

In The Holy Book, Allah (SWT) questions those who follow what has been taken for granted without thinking. Allah says: "When we ask them to follow what the Lord commands, they respond: 'We found our fathers lived by a rule of life and we on their tracks are guided'. What! Even if their fathers did not use their reasoning at all, nor were they truly guided" (Holy Qur'an, 1:170). So, I am not going to say that I found people in a situation and I am going to follow in their tracks. Rather, I am going to use my own mind, my reasoning, to think of a suitable way of conducting a research inquiry. I am not going to follow others without thinking. I might follow others and might take some things for granted but I need to use my mind, to think, to question, reflect and judge whether it makes sense for me or not.

On the other hand, Postmodernism seems to be a danger if I – as a teacher educator and as a Muslim as well – adopt it in its entirety. It is dangerous because Postmodernism (generally speaking) tends to deconstruct instead of construct. Actually, I cannot adopt it in its entirety. If I were to adopt it in its entirety, I should have to respect its characteristic of being suspicious by being suspicious of its tenets. This is a challenge in Postmodernism. Furthermore, I as a Muslim educator believe in absolute truth about, for example, the existence of God (Allah), although we are supposed to think and reflect about what God has created, not to be suspicious of his existence but to increase our faith. Moreover, as a teacher educator only deconstructing (including deconstructing my own deconstructing) might lead me into a chaotic state of mind such that the relevant concepts would not assist me to start doing my research. It would not help me to express meaningfully to my students. It would not assist me to aid my students to construct their own understandings and their knowledge. It might enable me to do so but only at the cost of my being in a constantly sceptical frame of mind. I do not know!!!

So, instead of embracing Postmodernism entirely I use some of its constructive features, or what has been called *constructive Postmodernism* (Schiralli, 1999) which would help me to achieve a stable base for my inquiry and hence to enhance my possibilities for cumulative and meaningful understanding.

First, Postmodernism is a set of perspectives employed by critical theorists (Desmond, 2011). It opens my mind (i) to think critically, and more importantly, freely about what I am doing without having to stick to following obediently a certain line of action, and (ii) to think carefully about what I have taken for granted in the way of conducting research. It is a new way to understand a new world. Therefore, the ideas of validity and reliability of research have become the subject of my sceptical view of what counts as such in typical and trusted research.

Second, Postmodernism brings to our attention the very important concept of *representation* (Denzin & Lincoln, 2000) which is associated with research based on the Arts (McNiff, 2008). Postmodernism welcomes me to use figurative forms such as pictures, poems and poetry to convey the meanings I want to express and to extend our understanding of *the other* (Bryman, 2004). It enables me to break the hegemonic grip of scientific research writing. It allows me to represent my inquiry in a non-conventional way; not tied to using an established scientific style of writing or the third person voice or conventional thesis structure. It encourages me to express my educational experience emotionally and my inquiry aesthetically. The reason for writing in an unconventional scientific manner is that I need to write in a way that allows readers to understand and resonate with my particular version of mathematics education (Denzin, 1997).

Third, Postmodernism encourages me to use (i) powerful new ways of reasoning, such as metaphorical and dialectical logics, which enable me to capture the complexity of teaching and learning by engaging in multi-schema envisioning; and (ii) new genres, such as narrative writing, that help me to richly depict the complexity of my experiences in mathematics education by speaking from my lived storied perspective, foregrounding its contexts, events and people; and poetic writing that helps me to represent my educational experience emotionally and aesthetically (Taylor, Taylor, & Luitel, 2012). By using alternative logics and genres, I am able to make new sense of my experiences in a complex study of mathematics education in Saudi Arabia.

I write auto/ethnography with a slash (/) between auto and ethnography as I want to show that there is a dialectical relationship between me as a researcher (auto) and the culture of the Saudi mathematics classroom (ethnography). Using the slash would help me to explore the balance between me and the classroom culture that I have been involved in; examining the influence that I made to the culture and the culture made to me. The slash makes me able to (critically) inquire into the mathematics classroom culture including its practices, beliefs and values through me; my stories and my experiences which are embedded in that culture (Roth, 2005).

Fourth, Postmodernism respects the diversity of (often conflicting) theories, attitudes, ideas, and human experiences. It does not seek a grand theory of human experience regardless of context. It involves building fragments of understanding developed in different contexts. Pluralism and difference are considered to be key aspects of its central principles (Polkinghorne, 1992). Postmodernism is about *philosophical relativity*. Truth, culture, ethics and politics are all relative within Postmodernism. So, "no idea or expression or belief can be more credible than any other because all ideas are equally valid" (Desmond, 2011, p. 154).

Although I have explained these paradigms separately, they are interconnected. I cannot, for example, talk about Postmodernism and, at the same time, keep aside Interpretivism and Criticalism. From an Integral perspective, each paradigm emerges from (and includes) earlier paradigms (Taylor et al., 2012).

My Poem to Positivism

Good bye positivism...
You always take a strong position...
Of how research should be done...
Reasons for research to be done...
How data are to be collected...
And how to be analysed.

Good bye positivism...
Let me take up another position...
Softer than your position...
That allows me to act positively...
And allows you to keep your position.

Good bye positivism...
I'm not meaning that for good...
We still are excellent friends...
Although we do not have the same mind...
We are still good friends.

Good bye positivism...
We both do research...
In the field of education...
Our focuses are different...
As our purposes are different ...
As we think differently.

Bye-bye positivism...
By the way...
There are others who like you...
But they have different names...
You know, you're all the same...
Say the same...
Think the same...
You look different, but you are the same.

Good bye positivism...
Convey my farewell...
To those who are parallel to you...
To name a few:...

Good bye empiricism…
God bye objectivism…
Good bye all tough conditions.

Good bye positivism…
But to be more specific…
Good bye to your hegemony…
Only your hegemony…
You are still around by virtue of your genes…
We cannot remove them…
But retain positively…
Being thoughtful…Seeing mindfully ☺

INTEGRALISM

Integralism tends to combine apparently different (or even seemingly contradictory or conflicted) perspectives to co-exist in a balanced relationship. Integralism is about developing the ability to conceptualise everything as a whole. Integralism is a *vision-logic* that transcends rational thought and involves a great deal of meditation for non-dualistic (non-polarised) awareness. Integralism is a vision-logic that "supports an integrated personality"…when vision-logic "is the basis of actual interior transformation" (Wilber, 2011, p. 287). It is a conceptually inclusive mode of reasoning (Taylor, 2014) that stimulates integration among a variety of realisations, and evokes the relationships between one's sense of past, present and future, self and other, particular and general, and instance and type.

Integralism allows me to combine Interpretivism, Criticalism and Postmodernism in order to construct my critical auto/ethnographic inquiry. This comprehensive perspective gives different epistemologies the same status. For my research – which is not restricted to only one worldview – I take several elements from different worldviews to produce and generate *my own methodology*, which – for me – fits the aims of my research. The reason for not following only one paradigm is that I do not believe that Saudi educational reality is unitary. It does not make sense to me that we all should perceive reality from a single point of view. There are multiple perceptions of Saudi educational realities. So, to perceive reality, I need to employ multiple perspectives which can be combined by adopting a *multi-paradigmatic research design space* (Taylor, 2008) that provides me with what I need to construct my hybrid research methodology. In my research, I need to interpret an event, criticize an idea, adopt uncommon representations, and envision alternative cultures. I need a wide-ranging perspective that enables me to envisage an inclusive mathematics education culture.

Integralism is really what I feel I need in the culture of mathematics education in Saudi Arabia. I thank Postmodernism for promoting a plurality of views and treating these views with the same status. However, Integralism takes one more step by not only accepting the variety of views but by bringing the different views to co-exist AND to cooperate in order to build a more inclusive view, and more so, to argue that a view cannot be completely understood unless the opposite point of view is considered. A student-centred teaching approach, for example, needs to be understood in relation to a teacher-centred approach. Both approaches need to work together to provide a more comprehensive approach to Saudi mathematics education. Metaphorically speaking, I would say that ideas, views or perspectives are colours. Each colour, red, blue, green…has its own quality and is the favourite for some people. Bringing the colours together constitutes a rainbow. And a rainbow seems to be what Saudi mathematics education culture needs.

Culturally speaking, people tend to vary in their views and it is likely that they always will. Allah said: "And if your Lord had willed, He could have made mankind one community; but they will not cease to differ" (Holy Qur'an, 11:118). The best way to transcend the differences could be by accepting them as they are, as Postmodernism suggests with the view to promoting pluralism. However, to bring unity in diversity, an inclusive view is required. It is important to say that an inclusive view does not mean that each different view has to give up its own ideologies or principles, but it does mean that (i) each one focuses on similarities more than on differences, (ii) each one focuses on moral values more than on specific procedures, and (iii) each one focuses on purposes more than on methods. The goal is to build a more inclusive view and cooperative vision in the field of Saudi mathematics education rather than to produce a single privileged view. "A theory of everything" needs to be at hand, in which "an integral vision offers considerably more wholeness than the slice-and-dice alternatives" (Wilber, 2000, p. xii).

CRITICAL AUTO/ETHNOGRAPHY

My experiences in school life are neither simple nor linear; they are rich and complex in quality. The richness, complexity and the quality of my school life cannot be captured by quantitative tools and methods alone. It entails me – Naif Alsulami' a researcher and learner – to use an alternative form of inquiry to capture them. Drawing on the aforementioned paradigms I construct a critical auto/ethnographic methodology.

This methodology allows me to focus on myself (auto), Saudi mathematics education culture (ethno) and the inquiry process (graphy) (Reed-Danahay, 1997). Auto/ethnography connects my personality to Saudi education culture and, in the process, the two concepts relate to each other dialectically. It allows me to breach the conventional separation of myself from my research by making myself both the object and the instrument in conducting research (Ellis & Bochner, 2000).

Critical auto/ethnography, however, seems to be sometimes a loose term. It can be used with a somewhat different application in varied research situations. There are some commonly used terms that provide a sense of the range of methodologies associated with autoethnography (Ellis & Bochner, 2000). Critical auto/ethnography can be used, for example, as a narrative inquiry. Critical auto/ethnographers are not like objectivists. They are very flexible in functioning in accordance with several terms of inquiries. I found that Taylor's (2010) definition is appropriate to me: "Critical auto/ethnography is situated at the nexus of ethnography, writing as inquiry, arts-based research, narrative inquiry, evocative autoethnography, anthropological poetics, philosophical inquiry, critical hermeneutics and practitioner inquiry" (p. 7). So, critical auto/ethnography can be understood as non-positivist research.

Critical auto/ethnography provides me with an approach to immerse myself deeply in the moments of my (academic as well as personal) life, to understand them closely and critically. It makes my life and experiences in school the focus of the research (Reed-Danahay, 1997). So, I am allowed to make my own experiences, in my various roles as a pre-service mathematics teacher and an experienced mathematics teacher, a "topic of investigation in its own right" (Ellis & Bochner, 2000, p. 733). My experiences have not been just as an isolated person; rather they have come from interactions with others who then became part of my experience. So, the experiences of others may be involved in the inquiry. Moreover, my experiences and those of others were not isolated from our society; they were embedded and reflected within it. So, features of our society and their influence on us may also be embedded in the inquiry.

Furthermore, this approach allows me to refer to our Holy Book (The Qur'an) and our Prophet Mohammad (PBUH); that we are inspired by them to reveal and demonstrate the deep culture behind our experiences, noting that our social culture in Saudi Arabia is derived from Islamic culture in general. This approach provides me with an avenue for doing something meaningful for both myself and the world surrounding me (Ellis & Bochner, 2000).

My experiences are not static; they are changing and evolving. They are unique and should be studied in their contexts; they are not fully generalizable (Cohen et al., 2000). Therefore, this methodology allows me to emphasize significant details and necessary accessories surrounding my experiences with mathematics education. They are very important and crucial in contextual understanding (Bryman, 2001).

This transformative approach to educational research requests me to be the one who is generating the data through stories, gathering information and evidence relating to my research topic, presenting my past and present personal experiences and those of the participants in an actual school setting, and to discuss the meaning of those stories and experiences (Creswell, 2008) by reflecting critically upon them in order to construct a deep understanding about them. I need this kind of understanding due to the complexity of my educational inquiry. In this type of research, I see myself as a self-ethnographer as I am sharing my stories with others in mathematics classrooms. My subjectivity and personal accountability are dynamic in this approach. It goes without saying that my aim is to explain the complexity of experiences through verbal description rather than testing hypotheses with numerical value.

What makes this approach to knowledge production legitimate is that it is inspired by The Holy Qur'an. In the Qur'an, there is a chapter (28) by the name of Al-Qasas [Narratives/Stories]. The entire chapter (12), named Yusuf [Joseph], has been devoted to the story of Yusuf [Joseph], Yaqub [Jacob], Zulaikha and the brothers. In the beginning of the chapter, Allah (SWT) says: "We narrate to you, O Prophet, the most excellent of the narratives by (means of) what We have revealed to you in this Qur'an" (Holy Qur'an, 12:3). In the concluding verse of this chapter, Allah says: "In their stories there is certainly a lesson for men of understanding. It is not a narrative which could be falsified, but a verification of what is before it and a distinct explanation of all things and a guide and a mercy to a people who believe" (Holy Qur'an, 12:111). In several places in the Qur'an Allah (SWT), after telling a story, *says that they may reflect, perhaps they may understand*. These features are characteristics of transformative learning which lie at the heart of transformative educational research.

MY WRITING...

Critical auto/ethnography considers the act of writing as: a method of inquiry (Taylor, 2010); as a method of generating my data; and, as a way of finding out more about myself and my topic. Writing is a way of getting to know. I inquire at the same time as I am writing (Richardson, 2000).

The Power of Writing

It is vital writing...Not static at all
Here is my own voice...Not the omniscient one
I'm writing in the first voice...Not the third one.

My voice is made known...Not hidden
I'm an instrument...Not an impediment
I'm "onymous"...Not anonymous.

My research should be read...Not scanned
Its meaning...In the reading
My attention...Turns to writing...Not boring
Never express precisely...Completely
Yet, I keep on going...In my writing.

Writing is viable...Not for reliable
Wiring is expressive...Don't take it for granted
Writing is fun...Not full of grief.

Writing is my life...As I write about my life
Writing presents my voice...As I write my experience.

Who you are...Do you know?
When you write...You may know!!

Writing about myself…To find out about myself
Writing my stories…To see myself.

I write unknown to be known
I write to know what was unknown
I write to know…what I didn't know.

In my past learning…
I learned to write what I know…But didn't know how to write
I learned to write what I knew…I learned to know before I wrote
I learned to write…But not to really know
My writing was about what I already know

What if I write to know…
Write what I don't know to know…
Write what is unknown to be known.

My writing has different ways…my life has different stories
Writing in different ways…means considering new aspects of my life.

I write about myself…From myself…To understand myself
I wanna make a difference…About my experience

Should it be done academically (objectively)??…But why??!!
Why not narratively!!…Why not poetically!!…Why not evocatively!!…
Emotionally!!…Strikingly!!
Why not??!!!…So,…Let's do it.

CLOSING

The power of this approach seems to be most obvious in its ability to enable us to think critically and reflectively to deeply understand ourselves first (including our perceptions and our professional practice) before we understand others. It awakens us to the status quo of the mathematics classroom culture we have been involved in. Critical auto/ethnography empowers us to be emancipated from restrictions which unconsciously were made by ourselves. Critical auto/ethnography can be used as a transformative learning tool for Saudi mathematics education researchers to transform their professionalism. The approach is unconventional in that is based on the researchers themselves, their personal lived experiences and their educational culture. Critical auto/ethnography enables educational researchers, especially novices, to be involved firsthand in a process of transformative learning which lies at the heart of transformative education.

NOTE

[1] Muslims say PBUH (peace be upon him) after mentioning the Prophet, and they say SWT (Subhanahu Wa Ta'ala) after mentioning Allah, which translates as Glory to Him, the exalted.

REFERENCES

Alsulami, N. M. (2014). *Transforming Saudi mathematics education culture: An arts-based critical autoethnographic inquiry* (PhD thesis). Curtin University, Perth, Australia.

Bryman, A. (2004). *Social research methods* (2nd ed.). Oxford: Oxford University Press.

Cohen, L., Manion, L., & Morrison, K. (2000). *Research methods in education* (5th ed.). London: RoutledgeFalmer.

Creswell, J. W. (2008). *Educational research: Planning, conducting, and evaluating quantitative and qualitative research* (3rd ed.). Upper Saddle River, NJ: Pearson.

Denzin, N. K. (1997). *Interpretive ethnography: Ethnographic practices for the 21st century.* London: Sage Publications.

Denzin, N. K., & Lincoln, Y. S. (2000). Introduction: The discipline and practice of qualitative research. In N. K. Denzin & Y. S. Lincoln (Eds.), *Handbook of qualitative research* (2nd ed., pp. 1–28). Thousand Oaks, CA: Sage Publications.

Desmond, K. K. (2011). *Ideas about art.* Chichester: Wiley-Blackwell.

Ellis, C., & Bochner, A. P. (2000). Autoethnography, personal narrative, reflexivity: Researcher as subject. In N. K. Denzin & Y. S. Lincoln (Eds.), *Handbook of qualitative research* (2nd ed., pp. 733–768). Thousand Oaks, CA: Sage Publications.

Freire, P. (2005). *Pedagogy of the oppressed* (30th anniversary ed.) (M. B. Ramos, Trans, & D. Macedo, Intro.). New York, NY: Continuum. (Original work published in 1973)

Guba, E. G., & Lincoln, Y. S. (1994). Competing paradigms in qualitative research. In N. K. Denzin & Y. S. Lincoln (Eds.), *Handbook of qualitative research* (pp. 105–117). Thousand Oaks, CA: Sage Publications.

Kincheloe, J. L., & Tobin, K. (2009). The much-exaggerated death of positivism. *Cultural Studies of Science Education, 4*, 513–528.

Krauss, S. E. (2005). Research paradigms and meaning making: A primer. *The Qualitative Report, 10*(4), 758–770. Retrieved from http://www.nova.edu/ssss/QR/QR10-4/krauss.pdf

McNiff, S. (2008). Arts-based research. In J. G. Knowles & A. L. Cole (Eds.), *Handbook of the arts in qualitative research: Perspectives, methodologies, examples, and issues* (pp. 29–40). Thousand Oaks, CA: Sage Publications.

Meynell, H. A. (1999). *Postmodernism and the new enlightenment.* Washington, DC: The Catholic University of America Press.

Orlikowski, W. J., & Baroudi, J. J. (1991). Studying information technology in organizations: Research approaches and assumptions. *Information Systems Research, 2*(1), 1–28.

Polkinghorne, D. E. (1992). Postmodern epistemology of practice. In S. Kvale (Ed.), *Psychology and postmodernism* (pp. 146–165). London: Sage Publications.

Reed-Danahay, D. (1997). Introduction. In D. Reed-Danahay (Ed.), *Auto/ethnography: Rewriting the self and the social* (pp. 1–17). Oxford: Berg.

Richardson, L. (2000). Writing: A method of inquiry. In N. Denzin & Y. Lincoln (Eds.), *Handbook of qualitative research* (2nd ed., pp. 923–948). Thousand Oaks, CA: Sage Publications.

Roth, W.-M. (Ed.). (2005). *Auto/biography and auto/ethnography: Praxis of research method.* Rotterdam, The Netherlands: Sense Publishers.

Schiralli, M. (1999). *Constructive postmodernism: Toward renewal in cultural and literary studies.* Westport, CT: Greenwood Publishing Group.

St. Pierre, E. A. (2000). The call for intelligibility in postmodern educational research. *Educational Researcher, 29*(5), 25–28.

Taylor, P. C. (2008). Multi-paradigmatic research design spaces for cultural studies researchers embodying postcolonial theorising. *Cultural Studies of Science Education, 3*, 881–890.

Taylor, P. C. (2010, September 14–16). *Transformative educational research for culturally inclusive teaching.* Paper presented at the 7th International Conference on Intercultural Competence, Khabarovsk, Far East Russia.

Taylor, P. C. (2014). Contemporary qualitative research: Towards an integral research perspective. In N. G. Lederman & S. K. Abell (Eds.), *Handbook of research on science education* (Vol. 2, pp. 38–54). New York, NY: Routledge

Taylor, P. C., Taylor, E., & Luitel, B. C. (2012). Multi-paradigmatic transformative research as/for teacher education: An integral perspective. In B. J. Fraser, K. G. Tobin, & C. J. McRobbie (Eds.), *Second international handbook of science education* (pp. 373–387). Dordrecht: Springer.

Vinden, P. G. (1999). Gathering up the fragments after positivism: Can Ratner make us whole again? *Culture & Psychology, 5*(2), 223–238.

Wilber, K. (2011). *A brief history of everything* (Rev. ed.). Boston, MA: Shambhala.

Willis, J. W. (2007). *Foundations of qualitative research: Interpretive and critical approaches.* Thousand Oaks, CA: Sage Publications.

ABOUT THE AUTHOR

Naif Mastoor Alsulami is my full Arabic name. I was born in Jeddah, the Kingdom of Saudi Arabia. I hold a PhD in Mathematics Education from Curtin University, Perth, Australia. I am currently teaching postgrad students at University of Jeddah where I am also the Vice-Dean of Graduate Studies. My main research interests lie in the field of Transformative Education, Transformative Research; Critical Auto/ethnography in particular, and Professional Development of teachers in Higher Education.

SHASHIDHAR BELBASE

7. CONTEMPLATING MY AUTOETHNOGRAPHY

From Idiosyncracy to Retrospection

My Early Mathematics: Natural Mathematics
Pebbles of diverse faces and color
Metaphors of living cattle
Pairing a big with a small
Representing the caring mother
One-to-one correspondence
Perfect natural game
Odd was out from the set
What a beautiful consequence
Pure… and pure and tranquil
No symbols, scripts or artificiality
Super math with supreme reality
Full of joy and cosmos within a mini feel

In this chapter, I contemplate an autoethnographic inquiry that I designed and conducted for an MPhil in Education at Kathmandu University: My Journey Of Learning And Teaching Mathematics From Traditionalism To Constructivism: A Portrayal Of Pedagogic Metamorphosis (Belbase, 2006), which I refer to here simply as My Autoethnography. In writing this chapter, I bridged from the idiosyncracy of my current academic journey as a researcher, teacher and learner to my distant self of over a decade ago, and back further to my childhood, which was the subject of my original inquiry. The experience of connecting my current self to my past self felt liberating; a transformative experience, as if in a dream, the effect of which was to make my mind more open, receptive and enlightened.

I commence the chapter by reflecting autobiographically on the experience of designing and conducting my autoethnographic inquiry, marked by four milestones: making a connection with mentors, reciting a poetic narrative, writing the research proposal, and submitting the dissertation for examination. Next, I present an extract from the dissertation – Relational Parallels – an evocative narrative that illustrates how I recollected and reflected on key moments of my early childhood experience. Following this, I analyse my autoethnographic inquiry through three conceptual lenses – methodological, relational and ethical. Finally, through these lenses I consider the merits and limitations of my autoethnographic inquiry. I conclude the chapter with a reflection and a poetic reminiscence.

REVISITING HISTORY

The charisma of early mathematics of pebbles and clay models of cows started for me as a 3-year old in the Spring of 1975 with sprouting blossoms of apricot in front of my house at Karange Kot, Dang, Nepal. With wonders of the changing seasons and surroundings, I used to sit at the east door of my small hut on a hillside when mother went to collect firewood and fodder for our cows. I collected pebbles to represent animals, family members, and motorcars. The clay models were my favorite play items. I compared, contrasted, counted, grouped, regrouped, and selected them for different purposes. This was how my journey of learning mathematics started unknowingly from my childhood. The poetic evocation at the beginning of this chapter – My Early Mathematics: Natural Mathematics – evokes my early childhood experience with mathematics related play.

This was a game-changing poem that I recited in a postgraduate research class at the School of Education, Kathmandu University (KUSOED) in 2006. The poem emanated from my inner temperament, articulating an artfulness and mesmerizing part of my narrative self. It was the foundation of My Autoethnography, in which I embraced the veracity of my life as a freely playing boy, a student, a teacher, and a neophyte researcher. The poem was not just a virtuous composition but was an embodied-self. It was myself that evolved through the poiesis of the text in search of the meaning of "who am I?".

My early schooling went through many uncertainties. I dropped out in grade one. I drowned in a river without knowing its depth. I rejoined the classroom. I was bullied. I encountered a ghost that almost killed me, but it turned out to be a horse. I balanced between self-reliance and cooperative/collaborative study until high school. I transitioned through youthful emotions that almost detached me from study. The deteriorating health of my father was an economic challenge to the continuation of my study. I began tutoring students to earn enough for college study. A desperate interest in many disciplines – science, mathematics, management, law – divided my focus, though it provided me a unique perspective to look at challenges and grow in all possible ways. I began teaching in schools after my undergraduate degree. Later, I was extremely busy teaching at different schools and colleges, earning the reputation of "helmet teacher": a busy teacher racing on a motorbike from one school to another to catch-up with many periods of teaching. I accepted a position in a relatively remote district where I encountered a war-torn political crisis. I continued searching for an avenue to grow further. I joined KUSOED as an MPhil scholar in 2005. Later in the same year, I began teaching as a full-time faculty.

It was some time in 2006. I was in the final semester of my MPhil when Dr Peter Taylor from Curtin University of Technology visited KUSOED. I asked Dr Bal Chandra Luitel, then assistant professor and author of his own autoethnography

(Luitel, 2003), if Peter and he could help to guide my autoethnographic dissertation writing. This conversation was the first milestone in My Autoethnography which kindled the thought process about myself as an agent in narrative and poetic form (Reese, Yan, Jack, & Hayne, 2010).

That evening, I thought about my possible research. The first thing that came to my mind was to reveal "who I am". I wrote a brief autobiography of a remote village boy, a learner of mathematics in school, and then in university. I also wrote about my experience of teaching mathematics. The opening line of my autobiography was My Early Mathematics: Natural Mathematics, which is the title of the above poem.

The next evening, Peter was to deliver a guest lecture on his paper, *Mythmaking and Mythbreaking in the Mathematics Classroom* (Taylor, 1996). Before the class, I handed my first autobiographical writing to him. I was anxious about how he would react. His first reaction was, "It's terrific, Shashi!", and he asked me, "Can I use your poem in today's discussion in the class?" I was overwhelmed by this positive response. During the class, he projected my poem on a PowerPoint slide and asked me to recite it to the class. I was not sure how the other students felt about my poem, but it was a good experience to receive a positive response from my mentors. This was the second milestone in My Autoethnography, which helped to create my self-identity through poetic agency, allowing me to express the "passion and spirit I had long suppressed" (Spry, 2001, p. 708).

At that time, Nepal's political history was unfolding with friction between the political parties and King Gyanendra Bikram Shah after he had assumed power for the second time by dismissing the democratic government. The seven-party alliance and the underground Communist Party of Nepal Maoist jointly staged protests and strikes in the country in April 2006. The government imposed a curfew in cities throughout Nepal. KUSOED classes were cancelled. Outside my residence there was a strict curfew. I could go out only for an hour in the evening to buy daily essentials. I continued writing my dissertation proposal. Frequently I could hear the sound of political slogans in favour of democracy and against the monarch. There were also loud sounds of police firing tear gas shells. The protests continued for days amid the curfew and clashes between government forces and agitating parties. This was the incubation of Federal Democratic Nepal. At the same time, this was an evolution of my being as a neophyte researcher.

Designing a legitimate research question and associated research method was a tremendous challenge for me. Reading chapters from Denzin and Lincoln (2005) helped me to understand the tacit nature of qualitative research and the difficulty in making the tacit explicit. Reading and reflecting on "writing as researching" (Luitel, 2003) motivated me to think, "Can my autobiographical vignettes be research texts?" I thought that if other researchers can talk to me or interview me and use the texts as data, why should I not use my texts as data for interpretation, connecting and theorizing these self-experiential evocative narratives. I was interested in unpacking my academic journey as a theatrical, staged, poetic and rhythmic account of the experienced other. Making myself as the other in my own writing (without objectifying) and connecting it to social and cultural contexts, I outlined the purpose of the study as exploring critical moments of my life and giving meaning to them. I expressed this as a research question: "What are the socio-cultural contexts of teaching and learning mathematics in Nepal and how do they influence pedagogical practices?".

I continued writing the research proposal, confining myself at home for a few days. When I was writing, especially in a poetic sense, I felt a rhythm within me. When I listened to music while writing I felt more focused with intense thinking within the musical rhythm. I completed a draft of the research proposal and wanted to discuss it with my mentors, but they were in Dhulikhel witnessing the pathetic violation of human rights and suppression of people's aspirations for democracy by the then government of Nepal (Luitel & Taylor, 2007). I sent the proposal to the university's Research Committee. The positive response to the proposal encouraged me to continue writing evocative narratives, poems and dialogues, making theoretical links to my lived mathematical experiences. This was the third milestone in My Autoethnography.

Eventually, the political situation in Nepal turned to peace with democracy when the King reinstated the parliament. Educational institutions resumed their normal routines, and I continued teaching at KUSOED and writing my dissertation. I crafted chapters by considering myself as an insider witness of the sociocultural contexts in which I had been performing in classrooms as a learner, a teacher, and a teacher-as-learner. While doing this, it was important to consider whether the evocative narratives truly represented these contexts. It was also important to assess whether my autobiographical semi-fictive writing was a legitimate way to make a connection between theory and professional practice (Denzin & Lincoln, 2005). I tried to portray my lived experience through the narratives in a way that would resonate with my reader's experience and elicit their "pedagogical thoughtfulness" (van Manen, 1990).

In 2006, I defended my MPhil dissertation. This was the fourth milestone which helped to help open the door to autoethnography as a tool for researching and teaching for transformative education in Nepal (Belbase, Luitel, & Taylor, 2008). Since then, many Nepali scholars have used autoethnographic methods to complete master's dissertations (e.g., Shrestha, 2011) and doctoral theses (e.g., Qutoshi, 2016).

Next, I illustrate a state of meta-consciousness that I experienced during the writing of My Autoethnography, a state that connected my adulthood to my childhood joyful play and that resonated with my daughter's childhood play in the moment of writing. I interpreted this relational parallel as a reverberation of "tandav", Fritjof Capra's (1989) eternal dance.

RELATIONAL PARALLELS

Dollies, toy-cars, animal models, a mini-piano, some rubber balls, and Lego blocks are around her. Anjila (in her third year) seems very busy assembling different models from the blocks. She makes a tall building; dismantles it and makes a boat out of it and puts two babies, Pintoo and Mintoo, on it and sails on a virtual river (she imagines a river on the floor carpet). She hums gentle songs. Frequently my eyes go to her genuine, innocent and perfectly natural play as I am reading a book by Fritjof Capra (1989), The Tao of Physics: An Exploration of the Parallels Between Modern Physics and Eastern Mysticism.

> The particle interactions give rise to the stable structures which build up the material world, which again do not remain static, but oscillate in rhythmic movements. The whole universe is thus engaged in endless motion and activity; in a continual cosmic dance of energy. (p. 270)

Anjila throws a Lego block as it does not fit properly with others and she softly sobs. She takes a piece away and takes another and tries to construct something meaningful that pleases her. She chooses colors, shapes or forms that fit together (Fig 7.1). She constructs patterned objects with a sense of meaningful play. She continues by trial and error fitting and unfitting the pieces, examining which model resonates with an animal or a house or car or an object of her choice. She sobs again when something goes wrong.

Figure 7.1. Anjila's play with lego models

I stop reading the book and pick her up in my arms. I tell her to play with toys and dollies. She starts moving a car on the floor with a dolly in one hand. I turn to the next page of the book that describes the eternality of creation and destruction, in a rhythmic cycle.

> This dance involves an enormous variety of patterns but, surprisingly, they fall into a few distinct categories. The study of the subatomic particles and their interactions thus reveals a great deal of order…The dance of Shiva symbolizes not only the cosmic cycles of creation and destruction, but also the daily rhythm of birth and death which is seen in Hindu mysticism as the basis of all existence. At the same time, Shiva reminds us that the manifold forms in the world are Maya – not fundamental, but illusory and ever changing – as he keeps creating and dissolving them in the ceaseless flow of his dance. (p. 271)

I feel the dance within me, in my childhood, and in Anjila's play. I see myself in two different times – scientific time and meta-time – and in two different spaces – scientific space and meta-space – in the dance. I read about manifold forms of the tandav, the eternal dance. I hear the rhythm of an eternal echo. It is reverberating, timelessly and from nowhere. Anjila is a little distance from me and I hear her childish hum as she produces the sounds of her car. She is pushing a red car up the corridor ("Hui...n, hui...n..."). Again, I focus on reading Capra (1989) which is very engaging.

While Anjila is playing with Lego blocks, I remember a day of my childhood. I am in my childhood within the present moment of adulthood. The former, a meta-time that never returns, has a profound influence on "who I was, who I am, and who I will be". The tacit childhood play time in my memory keeps me conscious of the transient moment, a deep sense of connection with and knowledge of the self-other relation. I experience two kinds of time – my current time (of adulthood) and the meta-time of my childhood. My childhood time is concurrent with Anjila's time. I feel the same way as a child. I am a child for a moment. I am moving a truck made of clay. I hum when it is climbing up and jolting ("Dhueen..........Dhueen"). The truck overcomes the jolting. It turns left and right along the spiral road. I am pulling it with a cotton thread. The truck reaches the rocky mountain. I load it with pebbles. Then, I pull it with a rope to a destination. When I go to my childhood memory, I loosen my grip and the book (that I am reading) falls to the right, but it is still in my grasp. Again, memory returns in a flashback. Suddenly, a shadow appears from behind me. My truck is brutally squashed under a giant foot and crushed to pieces. Then it flies away as if it is a football with wheels and other pieces separated. I lie down on the ground, sobbing in mourning at the demise of my truck, my creation, my science and my mathematics. I lose my most favourite truck.

I am with tears in my eyes when Anjila comes to me with a wheel off her car. I wipe her tears (hiding mine) with a handkerchief and mend the car. She smiles at me and goes back to play. My book is lying to the right of me with page 270 facing up, "The Parallels".

It occurs to me that the temporal and spatial connection through childish play is a parallel of meta-time and meta-space. It is a parallel of meta-time that can only be felt through conscious experience, but cannot be measured in an absolute sense. The parallel of meta-space is a space within the sphere of experience we have the moment we rejoice in the play, an idiosyncratic space. It is a space which brings us together at the same place with a similar experience of the objects around us (e.g., play items) at the same time, in a rhythm of joy and anguish, destruction and creation.

Is there a coincidence between Anjila's play with her toy car, my play with a clay-made truck and the eternal tandav? I try to link the mathematical notion in a very subtle way with the Anjila's toy car and my clay-made truck. The childhood play with favourite objects that involves creation and destruction of models and remodeling them has a great significance in early childhood mathematics. Perhaps, these experiences from early childhood play can be linked with the cosmic cycle of creation and destruction. I interpret this relationship as a parallel (i.e., relational parallel) of mathematical sensibility by virtue of Anjila's play relative to my early experiences.

The sense of tandav may symbolize the interface between existence and non-existence, that is, I did not exist before I was born, I exist now and so I am writing, and I will not exist after I die. Hence, our lives have a thin line between existence and nonexistence, in a rhythm within the cycle of eternal tandav. My play does not exist in the moment when Anjila is playing, but in the conscious meta-time and meta-space it brings me to Anjila's time and space, despite our differences. In the rhythm of tandav, existence and non-existence blur and the interface dissolves. My interpretation of tandav is neither spiritual nor religious nor cultural, but is meta-conscious thinking, and constitutes being and non-being within the rhythmic convolution of time and space. I used the metaphor of tandav to observe and interpret the parallel childhood experiences that witnessed the cycle of creation and destruction of things (of play items) leading to a salvation of *mana* or *chitta* (mind) with manifestation of periodic pain and pleasure.

A Reflection

To me, learning, teaching, and constructing mathematics should, perhaps, be considerate of the tacit nature of the assumptions we make, the relations we develop, and should contemplate further those relations to the abstraction of meaning at a higher dimension. I consider that there is the possibility of linking abstract meaning of learning as a process of constructing the "embodied self" (Cassam, 2011). The embodied self culminates in self-awareness or self-consciousness of what we do or how we operate in an event or play. The operational functions of mathematics in children's play may provide a rich context to relate different entities in a model to explain the world (a relational world) under certain naïve assumptions (axioms) and reasoning based on those assumptions even from childhood. It can be a rich area of research in mathematics and mathematics education.

I interpret the notion of relational parallels in a metaphysical sense in the form of meta-time and meta-space. I conceive the flow of energy within us and outside (in the external world) in the form of Shiva's tandav (in a symbolic form) within the blurred interface of existence and non-existence. Here, I see a thin line between what exists and what does not exist, at least metaphysically. This thinking helped me to interpret the spatio-temporal and self-other relation (e.g., Anjila's childhood play with mine, phenomenologically and metaphysically). The narrative of relational parallels, though it was semi-fictive and imaginative, served as a context to make sense of actions in terms of ways we perform them, build our relations in the world, and reason rationally for transformative effect.

Next, I critically analyse the narratives embedded in My Autoethnography through three distinct conceptual lenses—methodological, relational and ethical. These lenses are based on perspectives and paradigms of doing research in the context of teaching and learning mathematics, but they may also relate to other disciplines. These lenses represent current standpoints about my experience of conducting an autoethnography.

THREE LENSES FOR CRITICAL REFLECTION

Our thoughts, perceptions and perspectives may change over time. Our personal ontology and epistemology may shift as our identity changes with new experiences, knowledge and professional practice (Burke, 2006). As a result, our interpretation of events, actions and phenomena may also change. From the perspective of "radical constructivism", these changes may occur with assimilation and accommodation of the new experiential schemes and adaptation to more sophisticated schemes by reorganizing the experiential world through enhanced participation, interaction and dialogical relations with others (von Glasersfeld, 1995).

Hence, my re-interpretation of My Autoethnography (undertaken over a decade later) is both a cognitive and adaptive function (Belbase, 2015). It is a cognitive function in the sense that it is not a conception that occurred at one point in time, but was a process of assimilating and accommodating the ideas of autoethnography from mentors and literature. While doing this, I had to be self-adaptive to the knowledge of qualitative research, in general, and autoethnography, in particular.

My critical stance on My Autoethnography is no way to disgrace it but to strengthen the approach by raising awareness of possible issues related to method, process and rationality that may otherwise hinder or deteriorate its transformative potential.

Methodological Lens

I observe three elements in the methodological lens of My Autoethnography: What to do? How to do it? Why do it? In undertaking the inquiry, I constructed narratives of my experience of informal mathematics as grounds for formal mathematics. The narratives recollected memories of my childhood. This process connected me to a remote village on a hillside where I grew up, played and enjoyed the moments of my childhood. The narratives contextualized the moment of the memory in a musical flow that invigorated the poetic spring within me. This process transformed me from a prosaic/linear thinker into a poetic self-reflexive narrator. A "storied self" merged into a poetic self in the poem, My Early Mathematics: Natural Mathematics. The narratives of the Relational Parallels depict a sense of connection between my childhood and my daughter's world of play.

Relational Lens

I anticipate four aspects in the relational lens of My Autoethnography: Who are involved? What is the relationship? Why relationship matters? How to balance the relationship? Autoethnography portrays "interrelationships between autobiographies, lived educational experiences, and wider social and cultural concerns" (Pillay et al., 2016, p. 1). The researcher may explore a myriad of relational aspects – compatible or incompatible, dynamic or static, receptive or unreceptive, perceptive or unperceptive, collaborative or noncollaborative – to weave stories across three dimensions – time, place and culture — of one's lifeworld (Pillay, Naicker, & Pithouse-Morgan, 2016). Hence, autoethnography is all about the "relational consciousness" of self and other in relation to events, objects and actions to make sense of lived experiences (Timm, 2016).

My Autoethnography depicts the relation of being a child, a student at different levels, and a teacher within the frame of time as a dimension of change because it was possible to observe similar/different experiences from a different time-frame (Mendez, 2013). The episodic expressions of my childhood experience of playing with natural things compared to my daughter's play with artificial artifacts demonstrates a temporal aspect of two kinds of life within the same stage: one in the remote past and the other in the relative present.

While doing this, I tried to balance the artistic expressions of lived experience with the aesthetic aspect of the lifeworld as part of Maya (illusion) or beyond it, a delusion (Barleet, 2013). Maya within the experience of meta-time and meta-space of childhood play was an experience of meta-consciousness, some may call it divinity or eternity or even virtual reality in making sense of these relations (Thompson, 2003). I used the metaphor of Maya to explain my life-world experiences as nothing more than illusion or virtual reality that we create in mana or chitta (mind) for which there is no real ontological existence since one's pain could be another's pleasure, and vice-versa, due to differences in interpretation of such experiences.

Ethical Lens

I focus on three key factors in the ethical lens: What is the power relation? How to balance power? How to protect self and other identity? One of the most important aspects of autoethnography that I considered was "power" (Richards, 2016). In My Autoethnography, I question "the politics and poetics of representation" (Reed-Danahay, 1997, p. 3). Questions included issues of identity and selfhood, voice and authenticity, cultural displacement, power and privilege, equity and justice, and liberation (Reed-Danahay, 1997).

I agree that an autoethnographer possesses dual identity or selfhood in the research – as the subject who studies and as the object whom he or she studies. The subject-object boundary blurs in the process of doing autoethnography. I also possessed other identities depending on my gender, professional life, family relations, social and political power and privilege. Hence, I embodied "multiple and shifting identities" (Reed-Danahay, 1997, p. 3).

Other issues in My Autoethnography are "voice" and "authenticity" which are related to the construction of myself in relation to the other (Benolt, 2015).

Whose voice did my autoethnography represent? How did it represent the voice of the author (me)? How did it represent the voice of the other? These questions, to me, are related to the privilege of voice inscribed in the ethnographer's reflexive accounts of experience. These reflexive accounts present an insider perspective which I consider to be more authentic than that of an outsider (Reed-Danahay, 1997).

In writing this chapter, my re-interpretation of the narratives of My Autoethnography, from the perspective of methodological, relational and ethical lenses, have helped me to consider the merits and caveats of My Autoethnography. The value of doing autoethnography lies in the issues that it focuses on, the truthfulness of the narrative voices, and the ability to touch the experience of the other (e.g., the reader). The caveats may arise from issues such as a poor fit between the stories and context and theory, the identity (with power) and ownership of the researcher over the stories, and the construction of a co-evolving space for the author-researcher as a story teller and the reader as the contributor to the meaning of the stories in his/her life. In this sense, the question of whose stories (or even songs) does the researcher unveil and how these stories or poetic expressions connect lives, emotions and experiences may add to ethical, relational and methodological dimensions of an autoethnography.

MERITS AND CAVEATS

Every research method, including autoethnography, comes with some advantages and limitations. However, most research papers on autoethnography rarely discuss limitations of the method itself. Here, I reflect on some of the merits and caveats of my practice of this approach based on the three lenses discussed above.

Merits of My Autoethnography

In my experience, the most significant merits of performing My Autoethnography were access to a private world, a sense of self-emancipation, and conversation and connection.

Access to a private world. While performing My Autoethnography I found many advantages of this method. First, it provided access to my private world (Mendez, 2013) through self-reflective and reflexive thinking and writing about learning and teaching mathematics and other disciplines. It helped me to gaze into my inner world. It helped me to break the boundary between my private world and the public world, to some extent, while connecting my personal stories to social and cultural contexts to make sense of my experiences.

Second, it provided rich data about issues of learning and teaching mathematics from my childhood to university level. I crafted reflective and reflexive vignettes, poems and journals, making sense of my experiences during different stages of my life as a learner and teacher. I touched upon the past by combining recollection, creative imagination, and artistic manipulation of experiences through semi-fictive writing.

Autoethnography was an ideal process for both gazing inward and connecting to the outward, and vice-versa. It provided me with rich experiential data because I called upon my own learning and teaching experiences and wrote narratives to portray the specific phenomena under study (Mendez, 2013). My stories could possibly contribute to others' lives by helping them to reflect on their experiences and pedagogical practices, generate pedagogical thoughtfulness, and empathise with shared meanings and values (Hayler, 2011). I found it helpful to present my voice in first-person accounts and confess my fragilities. The process liberated me from my own chains of self-limiting thought (Richards, 2008).

A sense of self-emancipation. One of the most significant advantages of doing My Autoethnography was my development of a sense of emancipation. The self-reflective and reflexive narratives, poems, and arts-based writing helped me to understand more deeply my role as a learner and a teacher at different stages of my life. It transformed my agency from a silent receiver and preacher of knowledge to an integral reflexive thinker (Ellis, 2004). The autoethnographic vignettes of different forms helped me make sense of personal experiences in the social, political, and cultural contexts of Nepal (Belbase, Luitel, & Taylor, 2008). My autoethnographic text was a mental recursion of time beyond scientific (Newtonian and Einsteinian) time through archives full of the emotions of past experiences, evaluations of contemporary teaching and learning practices, envisioning new courses of thinking and acting to transform my personal, professional and social actions (Roth, 2005). My autoethnographic writing was also a part of critical reflection on my practices as a teacher or teacher educator leading to professional development in the long run.

Embracing positivity. Autoethnography placed me in conversations – conversation with self and others, conversation between my practice and theory, and conversation between teaching and learning – informing each other and contributing to each other. The conversations helped me to embrace uncertainty, cope with unfavourable situations, take risks and learn from mistakes I had made, and pave a better way to move ahead. Autoethnography is a way to embrace positivity among different research paradigms and find a possible way to integrate multiple viewpoints, beliefs, and practices (Taylor, Taylor, & Luitel, 2012). I observed a change in my perceptions, beliefs, values and actions toward a more constructivist teaching approach, although I might not reach the level of integral aspects of transformative educational practice. It provided me with an opportunity to foster a commitment for advanced thinking, reasoning, writing and acting for change, although it might not be visible in many instances. Therefore, writing and performing My Autoethnography was a part of developing an understanding of different paradigms and perspectives in qualitative research, and qualitatively enhancing my personal experiences of learning and teaching mathematics in relation to the paradigms.

A process of transformation. Autoethnography is a way of living and being with blurred dual identities – one as a researcher and the other as a researched – both in the same time and space. When I wrote my stories, they were partly stories within culture, and hence they provided me with an insider view. For me, it was a radical shift in research practice to observe myself as a performer, observer and participant on the social stage and to recreate and transcend my identity as a traditional teacher towards a constructivist practitioner. Hence, autoethnography positioned me on a stage to find my professional roles, relations and identity in relation to others (Ellis & Bochner, 2014). I wrote my experiential stories in the socio-cultural and political environment of Nepal which helped me to gaze inward and outward and to position myself in the changed context.

Caveats of My Autoethnography

With all the benefits and strengths discussed above, My Autoethnography was not beyond limitations in terms of methods, processes and outcomes.

Self-contradiction. The focus of My Autoethnography was to present my stories as a foreground for highlighting major issues and practices of learning and teaching mathematics. It was a partial archive of my professional and personal self in context (Roth, 2005). However, the archive of my method of teaching as preaching was not connected to the learning of mathematics. Collaborative group work as a method of learning mathematics was not connected to classroom practice in a general sense. My narrative vignettes did not bring these methods together to form an integrated approach to teaching and learning mathematics. On reflection, I was too critical of the direct instruction method of teaching and too positive of self-organized collaborative learning groups. I did not find a link between these two approaches. I lost the sense of the foreground of my experience for portraying a theory-practice connection, and situated the broader social, cultural and political context in the background (Denshire, 2013). The loose connection between theory and practice contradicted my awareness of being both the researcher and the researched at the same time.

Complexity of meta-consciousness. Autoethnography allows fictive, imaginative, and reflective expressions in writing as an art form. With this in mind, I wrote reflexive narratives of my experiences in a rather mystical way such that my readers might easily get lost in the overall flow of the story. For example, I am not sure whether my readers can make sense of the Relational Parallels between a child's play and my reminiscence about Capra's tandav (a form of eternal dance). The emotional expression of losing a toy in childhood and its connection to tandav might seem too mystical for my readers; mystical in the sense of linking a material phenomenon of childhood play to the miracle of eternity in the dance.

Forceful connection. While writing autobiographical narratives and making connection to literature-based theories there is a possibility of making a forceful connection. On reflection, I realise that I synthesized my life stories in such a way that they fitted an extant theory or I sought a theory to make it fit the story. Both actions could have diverted me away from the main issues that I wanted to emphasize in giving meaning to my real-life experiences. The connection between the experience of my recursive mind and a related theory rejuvenated the imaginative world. Such an imaginative connection might not have a meaningful relation to learning and teaching mathematics and related activities in the classroom, although it might have a spiritual element (Long, 2008).

Self-indulgence. I wrote personal stories based on my lived experiences as student in other teachers' classrooms. Although these stories reveal thoughtful experiences of critical moments that might have some value in relation to learning mathematics, they are not explicit in terms of the concepts, procedures and processes of doing mathematics within and outside of the classroom. The stories are mostly descriptive expressions of events. An autoethnographer should be able to move beyond phenomenal description of events to present interpretive and critical accounts of activities, concepts, processes and outcomes (Denshire, 2013). I now feel that many of the stories presented in My Autoethnography reveal my self-indulgence in telling personal stories without considering their educational significance (Coffey, 1999).

Vulnerability with identity. My Autoethnography is a portrayal of my personal stories in relation to self and others. The stories are connected to social, cultural and political contexts, events and actions, to some extent, because they were not created (or experienced) on purpose but co-evolved with contexts. While writing my narrative vignettes I disclosed sensitive issues (related to identity and values) in my relationships with students, teachers and family members. In the flow of writing autobiographical vignettes peak emotions can be attached to recollected experiences. However, these emotions might not be permanent beliefs, but are momentary and contextual; a particular emotional experience at one time might not have the same meaning or relevance at a later time. I did not feel comfortable revealing publicly sensitive issues of identity and personality relating to myself and others. I feel vulnerable about potentially being caught up in relational disputes due to self-disclosure of issues that might be misinterpreted by my readers (Allen-Collinson, 2012) and that may have implications for ethical issues of privacy.

Ethics of privacy. When I told my stories, I told stories of people who are/were connected closely to my life as a friend, relative, teacher, student and in other ways. Therefore, these are not just my private stories but are stories of the "ethnographic other" (Roth, 2010). When I recounted my stories in public through writing they were no longer private. That means the stories that I wrote for others to read were out there in public making my privacy a public entity, with all that could come with it. For example, I wrote a story about a teacher and his teaching of mathematics. Anyone who knows the school, the teachers, and the context might discover the identity of the teacher. Then, my story would no longer be my private story. It is a story about the teacher, a story about the school, and the story of all who are connected. This can be a serious ethical issue of disclosing the other through personal stories (Allen-Collinson, 2012), especially when it refers to one's personality and identity. I also portrayed relational experiences of observing my daughter in her play and interpreted it in relation to my childhood experience and then related to a theory of cognition and meta-cognition. Using a family member as visible or invisible subject of study without obtaining informed consent (even as a parent) is an ethical issue for autoethnographers (Roth, 2010). Hence, some confessional stories that I wrote about myself might eventually return and have a negative effect on the other (Derrida, 1998).

Crisis of dual-identity. My claim that doing autoethnography involved observing myself as a performer and performing on stage as an observer-participant might seem counter intuitive to my readers. It may raise the question: "How can 'I' be an observer and an observed at the same time?" It seems unlikely that I can be two persons at the same time in the idiosyncracy of personal experience as the autoethnographer and the autoethnographed. When I am observing I am not observed and when I am observed I am not observing. I cannot see two persons within me in an idiosyncratic flow of experience. I must shift my position – one time being the observer and the other time being the observed. Therefore, to me, the conceptually blurred boundary did not unblur the existential crisis of the dual identity of observer and observed. This issue has not been made explicit in the literature on autoethnography, except for suggesting taking turns while staging the roles of researcher (observer) and researched (observed). Thus, first we go through certain situations with unusual experiences and then we observe those experiences as a researcher. This turn taking could ease the tension, to some extent, however the approach pushes the observed into the past and holds the observer in the present outside of meta-time and meta-space, which goes against the intent of autoethnography, which is to bring both into the same time and space (Bochner, 2016).

These limitations, however, should not be considered as weaknesses of the method of autoethnography, but as subtleties to embrace in performing autoethnography with power and possibility.

FINAL REFLECTION

Autoethnography is an inner voice, a human truth, and untold stories told to inform self and other of layered meanings. It is a way to interpret subtle experiences in a powerful way to contribute to humanity, compassion and co-existence. To me, it is a way to be responsible, ethical and considerate in building self-other relationships by portraying positive images of who we are and what we do.

In writing this chapter, I found some caveats of My Autoethnography associated with the extent of focus in writing the narratives, mystical expressions, semi-fictive and imaginative connections between events of different times, indulgence in personal stories forced to connect with extant theories, self-disclosure of sensitive issues, the crisis of blurred identity as an observer and observed, and ethical issues related to narrative expressions about others.

Despite these caveats, My Autoethnography helped me to see not only the past and present in a more fully conscious way, but also opened my eyes to envisioning the future in terms of learning and teaching mathematics and other disciplines. For me, the writing of narratives in My Autoethnography had merit in terms of gaining access to my personal private world, generating thick and rich experiential data, creating a variety of textual expressions, engaging in critical self-assessment of my professional work, and an elevated sense of emancipation.

In writing this chapter revisiting the method and process of autoethnography felt like a call to chisel the "praxeological wood" of wisdom to unveil the beauty of writing as revealing hidden "secrets" (Bochner, 2016). For me, to perform autoethnography is to embrace critical reflexivity within the complexity of living through different experiences and contemplating those experiences in meta-time and meta-space. Now, I shall conclude this chapter with a poetic revelation of My Autoethnography.

> For some, it is evocative
> Sometimes, hyper subjective
> For others, a legitimate strategy
> Transcending intersubjectivity.
> Vision of canonical action
> Inner 'self', a manifestation
> Amid frown and reaction
> In and out border, a ramification.
> Observed-observer, a tension
> Mental time and recursion
> In the distant 'self' and 'other'
> Kaleidoscopic collage of color.
> Searching the meaning of 'self'
> In the stories that others tell
> Nuances and rhythms of living
> A revelation and a healing.

REFERENCES

Allen-Collinson, J. (2012). Autoethnography: Situating personal sporting narratives in socio-cultural contexts. In K. Young & M. Atkinson (Eds.), *Qualitative research on sport and physical culture* (pp. 191–212). Bingley: Emerald Group Publishing Limited.

Barleet, B. L. (2013). Artful and embodied methods, modes of inquiry, and forms of representation. In S. H. Jones, T. E. Adams, & C. Ellis (Eds.), *Handbook of autoethnography* (pp. 443–464). London: Routledge.

Belbase, S. (2006). *My journey of learning and teaching mathematics from traditionalism to constructivism: A portrayal of pedagogical metamorphosis* (M. Phil. dissertation). Kathmandu University, Dhulikhel, Nepal.

Belbase, S. (2015). *Preservice mathematics teachers' beliefs about teaching geometric transformations using geometer's sketchpad* (Doctoral dissertation). University of Wyoming, Laramie, WY.

Belbase, S., Luitel, B. C., & Taylor, P. C. (2008). Autoethnography: A method of research and teaching for transformative education. *Journal of Education and Research, 1*(1), 86–95.

Benolt, B. A. (2015). *Understanding the teacher self: Learning through critical autoethnography* (Doctoral thesis). McGill University, Montreal, Canada.

Bochner, A. P. (2016, April 8). *The rise of autoethnography: Stretching boundaries, fashioning identities, healing wounds.* Paper presented at the GCA Keynote presentation, University of South Florida, Tampa, FL. Retrieved from https://www.youtube.com/watch?v=X3EJfPN9sIg

Burke, P. J. (2006). Identity change. *Social Psychology Quarterly, 69*(1), 81–96.

Capra, F. (1989). *The tao of physics: An exploration of the parallels between modern physics and eastern mysticism.* Boulder, CO: Shambhala Publications.

Cassam, Q. (2011). The embodied self. In S. Gallagher (Ed.), *Oxford handbook of the self* (pp. 139–157). Oxford: Oxford University Press.

Castor, L. (2015). "No shadows under us": Fictional freedom and real violations in Louise Erdrich's shadow tag. In K. W. Shands, G. G. Mikrut, D. R. Pattanaik, & K. Ferreira-Meyers (Eds.), *Writing the self: Essays on autobiography* (pp. 239–256). Sweden: Elanders.

Coffey, P. (1999). *The ethnographic self.* London: Sage Publications.

Denshire, S. (2013). Autoethnography. *Sociopedia.isa.* doi:10.1177/205684601351

Denzin, N. K., & Lincoln, Y. S. (Eds.). (2005). Discipline and practice of qualitative research. In *Sage handbook of qualitative research* (3rd ed., pp. 1–32). Thousand Oaks, CA: Sage Publications.

Derrida, J. (1998). *Monolingualism of the other; or, the prosthesis of origin.* Stanford, CA: Stanford University Press.

Ellis, C. (2004). *The ethnographic I: A methodological novel about autoethnography.* Walnut Creek, CA: Altamira.

Ellis, C., & Bochner, A. P. (2014, April 28). *Autoethnography in qualitative inquiry.* Retrieved from https://www.youtube.com/watch?v=FKZ-wuJ_vnQ

Hayler, M. (2011). *Autoethnography, self-narrative and teacher education: Studies in professional life and work* (Vol. 5). Rotterdam, The Netherlands: Sense Publishers.

Hitchcock, G., & Hughes, D. (1995). *Research and the teacher* (2nd ed.). London: Routledge.

Jones, S. H., Adams, T., & Ellis, C. (Eds.). (2013). *Handbook of autoethnography.* Walnut Creek, CA: Left Coast Press.

Long, L. (2008). Narrative autoethnography and the promotion of spiritual well-being in teacher research and practice. *Pastoral Care in Education: An International Journal of Personal, Social and Emotional Development, 26*(3), 187–196.

Luitel, B. C. (2003). *Narrative explorations of Nepali mathematics curriculum landscapes: An epic journey* (Master's dissertation). Curtin University of Technology, Perth, Western Australia.

Luitel, B. C., & Taylor, P. C. (2007). The shanai, the pseudosphere and other imaginings: Envisioning culturally contextualized mathematics education. *Cultural Studies of Science Education, 2*(3), 621–655.

Mendez, M. (2013). Autoethnography as a research method: Advantages, limitations and criticisms. *Colombia Applied Linguistic Journal, 15*(2), 279–287.

Nicotera, A. M. (1999). The woman academic as subject/object/self: Dismantling the illusion of duality. *Communication Theory, 9*(4), 430–464.

Pavlenko, A. (2002). Narrative study: Whose story is it anyway? *TESOL Quarterly, 36*, 213–218.

Pillay, D., Naicker, I., & Pithouse-Morgan, K. (Eds.). (2016). *Academic autoethnographies: Inside teaching in higher education.* Rotterdam, The Netherlands: Sense Publishers.

Pithouse-Morgan, K., & Samaras, A. P. (Eds.). (2015). *Polyvocal professional learning through self-study.* Rotterdam, The Netherlands: Sense Publishers.

Pompper, D. (2010). Reseacher-researched differences: Adapting an autoethnographic approach for addressing the racial matching issue. *Journal of Research Practice, 6*(1), Article M6.

Quicke, J. (2008). *Inclusion and psychological intervention in schools: A critical autoethnography.* Dordrecht: Springer Publications.

Qutoshi, S. B. (2016). *Creating living-educational-theory: A journey towards transformative teacher education in Pakistan* (Doctoral thesis). Kathmandu University, Dhulikhel, Nepal.

Reed-Danahay, D. E. (1997). Introduction. In D. E. Reed-Danahay (Ed.), *Auto/ethnography: Rewriting the self and the social* (pp. 1–17). Oxford: Berg.

Reese, R., Yan, C., Jack, F., & Hayne, H. (2010). Emerging identities: Narrative and self from early childhood to early adolescence. In K. C. McLean & M. Pasupathi (Eds.), *Narrative development in adolescence* (pp. 23–43). New York, NY: Springer. doi:10.1007/978-0-387-89825-4_2

Richards, R. (2008). Writing the othered self: Autoethnography and the problem of objectification in writing about illness and disability. *Qualitative Health Research, 1*, 1717–1728.

Richards, R. (2016). Subject to interpretation: Autoethnography and the ethics of writing about the embodied self. In D. Pillay, I. Naicker, & K. Pithouse-Morgan (Eds.), *Academic autoethnographies: Inside teaching in higher education* (pp. 163–174). Rotterdam, The Netherlands: Sense Publishers.

Roth, W.-M. (2005). Auto/biography and auto/ethnography: Finding the generalized other in the self. In W.-M. Roth (Ed.), *Auto/biography and auto/ethnography: Praxis of research method* (pp. 3–19). Rotterdam, The Netherlands: Sense Publishers.

Roth, W.-M. (2010). Auto/ethnography and the question of ethics. *FORUM: Qualitative Social Research, 10*(1), Article 38.

Shrestha, I. M. (2011). *My journey of learning and teaching: A trans/formation from culturally decontextualized to contextualized mathematics education* (Master's dissertation). Kathmandu University, Dhulikhel, Nepal.

Spry, T. (2001). Performing autoethnography: An embodied methodological praxis. *Qualitative Inquiry, 7*(6), 706–732.

Taylor, P. C. (1996). Mythmaking and mythbreaking in the mathematics classroom. *Educational Studies in Mathematics, 31*(1, 2), 151–173.

Taylor, P. C., Taylor, E., & Luitel, B. C. (2012). Multi-paradigmatic transformative research as/for teacher education: An integral perspective. In B. J. Fraser, K. Tobin, & C. J. McRobbie (Eds.), *Second international handbook of science education* (pp. 373–387). Dordrecht: Springer Publications.

Thompson, R. L. (2003). *Maya: The world as virtual reality.* Alachua, FL: Govardhan Hill Publishing.

Timm, D. N. (2016). From exclusion through inclusion to being in my element. In D. Pillay, I. Naicker, & K. Pithouse-Morgan (Eds.), *Academic autoethnographies: Inside teaching in higher education* (pp. 95–116). Rotterdam, The Netherlands: Sense Publishers.

Van Manen, M. (1990). *Researching lived experience: Human science for an action sensitive pedagogy.* Albany, NY: State University of New York.

Von Glasersfeld, E. (1995). *Radical constructivism: A way of knowing and learning.* New York, NY: RoutledgeFalmer.

Wall, S. (2008). Easier said than done: Writing an autoethnography. *International Journal of Qualitative Methods, 7*(1), 38–53.

ABOUT THE AUTHOR

Shashidhar Belbase was born in the mid-western region of Nepal. He earned his PhD from the University of Wyoming, Laramie, WY in USA. He is currently teaching at University College, Zayed University in Dubai, UAE as a regular faculty and School of Education, Kathmandu University, Nepal as a visiting faculty. His research interests range from environmental issues to mathematics education.

PART 3

TRANSFORMING CULTURALLY SITUATED SELVES

ALBERTO FELISBERTO CUPANE

8. EXCAVATING MY CULTURAL IDENTITY

Promoting Local Culture and Stability in a Post/Colonial Era

I was born in Gaza, in the rural north of Mozambique, and grew up in Maputo, the capital city, where I completed my schooling and undergraduate education. This trajectory enabled me to speak Changana (my mother tongue), Ronga (the main language spoken in Maputo) and Portuguese (the official language of Mozambique). I have been teaching physical science in Mozambique since 1983 in technical agriculture high schools, public and private universities, and secondary schools. I completed postgraduate studies (Masters and PhD) in Australia, which enabled me to speak English and be enlightened about how to promote Mozambican culture in the science classroom. As a teacher, and later a teacher educator, my main concern has been to understand myself and how I can help my people.

Mozambique, like many other post/colonial countries, is facing huge developmental challenges. We gained independence from Portugal in 1992, then faced a civil war for 16 years, changed to a multiparty country, recently discovered mineral resources, gas and petrol, and now have huge investments from several parts of the world, just to name a few national factors that are transforming the country. At the international level, I can list other factors impacting our country, such as climate change, globalization and digital communications. So, how can we manage these massive transformations? What values are we taking into account? How do we collaborate with others in these transformations? Who are we?

A major vector that fosters our values is an education system that was established by the colonial power 500 years ago. Since independence, however, we have been making only cosmetic transformations to this system. Could we do things differently by wishing to educate a citizen who is at peace with himself, with his/her culture, with the culture of other Mozambicans, and foremost who is a world citizen? How can we develop a teacher education system whose main aim is to enable student-teachers to "know the self who teaches" (Palmer, 1998) so that they can help students throughout Mozambique to develop resilient cultural identities.

In this chapter, I argue that the transformation needs to start with Mozambican teacher educators, such as me. Understanding my identity would help me to clarify my view of the curricula that we should have in Mozambique because, in my opinion, we are not only in a free-market period, but there is an overlap with previous times, in a hegemonic way. We are living simultaneously in a traditional, modern and postmodern society. By making clear who I am and which curricula are adequate for our complex situation, my colleagues and students may benefit as they are likely to be facing the same problems of curricula and identity.

WHO AM I?

I was born at the end of the colonial era in Mozambique which was colonized for nearly 500 years by Portugal. During this period, Mozambicans were inculcated with the belief that they were indigenous, Black, inferior human beings with a culture that cannot be understood by the colonizers, leading Mozambicans to live in poverty and obscurity. However, my induction into "World Modern Science" was started by the colonizers in a political environment where it did not make sense to ask "Who am I?" because our official identity was established some centuries ago. World Modern Science is the designation, from my perspective, for what has been called "Modern Science", "Western Science" and "European Science". I believe that World Modern Science results from the contribution of all cultures, nations, women and men from all over the world. My induction into World Modern Science was characterized by seeing science as a foreign language that had nothing to do with my life. I was obliged to master it in order to survive: rote learning characterized by memorization was a major part of my learning experience. This experience did not allow me to ask more important questions: *(a) who are my students? and (b) who are we Mozambicans?*

I engaged with these questions during postgraduate studies in an Australian university. Initially I tried to understand them from my ingrained positivist perspective: I just needed to detach myself and see me as others see me, to describe my students and my people as an outsider using the third-person passive voice. My hope was that by addressing these questions I could also explain why my former student-teachers were not making good use of the "locally available materials technique" in their classrooms, as I had taught them. But it did not work out. I felt wedged, and to progress it was necessary, as I learned later, to take the questions personally. The opportunity to do so arose during my masters and doctoral research in which I drew on multiple epistemologies to conduct arts-based, critical, interpretive auto/ethnographic inquiries (Cupane, 2003, 2008).

However, to answer these questions from my point of view involved going through a process of reviving the pain and difficulties that I had experienced during the earlier time when I had been colonized and acculturated into so-called Western science. My first response was that my people, my students, and I are "indigenous". Then, the disparaging colonial meaning of indigenous came to my mind and I questioned: *Am I really an indigene? Does a Mozambican indigene know how to read and write? How can I be an indigene if I am in Australia?* Then I realised that these questions were expressing my anger at being humiliated by being considered indigenous. For days, I doubted whether I would be able to talk about indigeneity because of the colonial influence attached to bad personal memories. It took me several months to decide that this is the greatest opportunity in my life to deconstruct the meaning of indigenous and help myself, first and foremost, as a Mozambican citizen and science teacher educator.

I started to search for a research question that could address my problem with indigeneity, especially the question I was facing in the field of science education of being considered indigenous. Hence, I continued to question myself: *(a) I have been indigenous for five centuries – how long will I remain indigenous? (b) Does identity in general change? (c) What is identity? (d) Does it make sense to teach other indigenous people while using a colonizer curriculum? (e) Who am I? Do I have one or more identities?*

My first assumption was that by showing how my identities were influenced and, in some way, imposed by various curricula used in Mozambique, I could help science teachers, curriculum planners and schools to reflect on and re-evaluate how to teach science, which science to teach, and how to influence Mozambican students' emerging identities. The second assumption was the necessity to know culturally Mozambicans. The exploration of my identity would serve this purpose because it was, at the same time, the exploration of the identity of my Changana ethnic group and the identities of the different communities in which I have lived.

In Mozambique today we are challenging the accepted notion of identity in order to accommodate diversity and pluralism in education. So, *what is "identity"?* and, in particular, *what is my identity?* and *is it possible to promote cultural identity?* These questions seemed to encompass my dilemma with the indigeneity concept and promised to help me focus on my future praxis as a science teacher educator. They constitute the major questions that I addressed in my inquiry by using George Hegel's transcendent "dialectical thinking"

DIALECTICAL THINKING

Dialectical thinking, as proposed by Hegel, is a construction of entities (things, ideas, theories, beliefs, relationships) that provides less inadequacy or inconsistency. Inadequacy or inconsistency is illustrated by the negation or contradiction that each entity contains (Spencer & Krauze, 1996). The notion of dialectical philosophy is well illustrated by the following examples: (a) light makes sense because of its opposite (darkness); (b) the sense of love is given by the apparent absence of hate; (c) peace and war cannot exist separately. Thinking about the existence of opposites, it is possible to conclude that each of them contains the other.

Dialectical thinking is one philosophy among many others that places emphasis on transformation. It distinguishes itself by stating that transformation takes place in the clash of opposition within the entity, which is easily understood because of the intimacy of opposites. The opposites that exist in each entity cannot be suppressed because they constitute the condition for the very existence of the entity.

To explore my identity, I used the "triadic form" of dialectical thinking, as suggested by Hegel, in which my thesis is "my identity is fixed", my antithesis is "my identity is always changing". My endeavour to resolve this contradiction

Table 8.1. Triadic form of dialectical thinking

Thesis	Antithesis	Synthesis
An entity is built and, on reflection, proves itself unsatisfactory, incomplete, or contradictory.	The affirmation of thesis negation which also, on reflection, proves to be inadequate.	The search for an entity with fewer contradictions.

involved a synthesis that generated a more coherent identity. In general terms, the triadic structure is shown in Table 8.1.

THESIS: MY IDENTITY IS FIXED

The Artificial Environment of Colonialism

Colonial curricula were based on "essentialism" which is an assumed set of fixed and exclusive characteristics that define the establishment of a given category (Ashcroft, Griffiths, & Tiffin, 2000). A category can be, for example, Indigenous people, Africans, Americans, Europeans, Asians, White or Black people, women, men, Muslims or Catholics. The notion of essentialism was established historically by cultural anthropologists in an effort to name and categorize indigeneity. The notion of "essentialist authenticity" views indigeneity as non–existent in modern life. In this view, participants in modern life are false or adulterated; the prolonged interaction between Western and I(i)ndigenous people has destroyed the purity of the Indigenous people (Semali & Kincheloe, 1999). In other words, Mozambicans who existed before the 15th Century are more Mozambican than you or me because Portuguese colonialism appeared in our country at that time and now we are a product of impurification.

Obviously, not every indigenous person has the same knowledge because everyone has different strengths, weaknesses and gifts. Essentialist ethnographers are looking for those who fully represent their culture in order to learn indigenous knowledge from them. However, this is a new racism: "racism based on ideas of cultural difference rather than on claims to biological superiority" (Bilton et al., 2002, p. 178).

Essentialist policy in South Africa during the Apartheid era was responsible for ethnic and racial segregation. The intention was to keep "pure" all races, to avoid contamination among races and ethnic groups. In this way, each ethnic group was reserved a certain territory in which to live, and the medium of instruction and communication was the ethnic language. However, I question whether South Africans were *really* Africans simply because they were obliged to live in ghettos? Is the culture kept intact in the ghetto, which serves as a symbol of oppression?

In Mozambique, in contrast to the events in South Africa, we indigenous were manipulated to acculturate and assimilate the colonizer culture. The chief aim of

Portuguese colonialism was to turn indigenous people into Portuguese. At that time, Mozambique was called "Portugal Ultramar", which translates as "Portugal beyond the Sea". I remember that in my childhood Mozambicans were divided into those who were assimilated and those who were non-assimilated. To be assimilated meant that you had grasped some Portuguese manners and ways of doing things; a certificate (pass) was issued to confirm this assimilation. It was not a peaceful process. In the presence of the colonizer the assimilated were obliged to behave according to the colonizer's rules. For example, it was considered unacceptable to finish the food on your plate, a *faux pas* in Portuguese etiquette. This was necessary even at home, especially in the presence of strangers.

This is the process of living in contradiction: doing what you do not want to do, saying what you do not want to say, and feeling what you do not want to feel. This is assuming the identity the colonizer wants you to have. To what extent has this phenomenon adulterated people? While in Western culture it is polite to accept a compliment with "thankyou", in contemporary Mozambican culture it is not. You must refuse it by saying something negative. For example, if someone says: "You have a beautiful house", you need to answer something like: "Oh yes, but I still have to pay for it". Has the refusal to accept compliments resulted from the dilemma of being Black and White at the same time? How is this dilemma reflected in other aspects of our social life?

Nevertheless, I strongly disagree with the essentialist assumption that the colonizers are the ones who made me lose my African identity. How can I maintain this stance if the colonizers were there and caused many tribulations and changes to occur? Yes, colonizers were there and instigated many changes but they were not the sole authors of these changes. The colonized are also authors of their changed (and changing) culture. I have changed my identity in part because of colonization. Colonizers, in their imperial and racist efforts, helped to create a false identity by using a "universal discourse". This official discourse was characterized by declarations, mimicry, attitudes and clothes that convey identification. Both the colonizer and colonized identities have been imposed and contested through formal and informal education ever since the arrival of colonizers in Mozambique in the 15th century.

The Influence of Colonial Curricula

My identity has formed and evolved within the multiple contexts of being colonized, being independent, some years later being frightened because of civil war, and now being a researcher within my contemporary cultural context and living in a peaceful country. During these four periods, I have been struggling to decide what identifies me and what should guide my life. During these times, I assumed a collective identity because of my social interactions. This collective identity is given and maintained by discourses that induce pride. By contrast, the official discourse during the colonial era determined that my identity was characterised by submission, ignorance, humility and acceptance of fatality.

Colonial authorities used the Catholic Church to support the official discourse, particularly after the fall of the First Republic and through the "Estado Novo" (1926–1974). Although the State was separated from the Church, legal amendments were made to introduce Christian values into the teacher training and learning/teaching process. The main goals of school were to help people read, write and count well, have moral values and love Portugal. If teacher training and the learning/teaching process went beyond this it was seen as too much pedagogy for teachers and unhealthy for children, particularly if they lived in rural areas. One form of discourse in the teacher training and learning/teaching process was the cultivation of humility. According to this discourse, God is the One responsible for the distribution of riches. The poor who love God and are hardworking are happier than other people who are constantly worrying about their money.

Colonialism within education was evident in the dual elementary education system. The first system, "Escolas de Ensino Official", comprised government schools set up for White and Coloured people and assimilated Blacks. The second system, "Escolas de Adaptação", were "adaptation" schools attended by the non-assimilated majority of Black Mozambicans. The two systems had the same curriculum but for non-assimilated Black students school ended at grade 3 while for Whites, Coloureds and assimilated Blacks school continued to grade 4. Children started to attend school at 8 or 9 years old but no-one who was more than 13 years old was allowed to enter grade 4. In other words, by law Black students could progress to the Escolas de Ensino Official but the same law made it impossible to do so.

Contradictions within Essentialism

One of the contradictions within the essentialist view concerns the failure to account for fixed identity changing. Essentialists identify people by their skills, colour of skin and place of birth, among other non-human characteristics. For example, if you are Black and use plant leaves to heal then you are labelled as indigenous, whereas White doctors using pills that come from the same leaves are not labelled as indigenous. The knowledge of healing with plant leaves, like any knowledge, improves with practice; hence, to characterise people by their skills does not necessarily tell you who they are or what they can do. Furthermore, imposed identity cannot last forever. If categorisations such as Indigenous, Africans, Americans, Europeans, Asians, White or Black, women, men, Muslims, or Catholics are fixed, then we could not have the changes that we continue to have. For example, in Mozambique people who were called indigenous and who were seen historically as the ones serving the colonialists today are the ones ruling Mozambique. Likewise, assimilation, although set up to foster Portuguese culture, was used by Mozambicans to resist Portuguese colonialism. When out of the immediate influence of Portuguese, local people felt safe and often behaved more like Africans.

The war of liberation from Portugal was a major stimulus for Africans to change their attitudes towards the colonizer culture, at least in relation to the use of the majority of facilities introduced by the colonizer: schools and hospitals, Western knowledge, medicines, cars and clothes. The liberation war raised the need to quickly control the usage of these facilities because of their efficiency. In this process, the African culture did not remain the same, particularly the indigenous identity found in colonial and Catholic discourse. One example is the colonizer's (Portuguese) language, which was used to oppress, humiliate and insult the "natives". With the onset of war Portuguese language acquired new significance. It was the only language (today it is still the same) that could be used all over the country for communication among people from different ethnic (language) groups. Thus, the colonizer language became a liberating instrument and reluctance to learn the oppressor language largely vanished. The major implication is that this language was modified to allow the new users to express themselves. Indeed, it was modified in terms of pronunciation, grammar and vocabulary, becoming in this way a cultural artefact.

The war of liberation involved all members of society and many relationships changed. For example, before the war marriages were arranged by parents; however, during and after the war girls struggled side by side with boys, and today they are the ones who present their relationships to their parents, usually with a first born as a present. In this process, the male voice loses its dominance and the female voice also loses its submissiveness.

Indigenous knowledge expanded on the back of colonialism, but essentialists are interested only in so-called pure knowledge which has not yet been "contaminated". This is a romanticisation of the concept of indigenous knowledge (Semali & Kincheloe, 1999). According to Hornby (2000), romanticisation means to make things more attractive or interesting than they really are and to forbid development or change.

The notion of purity advocated by essentialists prohibits development of indigeneity, categorizing it as "freedom/nature" and European culture as "culture/reason". For essentialists, these two knowledge systems do not interact. Local knowledge is understood as primitive and as an important focus of academic knowledge, but never as the other kind of academic knowledge that can be studied at school.

The notion of essentialism is underpinned also by the belief that indigenous culture was influenced only by colonialism. However, this is a myth. For example, before the arrival of Europeans in Australia the Aboriginal people were influenced by Indonesians, and vice versa. The same can be applied in Mozambique, as the area was settled by African internal immigration well before the arrival of the colonial power.

After making explicit what I was feeling I was relieved for a time. I realised that my identity is not and cannot be fixed. If I was indigenous in the way described by colonizers I would never have learned so-called Western science. It was clear to me that essentialism had served colonial interests and that I had overcome this barrier by being educated and educating myself. After a few moments of relief, however, the storms came as I questioned my professional self: *Am I a colonizer by not allowing other knowledge than Western science in my science classroom? What is my knowledge? How would I justify the inclusion of knowledge that exists within our many ethnic groups?* In response, I moved to the next step in the triadic structure of dialectical thinking (antithesis) and adopted a "nonessentialist" perspective for my ongoing inquiry.

ANTITHESIS: MY IDENTITY IS ALWAYS CHANGING

Nonessentialism views culture as a dynamic process that can be observed differently by different observers: "The cultural position of the observer helps construct the description of such cultural dynamics" (Semali & Kincheloe, 1999, p. 23). The source of dynamism can be intra group, inter group (border crossing), or both. Individuals learn things from their culture and from other cultures and export their knowledge to other cultures. This explains why no one is culturally pure and why all of us are absorbed in and participate in a subset of cultures. Identities "are historically constructed, always in process, constantly dealing with intersections involving categories of status, religion, race, class and gender" (Semali & Kincheloe, 1999, p. 23). This is in contrast to the essentialist belief that there are fixed and stable identities. The following summarises the contrasting aspects of essentialism and nonessentialism.

Does the Knowledge Belong to the People or to the Land?

The immediate implication for the field of science education is that there is no reason to exclude any form of knowledge of the physical world from the science classroom as, according to the nonessentialist view, the physical world is explained by different knowledges all of which are equally limited and valid. Hence, my indigenous knowledge can and should be included in the science classroom. This stance is completely different from the one into which I have been educated and am teaching from, namely, that Western science is universally valid and provides responses for everything. If there is any event or phenomenon that does not have an explanation it is only because scientists have not yet looked or they are still looking.

For nonessentialists, each knowledge system is constrained by its context and culture; and hence universal truth cannot be achieved. The first consequence of this proposition is that all knowledge, at least in its initial stage of development, could be considered local. Hence, local knowledge can become global knowledge, as is

Table 8.2. Essentialism and nonessentialism

Identity is Fixed (Essentialism)	Identity is Changing (Nonessentialism)
• Skin colour, place of birth, sex, religion determines undoubtedly our identity • Reality is explained by a metanarrative	• Skin colour, place of birth, sex, religion do not determine our identity • Refuses metanarrative

happening with World Modern Science. I argue that local and global knowledges, especially World Modern Science, are distinguishable only by their locations.

In the context of Mozambique, the expression "local" served, first and foremost, the colonisers' interest of them being distinct from the native people. I cannot find an equivalent word in Changana. I understand local as being attached to a certain place; in Changana we have expressions such as "vinhy va tiku" (the owners of the land) and "vavandabwara" (without land), the latter being an offensive term in my culture. I am calling your attention to the fact that, from the native perspective, *natives have the land*, whereas from the coloniser perspective the opposite is true: *the lands have natives*.

Another of the colonisers' interests served by the expression "local" was to show that colonizers brought with them an improvement to our lives; for example, better ways of teaching, moving and healing, and other forms of knowledge. Hence, all types of manoeuvres were made to reject indigenous knowledge; and unfortunately, this is still happening nowadays with the protagonists being "compradors" and with the hegemonic presence of colonizers. A comprador is a local person who identifies with colonial values. S/he is interested in maintaining her/his social status and is not interested in changing the colonial system (Ashcroft, Griffiths, & Tiffin, 2000).

World Modern Science did not evolve simultaneously across the whole globe; rather, it developed at certain locations, and at that time it was local, just like other indigenous knowledge. Then the parts of that World Modern Science were joined, exported, imposed and developed, becoming in this way the property of humankind. It is not in my mind to say that World Modern Science belongs to every woman and man who exists on Earth; I claim that World Modern Science belongs to those who have been inducted into it. A highly visible group would be (Western) science teachers and science teacher educators. This group of practitioners of World Modern Science exists all over the world. This was the fact that inspired me to designate this science as World Modern Science.

Knowledge Should be Given Importance to be Developed

The development achieved by World Modern Science through the co-participation of women and men from all cultures throughout the world appeals and suggests that Mozambican indigenous knowledge needs to be included in the science classroom in order for it to be developed in a similar manner. But how do we do this without human resources and material? I see this as a challenge, not an impediment.

The second consequence of the proposition that "each knowledge system is constrained by its context and culture" is that (a) the World Modern Science we are teaching in the science classroom in Mozambique is valid within its cultural domain and (b) its hegemony in Mozambique is given by being promoted at the expense of other cultures, especially local cultures. In Mozambique, the promotion of the culture of World Modern Science was done mainly by the colonial power (inside and outside of the science classroom), making sure that the natives hated their culture.

The imperialist form of promoting World Modern Science is covered by the colonizers' altruistic slogan that "they are giving others their way of pursuing the Truth", while eradicating the receiver's culture which apparently does not lead to the Truth. In the words of Bilton et al. (2002, p. 433):

> Modernity involved the pursuit of objective truth. Once armed with this truth, modernisers saw it as their duty to become missionaries – to oppose falsehoods. Thus, the standard bearers of science have marched against other forms of knowledge, crusaders on behalf of freedom from ignorance.

So, for me the question arises: *Is the contemporary promotion of World Modern Science in Mozambican science classrooms a continuation of the imperialism started by the colonial power?* Imperialists affirm that Mozambique and other countries in the same situation pursue this form of scientific knowledge because of its perceived superiority over indigenous knowledge. Thus, imperialists of knowledge employ an extremist argument against the principle of equity of cultures. In this way, imperialists argue that different cultures should not be equally accepted because of the possible inequalities that they can incorporate.

Although apparently sound, this argument does not address what is proposed by nonessentialism. Nonessentialism supports my proposal of giving equal value and status to different cultures and knowledges around the world. Racism, sexism, and religious intolerance exist within and among all cultures. The question, in my opinion, is not the acceptance of those awful aspects but how we make them explicit without replacing the local culture by an imposed one. The acceptance of all epistemologies would emphasize that all are valid and can contribute in different ways to general well-being.

My understanding of nonessentialism supports what is happening in Mozambique, where ethnicity is mixed in such a way that couples from different ethnic groups are the norm rather than the exception. Nonessentialism affirms that this is good because each of us Mozambicans is exposed to different knowledges, habits and customs, and we need to understand that the world does not end at the end of our garden. One of the consequences of being exposed to different cultures is that we can go beyond the end of that garden if we wish.

I am questioning how many of us in Mozambique see this healthy and peaceful amalgamation of ethnic groups as a source of international and universal values for our education system. It seems to me that when we decide that it is good to know more than one language we usually opt for English, French, Spanish, German or other European languages, instead of one of the languages of our ethnic groups. According to nonessentialism, Mozambican languages are not chosen because of our alienation from our own culture.

The inclusion of knowledges incorporated among the different ethnic groups in Mozambique can help to challenge students and teachers to analyse the ethics inherent in that knowledge, the power relationships in our ethnic groups, and the manifestation of neo-colonialism throughout Mozambique. In this way, local knowledges can help to address the issue of social justice in our society and can help each of us to be proud of his/her identity.

Reconsidering Identity

Identity is characterised by the way that things such as family, religion, political agency, education and human rights have significance for the individual as self-connected to human aspirations in a given space. In other words, my way of teaching science and taking care of my family, for example, identifies me when it makes sense also to my local community. This way of teaching science and taking care of family is likely replicated elsewhere. Hence, despite my colour and location I can be characterised in the same way as people having different colour and locations from mine.

Anna Sfard and Anna Prusak (2005) suggest that our identities can be known by the stories told by individuals. For them, identity results from everyday interactions and decisions taken in everyday life. This notion of identity states that "human beings are active agents who play decisive roles in determining the dynamics of social life and in shaping individual activities" (p. 15). This notion of identity can help to unravel how the processes of failing or succeeding occur in school.

> People tell others who they are, but even more importantly, they tell themselves and they try to act as though they are who they say they are. These self-understandings, especially those with strong emotional resonance for the teller, are what we refer to as identities. (p. 16)

However, the weakness of this definition is that only the individual can characterise him or herself. A number of elements (including grades, test results, certificates, passports, diagnoses, licenses, diplomas, titles and ranks) are available to tell others who the individual is. However, even this alternative does not seem to be adequate for describing identity because of its reductionism (Golmohamad, 2004).

Nonessentialists view each identity on the planet as changing systematically. The identity of each of us is changing because in every single moment we are acquiring new experience/knowledge through what we see, think or learn in, for example, the science classroom; consequently, it is possible for different people to acquire the same identity. It does not matter where you were born – Africa, Europe or Asia – you have a certain identity according to the value that you place on things. This identity changes simultaneously with your change in referred values.

Nonessentialism agrees with essentialism in relation to the existence of characteristics that identify individuals, people and communities but refuses the immutability of these characteristics. For me, this theory explains why individuals, people and communities change their opinion about different issues throughout their lives. It explains also why foreigners can become Mozambicans, to fight and die for the development of our country. Nonessentialism also explains the ongoing stability of our (evolving) mixed ethnic groups which, for me, is an example of how different people can live together.

Table 8.3. Essentialism, nonessentialism and non/essentialism

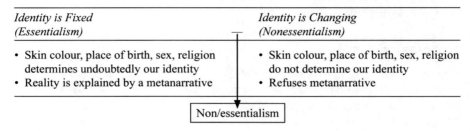

However, nonessentialism creates the dilemma of accepting or rejecting its tenets. On the one hand, it frees me from the colonial fossilization of calling me indigenous, and allows me to bring into the science classroom knowledges other than so-called Western science and to analyse and find out what are the inequalities in my community. On the other hand, it affirms that "I am changing continuously". How can it be so, as I feel that I am still the same and everyone who knows me recognises me. I am sure I can accept discreet changes but perpetual change suggests the revolting idea of permanent instability. These feelings of unease notwithstanding, I cannot identify any contradiction within nonessentialism, only some questions that I could not answer by applying this theory:

- What makes me motivated to change from one identity to another, considering that both are equally acceptable?
- How many identities do I have?
- If I am changing from one identity to another, I am assuming in all of them a different status; so, are there preferred identities?
- Given that identities are different, does it make sense to segregate and classify people?

Therefore, I proceed with my dialectical thinking, aiming to answer these questions and to resolve the dilemma of permanent instability. The synthesis in the triadic structure could be "non/essentialism", where the 'slash' denotes the dialectical relationship between nonessentialism and essentialism. My understanding of non/essentialism is that I am moving back and forth strategically (Ashcroft et al., 2000) between nonessentialism and essentialism.

NON/ESSENTIALISM

Non/essentialism is a symbiosis of essentialism and nonessentialism. It is "strategic essentialism" because, as I will argue, many interests for the individual and society can only be satisfied by using an essentialist concept of identity. In Mozambique, examples of political interests satisfied by acting strategically in accordance with an essentialist perspective include both the expansion of imperialism and the war of liberation, wherein each group assumed the fixed identity of exploiter or exploited. At the individual level, this included what to eat, what to do, and how to live in an environment. According to Ashcroft, Griffiths, and Tiffin (2000), strategic essentialism has been used by "national liberation theorists" such as Fanon, Cabral and James.

Non/essentialism asserts that there exists a set of characteristics that identify individuals, ethnic groups and communities, but it also asserts that these characteristics are not fixed. Changes to these characteristics vary from individual to individual; hence, although some exceptions occur, individuals are different from one another. Nevertheless, within a community all individuals share the same rights and obligations. The differences among individuals problematize firmly established concepts such as Africans, Europeans, colonisers, colonised, and ethnic group. This mutability suggests that individuals and groups can move back and forth between various ethnic groups and communities, within and outside of their countries. It explains also why individuals, ethnic groups and communities do not hold always the same view about themselves and the world around them.

Our identities differ because we do not make identical sense of our experiences; like others, our identities "[are] actively constituted and negotiated" (Bilton et al., 2002, p. 182). In this way, all individuals are indigenous. Each of us was born in a given place and all of us in the end are dependent on Nature. Furthermore, colour, gender, age, location of birth, class, race, religion, language, and spirituality are not adequate for distinguishing people, because identity is not limited to these dimensions.

In the literature, confluence of different identities is called "cultural hybridity" (Ashcroft, Griffiths, & Tiffin, 2000). Non/essentialist theory helps me to make sense of this concept which has created emotional and never-ending debates. To fully understand the concept requires us to resolve dichotomies such as "local/universal" and "I/other". However, these binaries raise complex issues that cannot be resolved by dichotomous thinking. Nevertheless, these binaries can be resolved if we promote a dialectical co-existence of different cultures in hybrid space.

According to non/essentialism, when individuals, ethnic groups and communities are comfortable with their identity this constitutes their "essence"; consequently, they can be characterised by a set of determining features. When they change their identities simply move strategically to another "essential identity". In this way, non/essentialism is based on individual agency. For example, it affirms that we Mozambicans perceived the identity imposed by the colonial power (essentialism), then we refused it (nonessentialism), and then we assumed the identity of the exploited (strategic essentialism).

Non/essentialists accept that in Mozambique we have strongly interconnected groups and, consequently, we have a multicultural setting where each culture is evolving gradually, rather than every single second as implied by nonessentialism. For non/essentialists, indigenous knowledge should be one of the referents in the teaching process as a way of deepening the understanding of our context and the relationship that we have with the rest of the world. Another justification to include indigenous culture in the science classroom is that culture differs from ethnic group to ethnic group and from place to place. Students should be, first of all, informed about different cultures and, secondly, helped to move from one culture to another if they want to. Hence, some of the roles of indigenous knowledge in education can be:

- To contribute to students being well-informed and able to make good decisions about their lives.
- To enable students to see what they have in common as well as their differences.
- To understand science from a broader perspective.

Non/essentialism also explains why the unrealistic teaching of science that does not have a connection with our own lives is 'successful', as demonstrated by me, my colleagues and students. We assumed that we were ignorant, that we needed to be informed and that we had mastered new scientific knowledge, albeit through more or less memorization. To achieve this success we imagined living in a perfect world where scientific principles and laws are universally valid. The problem is that when we wake up from this imagined world we are lost in the world outside of the science classroom where we apply a constant force to produce motion with constant speed and where we use mass (kg) to refer to weight (Newtons).

'WHO AM I?' REVISITED

Using the triadic structure of dialectical thinking I can now answer more meaningfully the question of '*Who am I?*' and draw out the implications for science teacher education.

Non/essentialism helps me to understand that my identities do exist (essentialism) and are changing (nonessentialism) gradually (non/essentialism). Non/essentialism also helps me to contemplate why, as a science educator, I should include indigenous knowledge in my teaching. Non/essentialism helps me to understand that "indigenous" is a category created by essentialists that I can use for my own interests. In relation to this term, I have concluded that the colonizers and colonized and, by extension, all individuals worldwide, are indigenous. At the end of the day, we were born in a given place and have habits and customs that are peculiar to others. There is nothing inherently wrong with or to be ashamed of being indigenous. This stance represents a new way of viewing my identity. Before, when I was ashamed of being indigenous, I used to think that indigenous people lived in the countryside, not in cities ruled by the Western style of living.

In my old (essentialist) view, I am indigenous when I am in the countryside eating the food cooked by my grandmother, speaking my mother tongue (Changana), educating ourselves and the youth through stories, and discussing where to start to collect cashew nuts: this is living the life of my ethnic group. And I am not indigenous when I am in the city educating my student-teachers about teaching World Modern Science, perhaps because we city dwellers, based on what we are doing and where we are now, cannot easily relate to that other life. And when I am a father at home taking care of my children I am not a father at the hospital when I queue to see a nurse. And if I am Changana within my ethnic group I am not Changana when I learn Macua habits and traditions.

The main problem with this old view is that it compels me to be independent within each of my identities: Changana, teacher, father, patient. But this never actually happens. I have solved the contradiction of being independent within each identity, while assuming responsibilities in other identities, by thinking that it does not really matter what I am doing or where I am: I am the same person.

My new view of identity (non/essentialism) helps to explain the existence of two types of identity – fixed and changeable – but does not help to explain the feeling of being the same person. Is this a limitation of the use of the triadic structure of dialectical thinking? What is the importance of explaining the feeling of being the same person in the field of science education? In Mozambique, it is important because, in this way, I see that the Maconde, Machangana, Macua ethnic groups, just to name a few, and consequently, Maconde Knowledge, Machangana Knowledge, Macua Knowledge and, by extension, Western Knowledge, are fictitious constructions. What we have are human beings born in certain contexts and cultures, which does not make them the sole owners of those contexts and cultures. Furthermore, these human beings can decide to live in a sustainable way wherever they want to and science education can contribute to their purpose if designed with that purpose in mind. In short, although I am always the same person I need to be helped by science education to do the different and complex activities in my life (changing identity) and to live with others in and outside of my ethnic group and country (changing identity).

I AM THE ONE WHO I AM

I was given a name to personalize my ancestors
I was colonized to build foreigners' wealth
I was taught science, Western science, to think as a Westerner
I am given back my freedom with the physical expulsion of the colonizers
I am told that I am the One who now determines events in my life

I am the One who has seen the dreams coming true
Is it true that colonizers who have been there for 500 years have vanished?
Is it true that my people and I won't fear any more the White skin?
Is it true that we won't have any more secret teaching?
Is it true that our traditions will flourish freely?

To what extent was I moulded by my parents, family, ethnic group, and society?
To what extent have I made myself?
I wouldn't like to betray my parents, family, ethnic group, and society
I wouldn't like to betray my conquered values
Who am I?

I am looking for myself within the city in which I live
I am looking for myself within the rural areas where my roots are
I am looking for myself within Western culture
I am looking for myself within my ethnic and African culture
I am looking but the images do not match who I think I am

I am thinking that all of these are constraints on my freedom
I would like to be a World citizen
I would like to be a freedom thinker
I would like to not be constrained by my tradition, colonizers, or Western science
I would like to be what I am

I fought for my freedom
I have used Western science to show its oppression of me
I have used my costumes and traditions to show their oppression of me
I am struggling to be enculturated in my own local-indigenous science
I am wondering if I will succeed in getting rid of Western science, local-indigenous costumes and traditions, and colonialism.
I would like to be what I am

My fight has evolved
I am also identified by colonialism, indigeneity, and Western science
I was never identified by mountains, panoramas and emotions
I have languages and traditions that were never given value to be taught in school
I have evolved to have an integrated science in my classroom
I would like to teach who I am

How can I teach you without knowing who you think you are?
How can we create a better world without sharing the meaning of 'better'?
How can we describe to each of us who we think we are?
How can we accept discovering that we are wrong?
I think we are just Awareness/Emptiness
What do you think?

My poem is both a product and an instrument of my inquiry. It shows me where I started my doctoral studies and where I am now whilst seeking to evoke readers' knowledge of how they have faced the struggle of identity in their own lives.

What engages me in this poem is its ability to show how uncomfortable I was with myself when I began my research, and as this study developed I ended up accepting myself. The poem shows that I was focussing only on some aspects of my 'initial starting point' and now I see it in its complexity. I have said, for example, "I am also identified by colonialism, indigeneity, and Western science". At the beginning of my inquiry, colonizers were only the 'others', indigeneity was a symbol of being oppressed, and Western science was something that I could worship as the answer provider.

Now I am aware that these are all part of me; I am also part of the problem. My struggle now is to continue to transform or consolidate parts of the identities of me that I have just discovered. Being identified by colonialism is one of the identities that I do not want to wear. I am not saying that from now on I will not be identified by colonialism, but instead that I am *struggling* to not be identified by colonialism. I am identified by colonialism when I refuse to acknowledge the existence of my own culture, language, science and a view of the world that is different from the Western view. I am identified by colonialism when I struggle to promote my ethnic group at the expense of other ethnic groups in Mozambique. I am identified by colonialism when I think that the Portuguese language I speak belongs to Portuguese people while Mozambicans are creating it in our own mould with pronunciation, vocabulary and grammar that can hardly be understood by Portuguese people. I believe that to suppress this colonial identity does not serve my interests; hence, Mozambicans need to engage in a dialogue to understand which interests are being served and why. Unfortunately, we cannot do everything at the same time.

My final comment about this poem is that it has the characteristic of being an instrument of inquiry. The poem illustrates my belief that true inquiry goes beyond traditional interviews where the participants have fixed roles; that is, asking questions and providing answers. In a post/modern interview these roles are not fixed (Kvale, 1996). In my poem, although I am the one who is inquiring, I have started by telling my reader in an evocative manner how my identity was defined by various influences and how I now conceptualise my sense of identity. I end with a concise open question. This shows how I see my research as a contribution to dialogue about education in Mozambique and the rest of the world.

REFERENCES

Ashcroft, B., Griffiths, G., & Tiffin, H. (2000). *Post-colonial studies: The key concepts*. New York, NY: Routledge.
Bilton, T., Bonnett, K., Jones, P., Lawson, T., Skinner, D., Stanworth, M., & Webster, A. (2002). *Introductory sociology* (4th ed.). New York, NY: Palgrave Macmillan.
Cupane, A. F. (2003). *The use of everyday materials in the science classroom in Mozambique: An interpretive inquiry* (Unpublished masters dissertation). Science and Mathematics Education Centre, Curtin University of Technology, Perth, Australia.
Cupane, A. F. (2008). *Towards a culture-sensitive pedagogy of physics teacher education in Mozambique* (Unpublished thesis dissertation). Curtin University of Technology, Perth, Australia.
Golmohamad, M. (2004). World citizenship, identity and the notion of an integrated self. *Studies in Philosophy and Education, 23*, 131–148.
Hornby, A. S. (2000). *Oxford advanced learner's dictionary* (6th ed.). New York, NY: Oxford University Press.
Kvale, S. (1996). *Inter/views*. Thousand Oaks, CA: Sage Publications.
Palmer, P. J. (1998). *The courage to teach*. San Francisco, CA: Jossey-Bass.
Semali, L. M. (1999). Community as classroom: Dilemmas of valuing African indigenous in education. *International Review of Education, 45*(3–4), 305–319.
Semali, L. M., & Kincheloe, J. L. (1999). What is indigenous knowledge and why should we study it? In L. M. Semali & J. L. Kincheloe (Eds.), *What is indigenous knowledge? Voices from the academy* (pp. 3–57). New York, NY: Falmer Press.

ALBERTO FELISBERTO CUPANE

Sfard, A., & Prusak, A. (2005). Telling identities: In search of an analytic tool for investigating learning as a culturally shaped activity. *Educational Researcher, 34*(4), 14–22.
Spencer, L., & Krauze, A. (1996). *Hegel for beginners*. Retrieved December 24, 2017, from https://www.marxists.org/reference/archive/hegel/help/easy.htm
Taylor, P. C. (2006). Forum: Alternative perspectives towards culturally inclusive science teacher education. *Cultural Studies of Science Education, 1*(1), 189–208.

ABOUT THE AUTHOR

My name is **Alberto Felisberto Cupane** (Cupane). I concluded my Masters and PhD at Science and Mathematics Education Centre, Curtin University of Technology, Perth, Australia in 2007. I have been a high school science/mathematics teacher (since 1983) and science teacher educator (since 1992) in Mozambique. As a science teacher educator, I have been teaching undergraduate students in the Physics Department at Pedagogical University in Maputo, preparing them to become science teachers. Although I became a teacher by chance, now I cannot dissociate myself from the teaching/learning process. Therefore, my wish is to continue to be a teacher for the rest of my life. Currently I am looking after postgraduate studies in Centro de Pós-graduação At Universidade Pedagógica (UP) – (Pedagogical University). I am also teaching at Master's Degree several units including Innovative Research Methods, Mechanics and Electricity laboratories. I have published several books on physics teaching for grades 8 and 9 used in our national education system. My research interest focuses on transformative research related to identity, culture, emancipation, feminism, language, and science teaching.

SADRUDDIN BAHADUR QUTOSHI

9. CULTURAL-SELF KNOWING

Transforming Self and Others

Went through a journey without I
There, my heart opened up to joy without I
Why do you stay in prison
When the door is so wide open
Escape from the black cloud
that surrounds you
Then you will see your own light
As radiant as the full moon
Occupy yourself with your own
Inward self

(Rumi)

Once I was a doctoral scholar at Kathmandu University School of Education (KUSOED) where I came to know how to explore the self by using unconventional ways of conducting *research as knowing thyself* (metaphorically speaking) My mentor, Dr Bal Chandra Luitel, was teaching a course in which his discussions on innovative multi-epistemic transformative research design inspired me. I began to deconstruct my own view of *research as proving* together with other ingrained positivistic assumptions. Philosophically speaking, the innovative approaches to teacher education research were embedded in William Pinar's (2004) view of empowering learners via writing autobiographically.

My initial reaction was to feel a great threat to my identity as a positivistic researcher who had been enculturated within a dualistic mindset of *research as qualitative and quantitative* or *research as mixed methods*. However, I gradually came to realize the enabling practices of a culturally empowering view of educational research as a transformative enterprise that challenges the realist agenda of research. This realization led me to construct a new identity as a transformative teacher educator and researcher for Pakistan, my own country.

During my doctoral research, I reflected on culturally responsive and empowering approaches to knowing and realized that in my home university existing practices lagged behind such a liberating view of educational research (Qutoshi, 2016a). Because my own schooling had not helped me to think beyond the boundaries of what I was taught, I (and my fellow researchers) had relied on taken-for-granted ways of conducting *research as reproducing the status quo*. I began to write narratives about these practices, addressing questions of the kind: 'Why culturally disempowering and disengaged learning could not help me (and my fellow learners) to escape from the positivistic box of thinking and doing?' My reflective writing was designed to invite my readers (my colleagues) to take the journey of interrogating the nature of the dominant educational practices in our country. Reflecting critically on the limitations of canonical ways of rendering the *researcher as disengaged self* enabled me to focus my doctoral inquiry on my personal-professional development; a transformative process of becoming aware of the limitations and possibilities embedded in my practice. Today, the outcomes of this research are enabling me to facilitate the development of my own students (pre-service teachers) as transformative learners.

Thus, the purpose of this chapter is to illustrate how, during my doctoral research, I engaged in cultural-self knowing in relation to my personal-professional lifeworld embedded in the classroom, the university, and the cultural context of Pakistan. During my critical auto/ethnographic inquiry, I reconstructed my identity as a transformative learner in the interests of empowering my students (pre-service teachers) as critical reflective practitioners. First, I explain where the motivation came from to undertake this very challenging, and at time confronting, journey.

EMBRACING CARING PEDAGOGY

My exposure to an open view of educational research practice encouraged me to think beyond the conventional requirement of doctoral research as completing the thesis without paying attention to my professional growth as a teacher educator. Later, this innovative experience led me to engage with myself and postgraduate students in my home university (Karakorum International University, Pakistan) through ongoing professional endeavors to initiate new ways of thinking and doing research. In particular, research as constructing a new identity, as reconceptualizing self, and as developing an oppositional stance.

Today, when I reflect on my interactions and engagements with KUSOED fraternity (especially those engaged in the transformative educational research community) I feel that if I had not had such a learning opportunity to embrace research as and for transformative professional development then I would not now be able to contribute to self and others in such an empowering way. To me, educational research as and for transforming has the power to liberate both teacher and learner from conventional practices, thereby encouraging them to become innovative in their views and actions. I sincerely give credit to the cultural context of KUSOED which enabled me to envision a liberating view of teacher education for my country. This has led me to believe that leadership at different levels, especially teacher as leader at the classroom level, and heads at departmental and institutional levels, and beyond, need to reflect on cultural views and practices to create a caring and enabling culture that fosters transformation.

When I reflect on that situation, I can understand how generously KUSOED bestowed love, care and support (both academic and social-moral within a scaffolding culture) that empowered me in many ways. For example, I did not find my professors avoiding me (by saying, for example, "You can come in your own time, or some other time, I have no time now, you should get prior time to come and discuss things relevant to my subject"). Instead, they appreciated me for seeking their views when I needed clarification. One of the outcomes of such an appreciative and empowering approach to supporting mentees has been to lead me to contribute to my own students at my university to raise their consciousness as caring teacher educators.

After rejoining my home university, while teaching a course on Critical Thinking to Master of Arts students I encourage them to be critically reflective practitioners and challenge both self and others, including me, who was/is their teacher. Initially I found my students in a state of chaos to adopt such a critical stance in their lives (i.e., in their academic discourses) to challenge their own views and those of others, especially their teacher's views. This is because the conventional educational practices in their lives have enculturated them with the myth of the teacher (as a learned person, senior, and elder) as always being right and students as having to accept whatever their teachers tell them (metaphorically teachers as re/tellers, transmitters and/or translators) to do in their lives.

However, with my continuous encouragement, support and engagement in critical reflection on our cultural practices in the classroom, in the university and in our country's context, I see my students moving gradually in the direction of becoming reflective practitioners. For instance, Shahban, a student in my Master's Critical Thinking class, expressed this view to fellow students when reflecting on his failure in a semester exam.

> As a general practice within our everyday life, it is normal to celebrate success with full of joy and failure with shock, and sometimes shedding tears over failure. Knowing about my failure in the exam was a shocking news for me, however, soon after I began to recall the moments of our discussion on how to become a critically reflective practitioner, and this enabled me to become cool. I came to realize that I need to focus on improving my learning by critically reflecting on how I learn the way I am learning rather than focusing on how to get good marks in the exam.

The student seems to be advising his colleagues in the light of his own life experience and his learning through critical reflections with the sentiment: "learn to study to become competent in your field rather than to get good marks in the exam". To me, such changes in my students and their way of looking unconventionally at self and others within the cultural practices of the classroom and beyond is a moment of hope that enables me to envision a future of learners engaged in transformative learning. This is the outcome of a caring and empowering pedagogy that enables learners to disrupt taken-for-granted assumptions and construct new perspectives (Mezirow, 2000).

SADRUDDIN BAHADUR QUTOSHI

EMBRACING MULTI-EPISTEMIC RESEARCH DESIGN

During my doctoral program, I became dissatisfied with the conventional role of the *researcher as disengaged self*. The agenda of positivism disengages researchers by using third person language in order to avoid their subjectivities, thereby avoiding innovative and creative thinking. Thus, the researcher as disengaged self has no voice with respect to his or her own feelings, perceptions and experiences. The fixed rules of positivist research bind the researcher to collect and analyse data by pretending that the researcher is entirely external. By contrast, a liberating view of educational research enables and encourages practitioner-researchers to use innovative ways of knowing by thinking beyond the boundaries of positivism.

I came to understand that cultural-self knowing is a complex phenomenon that demands an un/conventional approach to knowing within a complex multi-epistemic research design. I use the '/' symbol to refer to the dialectical method of combining conventional research methods (e.g., English grammar rules, chapter structure, prosaic flow) and unconventional research methods (e.g., personal narratives, autobiographical voice, arts-based genres). Thus, autoethnography as cultural self-knowing was a lens through which I contemplated the complex, undetached, fluid self in micro (classroom), mini (university) and macro (country) cultural settings.

With this multi-dimensional lens I asked questions such as: Who am I? Why have I been working in the field of teaching? How am I contributing in the field? What is the role of cultural self-knowing in contributing and/or hindering my way of becoming a change agent for education as a means for empowerment? How can I make my fellow teacher educators and researchers realize the power of an open view of education? In what ways can they help themselves and others with whom they work? In so doing, my critical reflective inquiry led me to focus on the question: What is cultural-self knowing and how can it enable me to foster transformative learning of self and beyond?

While seeking multiple contextualized meanings of cultural-self knowing – knowing my lifeworld as a practitioner-teacher, as a teacher educator/researcher, as a reflective practitioner, and as a learner – I came across another emergent question: How do my students see me as a teacher and themselves as learners? In so contemplating, I began reflecting on others who have experienced (metaphorically speaking) *leadership as dictating*, *curriculum as textbooks*, *teaching as transmitting*, *assessment as upgrading*, and *research as proving* (Qutoshi, 2016a). These limited views of education and research practices have developed an inhibiting mindset in both teachers and learners, including my former self.

With a focus on cultural-self knowing, I challenged conventional approaches to education and research and employed autoethnography to frame a complex research design. I used the lens of critical self-reflection within the paradigm of *criticalism*; raised awareness about issues related to cultural-self knowing at classroom level, university level, and country level by employing *interpretivism* and *postmodernism*; and searched for evidence of how cultural-self knowing contributes to

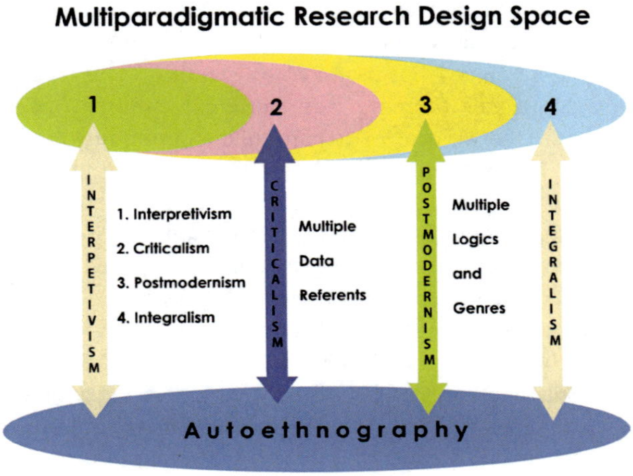

Multiparadigmatic Research Design Space

Figure 9.1. Multi-paradigmatic research design space

transformative learning, using multiple logics and genres within *integralism* which promotes the epistemic power of a *multi-paradigmatic* research design (Taylor, Taylor, & Luitel, 2012).

Engaging self as researcher in a multi-epistemic process of knowing helped me to develop capacities at different levels. For instance, such knowing helped me to explore my inner self as a person and a professional teacher educator and researcher and my external self as a social change agent in various cultural settings. Exploring my identity enabled me to explore how the knowing self within a particular cultural context (such as a school, a university, and communities in Hunza where I was born, and Gilgit, Islamabad, Lahore and Karachi where I lived, studied and worked) can develop a consciousness that contributes to becoming a transformative learner.

EMBRACING MY LIVED IDENTITY

Let me delve into the realm of my own experiential take on cultural-self knowing from the vantage point of a male Muslim Pakistani national. This is to demonstrate ways in which this particular identity influenced my life as a professional teacher educator and researcher. I speak Urdu as my national language along with *Brushaski* – one of the world's unique languages as my mother tongue which is spoken in central Hunza (my home city), Nagar and Yaseen valleys with slightly different dialects. Unconsciously in my everyday practices (both educative and social life activities) this identity brings forth powerful insights into my worldview as a teacher educator and researcher in the field and as a social worker.

During my research I reflected on my cultural self and came to realise that I was an advantaged person within the cultural setting of my hometown, Altit. I asked a host of questions: In what ways did my parents, especially my elder brother (Mr. Badruddin, a software developer), extend their full support (even in hard times) during my student life? How I felt proud of self and my family for being blessed, compared to my colleagues (coming from different cultures)? Why a particular family culture and/or the culture of a particular community holds such values, compared to others? In what ways did such values of support influence my life as a student? I realized that my unique cultural identity contributed embodied values of practice, such as being proud of self as a learned person, while living with people in a culturally decontextualized world where students are exposed to teaching, learning and research within a narrowly conceived view of education.

Cultural-self knowing opened a space for me to think critically about my worldview. I wrote life stories that contributed to knowing about the nature of my own and my colleagues' established beliefs in hierarchical and dictatorial leadership, and our practices of teaching, learning and research that we performed under the auspices of a closed vision of education. It was important to explore how my lived identity influenced my own learning and the learning of others, including my students at the university (Whitehead, 2015).

I came to realize that without exploring self I could not make a difference to the lives of my students. For example, if I could not lead my students with encouragement then I would not enable them to make good sense of their learning. I noticed that my transformed approach to enabling my learners – engaging with their critical questions over their own ways of learning and the learning of others, putting questions to their teachers, and even challenging their elders (i.e., teachers) – was helping them to become critically reflective practitioners.

With such an encouraging and empowering view of teaching (teaching as liberating), my narratives of teaching and learning carry insights that can raise *pedagogical thoughtfulness* (van Manen, 1991) in my readers – teachers and teacher educators and researchers. Thus, they might come to know whether their pedagogies are based on teaching as transmitting or teaching as liberating. In so doing, teachers (including myself) may start reconstructing their lived identities. For example, how they perceive their roles and engage in the practice of teaching, supervising research students, and learning about learning so as to enable students to become consciously knowing learners, rather than blind followers with the notion of learning as receiving. Engaging in cultural self-knowing about my own complex lifeworld was aligned with an emancipatory social interest.

EMBRACING MY COMMUNAL SELF

I came to know that cultural-self knowing involves becoming aware of the components of my culture (Mezirow, 1978; Taylor, 2000). When I say my culture, I mean a culture that can be classified at three different levels: (i) *mega culture* – the culture of my country and my religious background with a broader Muslim culture which in/directly influences my world views; (ii) *mini culture* – the culture of the organization where I work, with a diverse group of people (how they perceive their roles and responsibilities of their jobs and what are their practices within a particular environment, in what ways organizational leadership is aware of creating a conducive learning environment and its impact on job performance of the people in organization; and (iii) *micro culture* – a culture of the classroom where I teach, and the family culture in which I live.

With this realization, I started thinking about and understanding and valuing the values (especially my embodied values of practice in my everyday life), customs, rites and rituals, ceremonies and events (which I celebrate un/consciously), to name but a few, as components of my wider culture. The question arose of how these components could help me make sense of knowing my role as a teacher educator, researcher and supervisor who influences the learning of self and others in the field of teacher education. To do this, I came to realize how important it is to explore my personal and professional identities in a *rational* manner (Mezirow, 1978) as well as in an *extrarational* way (Boyd, 1991) to make better sense of my lifeworld.

Arriving at this point of my soulful inquiry, I explored the complex undetached-fluid-self (Qutoshi, 2016) through my everyday activities embedded within my beliefs and my exposure to my knowledge, skills and attitudes while living in particular cultural settings. To me, this is what cultural-self knowing is all about, that is, understanding the personal-professional (as a person and as a professional teacher educator, researcher and supervisor) and spiritual dimensions of learning. To me, the spiritual dimensions of learning appear to be a way of thinking, being and becoming as a person who contributes something good for sociocultural others (including self). Therefore, it is rooted in cultural, religious and other practices which sensitize the individual to develop a deep level of thinking leading towards liberation from limited worldviews (Qutoshi, 2016).

Knowing my life as part of the life outside the 'I' – including my family members, my colleagues and students where I work, and the society where I live and have interactions with other people outside of the immediate society – brought a shift in consciousness that altered my way of being in the world (Mezirow, 1978). Knowing the fluid nature of self – not only the single self but also self as part of others – is experienced at the communal level. However, knowing the self with such an inclusive lens seems to be missing, or at least is unexplored, in postcolonial studies of countries such as Pakistan. Let me tell you what the meaning of knowing at the communal level is and how knowing at the communal level contributes to transformation of self and others while living and working in a particular cultural setting.

My perceived meaning of the communal is to engage in knowing a community of teaching and learning: student-teachers and their relationships and other co-workers. For instance, in the classroom the academic needs to develop a sense of being aware of every learner and his/her capacity to learn. To this end, I started to think about my positionality from both *soft* and *hard* aspects of the classroom culture. I developed my own view of the soft aspects of the culture which are my interactions with learners – how do I encourage and/or discourage my students un/consciously? – my observations in class about how students feel and think, their levels of participation and responses, to name but a few. Whereas, the hard aspects of classroom cultural ingredients and the environmental settings are seating arrangements (quality of chairs and tables), classroom climate (location, ventilation, lighting, placement of other resources in class and color), and the availability and accessibility of required physical resources.

As a teacher, I began to feel that it was vital for me to develop consciousness about such aspects of the classroom culture in order to provide maximum support, care and empowerment required for my student-teachers' transformation. To me, such a way of knowing my life as a teacher (i.e., cultural self-knowing) is complex and spiral in nature, rather than a simple linear form of learning. To learn about self and others demands an innovative and multi-epistemic research approach.

ڈھونڈتا پھرتا ہوں اے اقبال اپنے آپ کو
آپ ہی گویا مسافر آپ ہی منزل ہوں میں

O Iqbal! I am in constant search for myself
I am the traveler as well as the destination

In a poem on Khudi (i.e., self-exploration), Allama Muhammad Iqbal, a famous Pakistani poet-philosopher, reflected on self as both destination and traveller (Iqbal, 1905). In a similar vein, Jalalluddin Rumi (King, 2014) cautions knowers (including himself) to explore the ego, yourself, because self is itself a universe that contains you. Arriving at this point of exploration where the knower is a traveller and the destination is self and beyond, I came up with a few metaphoric expressions to characterize cultural-self knowing as an epistemic approach to transformative learning for sustainable futures. As a teacher educator and researcher, the notion of cultural self-knowing appears to be embedded within the philosophy of a living educational perspective.

EMBRACING CRITICAL REFLEXIVITY

With the notion of transforming my practices of teaching, learning and research, I came across the *living educational theory* perspective of Jack Whitehead (1989) which further enabled me to reflect on my perceptions and practices, and develop my own living educational theory. The focus of developing a living educational theory is embedded within the philosophy of cultural-self knowing based on questions of the kind: "How do I improve my practice?" (Whitehead, 1989, p. 1) In developing my own living educational theory, I engaged in critical self-reflection on my practices from the standpoint of my embodied values.

When I reflected on my embodied values – "my intention of doing good for others, humility for humanity, care of self and others with ecological consciousness, love and peace" (Qutoshi, 2016b, p. 3) – I began to identify my living contradictions, that is, the difference between what I value and what I practically do. These contradictions served as explanatory principles of my living educational theory.

This process can be understood as digging at a deeper level of thinking to make better sense of one's own (and others') actions, thereby opening both inner and outer worlds to the complex, undetached, fluid self, especially from the standpoint of questions such as: what are our values and how do we practice?

From a critical theory perspective, cultural-self knowing is a powerful learning experience that creates conditions to be critical towards self and others for the common good. To this end, creating such conditions is necessary to provide a common space for all to make better sense of being in the world with an emancipatory intention (Singh & Devine, 2013). I believe that one needs to be very clear about a common view of culture in order to create a space that encourages more dialogue and discourse (Dirkx, 2008, 2012) for creating a universal brotherhood (here I am thinking about humanity around the globe). To achieve such a noble transformative objective one needs to be very much sensitive towards cultural-self knowing through the lens of critical reflexivity.

Critical Reflexivity

It is the bell that awakens sleeping fellows
Enabling critique of self and others

It is the philosophy of action, not just words
Helping together self and others

It is the epistemology of lived identity construction
Raising creativity, reducing rigidity

It is the rider for past to engage in present
Opening windows, both past and recent

It is the mirror of one's inside-out to envision the future
Infusing thrust for explorative adventure

It is the driller to create cracks in frozen rocks
Enabling light to pass through to the other side

It changes those who are loyal to self and beyond
Enlightening one's heart and mind

It is the agent of change, not traditional inquiry
Empowering self and others for emancipation

It is discourse for a sustainable future
Bringing transformation to the lives of self and others

My critical self-reflective inquiry enabled me to experience cultural-self knowing as a complex process of exploring self and beyond. It is multifaceted, complex and spiral in nature from the vantage point of emancipation for the common good. To me, the essence of cultural-self knowing is embedded within the philosophy of fighting against ignorance by engaging in critical reflective thinking about the lifeworld.

In so doing, one raises awareness and develops consciousness within self and others to create common spaces for better ways of living and being in the world.

EMBRACING TRANSFORMATIVE LEARNING

I remember when my supervisor engaged me in writing narratives on my teaching and learning related practices after exposure to reflexivity as an epistemic approach. I found it very challenging. It was not easy for a researcher like me to come out of my strongly held assumptions to develop new perspectives (Mezirow, 2012) using such a powerful epistemic approach. I had been enculturated by a postcolonial regime into the Western modern worldview.

However, with constant struggle and empowerment, I started using the lens of critical reflexivity which enabled me to critique my own limited views of educational leadership, curriculum, pedagogy and assessment, and research practices as five key thematic areas of my doctoral study. While exploring self within a holistic approach to teacher education, I engaged in mini-, micro- and macro-cultural explorations of my educative practices and worldview. Designing and developing an un/conventional research design was challenging, but in so doing it enabled me to find multiple opportunities to transform my practices. I challenged my own positionality and taken-for-granted identity as a professional teacher educator, researcher, curriculum developer, educational technologist, and research supervisor in the field of teacher education in the context of my own country.

Who Is the 'I' that Teaches?

Writing narratively from such a standpoint constitutes a *confessional* approach (van Manen, 1991) to exploring one's personal-professional lifeworld. When I explored my lifeworld I came to realize in what ways my teacher-centred approach to teaching during the early period of my university teaching both facilitated and incapacitated my students. Let me share my perspective on the teacher's dominating approach to pedagogy.

> What [Eliot] Eisner calls *structural violence* indirectly makes learners voiceless and passive receivers of information through a telling and transferring mode of teaching in a very formal setting. This view of my teaching and those of the others in the context of my country led me to ask questions of the kind, "how have I encountered key facets of definitional/informing pedagogies that disempower learners to develop a broader view of learning to understand a real-life situation?" (Qutoshi, 2016a, p. 45)

During my critical-self knowing inquiry I came to realise that without being aware of my classroom culture and challenging my taken-for-granted assumptions to teaching and learning, I could not explore the 'I' who was teaching. Now, after having engaged in extensive critical self-reflection, I can honestly confess how difficult it was to challenge this 'I' who was exposed to schooling in a postcolonial regime. There, I had experienced the culture of *leadership as dictating, curriculum as textbooks, teaching as telling, assessment as promotion,* and *research as positivism.* My scholarly reflections led me to infer that as a student I had experienced school, college and university life under a narrowly conceived view of education that Habermas (1972) calls the *technical interest.* It was the outcome of such an education that had dominated my thinking, feelings and actions as a teacher. Let me illustrate this technical teaching approach by sharing a dialogue with a student of mine at that time (J. A. Noori, personal communication, June 16, 2012).

I: Students you know it's the last week of this semester, and I have almost done my teaching in this course [ICT in Education].

U: Sir, I am afraid how we can make our preparations for getting good marks in exams.

I: What do you mean by this...?

U: You know, sir, you have covered a lot of topics in this course. The topics are very difficult to understand. Whereas, in other subjects we have studied the limited course content that appears easy for us to prepare for the exam.

I: What is the problem with you in this subject as I have taught everything you know!

U: Sir, yes, you have taught a lot of topics and I am confused with this stuff. Because you have taught theory only not provided an opportunity for practice in a lab. You know, sir, we have no computer lab to practice that could be the reason we are in trouble!

I: It's shocking for me. If you were not clear about the topics then why did you not ask me at that time when I was asking you in class?

U: Sir, at that time we thought that was easy. But now we are confused.

I: Are you crazy? Is this the time to ask me about this problem when we are going to conduct exams in a few days?

FINAL REMARKS

A major outcome of my doctoral research is an understanding that a key purpose of cultural-self knowing is to become consciously sensitive towards my own teaching and learning practices, and that we can transform our practices by using multi-epistemic lenses rather than relying on canonical ways of knowing. To this end, we (including the academic community) need to be serious about ways that enable us to challenge our unwittingly assimilated assumptions. When I started challenging my own assumptions I came to realize that I had been unaware of and unconscious about my own classroom culture. At that moment, I realized that our knowing needs to be based on liberation from ignorance, from rigidity in our approaches to knowing, and from one-size-fits-all notions of thinking, believing and acting. To achieve this goal we need to raise awareness about humanity with humility. Such a concerted endeavor can lead individuals, groups, academic organizations, societies and nations towards transformation for a sustainable future.

Cultural-self knowing is of fundamental importance for educators in higher education institutions in order to create conditions favorable for fostering transformative learning. However, in the current situation such conditions appear to be missing; instead, we (educators wielding a dominant colonial discourse) try to impose our own ideas, views and rules via a positivist style that badly hampers the creativity of our adult graduates. I believe that without fostering transformative learning at the classroom level claiming to be educators makes no sense and does not meet the demands and needs of 21st century graduates: technologically connected and independent learners armed with multiple ways of knowing.

REFERENCES

Boyd, R. D. (Ed.). (1991). *Personal transformations in small groups: A Jungian perspective*. London: Routledge.
Boyd, R. D., & Myers, J. G. (1988). Transformative education. *International Journal of Lifelong Education, 7*(4), 261–284.
Dirkx, J. M. (Ed.). (2008). *Adult learning and the emotional self. New directions for adult and continuing education*. San Francisco, CA: Jossey-Bass.
Dirkx, J. M. (2012). Nurturing soul work: A Jungian approach to transformative learning. In E. W. Taylor & P. Cranton (Eds.), *The handbook of transformative learning: Theory research and practice* (pp. 131–146). San Francisco, CA: Jossey-Bass.
Habermas, J. (1972). *Knowledge and human interests* (2nd ed.). London: Heinemann.
Iqbal, A. M. (1905). *Bang-e-Dra*. Retrieved from http://iqbalurdu.blogspot.com/2011/03/bang-e-dra-061-sakhtiyan-kerta-hun-dil.html
Kreber, C. (2012). Critical reflection and transformative learning. In E. W. Taylor & P. Cranton (Eds.), *The handbook of transformative learning: Theory research and practice* (pp. 323–341). San Francisco, CA: Jossey-Bass.
Mezirow, J. (1978). Perspective transformation. *Adult Education Quarterly, 28*, 100–110.
Mezirow, J. (2012). Learning to think like an adult: Core concepts of transformation theory. In E. W. Taylor, P. Cranton, & Associates (Eds.), *The handbook of transformative learning: Theory research and practice*. San Francisco, CA: Jossey-Bass.
Moneypenny, P. (2013). *A poststructural autoethnography: Self as event* (Unpublished master thesis). University of Waikato, Hamilton, New Zealand.
Qutoshi, S. B. (2014). *Reengineering higher education with technologies: A case study of use of computer technologies in teacher education at Karakorum international university Pakistan*. Paper presented at IT Conference for a Smart Society, Computer Association of Nepal, Kathmandu.
Qutoshi, S. B. (2016a). *Creating living educational theory: A journey towards transformative teacher education in Pakistan* (Unpublished doctoral thesis). Kathmandu University, Nepal.
Qutoshi, S. B. (2016b). Creating my own living-educational-theory: An autoethnographic-soulful inquiry. *Educational Journal of Living Theories, 9*(2), 60–86. Retrieved from http://ejolts.net/node/287
Rumi, J. (undated). 1st poem. In A. King (2014), *Freedom from yourself: Rumi's selected poems from Divan Shams Tabrizi* (pp. 1–2). Bloomington, IN: Balboa Press.

Singh, A., & Devine, M. (Eds.). (2013). *Rural transformation and New Foundland and Labrador diaspora: Grandparents, grandparenting, community and school relations*. Rotterdam, The Netherlands: Sense Publishers.

Taylor, E. W. (2000). Fostering transformative learning in the adult education classroom. *The Canadian Journal of the Study of Adult Education, 14*, 1–28.

Taylor, P. C. (2013). Research as transformative learning for meaning-centred professional development. In O. Kovbasyuk & P. Blessinger (Eds.), *Meaning-centred education: International perspectives and explorations in higher education* (pp. 168–185). New York, NY: Routledge.

Taylor, P. C. (2015). Transformative science education. In R. Gunstone (Ed.), *Encyclopedia of science education* (pp. 1079–1082). Dordrecht: Springer.

Taylor, P. C., Taylor, E., & Luitel, B. C. (2012). Multi-paradigmatic transformative research as/for teacher education: An integral perspective. In B. J. Fraser, K. G. Tobin, & C. J. McRobbie (Eds.), *Second international handbook of science education* (pp. 373–387). Dordrecht: Springer.

Tisdell, E. J. (2008). *Spirituality and adult education learning* (New directions for adult and continuing education, No. 119). San Francisco, CA: Jossey-Bass.

Whitehead, J. (1989). Creating a living educational theory from questions of the kind, "how do I improve my practice?" *Cambridge Journal of Education, 19*(1), 41–52.

Whitehead, J. (2015). The practice of helping students to find their first person voice in creating living-theories for education. In H. Bradbury (Ed.), *The Sage handbook of action research* (3rd ed., pp. 247–255). London: Sage Publications.

ABOUT THE AUTHOR

My name is **Sadruddin Bahadur Qutoshi**. I was born and grew up in Altit, Hunza, in the North of Pakistan. I founded the Transformative Teacher Education and Research Program in Pakistan by developing my own living-educational-theory of practice. I was awarded my PhD in Educational Leadership by Kathmandu University, Nepal. I am currently serving as an Assistant Professor of Teacher Education at the Faculty of Education, Karakorum International University, Pakistan. I am teaching critical thinking, educational leadership, curriculum, assessment and educational technology (Master of Education) and qualitative research in education (MPhil in Education). I am the coordinator of the Master Degree program and convener of the Faculty of Education for Self-Assessment Reports for different programs. My research interests focus on teacher education leadership, curriculum and pedagogy, assessment and research practice. I also take an interest in social justice, peace, spirituality and identity and cultural studies. Since 2013, my publications are in the areas of leading learning organization, leadership in school improvement, learner-centred pedagogies, and technologies in education.

HISASHI OTSUJI

10. WHERE DO I COME FROM? WHAT AM I? WHERE AM I GOING?

How the Grandson of a Mahayana Buddhism Priest Became a Science Educator

In this chapter, I would like to talk about me, as a case study, a person who teaches science education methodology and general introduction to education in the College of Science and Engineering of a private university in Japan. I was born the grandson of a Buddhism priest in the mid 1960s. How did I, someone that seemed to have the opposite cultural background, become a science educator? This has been the main research question of my doctoral research. You will see in this chapter that I have been struggling to bridge binary cultures: West and East, qualitative and quantitative, theory and practice, research and practice. This process not only traces my transformation but also recognises the self in the web of related wholeness.

I have two questions. Do you know a painting by Paul Gaugin, titled "D'où venons-nous? Que sommes-nous? Où allons-nous?" The title of this chapter was named after this painting. However, I feel a little discomfort with this title because it seems to imply a linear image of a lifetime. Then, I ask you a second question. Do you believe in reincarnation? For me, I do not really believe in it, but sometimes I feel that this image of a big circulation and web of co-relationships works well.

In this chapter I draw on the critical auto/ethnography of my doctoral research which has enabled me to investigate my "own cultural situatedness from the unique standpoint of both a cultural insider and border crosser, excavating the way in which [my] professional identity has been shaped". The inquiry enabled me "to explore [my] culturally embedded identities, to excavate and portray multi-hued accounts of [my] lived experiences, to generate critical reflexivity with which to deconstruct the hegemonic grip of [my] cultural history, to envisage with optimism, passion and commitment a culturally diverse and inclusive world, and to engage…readers in moments of pedagogical thoughtfulness" (Taylor, Taylor, & Luitel, 2012). In this chapter, you may recognize the different value systems that have surrounded me throughout my life. The chapter addresses two key themes:

- Transitioning as a novice researcher from positivism to new research paradigms.
- Excavating and reconceptualising my cultural-teaching identity.

HISASHI OTSUJI

EPISODE 1: REFLECTION ON OLD MEMORIES

Noisy Silence in LEGO Play

What is your oldest memory? For me, I clearly remember stirring a big tin container. It was my treasure box because it was full of LEGO puzzle pieces. Because my mother was a nurse she often went to the hospital to take care of her parents in law before I went to school. I accompanied my mother and almost every time she bought me a small package of LEGO pieces. I enjoyed assembling LEGO in the hallway of the hospital. For my mother, that was the way to treat me, not as a boy sitting quietly on bench with nothing to do. This was why I had plenty of LEGO pieces in the tin box.

Imagine that the boy is quietly sitting on a tatami mat on a humid summer day and is stirring the plastic pieces, making a big noise. Generally, you may imagine that his mother would appear and shout, "Quiet!", because such an imagined character typically focusses only on what is observed. On the contrary, my mother sewed or ironed sitting beside me in silence, and there were a lot of activities going on in the boy's mind. I was making something that I was aiming at. So, I had a plan, looking to the future. I was searching for a certain piece of a certain size and colour to assemble. So, I referred to my memory of using the piece before, looking back to the past. In the noisy silence there was a discourse within the self.

When I teach *the discovery of children* in the history of Western education to teacher candidates, I introduce this story as well as the writings of Jean-Jacques Rousseau, Ellen Key and Philippe Ariès, who are recognized as the discoverers of the child in the Western history of education. To be a teacher it is important to be sensitive with a strong imagination about the workings of children's minds (Otsuji, 2016). As I mentioned above, a narrative approach, based on the qualitative research paradigm, shows us a kind of powerful reality. On the other hand, behaviorism, which is based on positivism, is another type of powerful scientific approach that captures visible phenomena (mostly numerically measurable) and adopts the objective and logical approach (Rohmann, 1999). In this chapter I take the former approach.

Fate

I was born the grandson of a Buddhist priest in a Tokyo suburb. Since the temple was relatively old and served as a land mark for the community, I felt pressure to behave nicely all the time, not to raise any disgrace for the temple, and I felt pride at being a member of this family. The name of the temple is Dai-en-ji – the temple of big circle – which in Zen Buddhism represents an wholistic worldview, repeated relationships and the web of causality.

Fate might have affected my character. As a young boy, I gained the way to behave with dexterity, sensitively perceiving or predicting others' facial expressions. Saying "Quiet!" to my classmates, I often prevented the whole class from incurring the anger of our home-room teacher in elementary school days.

Since my parents were a secondary art teacher and a nurse (both occupations are appreciated by students and patients), it was natural for their son to select a job in the field of education, to serve others.

I saw my father teach junior high school students. Also, I saw my grandfather and uncle preach in front of people. I could not understand their meaning at all when I was a boy. However, my readiness to talk in front of people in the future might have emerged at that time. The first image of a teacher was to deliver knowledge to people. This was developed naturally in my early days.

Dissection of a Flower

Let me quickly insert an episode of my elementary school days, which is very much concerned with cultural identity. It is an old memory of when I first took a lesson in the science lab at school (Otsuji & Taylor, 2007).

The lesson was the dissection of a flower. Tweezers, drawing paper, and a flower were distributed. When I picked up a petal with the cold tweezers, I said, "Ite! (Ouch!)". The drawing paper turned into a dissecting table of flower parts. After putting the parts of the flower on the paper and counting the number of parts, I was waiting for the teacher to pass out glue to each group. I thought we would turn the parts back into the flower's original shape. However, against my expectations, the teacher told us to wrap them up and throw them into the bin. I was very upset. After wrapping them carefully and gently putting them in the bin, I joined my hands to pray naturally in front of the bin. My friends followed me, lining up behind to pray. When I went home after school I could not look at the flowers along the path. They looked like a ghost to me. I just ran and passed by without looking at the flowers. From a scientific and educational point of view, the lesson aimed at making students notice the rule of the number of petals and stamens and the structure of the flower. On the other hand, from the children's view, if you only count the numbers it was not necessary to kill the flower.

You may have already noticed the necessity of a cultural point of view in science education. It is possible to consider a confrontational axis, such as the difference between the sensitive world of children and the scientific world, the aim of the teacher's plan and the effect on the children, the images of Nature of the East and the West. At least, the teacher's job is not limited to simply enhancing understanding of scientific knowledge. We will come back to this point later.

Double Meaning of Sacrificing the Self to Serve Others

I have found that not all young applicants who wish to become teachers share the fundamental motivation of sacrificing the self to serve others. Some students have a dream to be the coach of a sports club activity (such after-school activity is so popular in my country that an international comparative survey revealed Japanese teachers' working hours are the longest) (OECD, 2013). And most students aim to be an active performer who transfers knowledge and skills while standing in front of the children. Conversely, if a teacher really wants to serve students, to develop their abilities, he/she had better erase this primitive objective and think how to make contact with children in each and every moment. Serving students denies one's selfish eagerness and, instead, supports thoughtful action and inaction. Ellen Key argued that "the great secret of education lies hidden in the maxim, 'do not educate'?" (Key, 1909, p. 109).

Sacrificing the self for children has a double meaning. First, it literally means to work for students with the same eagerness as in many other occupations. This is observable. The second deeper meaning is denying or restricting the teacher's wish to actively work for children (i.e., sacrificing the self); he/she consciously selects the best way at each and every moment. It does not mean taking explicit action immediately for the child, but sometimes to choose not to teach based on the child's propensity. Let me continue how I became a teacher trainer holding such a notion.

EPISODE II: EXPERIENCES THAT SHATTERED MY PRECONCEPTIONS

When I enrolled in the elementary teacher training course of Chiba University in the mid 1980s, I had the ambition to be the best teacher in Japan and to write a school textbook in the future. I did not have any philosophy and kept the primitive image of teacher as deliverer of scientific knowledge. It was the time when STS (now socio-scientific) issues had been raised in the research of science education field (Ziman, 1980). I remember not only global warming but many issues, such as deforestation, population explosion, environmental hormones, desertification and AIDS, were highlighted as alarming at that time. There was also an argument about the role of science education on these issues. It was said that science education had not played an important role in helping to prevent or solve these issues. The STS movement was based on the paradigm of criticalism, which "concerns with social justice, bio-cultural diversity and sustainable eco-systems" (Taylor, Taylor, & Luitel, 2012). On the one hand, there was an easy way of thinking that scientific knowledge might solve social issues but, on the other hand, there was also an advocating voice to firmly recognize the double-edged sword of science. For me, I was so interested that I wrote a bachelor's thesis about STS education. However, I could not become enthusiastic because: (1) I thought pointing out these issues is like threatening, and threatening cannot be a major motivation for children to study; (2) the social issues related to science were not new for me who had been grown in Japan which had been attacked by atomic bombs in the 1940s, and experienced pollution diseases since the 1950s. People had become indifferent and numb; and (3) personally I was trained in an attached school as a student teacher at that time and I was more interested in the practical aspect of science education.

Being a student-teacher was a huge event for me as my image of teaching dramatically changed from idealism to pragmatism (Ornstein & Hunkins, 2012). In the pragmatism of John Dewey, "experience emerges in a continual interaction between people and environment and, accordingly, this process constitutes both the subjects and the objects of inquiry" (Greenwood & Levin, 2000, p. 95). Below, I list what I learned through practical training and part-time teaching. These were just proverbs for me when I first heard them, however, the meanings expanded as my understanding of education progressed and they became principles of good teaching.

Principles of Good Teaching

"Teacher does not teach, but waits". I noticed this was similar to Ellen Key's maxim. Teachers in the attached school did not mention Ellen Key. They might not have known Ellen Key, however, they had reached the same conclusion. I learned a similar lesson from a senior teacher when I taught general earth science as a part-time teacher to bright high school students in the early 1990s. He said, "Think what not to teach". I understood that this means, between the lines, to prepare a lot, make a story, and select what not to teach.

"Teacher does not teach. School textbook neither. But the experiment teaches the answer". This is the favorite phrase of Mr. Fujio Hiramatsu who has been leading the practice of elementary science teaching in my country. I will come back to this phrase later in this chapter.

"Guess and follow the natural flow of children's thinking". A teacher of the attached elementary school kept mentioning this maxim many times. Children's inquiry and learning are an endless flow. I think this statement which respects the autonomy of children shares the common direction of Johann Pestalozzi, John Dewey, William Kilpatrick and Helen Parkhurst. The student-oriented approach was brought from Oswego, the USA, in the 1870s by the last samurai, Hideo Takamine, the father of the normal university in my country.

"Not to teach what students can gain by themselves". This reminds me of the notion of the ZPD, or the Zone of Proximal Development, of Lev Vygotsky. Although Vygotsky might have appreciated the positive role of teacher's involvement, for me this statement illustrates that a child freely explores in the warm atmosphere of the teacher. I do not deny either of them. Sometimes the former gains approval and the latter gets backing at another time.

"One board in one lesson". This is typical in elementary school. Teachers should complete and provide a well-organized blackboard when the class ends, for students to reflect on the aim, the methods, the results and conclusion. Many of the students' inquiries stand on the platform of positivism.

"Evaluate how students changed". What is evaluated is not the observable performance of teachers but the invisible mind work or change in children. Even though the national best teacher performs very well, if all students are falling asleep

such a class is meaningless. Ellen Key's and Japanese teachers' maxims are to warn the teacher who is full of enthusiasm but lacks consideration.

"Share an idea with classmates". When a teacher supports and enhances students' debate he/she sometimes praises with a single comment, such as "Good point" or "Good question". For the student whose comment was appreciated he/she would be positive toward school activities. Most of the other students might praise the comment and the classroom transforms into a better society, little by little. Of course, it is natural that some students rebel or envy the "good students", like Draco Malfoy of Harry Potter. However, teachers need to deepen the discussion. Higher expectations of teachers lead to higher performance of students. It is very important to widen the focus from the individual learner to the learners as a group. In the 1980s, we experienced the emergence of social constructivism which focused on the relationship of learners and the environment, after earlier constructivist research that had focused mainly on individual learning.

In teacher training programs the above principles are significant for my teacher candidates. Since many novice teachers initially do not care to observe their students' faces, these teachings serve as guidelines for such candidates. For example, I instruct my teacher candidates that after receiving a good comment from a child do not proceed immediately by saying, "Good! Then...". Classroom teaching does not consist of one-to-one teacher-student relationships. Instead, talk to all students: "How many understand what she said? She raised a very important point. Say it again to all please?" Giving students such an opportunity plays an important role in enhancing not only their understanding of the lesson content but also the humanistic ties of the group and their attitude toward democracy. Many talented teachers look forward to how much their student group grows in this way during the year.

Experiences Abroad

In the late 1980s, I had the opportunity to spend half a year as an intern in British Columbia, Canada. I stayed in teachers' homes, visited local schools, and introduced Japanese culture to Canadian students in grades 3 to 12. I found many differences between schools in Canada and Japan. For example, Japanese teachers drew lines on the school yard to make an athletics track, but Canadians did not. The Japanese staff room was a chaos of papers, but there were only tables, chairs and refrigerators in the Western staff room. Classroom windows were larger in Japan, facing mainly to the south. Since most Japanese people are right-handed, students study facing west. Canadian people seemed not to be concerned about the sunlight and direction.

I also found similar ways of teaching and teachers' attitudes across the Pacific Ocean. I was observing a practical class in an outdoor school. When the teacher explained the method of how to fertilize fish, he said:

We need to strike the salmon and stun them. We get fresh sperm out of the male salmon by squeezing. They are released back to the river afterwards. And we need to cut the female's belly to take out thousands of eggs.

Students went into a panic, and the teacher continued:

I do not want to hear your shouting and laughing. This is the treatment. Why have salmon swum up to our stream here after a very long swim? To? To spawn. Yes. This is the treatment of human beings to, to what? To help their wish. We help the parent salmons' wish, which is very much a sacred time. If you don't want to watch the moment just close your eyes or face sideways in silence. That's fine.

I was so impressed by the teacher's deep, careful treatment toward life and the students. As I mentioned in the episode of the dissection of flowers, teachers should be careful when they treat and teach about living things. This educational facility was later honoured as the best environmental learning facility in Canada.

So, during my 20s I trained in and out of my country. These events broke my shell and de-constructed my inner life in Japan, my image of children, and the way of teaching. It may have been a preparation period.

EPISODE III: WORKING AS A TEACHER TRAINER

Most of the university students who graduate from colleges of education in Japan become teachers in public schools. However, I felt that I had something more to study before standing in front of young students. So, I enrolled in a master's degree program at Chiba University. My master's dissertation focused on the issue of the relationship between human beings and nature in the context of the high school science education curriculum. It was 1991 when the new textbooks were introduced after the course of study had been revised. I conducted a survey targeting high school science teachers to reveal their opinions about this issue. It was not high impact research, but I was satisfied with the result. I revealed high school teachers' wishes and the gap between their wishes and what they were teaching. They certainly had a wish to talk to students about social issues related to science, however, they faced some barriers. I summarised them as the three "Js" that prevented high school science teachers from teaching integrated content: Junbi (preparation or materials), Jikan (time, no time to teach the new unit), and Juken (entrance examination to university). The motive for my master's dissertation was aligned with the criticalism paradigm and the survey methodology was based on positivism.

After the master's degree I had the hope of getting a research job in a university. However, I felt that I lacked scientific methodologies for teaching and researching in higher education institutes. This was why I moved to the Educational Technology Centre of the Tokyo Institute of Technology, to obtain powerful quantitative approaches of positivism. Initially, I thought my knowledge, skills and attitude as a science educator would be more powerful after they had been blended with the methodologies of educational technology. I thought that such methodologies would be necessary for producing research papers after I got a job in a university. What did I learn? In my understanding, the engineering approach determines a problem, proposes a hypothesis, takes an appropriate action and test, evaluates with provided criteria, gives feedback, and modifies the hypothesis or model. The researchers of the scientific community seemed to believe that they can come close to the truth by repeating this cyclic procedure. Intuitively, I came to sympathize with the students who were subjected to immature treatment in these research studies, wondering "is this experimental lesson really for the students' benefit?" Therefore, I chose concept mapping as my theme which is used as an evaluation tool, based on positivism, and also serves as a learning method in practical situations. This theme seemed to be better for subject students. However, my previous experience prevented me from going further. I could not bridge the two cultures of research and practice at that time. I left there after three years of training.

In 1995, I was appointed lecturer at Ibaraki University and started to teach mainly elementary science education methodology. Since the job was more related to practical teaching and learning than cognitive research work, I was very satisfied. Several years later I had an opportunity to join the editorial board of a school science textbook. Thus, I could make one of my old dreams come true. Now, I am very satisfied with my former students who have become good science teachers. During their university days I arranged for them to meet Mr. Hiramatsu, the retired veteran science teacher. He kindly came to our university and instructed on the essence of science education. A few of these graduate students now work at attached schools of Chiba University and Ibaraki University. I was able to connect the upper generation to the next generation.

In parallel with my education duties, I have also been working on my own research activities. As I was interested in the practical aspects of science education, I wanted to know the roots of Mr. Hiramatsu's teaching practice. So, during my doctoral research I studied the history of Japanese science education. I found that the proverbs I had learned at the attached school in the 1980s were in accordance with the principles of Pestalozzi. And, as mentioned above, Hideo Takamine had introduced this theory, methodology and practice into Japan in the late 1870s. The following is the list of good teaching principles summarised by his teacher, Edward Austin Sheldon (1862, pp. 14–15):

1. Activity is a law of childhood. Accustom the child to do – educate the hand.
2. Cultivate the faculties in their natural order – first from the mind, then furnish it.
3. Begin with the senses, and never tell a child what he can discover for himself.
4. Reduce every subject to its elements – one difficulty at a time is enough for a child.
5. Proceed step by step. Be thorough. The measure of information is not what the teacher can give, but what the child can receive.

WHERE DO I COME FROM? WHAT AM I? WHERE AM I GOING?

6. Let every lesson have a point; either immediate or remote.
7. Develop the idea – then give the term – cultivate language.
8. Proceed from the known to the unknown – from the particular to the general – from the concrete to the abstract – from the simple to the more difficult.
9. First synthesis, then analysis – not the order of the subject, but the order of nature.

Even though this tradition was interrupted due to World War II, the flow was inherited particularly in a few attached elementary schools. Chiba University where I was trained as a student teacher is one of them, and Mr. Hiramatsu once taught there. This discovery was an unexpected coincidence, but I was able to know the roots of my own practical interests.

It was natural for me to shift from a quantitative to a qualitative research approach. But, at the time, there were no researchers who had adopted qualitative methodologies in science education in Japan. I think I was a stray sheep. I knocked on the doors of several researchers abroad and finally visited Science and Mathematics Education Centre of Curtin University where I met Dr. Peter Taylor. He proposed an auto/ethnographic methodology which gave me the light to penetrate the various elements related to science education that I was holding. The following is the definition I learned at that time.

> Autobiography...focuses on the researcher's own life-history, involves writing in the narrative first-person voice, and can give unique insights into the social and cultural forces shaping his/her own practice...helping the researcher to deal with his/her own biases prior to interpreting and representing the perspectives of other participants...reveal hidden cultural forces influencing the social structures of schooling, the curriculum and their own pedagogies...[it] commences with a descriptive account of key-issues and develops further into reflective thinking, generating new insights and heightening the researcher's sensitivities towards those issues, thereby enabling the researcher to see his/her research in the context of his/her biography and culture. (Taylor & Settelmaier, 2003, p. 233)

The encounter with auto/ethnography enabled and enhanced me to confront the self deeply. At the same time, it would be better to have a central theme to work with. Fortunately, I was given good advice by chance. It was a colleague, a professor of philosophy, who murmured that the teacher is like a Bodhisattva. At that moment I felt that I could see another light shining from far away.

Bodhisattva has a few meanings, but the most important concept in Mahayana Buddhism is the group of people in training for being awakened. This is ranked second to Tathagata (Buddha) which is the group of special persons who have already awakened. From this point of view, Bodhisattva postpones his own training and gives priority to save sentient beings. This image overlays the common ideal image of teachers in my country. The teacher is Bodhisattva. All my concerns seemed to be combined around this notion. The sacrificing attitude of teachers for students, or the virtue to share ideas with others, can be interpreted as the influence of Mahayana Buddhism in Japan.

Looking back at the self, I have been educated at Chiba University where Pestalozzi's thoughts, method and spirit were inherited unconsciously, and I have been tying together my seniors and juniors. I can find the self in the big circle of the flow of practical elementary science teachers in Japan. Situated in this circle and looking around, I notice that the name of my original temple – Dai-en-ji – had signified my long journey.

EPISODE IV: ARRIVING AT A NEW DESTINATION

Working in a college of education and training teacher candidates should have been what I wanted. However, I recently left Ibaraki University and moved to Toyo University which is one of the largest private universities in Japan (Toyo means "orient"). There were repulsion and attraction forces. Since the Ministry of Education of Japan gave the order to reform local national universities, some researchers who were good at coaching children were targeted to engage in community contributions to their university. However, I was not satisfied with the many meetings for these undesired reforms and many on-site activities. I prefer to be an expert who focuses on continuous and holistic human growth by teaching undergraduates. Also, I want freedom and time to concentrate on my interests, such as Japanese folk culture that helps with the search for cultural identity and disaster prevention education which can be interpreted as the interface between human beings and nature, environmental education or STS education, as well as my dissertation theme.

A particular condition at Toyo University strongly attracted me. It was the teaching duty to be in charge of general introduction to education for fresh students. It would be a challenging duty that I had not been involved in before, but I relished the challenge because I want to reorganize science education firmly in terms of the whole discussion around pedagogy. This is why I have mentioned several educational theorists in this chapter. I have just started and it will be a never-ending challenge.

In conclusion, I may have been making a bridge between two things. I tried to combine the previously seen pieces of LEGO with the puzzle being conceived. As an intern, I tried to be a bridge myself between Japan and Canada. When the science education field is divided into two regions of theory and practice, I prefer to be a bridge between them. Now I aim at establishing another bridge between science education and general educational theories for the next generation.

Recently I often visit the hospital to take care of my mother. Though I do not have a small kid to accompany me, I am thinking of how to hand over what I have received from the older generation to the next generation, more as a package of practical science education blended with general educational theories. For me, writing auto/ethnographically reminds me of stirring the big tin can of LEGO pieces. I look for pieces that I have experienced and pile them up into a meaningful work of art.

REFERENCES

Greenwood, D. J., & Levin, M., (2000). Reconstructing the relationship between universities and society through action research. In N. K. Denzin & Y. S. Lincoln (Eds.), *Handbook of qualitative research* (2nd ed., pp. 85–106). Thousand Oaks, CA: Sage Publications.

Key, E. (1909). *The century of the child*. New York, NY: Arno Press.

OECD. (2013). *Japan-country note, in Teaching and Learning International Survey (TALIS) 2013: An international perspective on teaching and learning*. Retrieved from http://dx.doi.org/10.1787/9789264196261-21-en

Ornstein, A. C., & Hunkins, F. P. (2012). *Curriculum: Foundations, principles, and issues* (6th ed.). Upper Saddle River, NJ: Pearson.

Otsuji, H. (2016, August). Fushigi no tane wo [Seeding the wonder]. In *The attached kindergarten of the college of education, Ibaraki university* (pp. 76–80), *Tanoshiku Asonde Kodomo wo Nobasu* [Growing children playing happily]. Tokyo: Fukumura Shuppan.

Otsuji, H., & Taylor, P. C. (2007, July). *Teacher as nurturer: Engaging pre-service science teachers in worldview learning*. Paper presented at the 2007 World Conference on Science & Technology Education, Perth.

Rohmann, C. (1999). *A world of ideas*. New York, NY: Ballantine Books.

Sheldon, E. A. (1862). *A manual of elementary instruction: For the use of public and private schools and normal classes, II. Pestalozzian plans and principles*. New York, NY: Charles Scribner.

Taylor, P. C., & Settelmaier, E. (2003). Critical autobiographical research for science educators. *Journal of Science Education Japan, 27*(4), 233–244.

Taylor, P. C., Taylor, E., & Luitel, B. C. (2012). Multi-paradigmatic transformative research as/for teacher education: An integral perspective. In K. G. Tobin, B. J. Fraser, & C. McRobbie (Eds.), *Second international handbook of science education* (pp. 373–387). Dordrecht: Springer.

Ziman, J. M. (1980). *Teaching and learning about science and society*. London: Cambridge University Press.

ABOUT THE AUTHOR

Hisashi Otsuji is my name. I grew up in a Zen Buddhism temple in a Tokyo suburb. Coincidentally I received practical training at the attached school of Chiba university where the Pestalozzian method of teaching was inherited. After I studied at Tokyo Institute of Technology, I turned to teach the methodology of science education at Ibaraki University. I am currently teaching at Toyo University, and I am also the Deputy Director of the Center for Teacher Certification Program. My main research interest focuses on the interface of human beings and nature.

MANGARATUA M. SIMANJORANG

11. BEING ANIMATED BY A TRANSFORMATIVE SOUL

Ethical Responsibility in Mathematics Education

My Dream – My Anxiety

When my eyes opened	When my eyes opened
When my ears widened	When my ears widened
My lips smiled	My lips trembled
My heart refreshed	My heart shrivelled
Green carpet made from tropical forests	Red carpet made from fire and blood
Lovely sounds are heard from nature	Horrific screams haunt in dreams
Kind surroundings hum friendly greetings	Harsh surroundings cruelly growl
What a blessing, need nothing else	Humanity decays till nothing less
My hands are opened widely	My hands are crossed on my chest
My feet are stepping happily	My feet are weak but can't rest
In response to the call	Who will respond to the call?
As will be done by all	Worried eyes, leery ears repel the call
Brother and friends	No friends, let alone brother
Together in difference	Difference means nightmare
Mindful of diversity	Distrustful of diversity
Keep growing in unity	Elicits exclusivity

Living and growing in diversity has enabled me to realize that diversity can become a strength as well as a weakness. Understanding differences has helped me sharpen myself and strengthen my standing in life. However, differences without respect can also lead to schism. Small conflicts fuelled by differences might grow into tragic conflict, as has happened in parts of Indonesia, such as Sampit in 2001 and Ambon in 1999. Remembering these horribly tragic conflicts makes it hard for me to breathe. Sometimes I cannot imagine, indeed am afraid to imagine, the future of my country if such conflicts continue.

But it is also true that differences in diversity can be a source of harmony. The sound of a piano itself is good to hear, however, when it comes together with different instruments it can help form the harmony of an orchestra. This depends on how each element relates to the other, whether dominating or respecting the other.

The way we respond to the other may determine the other's reaction, and vice versa. When I experience a positive feeling from the other I feel comfortable and open myself more. However, when I experience a negative feeling from the other then negative pressure from this feeling naturally pushes me to defend myself and close myself to the source of this pressure. Thus, it is important to reflect on our ability to respond to the other. This *response ability* is one of the interpretations of the term responsibility (Atweh & Brady, 2009). So, how should I respond to the other?

As a member of a society encountering the other is an unavoidable event. And as a social creature it is human nature to build relationships with others. However, conflict may occur in these relationships. Considering this I have a responsibility to the others in my community to form relationships that establish a harmonious social life. The responsibility that occurs in my relationships with others brings forth ethics. When I encounter the other, while I am being close to the other, ethics is born (Egéa-Kuehne, 2008). Since I have these relationships in my daily life then ethics is a must for me. Thus I am called to live ethically in my community.

However, to be called to live ethically is not sufficient in my position as a mathematics teacher educator in Universitas Negeri Medan, one of the public universities in Medan, Indonesia. As a lecturer in this university I also bring a responsibility to help the other, especially my students, to live ethically. So, a question arises in my mind: how can education help students to have a concern for ethical responsibility in their lives? Further, in my position as a mathematics educator this question leads me to consider how I can integrate ethics into mathematics education. But this chapter is not intended to answer these questions. Instead, I want to reveal how I was transformed in the process of conducting a doctoral research inquiry in which I sought answers to two questions: "What does being a researcher mean to me?", and "How am I transformed by doing this research?". These questions will guide the discussion offered throughout this chapter. Details can be found in my doctoral thesis (Simanjorang, 2016).

In this chapter I uncover some of the aspects of the methodology of my doctoral study and my reflections on the concept of ethics. These seemingly different aspects were closely related since the methodology enabled me to arrive at a new understanding of the concept of ethics. To be exact, the methodology enabled me to transform my view of ethics. Based on my newly conceptualised multi-paradigmatic research perspective (Taylor, Taylor, & Luitel, 2012), I designed a "philosophical-auto/ethnographic" methodology.

Auto/ethnography enabled me to connect my personal experiences to my cultural, social and political background (Ellis, 2004). This required me to express my whole self in order to better understand myself in relation to the culture to which I belong. By coming to understand myself I deepened my understanding of my culture, including the mathematics education culture that is a large part of my professional life. The symbol "/" in auto/ethnography represents a dialectical relationship between auto (the self) and ethnography (the other) "without one denying legitimacy of the other" (Taylor, Taylor, & Luitel, 2012).

The term *philosophical* signifies that I employed conceptual analysis that complemented my auto/ethnographical path. Philosophical inquiry is not necessarily about the empirical world, rather it is about the nature of our concepts about the empirical world, which makes philosophy a conceptual analysis (Daly, 2010). Through conceptual analysis I endeavoured to discover the elements that construct concepts and how they are related (Bunnin & Yu, 2004). The clearer the relationship becomes, the deeper the understanding I would have in this process. Frequently, the elements that construct a concept are also embedded in another concept that also may need to be analysed. In the process of discovering the relationship between elements and concepts I found that I grew along with my understanding. Hence, it is not an exaggeration to say that conceptual analysis is not merely a method that I employed to understand ethical concepts but also was a path of my growth as an ethical human being and professional educator. My choice of using conceptual analysis relates to my mathematical background. With this background, conceptual analysis had become part of my way of thinking before I started this inquiry. Hence, in accordance with the goal of better understanding myself and my culture, I chose to acknowledge this aspect of myself. My philosophical-auto/ethnographic methodology enabled me to learn and to be transformed in this study.

HOW DO I SEE RESEARCH?

As a postgraduate student, I designed and conducted a research study during my doctoral degree programme. Therefore, I could call myself a researcher. While doing this research I found myself learning many things. I was not only a researcher but also a learner. In this case, I was a learner not because I was a student but because I was doing research. I was a learner because I was a researcher.

The way I see research has changed over time. In the past, the term *research* was always related to data, especially ways to collect and analyze data. Earlier in my life, as a bachelor degree student, I understood research as merely a way to achieve graduation. Although I learned and benefited from that experience, it was merely a matter of fulfilling the requirement to graduate. Later, when I completed a master degree, I came to see research as a way to develop knowledge and advance understanding. Through research I can examine or verify an assumption or hypothesis. I can also use research to develop learning materials or evaluate an education program.

But as a doctoral research student, I had my eyes opened much wider. The reflective activity that I experienced during the research process helped me to cultivate *mindfulness*. Mindfulness is about being present in and aware of the moment (Tobin, 2016). To be right here right now, that is, engaged deeply with the present moment enabled me to gain more understanding of the moment (Hanh, 1996). By means of this understanding I came to realise that the more I learn the more I can see that the less knowledge I actually have. If I once felt confident and mature after my master degree, now I feel that I'm just a kid in this massive world of knowledge. I have come to realize that the greatest value of my research lies in my self-development. This realization then drew my interest to the idea of transformative research.

If doing research allows me to develop and improve myself then there is a transformative potential within the research itself. I would like to call this kind of research, which possesses a *transformative soul*, transformative research. Here I am using the term *soul* metaphorically, knowing that it may be interpreted differently based on our different standpoints or worldviews. As for me, I have been growing up under the influence of Catholicism, both in education and society; and thus traces of the influence of Catholicism may be found in my views. I understand soul as the life source that comes from God and represents the will of God. Soul is also seen as the innermost aspect of humans that holds the greatest value of being human as it spiritually animates the body in the image of God (Catechism of the Catholic Church Part 1, Sect. 2, Chap. 1, Par. 363). Humans become whole by body and soul. There is no living body without the soul, while the soul is incorporeal without the body. However, it is not that there are two different natures, body and soul, in one human; instead the union of body and soul creates a single nature (Catechism of the Catholic Church Part 1, Sect. 2, Chap. 1, Par. 365).

By using the term soul metaphorically, I am trying to draw a relationship between research and transformative ideas analogically with what I understand about the relationship of body and soul. Since there is no living body without a soul then research will lose its essence without a soul. As in the body and soul relationship, the transformative idea is not an additional character imbued into the research but is united with the research itself. In the transformative soul there is a will; a drive that would guide the whole research activity. The soul in research is a foundation that influences perspectives or assumptions. In this regard, if I claim that a particular research possesses a transformative soul then it means that the research uses the transformative idea as its very foundation. Then, what is this transformative idea?

Jack Mezirow provided the key to this idea as critical reflection on presumptions that emphasize our values or beliefs (Taylor, 2015). The transformative idea encourages us to critically rethink what we believe. Critical reflection may help us become more aware of ourselves, our society and our environment, which later may help us to consciously relate what we have in our inner and outer worlds (Taylor, 2015). This consciousness is necessary for us to be able to critically rethink and reshape the relationship between our inner and outer worlds in order to improve ourselves in the transformative process. In this regard, transformative research should allow all participants, including the researcher, to reconceptualize and reshape this relationship. In other words, it is not only respondents but also researcher who has an opportunity to transform. And this is how I became a learner as a researcher.

MY STANDPOINT AS A RESEARCHER IN DIFFERENT PARADIGMS

Our standpoint influences what we can see, and this is also the case in research. It seems that having a mathematics education background with the strong influence of statistical methods situated me not far from positivist and post-positivist research perspectives. I am not saying that every person with a similar background will have a similar view to mine, yet I can say that my background strongly influenced me. Research for me had always been about an effort to find the truth (Willis, 2007) or maybe get closer to the truth. By saying getting closer to the truth, I am embracing the doubt that ultimate truth has yet to be uncovered. At the same time, I had no doubt that the truth was out there to be uncovered (Guba, 1990). Hence, in spite of this doubt I can now say that I was more a post-positivist than positivist researcher who confidently affirmed that good research should result in a theory that reflects the truth (Willis, 2007).

I started my study with an action research design that would enable me to collaborate with a mathematics teacher and her students in year three of a primary school in my hometown. My goal was to enable the teacher to develop a practice of ethical responsibility in her own classroom practice. However, I soon discovered that my post-positivist research standpoint of objectivity and value-neutrality prevented me from intervening with my participants. I was like a fisherman who actively observes the fish swimming in the water while preventing myself from getting into the water, since it can disturb the water and the fish (Medina & Taylor, 2013). Furthermore, I realised that I lacked a proper foundation for explaining ethical responsibility in mathematics education. When I encountered these constraints I understood the limits of my ontological perspective, and I realised that it was neither the situation nor the time to attempt an in-depth explanation of the place of ethical responsibility in mathematics education. Hence, I switched my research orientation to a more soulful research paradigm that enabled me to develop a deeper understanding of ethical responsibility in the context of my own professional practice.

I realised that I needed to reflect critically on my own experiences in which I encounter the other. In other words, rather than looking for the truth *out there*, I started to consider searching for the truth inside myself. At this point I considered the different natures of truth, as mentioned by Lakoff and Johnson (2003): truth is relative to a person's conceptual system or, in other words, truth is based on our individual understanding. We gain our understanding of truth through meaning construction carried out in interpreting our experience (Taylor, 2015). Thus, I needed to consider the issue that each person can interpret experiences differently from others. In respect of this difference, I realized that it was not appropriate to impose my understandings on others, yet neither was it appropriate for me to take for granted the truth seen solely from another's point of view. So, I needed to critically inquire into and interpret my experiences while relating to the ideas of another person.

According to this conclusion, post-positivism was not appropriate as the principal paradigm for my research. My concern was that my subjectivity should not be avoided. Rather, I needed to bring it forward for careful consideration. Moreover, the ontology of my research was no longer that conceived in post-positivism, since I was seeking ontological understanding from inside myself, not merely from the objective measurable outside. Therefore, the epistemology of my research should correspond to this view as well; the rigid scientific approach was no longer appropriate. I could not separate myself conceptually from other participants in this research; instead, I wanted to gain more understanding through being closely related to the other. I wanted to understand not only from my point of view but also from the other's. I wanted to inquire and re-inquire into existing theories and practical understandings, especially mine, of ethics and mathematics education and their putative relationship. Hence, I decided to employ a multi-paradigmatic research approach, which is termed *critical-interpretive-postmodernism* (Taylor, Taylor, & Luitel, 2012). From this standpoint, I would not only get into the water, but also swim with the fish to get a clearer understanding of the nature of the fish and my relationship with them.

INFLUENCE OF A MULTI-PARADIGMATIC VIEW

How did a multi-paradigm standpoint influence me during my study? Learning about different paradigms and how they were developed historically enriched my viewpoint. It was when I undertook my master degree that I first heard about *mixed methods*, where a researcher employs qualitative and quantitative methods in the same study. At that time, I witnessed a doctoral candidate defending his choice of mixed methods in front of some professors who were questioning that choice. I remember one professor saying that it was impossible to combine quantitative and qualitative methods since they were based on different paradigms that embrace totally different philosophies. At that time I could see that even between the professors the application of mixed methods was debatable.

In this period of time, I was often trapped in truth bivalence, where there were only two choices: right or wrong, true or false, right or left, yes or no. Until now actually I find it is not easy for me to choose between these two choices. Sometimes I asked myself, "Which professor should I follow, the one that was against mixed methods or the other one?" Each of them raised a strong argument. However, if I reflect on the practice of mixed methods at that time, I might say that most of the researchers, postgraduate students of the university where I did my master degree, who practised mixed methods, were using a qualitative method in one part of the study and a quantitative method in another part. In other words, the methods were used separately. One method was used for one purpose or purposes and another one was used for other purpose(s). In this case, I might say that technically they employed two different methods, but in a philosophical or paradigmatic view they just used them differently. It could be said that there were two separate studies within one research. Apparently these two separate studies employed different methods. This practice actually is different from the idea of a multi-paradigmatic view.

New paradigms were not necessarily coming to replace the old ones, but they might complement one another. Quantitative methods, which come from the positivist paradigm, and qualitative methods, which come from the interpretive or post-positivist paradigms, might complement each other, since each of them has limitations derived from the paradigmatic view where they came from. Data from quantitative methods might highlight specific conditions that need more attention and to be responded to with further deep study using qualitative methods. At the end, such collaboration of different methods may produce a more complex and comprehensive result.

This understanding is nothing new. So, what actually did I learn from a multi-paradigmatic view? Of course, it is not only that different methods or paradigms can collaborate. What I learned is respect. Each idea or thought is worth valuing. With respect, I was able to switch my focus and learn some values. Instead of justifying between true-false or right-wrong choices I started to focus on value seeking. With this switched focus, instead of trying to find which argument or view about mixed methods was the right one between the professors, I started to try to find what valuable thoughts I could learn from their different views. As an example, the professor that asserted the philosophical base of a method raised the value of the root of a method. It reminded me not only to think at a technical level, how to use a method, but also to think at the philosophical level to have a deeper understanding of the method. In this case, it did not matter whether the professor chose to reject mixed methods or not. Instead, respecting what value I could learn from the professor's argument or statement was what matters. Finding this value helped me to have deeper understanding, which I could use later to make my own choice. Respect encouraged me to find possible values instead of merely judging between right and wrong. The willingness to learn this possible value led me to arrive at the idea of integrative ethics.

THE IDEA OF INTEGRATIVE ETHICS

In the process of studying how to integrate ethics into mathematics education, I reflected on various ethical views, which eventually brings me to an ethical view I call *integrative ethics*. Differences in ethics concepts show that there are a lot of ways to explain and approach ethics. The variety of concepts may be seen as well as a sign about how our views and understandings of ethics are limited. As we have found through history, as well as its followers every concept also came with its critics. Therefore, perhaps we need many concepts to describe ethics and not fewer (William, 2006). One concept exclusively may limit our understanding, while integrating concepts may extend it. Courage as a promoted characteristic of virtue ethics is also a character displayed by terrorists in their actions, and they are proud of this action. Duty or rule sometimes becomes an alibi for misconduct when it is blindly followed without conscience. Even the exclusivity of some religions, which are presumed to teach peace, also happen sometimes to be a reason for conflict. When virtue character stands alone we may have less guidance on how to act. While when merely duty leads our steps we may act without conscience. And the excessive fanaticism of one religion may loosen respect toward diversity. Do we not need courage, integrity and other characters to convey our duty, to fill our actions with our beliefs, to search for happiness for ourselves and for others?

That is why we need integration of these concepts of ethics. Integration will be able to reduce the incompleteness of each one when each stands alone. Consideration within this integration would cover the action and the person who acts, the principles and the person who implements them. An integrative ethics view asserts inclusivity against different views. Integrative ethics inclusively respects differences, which means being open to different views in a critical and respectful way. The term *different view* implicitly requires awareness about one's own position and how it may differ, or be similar, to the others' position. Without awareness it is impossible to recognize the differences, or similarities, between views. Hence, integrative ethics suggests the importance of awareness. So, what is the implication of this view for my study? If I was to embrace the integrative ethics view in my study then I should consider others' and my own awareness. My presence amongst the participants should help them to raise their awareness, and help me to raise my awareness as well. This awareness will be an *observer point* for both the participants and me to observe our surroundings in order to be able to take a step toward a particular direction.

Awareness is a necessary condition for integrative ethics, but it alone is not enough to gain the inclusive characteristic. My awareness about my position and how it is different to others' may be a good reason for me to exclude the others, which eventually situates me in an exclusive position. Therefore, awareness must be wrapped by respect. I choose the term *wrapped* because respect itself is a sign of awareness. By respecting I acknowledge the existence of differences. Respect is also a response, which shows my openness to the differences. By respecting I am not only aware but am also preventing myself from excluding any view that differs from my view. Furthermore, in order to grow in the inclusive state, I need to think critically about the differences that I am aware of. My further response regarding the differences should come from critical thinking. Critical thinking will be my vehicle to learn and grow in differences. Thinking critically also will raise my awareness and respect. By thinking critically about my own and others' views, I shall become more aware about my position. Thinking critically also brings me understanding about the other's position. This understanding will help me to respect the other even more consciously. So, apparently all these three factors are strengthening each other.

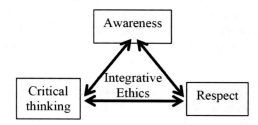

Figure 11.1. Integrative ethics based on awareness, respect and critical thinking

CRITICAL INCLUSIVITY – A QUALITY STANDARD FROM INTEGRATIVE ETHICS

So, how did my view of ethics influence my way of studying? How should this ethical view guide my research? When could I say that I have applied this view in my research practice? As part of the emergent process, these questions directed me to a consideration of generating a quality research standard that suited the view from integrative ethics. In this study, ethics was about how I should respond to the other and how I should relate to the other. Then the quality standard that might be promoted from this view is how I, as a researcher and moreover as myself, should relate to the participants in this study. Since I needed to inclusively respect the others' position then, in this study, I should not impose my own view on the others; rather, I need to respect their views. But what if I believe that there is something wrong with the others' view, should I leave it as it is? Should I contradict myself by respecting a view that goes against mine? Here, I need to be aware that what I believe is not necessarily what the other believes. I need to hold myself and think critically, what if it was my view that is not right? Questioning myself here does not necessarily mean doubting myself. It might act as a pointer for a better self-understanding, which might help me to reshape myself into a better person. There is also the possibility that, in the end, I might find that it is not about right or wrong, but is just different views within different structures.

Up to this point, I am still discussing the benefit of taking the integrative ethics position for myself; then, what is my contribution to the others? Thinking ethically means thinking about my responsibility to the others. How should I respond to the others in a way that may benefit the others? If I am aware that there are different views, then I should help the other (in this study, they are my participants), to become aware about the difference. As I mentioned earlier, awareness is the first step toward respect and critical thinking. Awareness would likely encourage my participants to take the next step toward critical thinking and respect. Being able to respect and think critically will empower the participants to choose freely. In this study, saying that the participants have freedom to choose is not enough. I need to encourage and empower them to choose freely.

The same strategy may be applied when I am introducing them to a new teaching approach. One may ask, "Is it not obvious that I need to tell the participants all about the new approach and they have nothing to do but to follow my instruction, since they know nothing about it?" Based on an inclusive view, even though I am introducing a new approach, I can't force them to use it in the same way that I would. Instead, they should have freedom to choose. I should help them to become aware and encourage them to think critically so that respect may be raised. Then they will be able to choose consciously. Encouraging them so they may become more aware, think critically and respect differences, which would empower them to choose consciously, is my ethical responsibility. It is not my place to change them. Change is not something that I force on the other. Changing is their part to choose, mine is encouraging and empowering.

MANGARATUA M. SIMANJORANG

CRITICAL SELF-REFLECTION AND SELF-AWARENESS THROUGH NARRATIVE INQUIRY

I have revealed so far, albeit briefly, how I learned and transformed by wandering in the vast area of theories while doing my research. In this culminating section, I am sharing how I was learning and was transformed by doing the research itself. For me, it was the method that I chose for the study that helped me to transform, just by doing it.

As a person I came to this study with inseparable ideology, values, and social/historical background. Being influenced by the interpretive and critical paradigms, I needed to consider my social and historical position as a vital element in doing my study (Carter, Lapum, Lavallee, & Martin, 2014) and to make sure that the ideology and values that I held entered intrinsically and inseparably into the methods, interpretations, and epistemology of my research (Carspecken, 1996). This position indicated that important factors were likely to be found in my own life story. So, I needed to uncover them. One way to do this was by narrating my life story, since in order to narrate my story I needed to recall the feelings, emotions, background and meaningful events related to my life story. Through narrative, I could elicit my life story, my experiences, in their complexity and richness (Webster & Mertova, 2007). This was the reason for me to choose *critical narrative inquiry* as the main method of my study. The process of my learning and transformation through this method could be represented by Escher's (1948) *drawing hands*.

I always love to see Escher's extraordinary work. Though I am not an art connoisseur, I have my own interpretation. In this picture I see two hands, and

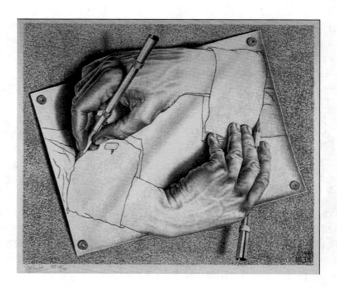

Figure 11.2. Drawing hands, by M. C. Escher

each hand draws the other hand. Both hands have plain two-dimensional and detailed three-dimensional parts. For me, these hands represent myself in my study. One hand represents myself that I understand, and the other is myself that I can tell about in my narrative story through the process of narrative inquiry. The more detailed the story about myself I tell in my narrative, the better the picture of myself I can show. This means that I can only tell my story well if I understand myself well, and the story itself helps me to understand more about myself by providing an opportunity for me to reflect on my story, which eventually reshapes myself. The more detailed the story I make about myself makes the story about myself not only more authentic but also better shapes my understanding about myself. Reciprocally, as my understanding of myself is getting better I can better tell the story about myself.

This process continuously recurred during the critical narrative inquiry within my autoethnographic methodology. In other words, I shaped and reshaped myself into a better person just by doing such research. That is the benefit of using narrative inquiry. It is a method to both represent and study experience (Connelly & Clandinin, 1990). With this method I had a great opportunity to reflect on my experiences and myself. It was in this critical reflexivity where the gate to transformation opened, since I had opportunities to question myself and understand myself. Reflexivity reminded me to engage with the moment in line with consciousness of my cultural, linguistic, political and ideological origins, and with the participants in my study (Cumming-Potvin, 2013). Indeed, I needed to be careful of the risk of becoming a narcissistic fad from an excess of reflexivity (Patai, 1994). But, as described by Davies et al. (2004, p. 386), "the reflexive process is elusive, exhausting and disruptive", but necessary to create meaning.

ENDING AND BEGINNING AGAIN

I grew in this research through the process of cultivating my knowledge and understanding. There are two main factors that allowed me to transform. Respect and openness to differences allowed me to enrich myself when I had access to a vast theoretical area, and the method that I engaged in during this process provided a great opportunity to improve myself. By accessing theories of paradigms and ethics I opened my eyes much wider and could understand my standpoint better while relating to others and to nature. Widened eyes along with critical reflexivity, suggested by the critical narrative inquiry method, encouraged me to respect differences and to attempt to learn positive values instead of merely justifying between right and wrong. Eventually, this attempt brought me to an understanding of a multi-paradigm view, which eventually resulted in the emergence of an integrative ethics view and critical inclusivity as an appropriate quality standard.

Experiencing different things helped me to know my position and myself better. In this process of knowing I improved myself. By doing research I constructed meaning, which allowed me to know better myself and the premises that underpinned and governed me. In this state I was better able to see that which exists that I had been ignoring. When I could thus see, I came to realize about differences and started to learn about relationships. Finding myself was not the end but the beginning of finding other selves, their differences and similarities, and learning how we relate to each other. This knowledge empowered me into becoming a critical being with a vision toward a better world, and having a commitment to action to make the vision real. By being a learner through researching I was transformed in my ways of knowing.

REFERENCES

Atweh, B., & Brady, K. (2009). Socially response-able mathematics education: Implications of an ethical approach. *Eurasia Journal of Mathematics, Science & Technology Education, 5*(2), 135–143.
Bunnin, N., & Yu, J. (2004). *The Blackwell dictionary of Western philosophy*. Oxford: Blackwell Publishing.
Carspecken, P. F. (1996). *Critical ethnography in educational research: A theoretical and practical guide*. New York, NY: Routledge.
Carter, C., Lapum, J. L., Lavallee, L. F., & Martin, L. S. (2014). Explicating positionality: A journey of dialogical and reflexive storytelling. *International Journal of Qualitative Methods, 13*, 362–376.
Catechism of the Catholic Church. Retrieved from http://www.vatican.va/archive/ENG0015/_P1B.HTM#LK
Connelly, F. M., & Clandinin, D. J. (1990). Stories of experience and narrative inquiry. *Educational Researcher, 19*(5), 2–14.
Cumming-Potvin, W. (2013). "New basics" and literacies: Deepening reflexivity in qualitative research. *Qualitative Research Journal, 13*(2), 214–230.
Daly, C. (2010). *An introduction to philosophical methods*. Canada: Broadview Press.
Davies, B., Browne, J., Gannon, S., Honan, E., Laws, C., Mueller-Rockstroh, B., & Bendix, E. (2004). The ambivalent practices of reflexivity. *Qualitative Inquiry, 10*(3), 360–389.
Egxea-Kuehne, D. (2008). *Levinas and education: At the intersection of faith and reason*. New York, NY: Routledge.
Ellis, C. (2004). *The ethnographic i: A methodological novel about autoethnography*. Walnut Creek, CA: AltaMira Press.
Guba, E. (1990). The alternative paradigm dialogue. In E. Guba (Ed.), *The paradigm dialogue* (pp. 17–27). Newbury Park, CA: Sage Publications.
Hanh, T. N. (1996). *The long road turns to joy: A guide to walking meditation*. Berkeley, CA: Parallax Press.
Lakoff, G., & Johnson, M. (2003). *Metaphors we live by*. Chicago, IL: University of Chicago.
Patai, D. (1994). (Response) when method becomes power. In A. Gitlen (Ed.), *Power and method* (pp. 61–73). New York, NY: Routledge.
Simanjorang, M. (2016). *Integrating ethics into mathematics education: A philosophical auto/ethnographic inquiry into Indonesian mathematics education* (Doctoral thesis). Murdoch University, Murdoch, West Australia, Australia.
Taylor, P. C. (2015). Constructivism. In R. Gunstone (Ed.), *Encyclopedia of science education* (pp. 218–224). Dordrecht: Springer.
Taylor, P. C. (2015). Transformative science education. In R. Gunstone (Ed.), *Encyclopedia of science education* (pp. 1079–1082). Dordrecht: Springer.
Taylor, P. C., Taylor, E., & Luitel, B. C. (2012). Multi-paradigmatic transformative research as/for teacher education: An integral perspective. In K. G. Tobin, B. J. Fraser, & C. McRobbie (Eds.), *Second international handbook of science education* (pp. 373–387). Dordrecht: Springer.
Tobin, K. (2016). Mindfulness as a way of life: Maintaining wellness through healthy living. In M. Powietrzynska & K. Tobin (Eds.), *Mindfulness and educating citizens for everyday life* (pp. 1–24). Boston, MA: Sense Publishers.

Webster, L., & Mertova, P. (2007). *An introduction to using critical event narrative analysis in research on learning and teaching*. London: Routledge.
Williams, B. (2006). *Ethics and the limits of philosophy*. London: Routledge.
Willis, J. W. (2007). *Foundations of qualitative research: Interpretive and critical approaches*. Thousand Oaks, CA: Sage Publications.

ABOUT THE AUTHOR

The name **Mangaratua M. Simanjorang** was bestowed upon me by my parents with the hope that I may bring blessings to people. I was born in a small city in North Sumatera province of Indonesia, called Pematangsiantar. I was blessed with the opportunity to finish my PhD study in mathematics education at Murdoch University, Australia. My research interest is integrating ethics into mathematics education. Currently I am teaching in the Science and Mathematics Faculty at Universitas Negeri Medan, Indonesia.

DORIS PILIRANI MTEMANG'OMBE

12. EXORCISING SATAN FROM THE SCIENCE CLASSROOM

Ending the Hereditary Syndrome of Science Teaching in Malawi

I am a learner who has been subjected to teacher-centred approaches from primary through tertiary education. As a kid, I thought that all knowledge rests in the teachers' heads; hence, I had nothing to share, especially in the eyes of the assumed most intelligent person, the teacher. Every time I walked into the classroom I knew I was one of the best observers. I do not remember having a class discussion, not even study groups. If one found new knowledge, it was not shared as it was a tool to surpass other students. My school days were filled with a competitive attitude; since if I shared my knowledge with a fellow student then it automatically meant selling my right to scoop the top position in class; and failure in class invited mockery from fellow students as well as the teacher. The underlying belief was that mocking failure would help students to work hard. Somehow it worked for us, but on the other hand it encouraged a cheating behaviour in students; for most of us, we used to memorize the concepts, not necessarily understanding and applying them.

We used to enjoy the lessons in other subjects, while for Science and Mathematics it was one big misery of classroom attendance. We thought the teachers in other subjects were good and experienced, while for the science and mathematics teachers we used to say, "They don't know how to teach that's why we are failing to understand", and we nicknamed them, 'Satan among the saints.' I used to ask myself, "Why is it that these teachers do not realize that they are killing the spirit of studying science in most students? Is it that they don't realize it or they enjoy doing it?" Sometimes I thought that maybe in their teacher training they are told to do so.

MY AUTO/ETHNOGRAPHIC INQUIRY

I am a Science and Technical teacher educator based at the University of Malawi, Polytechnic. My major role is to guide pre-service teachers in science content and methods of teaching so that after training they should be able to teach Science, Mathematics and Technical subjects in secondary schools and colleges. I see my professional career as a journey shaped by different experiences that I met as a learner, pre-service teacher and teacher educator. In this chapter, I am sharing what I discovered in a quest to understand how past classroom experiences impact teachers' practices and professional development.

In uncovering my experiences through meaningful reflection, I see myself interacting, contributing, observing and sharing; creating meaning and culture out of what I have been doing. My realities are grasped in the form of multiple mental constructions that I have socially created in interactions in my natural setting. These realities are collaboratively constructed from ontological relativism and later built up as subjectively created findings – my epistemology (Guba & Lincoln, 1994). I am not only sharing the stories but rather constructing a moral vision of my practice through a critical auto/ethnographic methodology (Mtemang'ombe, 2012). I have used my life history experiences through writing as inquiry and personal reflection to examine critically my past learning experiences and how they have affected my professional practice. During this inquiry, I was wondering:

1. How do my past experiences as a learner in science influence my current constructivist teaching practices?
2. How can I, as a teacher educator, embed students' cultural beliefs in my teaching practice to improve the quality of students' engagement in a science class?
3. How do I frame the future of constructivist science teaching in teacher education within Malawian cultural prospects?

The main purpose of this chapter is to bring a realistic view to my readers, especially in developing and fostering reflexivity and imaginative thinking, as well as nurturing changes in new research experiences to advance science teaching. It is my hope that this chapter will draw the attention of science educators who are still struggling to find answers to how they can accommodate modern educational and research practices alongside students' personal and socio-cultural perspectives. But first, some background context.

POLITICAL & PEDAGOGICAL CONTEXT

The Malawi education system found its course through the first missionaries. From the 1800s until 1964 the country was colonized by Britain. Due to language barriers, some Malawians were trained as teachers in order to teach others how to read and write, but the training was cosmetic and many were unqualified. These trained teachers relied on the use of teacher-centred approaches – as the learning culture within society was through imitation, observation and memorization (Banda, 1982). The teachers held a conception that their students were completely unknowledgeable on academic grounds. Thus, teachers were assumed carriers of knowledge; and hence, society valued the decisions made by them.

As the foundations of the education system were made by the British, they influenced the development of the curriculum and structures of education. Much of the concepts to be learned were designed to produce a workforce that would help their colonial settlement and evangelism of Christianity. The emphasis of the curriculum was on vocational education, reading, writing and counting (Banda, 1982). The same structure and curriculum was adopted when Malawi broke the federation in 1963. Changes to the curriculum were made, however the methodologies for teaching and learning remained a constant factor since the practices were deeply rooted in the teachers. In my experience, even today very few teachers practice newly introduced learner-centred approaches that are taught in the methods class during pre-service teacher training.

Political influence in 1994 led to the introduction of free primary education – an adopted policy from the Western education system – which led to an influx of learners in the schools; hence, the pupil-teacher ratio rose rapidly (Ministry of Education & UNICEF, 1998). These increasing numbers contributed to a shortage of qualified teachers, especially science teachers. This resulted in mounting pressure on the Ministry of Education. Furthermore, due to large classes it was easier for teachers to use teacher-centred approaches, hence promoting continual use of traditional instruction.

TEACHERS TALK, STUDENTS LISTEN

The dream of every Malawian parent is to have their children attain education as it is believed that education is a lifetime wealth. With this belief in mind, my parents made it possible for me to enrol in a government primary school. I was so excited to go to school and was very eager to learn new ideas. I was thinking that through education I will be able to make sense of the conceptions I had for other things that I was just imagining, for instance scientific ideas; and possibly develop something that will be useful among my community. Contrary to my expectation, however, school life was a life-time prison full of rules and regulations; it was more or less like a military training camp.

> Eyes of a young mind
> So young and innocent
> Full of truth and justice
> So eager to get the root out of the ground
> Cruel storm covers the trunk with heavy rocks
> Innocent eyes filled with tears
> As the struggle to pull out the roots continues...

These lines represent young learners who are eager to explore their capabilities and are using their young ideas to work out problems, but eventually strong forces act against their application, and finally they are left with anxiety and depression. This is exactly the mode of teaching and learning I have been exposed to. Possibly you could ask me how it happened. Let me take you to my Standard 5 (in other societies they call it year 5 or grade 5) science class. Our class had only a few desks which were occupied by boys at the back of the room and the rest of us were seated on a floor facing the front; normally, boys were sitting at the back and girls in front; I guess there was a good reason for that. In front of the class we had a wall-mounted chalkboard and the teacher's desk and chair. Common items that one would easily notice on the teacher's desk were a whip and some text books.

Communication in class was directed by the teacher and only the teacher could make a decision about when a student could speak. If we dared to speak without being told it was considered as 'noise'; and hence, if we failed to point out the noise makers the whole class could possibly be punished for disobedience. Therefore, our newly learned conceptions were never clarified; they remained in us side by side with the content that was heaped on us, resulting in widespread failure to understand the scientific ideas we were being instructed in. Furthermore, we were supposed to communicate in English – which is not the local language – hence, besides struggling with academic content, we were also battling to understand the teacher's language, which made it even more difficult to understand the science concepts.

Literature indicates the importance of having an *ideal speech situation* (Taylor & Williams, 1992) which creates an environment where students voice their ideas in order to challenge and be challenged, and possibly clarify their misconceptions (Cobb, 1994). The hegemonic teaching practice that I am critically reflecting on is based on an implicit belief that superiors have the right of speech and no one can challenge that – similarly in our culture an elder is to be respected and their words rule. Hence, this prevents an ideal speech situation, and thus constructivist classroom practices, from being realised in practice. It should be noted that this belief has seen its way into the education system; hence, deconstructing this practice requires a deeper understanding of the hidden influences (Ashcroft, Griffiths, & Tiffin, 2000) that continue to control our practices. In addition to monotonous classroom communication, language barriers contribute to failure to create an ideal speech situation. This language struggle has been reported by other African scholars (e.g., in Portuguese–speaking Mozambique by Cupane, 2011), especially how it creates confusion within students' understanding of academic concepts. In Malawi there have been debates about making a decision about which language (among the local languages and English) should be used in class and at what level (Ministry of Education & UNICEF, 1998). Reaching consensus has proved to be difficult regarding future educational development and progression within global development strategies.

In my experience as a learner, most of the science lessons were teacher-centred; our major role was to listen, observe and take down notes. Our teacher always referred us to the textbook to analyse pictures and understand the concept for the sake of national examinations. But having few resources such pictures often were drawn on the chalkboard (think of the accuracy of the drawing compared to the actual textbook picture). Most of the scientific concepts were presented in more or less meaningful drawings with little explanation. We used to ask among ourselves, "Aren't there any items that we use in our culture that can demonstrate similar principles?"

What is the problem with Science? This is the question I used to ask myself as a learner. In our class, we liked Agriculture and Biology because most of the biological aspects concerned our health and environmental wellbeing, while for agriculture, our country being an agro-based nation, most of us used our home experience to relate to the classroom and textbook contents. The most interesting thing was the school garden where we used to demonstrate the activities learnt in class in practical ways. On the contrary, Science was the most hated subject as it seemed to have no connection to our lives. In our informal class meetings students pointed out their concerns about Science:

We have a garden for the Agriculture class, when are we having a museum for the Science class?

I am fed up with this class, am only here because the curriculum does not give me an option.

Do we learn science to understand or just because we are supposed to?

My dad forced me to do science because it has been so in his family.

I hate the person who suggested that we should be learning science in schools.

Science concepts could have been reasonable if we could use locally available examples.

However, our science teachers never considered gathering students' opinions to affect improvement of teaching and learning practices; and yet we had a lot of criticisms and suggestions. The moral behind such barriers in communication stems from a cultural norm that a young person cannot advise elders. Hence, in our Science class it seemed like it was only the teacher who understood what was happening in the classroom; for most of us we were just warming the seats for the day.

BRINGING EDUCATION TO ONE'S REALITY

Developing students' understanding of scientific concepts can be enhanced by meaningful connection to students' real-life experiences. For decades, research has been conducted in science education in order to improve students' understanding. One of the notable factors is a recommended shift in teaching practice that brings the reality of science into the classroom (Duit & Treagust, 1998) by analysing the needs of students within their social-cultural contexts. Other research findings indicate the importance of verbal interactions in class, between the teacher and students and among students (Gunstone, 1995). However, most of the examples in the Malawian science curriculum are drawn from a Western point of view; hence, giving students an alien feeling about the existence of science in local Malawian contexts. I am not necessarily devaluing Western examples, but rather I believe that our science education context should provide opportunities to explore relevant examples that suit the cultural understandings of students.

Dan's Nightmare

Critical reflection takes me back to one of many circumstances I have experienced as a learner. Dan was an intelligent young boy who was always in the top 3 positions in class. One day the science teacher told us that the next lesson will focus on 'change of matter'. Dan raised his hand and asked the teacher if we were required to bring any materials that could aid our lesson. I will present this conversation in a dialogue. Although it was touching and sorrowful, today I have picked up some important facts from this experience that helped me and my friends develop a better concept of a science teacher and the possibility of bringing our social-cultural reality to the science class.

Dan: May we bring some materials to aid our lesson?

Teacher: Do you think you are smarter than me?

Dan: No madam, I was just thinking…

Teacher: Thinking what? Are you the teacher in this class?

Dan: No, but I have this idea…

Teacher: What idea, you silly boy! Do you think being in the top 3 position gives you a guarantee that you are better and automatically have the teaching certificate? Wait until you reach Standard 8 and sit for the national exams, if you will ever make it you are lucky. In our time those who considered themselves intelligent were never selected to secondary school, they had to repeat several times in order to get selected.

Dan: Sorry madam, I just wanted to…

Teacher: Shut up!!!!! You, you…good for nothing…what? Ask your parents the type of education they attained during the White man's era. They were told not to speak when the teacher is speaking. Their responsibility was to listen to the teacher and imitate. Do you think a White man was stupid when he trained teachers to take away your ignorance? A teacher is the boss of the class; hence, I am the only person who knows what you are supposed to learn. All of you in this class, you should take note of that, but if you will not comply you better get out of my class and don't come back.

It is time, you can all go home, see you tomorrow.

By the time the teacher finished speaking Dan's shirt was wet with tears. We were all terrified and afraid to never speak again and just bury our ideas forever, or one day if we become teachers we will also have the freedom to speak our mind. We gathered around Dan and comforted him knowing that it could also be one of us in his shoes. Later in the day I asked Dan what he had wanted to say:

Me: What was it that you wanted to suggest to the teacher?

Dan: I was thinking that we could bring an ice block, matches, empty tin and some firewood.

Me: What for?

Dan: An experiment. Because ice is an example of a solid and if heated it will turn into water. Since water flows then we need a pot or tin to put the ice so that when heating it should not spill; but am not sure how we can change water into gas because gas is invisible.

Me: The same water, Dan...if it is heated for a long time it produces vapour and escapes into the sky' then that's gas. It is a good idea indeed, but do you think the teacher is having the same idea?

Dan: Am not sure because I know her social status, she don't have a refrigerator at her home, hence cannot think of ice, but you and me we have them in our homes, hence we could have brought an ice block.

Me: That is true, and also other students could think of other interesting examples.

Teaching and learning is meaningful if the communication between the students and the teacher creates an opportunity for exposing ideas to be challenged. This creates an environment to understand learner misconceptions and establish the underlying beliefs guiding the nature of prior knowledge in learners (Bodner, 1986). This then acts as a platform to establish strategies that could aid in helping learners understand the concepts. In relation to Dan's experience, the teacher's response demonstrates a behaviourist approach to teaching and learning, which has been the main mode of teaching practices in Malawi. Progressive educators (Ausubel, 1963) argue that a deep understanding of scientific ideas is attained if learners construct meaning from their perspective in relation to their prior knowledge.

In Malawi, there is a notable defect in transforming past educational practices into current practices, despite the many social-cultural changes in society. The reproductive nature of contemporary teaching practices is a mirror image of teachers' past experiences; hence, their teaching practice is based largely on being in the shoes of their own teachers (Adams, Luitel, Afonso, & Taylor, 2008); albeit, in some small ways they try to improve what they feel their teachers could have done for their own learning.

Another important issue is the influence of power on practice. Habermas (in Grundy, 1987) pointed out that implementing the *practical curriculum interest* gives individuals a voice. The practical interest illustrates individual understanding of the environment in order to interact with it, hence the focus is on self-creation of knowledge and being able to make one's own judgement. The interest will make sense only if individuals have power and ability to stand up on their own rather than be directed on what to do. In Malawi, teachers' practices have been shaped by imitating the colonial masters who were deemed to be the liberators of the African community from academic ignorance. The practice of following the leaders' directives influenced our teachers' practices and deprived us of the possibility of developing multiple ways of considering educational practices. Although it feels as though our country is decolonised, we are still colonised by the hidden powers that cause us to refer to them for our contemporary social practices.

Our first State President always referred to education as 'an eye-opener', in which he said it is not just a matter of learning academic concepts but that education should also sharpen our values and beliefs. Hashweh (1996) and Prawat (1992) pointed out the influence of non-academic classroom experiences that contribute a high percentage to our practices. My question is, "What values are we instilling in the learners we teach? If they become teachers, how can we justify the values they will demonstrate in class?" On the other hand, it might be that our teacher training program does not provide opportunities for other influences on personal praxis, apart from emphasizing prescribed theoretical contents.

THE PROFESSIONAL BREAKTHROUGH

My critical account of the Malawian teaching profession arises from an abiding urge to transform teaching practices. In the days of our youth we used to say that medical and teaching professionals are the cruellest, however we were ranking teaching as the top cruellest profession as it transformed human sympathetic attitude into that of an animal; acting without considering the impact of their practices on students' learning, hence most of us never aspired to be a teacher.

Surviving through primary and secondary teacher-centred educational practices that were based largely on *the technical curriculum interest* – which focuses on following rules without reason and influences reproduction of knowledge (Grundy, 1987) – it was time for me to choose a career for my life. Having a spirit of being different from other girls and being responsive to changes brought in by the new millennium, I decided to be amongst the few girls taking the challenge of joining the most feared profession among women, and also some men – mechanical engineering. People described it as the most difficult program, hence they were afraid of failing. For most girls, they feared that they might not get employed as the field was considered masculine. Having gone through the hassles of academic torture in this program I realised why people feared it. I figured out that it was not the content, but rather the teaching and learning experience – very similar to the one I endured in primary and secondary school. With this it was very difficult to understand the concepts, hence the failure rate was high.

> Oooooh!!!! My freedom,
> It has been threatened again
> With things that are senseless in my life.
> What can I do to make it through?
> The same difficulty I thought I am done away with
> Has resurfaced.
> I wondered, here (college teaching and learning practices) too?

Having a mature feeling and mind, it was difficult to accept being pushed around by the lecturers who, to show their superiority, were nailing us on examination papers. Luckily we made it through and joined the industry to regurgitate the knowledge we learnt.

It was very exciting to work in an environment where I was the only lady, and hence I was given opportunities to demonstrate my capabilities. However, I never felt satisfied when I remembered all the other girls out there. Unfortunately, they could not take the course I took as the dropout rate for science subjects was highest amongst females (Ministry of Education & UNICEF, 1998). One of the factors that contributed to high dropout was a cultural norm that encourages people to give up on challenging tasks, other than self-exposure to torture and embarrassment. In education this cultural norm impinges on constructivist theories of learning which recognise that each individual is different (Bodner, 1986) and that rates of understanding differ; hence, calling for multiple approaches to teaching and learning to influence development of understanding. How can we penetrate through this restrictive cultural norm to liberate those that are interested to study sciences but are restrained by the prevailing cultural consciousness (Ameyaw, Dei, & Raheem, 2012)?

Every time I went to work in the morning I looked at young kids with their bags on their shoulders on their way to school. I felt pity as a person who could possibly help to turn the tables upside down in the teaching profession. My mind raced for the girl child who had always aspired to be a scientist; but with no female science teachers or figureheads where will the motivation come from? With little opportunity to voice their opinion how can they express their challenges and fears? My passion grew and I ended up in a pre-service teacher training college.

I started my journey with full momentum with the aim of breaking the hegemonic practices that have long framed teaching and learning practices in Malawi. The language of the teachers appeared to be the same at all levels of my academic journey, bringing fear and hopelessness of accomplishing my goal. My fellow student-teacher, Nita, told me one day, "I wish I could go in front of the class and demonstrate to this physics teacher how a student-centred approach to teaching is conducted". She was talking with confidence from the lessons we had in the teaching methods class. Nita's loud thinking matched Jimmy's who always imitated how our Mathematics teacher was behaving in class. When he enters the class he never greets us, he straight away writes down the topic on the chalkboard and starts scribbling examples; every member of the class immediately copies them down, and the teacher's explanation follows later.

STEPPING INTO THE TEACHER'S SHOES

Seated at my study desk, I started reflecting on the teaching styles my teachers had been demonstrating to me, and on the meaning of being a teacher that I had constructed from my fellow students' comments. And I reflected on the content that I learnt in the methods class, which provided very few practical demonstrations of progressive theories of teaching and learning. With all these memories racing through my head, I asked myself, "What sort of teacher will I be?"

I felt terrified when our teaching practice coordinator told us that it is time for us to go for the actual teaching practice. That night I did not sleep; I was figuring what I will wear, the hair style I should do, the type of shoes I will put on, how I will twist my tongue to make my English language sound better, and many more. As I was thinking about this a vision of Mrs Banda (my primary school teacher) came to me; I smiled. She was always smart and well groomed; immediately I wanted to present myself like her. When I was thinking of my role as a teacher I couldn't figure out the best teacher that suited the theoretical learner-centred and constructivist concepts I had learnt in the methods class. However, I thought of being brave like Mr Kashoti (my Physical Science teacher in secondary school); who could jump up and down to make us laugh, and read stories of great scientists every time we had a class with him. Sometimes teaching time could elapse without him presenting any of the concepts he prepared for the lesson – we nicknamed him 'the story guy'.

On my first day as a science teacher, feeling like Mrs Banda and feeling brave like Mr Kashoti, I entered my science classroom at the technical college – year one students studying various trades: carpentry, plumbing, brick laying, and painting and decoration. I feared to face the students as I was having a feeling that probably they are feeling the same way I had felt in Science classes. I was terrified when I looked at their innocent faces; in their eyes I could read, "What has she brought us? Will it be different from others?" I greeted them and we exchanged introductions – there the fear ended. I felt relieved and had the courage to move another step – to the academic concepts. I started teaching and my teaching approach was based on improving how my teachers had been teaching me; hence, my model also largely emulated their practices. However, I completely forgot to apply the constructivist theories I learnt in the methods class as I felt like they could never work. In some circumstances I tried to apply them but I felt like they were alien to my values and beliefs; at times I would adopt a constructivist teaching perspective but mostly I just couldn't apply it, especially when the use of power helped in controlling the behaviour of students and forced them to know the content for the sake of the exam. One day a student asked me, "How can one be a good teacher?" I wondered why she asked me so; does it mean I am a good teacher or she wanted me to find out the qualities of a good teacher, to learn and apply them?

The power struggle in me was too much and I reflected on the main reason that I joined the teaching profession. I realised that my dream will not be accomplished at the level I was at – when the oppressed realise the need to free themselves they take the initiative and start to look for strategies (Freire, 1970) – I decided to try my luck to become a teacher trainer, which is where I am now. But what is the problem now?

MY TRANSFORMATIVE RESEARCH EXPERIENCE

Scholars have revealed the influence of personal beliefs on social practices (e.g., Britzman, 1986). These beliefs have multiple sources, including common practices within our community, observations, experiences and cultural norms (Savasci & Berlin, 2012). As I am writing now, I feel that I am being freed from the tensions that hindered my professional growth. Recognition of what I have been secretly holding as a principle guide for my practice has made me realise other aspects of teaching and learning. I can imagine the feeling Emilia Afonso, a science teacher educator in Mozambique, expressed about how she could foresee future possibilities in science education when she discovered that realising the inner-self empowers personal capabilities and provides an ego to try new approaches to facilitate learning of science (Afonso, 2007).

My fellow auto/ethnographers (e.g., Ellis, Adams, & Bochner, 2011) have pointed out the power of self-reflection on rethinking our practices. I once took it for granted but now I know what they mean. Through writing I feel a new me, with new understandings arising from constructing new meanings of different circumstances; deconstructing ideologies that framed my practices (Richardson, 2000). Much as it is important to teach the curriculum content, understanding why we are teaching such content gives an insight into the myth within that content (Ameyaw et al., 2012). Critical reflection on our understanding, focusing on our implicit beliefs, enables us to uncover facts that we created as ideal and to consider other possibilities within our reach. Through such practices we will be able to redefine our curriculum and accommodate diverse ideas from stakeholders; hence, the curriculum will be relevant to our local needs as well as meeting global standards.

I have come to appreciate that if we inculcate a postmodern curriculum perspective – where knowledge, values and human nature are recognised as key aspects to be addressed in transforming passive, receptive thinking – then we can enable students to discover and reconstruct their existing understanding, and be empowered to attain their chosen goals alongside the set educational goals (Cary, 2006). A postmodern curriculum perspective provides limitless possibilities for unfolding our understanding of what we believe is best for our ever-changing society; hence, we could transform our mindset about teaching and learning practices.

Enacting 'curriculum as currere' – where Pinar (2004, p. 413) defined 'currere' as "the individual experience in an educational context" – would provide opportunities for students to reflect on self-experiences and rethink, reconstruct and transform their mental constructions. This perspective can embrace an 'agenda for social reconstruction' (Fleener, 2002) where curriculum is perceived as being dynamic and socially responsive; hence, if societal changes are recognised in curriculum development educational outcomes will be experienced as more meaningful. As learners are empowered to contribute to curriculum design they come to recognise societal needs and future life expectations. If we do not recognise our societal needs then the curriculum, and consequently our world, will remain stagnant.

IS THE CHANGE INDEED A CHANGE?

As a teacher educator, I have several challenges that I need to pay attention to. I feel that I pose as a role model for some of my students and, at the same time, I have a responsibility to 'practice my words'. As I continually ask myself, "How can I remove the Satan in me to speak the same language with these saints?", I am seeing pre-service teachers emulating my teaching style, as I used to do. Will my practices encourage a 'factory model' of teaching and learning? I want to exercise my power in a different way.

> To some power is guns
> To some power is knives
> To some power is the ability to read, and write.
> To some power is control
> To some power is a fist
> To some, like Dr Martin Luther King Jr, power is words.
> To some power is like a trapped animal trying to get out of a cage
> To some power is love
> To some power is art
> To some power is money
> To me power is knowledge
> So what is power to you?
>
> (Edwina Matthews, 2003)

Numerous changes have been happening in teaching and learning practices, especially in classroom situations: new models of teaching and learning that focus on students' interactions with the teacher and among themselves (White, 1998); and different learning materials to aid the current technological practices across the world have been introduced in schools. But do we have new teachers that are well prepared to handle such changes? How do we embed current learner-focused teaching alongside our cultural beliefs? In the Malawian perspective, only elders' views are considered valid, yet in a constructivist classroom all views are valid and can be contested. Other metaphors we use habitually in our education system control so much of the way we think and act. As a child, I was continually told that "an empty tin makes a lot of noise". Naturally I would ask myself: "Does the teacher really expect me to talk, and what will others interpret of my noise?"

Change comes with responsibility both to the learner and the teacher; understanding the limits of power and the meaning we are creating out of it. We know that changing the classroom setting and introducing new materials is not enough to change individuals' long-standing practices (Taylor, 1996). I critically reflect on my experiences and prepare PowerPoint lessons to support my desired interactive teaching, but still the class is passive; since our traditional belief has been that being a good listener and observer models the best classroom achiever. Hence, we need to focus on the influences behind our teaching and learning practices.

We seem to be stuck in our old ways despite the many changes in education. Fleener (2002) advocates a vision of curriculum serving an agenda of societal reconstruction, which I sometimes feel is unrealistic, confusing and unattainable – but these feelings exist because our minds and practices have long been guided by traditional views of teaching and learning. While we have always looked at educational practices as a means to refine behaviours, we have provided few opportunities for learners to unfold their abilities and challenge their own thinking. It is high time that we asked: Whom are we educating for? For what purpose? And why? If we reflect on these questions we will find that we have good reasons for attaining education other than as a means to eradicate ignorance.

For some time now, I have considered the curriculum that we have recently reviewed. I have thought about the type of pre-service teacher we are aiming to produce – the content looks rich but does it provide for personal growth and development? Will the teaching methods class be enough to change their perspective on science teaching and learning? I feel strongly that to effect sustainability of constructivist approaches in our science classes, our curriculum needs to provide opportunities to enhance students' personal responsibility for their own learning. If we empower our students, and trust their input, this could be a breakthrough to the transformation of both ourselves and our students from the bondage of passive learners to creative, critical and imaginative thinkers.

Transformational practices give students diverse opportunities for self-learning, self-evaluation and exploration, and power to define their own learning and understanding (Spady, 1995). Sustainability of these modern educational practices could be attained if we encourage individual responsibility and empowerment; through which learners reflect on their experiences in relation to real-life practices and redefine their educational needs, as well as those of the system. Alongside self-responsibility, a sense of ownership triggers high-level scrutiny in response to the complexity of real-life experiences. Furthermore, learners would have a determination to transform, to produce their best, hence rendering their curriculum to be dynamic.

If we truly understand for whom we teach and for what reason, we could perhaps identify if we need to fit neatly into society or, instead, to advance our thinking and unfold our capabilities to create the world we desire. It is high time we realised that teaching and learning is not just a matter of transmitting knowledge, but rather is about unfolding our existing knowledge structures and putting them into practice. Postmodern views help us to step out of the box and open our eyes through self-realisation of our needs. These needs contribute to our curriculum in an integrated manner, providing multiple dimensions of analysing the relevance of educational practices. The dynamic aspect of the curriculum and the need to understand the relevance of educational practices for our Earthly sustainability gives an insight into the need for self-recognition of our situation and for employing several strategies to clarify our understanding – this then, moves beyond knowledge transfer.

WHERE IS THE SATAN?

Lessons Learnt

It has been a long journey for me; scrutinizing my past learning and teaching experiences, searching for a deeper understanding of my teaching practice and the context of science teaching and learning. Some might think that I have come to the end of my inquiry; but to me it is rather the beginning of a new life, profession and practice. I am looking forward to writing again on my experiences of the new understanding and meanings I have created, and discoveries I have encountered as I committed myself in this writing process.

Throughout my research writing I have unfolded new knowledge which I thought could never be relevant to my academic practice in the teaching profession. I have realised that encountering knowledge has no limit unless we give ourselves a limit. The knowledge I have gained through this writing process is worthwhile for my personal development, my practices, my colleagues who might be influenced by the transformation I am still encountering, and my readers who share my experiences in different contexts.

Apart from the rich knowledge I have discovered, I have also been enlightened about aspects that we continually neglect, that influence our practices. Understanding my experiences alongside constructivist and postcolonial theories, has made me realise the hidden ideologies that have influenced my practices. For ages, the teaching profession has focused on altering pedagogies to enhance understanding of science concepts. We rarely think of the contribution and impact of our beliefs and ideologies on the teaching and learning of science. When I reflected on the teacher training program that I went through, I remember all the teaching philosophies and strategies and how they changed over time; how the psychologists (Piaget, Vygostky) presented the psychomotor development and the importance of understanding these in education. But we lacked a focus on self-reflection and an account on the influence of beliefs and understanding of the self in our teacher training programs. I want to see a curriculum that does not only value content but also individual and personal responsibility, and that urges discovery and change.

Writing as a practice has helped me to critique the self and envision other possibilities. I have realised that beliefs are built by peoples' perceptions and the way they view the world. We are, I am, and you are agents of change. The practices that we have been practicing for a long time could be simply the result of emulating those we admire – 'I want to be like someone' – hence, we change our attitudes to fit into that someone's shoes. I have recognised that it is my responsibility to practice what I feel is impossible because in actual sense it is possible; but we are manipulated by group decisions. Having read an article by Taylor and Williams (1992), I realise that there is power in rethinking our understanding but only if we have a voice. I feel that our voice should extend to action – in doing so there is more learning – I feel ashamed that I never provided that opportunity to my students.

New Eyes on Research Methodology

I was rooted in the scientific ways of conducting research; hence, in presenting this chapter in the first-person voice I felt that I was 'off the track' of the research community. Every time I put my thoughts on paper I felt that I was committing a crime against the research community. But will this guilt last forever? My answer is 'No'; I built courage to try this new approach. I have been overwhelmed by the impact of this approach in stimulating my deep and critical thinking and understanding of the world in which I live. I felt that for once I have done something that is truly reflecting my inner abilities, rather than living and acting in the shadows of others because of the binding frames of rules and regulations. For once I feel connected to the work I have done, and I feel so much relieved from the bondage of conforming to rules and order. This new way of conducting research has really influenced my thinking and understanding; I have also started envisioning the future and the best ways to encourage and sustain strategies of making science classrooms attractive and enjoyable, as in other subjects.

Ideas Worth Considering

Experiences will always come as we live day by day. It is a matter of making use of those experiences to create the ideal environment that we admire. For this to materialise relies on the understanding of the self which can invoke deep thinking and reconstruction of different scenarios within our reach. I believe that if each teacher could spare time and reflect critically we can find a solution that can influence an end to mindless reproduction in teacher education.

Another important aspect is recognition of the limits of power in classroom practices. In my experience, teachers feel they possess maximum power to control classroom activities, and on the other hand students feel they have no control of their learning – they feel that their learning depends entirely on the teacher's competence. This hegemonic practice hinders students' potential creative ideas. If we could provide opportunities for both students and teachers to exercise power within their limits this could give rise to self-trust and shared responsibility; and also to sustainability of innovative educational practices for improving science teaching and learning.

It appears that there exists tension between lived experience and philosophies of teaching and learning. This creates a struggle to let go of the other, and teachers are forced to accommodate both, side by side. Unfortunately, the one with most influence dominates; hence, as teacher educators we have to be the first to understand the constraints that hinder our positive practical impact on our students. Recognition of these hindrances would enable us strategize how we can engage our students in several educational practices without transmitting our values in their experiences. In the common idiom – we learn much through experience – teacher practices could strongly influence students' values and beliefs. Hence, I feel that the sustainability of the implementation of modern teaching and learning methodologies depends greatly on praxis.

Sometime in My Future

I see young girls praising the beauty of science in their lives, singing with excitement about the relevance of science in their communities. An understanding of why we learn science could wash away the misery of a Science classroom with less resources and materials; and could influence a deeper understanding of science concepts. I am imagining myself entering a class and hearing different noises, and those noises sound like music to my ears. And out of those noises brilliant ideas that I had never thought of emerge from the students.

I see a collaborative culture in schools, where all those questions we have are considered as part of curriculum inputs. I am seeing the beauty of cultural recognition in a Science class and students' ambitions to promote our indigenous science in rectifying community challenges in our motherland. On the other hand, I am seeing confused minds about what counts as education. A conflict of classroom practices and cultural behaviours; where the community believes in order and use of power. We do not have to worry so much as most of the cultural ideologies were natured by our school practices. If we could only give a chance to the ideal speech situation we could accept that 'curriculum as a journey' mandates everyone to walk along using different strategies.

REFERENCES

Adams, J., Luitel, B. C., Afonso, E., & Taylor, P. C. (2008). A cogenerative inquiry using postcolonial theory to envisage culturally inclusive science education. *Cultural Studies of Science Education, 3*(4), 999–1019.

Afonso, E. (2007). *Developing a culturally inclusive philosophy of science teacher education in Mozambique* (PhD thesis). Curtin University of Technology, Perth, Australia.

Ameyaw, A. A., Dei, G. J. S., & Raheem, K. (2012). *Contemporary issues in African sciences and science education*. Rotterdam, The Netherlands: Sense Publishers.

Ashcroft, B., Griffiths, G., & Tiffin, H. (2000). *Post-colonial studies: The key concepts* (2nd ed.). London: Routledge.
Ausubel, D. P. (1963). Cognitive versus affective factors in the learning and retention of controvesial material. *Educational Psychology, 54*(2), 73–84.
Banda, K. N. (1982). *A brief history of education in Malawi*. Blantyre: Dzuka Publishing.
Bodner, G. M. (1986). Constructivism: A theory of knowledge. *Chemical Education, 63*(10), 873–878.
Britzman, D. P. (1986). Cultural myths in the making of a teacher: Biography and social structure in teacher education. *Havard Educational Review, 56*(4), 442–457.
Cary, L. (2006). From currere to curriculum spaces: Bringing together curriculum theory and educational research. *Journal of Curriculum and Pedagogy, 3*(2), 148–167.
Cobb, P. (1994). Constructivism in mathematics and science education. *Educational Researcher, 23*(7), 4. doi:10.3102/0013189X023007004
Cupane, A. (2011). Towards an understanding of the role of language in the science classroom and its association with cultural identity development in the context of Mozambique. *Cultural Studies of Science Education, 6*(2), 435–440.
Duit, R., & Treagust, D. F. (1998). Learning in science: From behaviourism towards social constructivism and beyond. In B. J. Fraser & K. G. Tobin (Eds.), *International handbook of science education* (pp. 3–25). Dordrecht: Kluwer.
Ellis, C., Adams, T. E., & Bochner, A. P. (2011). Autoethnography: An overview. *Forum: Qualitative Sozialforschung/Forum: Qualitative Social Research, 12*(1), 1–18.
Fleener, M. J. (2002). *Curriculum dynamics: Recreating heart*. New York, NY: Peter Lang.
Freire, P. (1970). *Pedagogy of the oppressed*. New York, NY: Herder & Herder.
Grundy, S. (1987). *Curriculum: Product or praxis?* London: Falmer Press.
Guba, E. G., & Lincoln, Y. S. (1994). Competing paradigms in qualitative research. In N. K. Denzin & Y. S. Lincoln (Eds.), *Handbook of qualitative research* (pp. 105–117). Thousand Oaks, CA: Sage Publications.
Gunstone, R. F. (1995). Constructivist learning and the teaching of science. In B. Hand & V. Prain (Eds.), *Teaching and learning in science: The constructivist classroom* (pp. 3–20). Sydney: Harcourt Brace.
Hashweh, M. (1996). Effects of science teachers' epistemological beliefs in teaching. *Journal of Research in Science Teaching, 33*(1), 47–63.
Matthews, E. (2003). *Power: Poem hunters*. Retrieved from https://www.poemhunter.com/poem/power-2/
Ministry of Education & UNICEF. (1998). *Free primary education: The Malawi experience, 1994–1998: A policy analysis study*. Malawi: Ministry of Education & UNICEF.
Mtemang'ombe, D. P. (2012). *Exorcising Satan from the science classroom in Malawi* (Unpublished masters dissertation). Curtin University, Perth, Australia.
Pinar, W. (2004). *Understanding curriculum: An introduction to the study of historical and contemporary curriculum discourses (Ch. Autobiography: A revolutionary act)*. New York, NY: Peter Lang.
Prawat, R. S. (1992). Teachers' beliefs about teaching and learning: A constructivist perspective. *American Journal of Education, 100*(3), 354–395.
Richardson, L. (2000). Writing: A method of inquiry. In N. K. Denzin & Y. S. Lincoln (Eds.), *Handbook of qualitative research* (2nd ed., pp. 923–948). Thousand Oaks, CA: Sage Publications.
Savasci, F., & Berlin, D. F. (2012). Science teacher beliefs and classroom practice related to constructivism in different school settings. *Journal of Science Teacher Education, 23*, 65–86.
Spady, W. (1995). We need more than educentric standards. *Educational Leadership, 53*(1), 82–83.
Taylor, P. C. (1996). Mythmaking and mythbreaking in the mathematics classroom. *Educational Studies in Mathematics, 31*(1–2), 151–173.
Taylor, P. C., & Williams, M. C. (1992). *Discourse towards balanced rationality in the high school mathematics classroom: Ideas from Habermas critical theory*. Paper presented at the Sociological and anthropological perspectives working subgroup of the seventh International Congress of Mathematics Educators (ICME-7), Quebec.
White, R. T. (1998). Research, theories of learning, principles of teaching and classroom practice: Examples and issues. *Studies in Science Education, 31*, 55–70.

ABOUT THE AUTHOR

My name is **Doris Pilirani Mtemang'ombe**, the third born in a family of five. I was born in Chikwawa district which is located in the southern region of Malawi. I hold a Master's degree in Science and Mathematics Education from Curtin University of Technology, Perth, Australia. I am a teacher educator at University of Malawi – The Polytechnic and have been heading the Technical Education Department for the past four years. My research interests include: Science and Technology classroom environment, Science and Technology teacher practices, Transformative education practices, Constructivism and Science and Technology Pedagogy.

PART 4
ENVISIONING TRANSFORMATIVE PEDAGOGIES

NENI MARIANA

13. A REFLECTIVE JOURNEY WITHIN FIVE WAYS OF TRANSFORMATIVE KNOWING

Indonesia, Islam, International

In my doctoral study I employed *transformative learning theory* as a tool for critical self-reflection and envisioning (Mariana, 2017). This theory of adult education enabled me – an Indonesian Muslim university lecturer – to reflect critically on my own frames of reference and to reveal how they have impacted my professional practices as a learner, a researcher, and a mathematics educator. The inquiry process raised my consciousness and enabled me to answer the question: What does it mean to be an Indonesian Muslim for my academic role as a mathematics educator?

To address this research question I conducted an *integrative auto|ethnography*. The slash ('|') signifies that the study was *coloured* at the same time by auto-ethnography and ethnography. Thus the slash indicates my *dialectical experience* (Roth, 2005) of considering my culturally situated personal experiences as well as those of my participants: Indonesian Muslim teachers of primary school mathematics. The term *integrative* means that there was an integration of three research paradigms that made this study interpretive and critical and involved various arts-based genres. This multidimensional approach enabled me to investigate my own beliefs and values as an Indonesian Muslim mathematics teacher educator. The narrative method of *writing as inquiry* enabled me to make visible my critical self-reflection process. While transcribing interview data and writing stories of my participants' experiences, I engaged deeply in the process of critical self-reflective thinking about my own experiences as a mathematics educator. As I approached the end of my research I came to realize that this inquiry had transformed me as a researcher, a teacher and a learner.

I had earlier found evidence that in primary schools in Surabaya, East Java, teachers feel lost when trying to implement the Indonesian national curriculum requirement to embed spiritual values and Indonesian cultural contexts in their teaching of mathematics. Many do not realize that the mathematics problems in textbooks and examinations are dominated by abstract questions and are embedded in contexts that do not enable students to learn good values. In particular, Indonesian Muslim teachers are struggling to find a connection between mathematical concepts and appropriate Islamic and Indonesian contexts that could bring Islamic values to students, rather than simply having students *counting candies in rows*. During this research, I conducted *inter/views* (Kvale & Brinkman, 2009) with some of these teachers to explore this pressing issue in relation to mathematics assessment. During this process, I witnessed these teachers transforming their pedagogical perspectives.

In this chapter, I would like to outline how five transformative ways of knowing – *cultural-self knowing, relational knowing, critical knowing, visionary and ethical knowing* and *knowing in action* – emerged gradually during my interactions with these teachers. This powerful transformative learning perspective enabled me to raise Indonesian Muslim teachers' consciousness about the significance of Islamic and Indonesian contexts for use with primary school children. This perspective had the effect of making me both a researcher and learner in this study, enabling me to reflect critically on my own understandings of Islamic values and Indonesian knowledge.

AUTO|ETHNOGRAPHIC BACKGROUND

A butterfly just escaped from its cocoon
It stays on the branch when the empty cocoon skin hangs on
It looks at the skin and sees its reflection

I have experienced being an Indonesian student who learnt school mathematics, as well as being a teacher who taught mathematics to students, and being a mathematics educator who teaches pre-service primary school teachers how to teach mathematics to Indonesian children. For my master's degree, I became an international student and learned about Realistic Mathematics Education (RME) which provides a space for cultural values and practices in mathematical contexts (Freudenthal, 1991). During this research experience I met the concept of *ethnomathematics* – introduced at a conference by Ubiratan D'Ambrosio (2007) – which focuses on excavating indigenous knowledge for local mathematical contexts. These experiences involved me in thinking about and reflecting on the Indonesian curriculum of primary school mathematics.

The Indonesian Curriculum (Act, 2013) states that in the main competencies of all subjects the cognitive aspects should be developed towards actions that reflect the child's faithful behaviour and noble character. This requires teachers to embed spiritual values and local cultures in all subjects at the primary level, including mathematics. Indonesia is a multi-religious/cultural country. In my doctoral thesis, I expressed the diversity of Indonesia in the following poem.

My Indonesia

Its area is 1,904,569 square kilometers,
and I live in about 55 square meters of it
Consisting of 17,508 islands, small and large

And I live in one of the biggest islands, Java
The distance from west to east, from Sabang to Merauke, is 5,428 kilometers
Enough to cover 10 European countries at once
Its coastline is 95,181 kilometers
about twice that of the Earth's circumference
More than 242 million people live there
And I am one of them
They speak about 742 different native languages
And I speak one of them, Javanese language
From 1,128 ethnic groups
And I come from one of them, Javanese
They eat thousands of traditional culinary foods
During my life, I have tried less than 1% of them
They hold 6 different religions
And I hold one of them, Islam

The mandate of the 2013 Curriculum is for each believer of the six main religions to understand and live the religious teachings that s/he embraces, and this should be embedded in all disciplines. Therefore, I became very interested in investigating what this mandate means for my understanding as an Indonesian Muslim mathematics teacher educator and what it means to Muslim teachers. I chose to work with Muslim teachers who have been working with Muslim students and/or in integrated Islamic schools.

I found that these teachers were struggling to implement this idea, especially in mathematics. A lot of examples have been provided for science, language studies, and social studies, but unfortunately not for mathematics. In reflecting on this shortcoming, I was thinking about myself and trying to understand what "embedding cultural and spiritual values in mathematics" might actually mean.

Are mathematical topics that we learn in primary school found when practising our cultures and religion? This particular question did not emerge before, even though I declared myself an RME educator and focused my interest on ethnomathematics; not until I was touched by the beautiful theory of transformative learning by Jack Mezirow (1997) and was conducting transformative research within a multi-paradigmatic research design (Taylor, Taylor, & Luitel, 2012).

During my doctoral study, while learning about transformative learning theory I became aware of my *frames of reference* which influence my professional practice. This theory of adult learning enabled me to reflect critically on my multiple roles as a learner, a mathematics educator, and a researcher, as well as on my daily practices as a Muslim and my traditional practices as a Javanese child. It made me realize that the mathematics that I had learned and taught so far was dominated by other cultures, called *foreign mathematics* by the Nepali scholar, Bal Chandra Luitel (2009). Therefore, I posed a critical self-reflective question:

What does it mean to be an Indonesian Muslim for my academic role as a mathematics educator?

In order to answer this question, I conducted an integrative auto|ethnographic inquiry under the *big umbrella* of transformative research. This form of research allowed me to speak out my hidden subjective voice as a person who was considering how her cultural and spiritual identity colours her worldview.

TRANSFORMATIVE LEARNING AND FIVE WAYS OF KNOWING

Transformative learning theory was introduced in 1978 by Jack Mezirow in the context of research on adult education (Kitchenham, 2008). The theory transformed in Mezirow's mind and has been influenced by many scholars, such as Jurgen Habermas, Thomas Kuhn and Paolo Freire. Mezirow's (1997) theory mentions frames of reference that influence adult learning. He explains that when adults learn something new they refer to their frames of reference, which include sets of values and beliefs, previous experiences or pre-knowledge, and cultural understandings.

During my doctoral study, I was often flashing back to my previous experiences. As a mathematics learner. I loved doing mathematics at school, even though the mathematics was not related to my daily experience. Meanwhile, as a Javanese kid, I practiced mathematics while I was playing traditional games with my friends. As a Muslim, I have been doing mathematics while practicing my religion. However, as a mathematics educator, I seemed to be in another world in which most of the time I am teaching foreign mathematics and enjoying its hegemony. There were particular moments during my interviews and writings when I was thinking about these two parallel worlds and, for the first time, seeing their connections. Consciously, I engaged in this thinking processes by working within the framework of five ways of transformative knowing articulated by Peter Taylor (2015): cultural-self knowing, relational knowing, critical knowing, visionary and ethical knowing, and knowing in action. I was using these ways of knowing as tools to engage in the reflection process. One by one, I was able to unfold my cultural identities as well as the hegemony framing my professional practices.

To me, these dimensions are not linear or in order, but are more like a cyclic process of engaging in critical self-reflection. The starting point might be different for each person, depending on her/his personal stage as s/he starts the reflective process. In my case, I started with cultural self-knowing because I was at the stage of identifying *who I am* and my worldview before I contemplated my professional practices. Together, these five ways of knowing enabled me to raise my consciousness and critical awareness and engage in mindfulness, encouraging me and my participants to act differently. This process not only enhanced our cognitive understanding but also empowered our emotional, spiritual and social potentials (see Figure 13.1).

Furthermore, I came to understand that finding the *me* self was a micro-scale perspective within the transformative process. During interactions with my teacher-participants, I experienced this view expanding toward a macro-perspective. From

A REFLECTIVE JOURNEY WITHIN FIVE WAYS OF TRANSFORMATIVE KNOWING

Figure 13.1. The cycle of five ways of transformative knowing

this macro-perspective the question of *who am I?* expanded to *who are we?*, as Indonesian Muslim teachers and/or as a nation. I found that such an expansion happened in each way of knowing. Thus, in the discussion of each way of knowing I have included both a micro-perspective and a macro-perspective.

CULTURAL-SELF KNOWING
(SELF-REALISATION)

I begin to see the fog
The fog becomes clearer as I've moved on throughout my study
The fog of hegemony
The fog that has made us unable to see our hands
I walked into it and tried to awaken everybody that they are in its middle
Nobody is aware
And that's why I keep moving on...
And I start with understanding Who I Am

The first step of my self-reflection began with becoming aware of the hegemony that dominated my worldview, by reflecting on my cultural identities as a Muslim, a Javanese and an Indonesian, managing my habits of mind, and being mindful of my actions in the outer world. The poem above was an expression of my critical self-reflection in understanding the self of me and its relationship with my outer world. Reflective questions developed as I talked to my teacher-participants and went through the effort of understanding our practices in teaching children mathematics:

- What is dominating our mathematics problems?
- Whose cultures appear in our mathematical contexts?
- What are the impacts of these values and lessons on my students?
- Why have we done this for many years without being aware of what these are all about?

Then I realized how these questions could only be answered by understanding my own self, by asking: *who am I?* This question led me to think critically about my cultural and spiritual understanding. Then, I also brought this question to my teacher-participants to ask them to think with. If *their* contexts are not appropriate in *our* cultures and seem foreign to us then do *we* as Muslims and Indonesians have more familiar contexts to serve in our mathematics classroom? I posed the following questions to the teachers.

- Why do I want to be involved with these issues?
- How important are they to showing our cultural and spiritual identities in our mathematics lessons?
- If it is important, how can I convince other teachers to do the same thing?
- How can I empower them to see the hegemony and pose the same critical questions in their professional practice?

In our discussions, I reminded them of the vision of their school; the unique identity they want to foster in students through their local school curriculum. I obtained the following response from teachers (T) and a vice principal (VP) of two integrated Islamic schools.

I: You are working in an Islamic school, aren't you? Do you have any obligation to embed religious contexts in lessons you teach?

T: Yes, we have a spiritual paradigm that should be implemented

I: Doesn't it include mathematics lessons?

T1: It should be, but...[pause] how?

T2: How to do that? What kind of Islamic concepts can be integrated with mathematics?

T3: How to teach Geometry using Islamic values?

T4: We teach symmetry to remind students how kind Allah is creating our body in symmetrical ways.

I: Do you know what kind of Islamic concept that has mathematics in it?

T1: I know about *faraidh* (the concept of Islamic inheritance). It has fractions.

T2: Ehmm...I think...*zakah* (obliged charity) uses percentage.

I: Do you think we can use it in our primary math lesson?

T: Yes, but we haven't thought about it before. It's a good idea.

I: Talking about the spiritual paradigm that underpins your school's vision, what kind of effort have you made as a vice principal?

VP: We train teachers and develop books that contain Islamic concepts and values.

I: As well as in math books?

VP: We've done well in science, but not in math. Our math books remain the same. We need expertise.

Furthermore, from a macro perspective I realised the need for us as a nation to undertake self-realisation of *who are we?*. This led me to pose a critical question in my inquiry about the history of mathematics teaching in *Nusantara* (i.e., Indonesia during the pre-colonial era), as well as during the colonial and post-colonial eras. Through this historical study I found that mathematics was taught informally and applicably in old *Nusantara* cultures and in Islamic *pesantren* (i.e., boarding schools). As the oldest traditional educational institution in *Nusantara* (Azra & Afrianty, 2005), *pesantren* did not provide mathematics and science as separate subjects (Zarkasyi, 2015). Further, through my religious excavation of the Quran I found that it was impossible to practice Islam without having mathematical knowledge. However, the European colonisation of Indonesia demolished this cultural and religious context in our mathematics education. Since then, *Western mathematics* has become hegemonic in the Indonesian mathematics curriculum.

Colonisation also brought dichotomised thinking into Indonesian Muslim scholars for many years, which strengthened the hegemony. Due to colonialism, for many decades our mathematics curriculum has been separated from other subjects. The main reason is that colonialism created dichotomised thinking between Islamic and non-Islamic knowledge (Suyatno, 2013). Thus, the 2013 Curriculum which tried to integrate religious values into all subjects was a huge leap in the Indonesian primary education system. From such history I could understand why Muslim teachers hardly found any connections between mathematical concepts and Islamic values for teaching mathematics in their integrated Islamic schools.

RELATIONAL KNOWING
(OPENING TO DIFFERENCE)

I see complexity inside me like I see in others
I see diversity inside me like I see in others
I see particular conditions surrounding me as I see with others
I see…the massive universe inside me where others belong too

The next step of my reflective process was learning how to make connections with my community, culturally different others and our natural world. Connecting with my own self was not an easy first task. I had to understand my own desires and the worldview that dominates my decisions. I needed to choose a desire that did not harm others and was beneficial for the community and the environment. I was learning to deal with myself. This perspective impacted my way of relating to my teacher-participants. I tried to put myself in their shoes and feel what they felt in their daily practices. When I saw that they were different from one to another, I started realizing that each person had unique characteristics. Therefore, I had to treat them properly and to consider their diversity. This made me do more listening than intervening during our conversations. I invited them to contemplate on their teaching practices, to think about their students' needs and various backgrounds:

> We know children are different, but why do we provide them with the same treatment in our mathematics classroom? When we start a new mathematical topic, why do we usually think that children are like empty papers? Why do we think that they do not have any understanding about the math topic? Is it right that they really come to our class with empty minds? Is it right that they do not have any experience at all in their daily life related to the math topic we will discuss?

By engaging in postmodern *InterViews* (Kvale & Brinkmann, 2009), I allowed myself to have light conversations with these teachers, thereby exposing their feelings and struggles. They began to reflect on their professional routines. During these conversations they were asking critical questions about the use of the mathematics that they have to teach their students. They began to consider that the mathematics they taught should be meaningful and applicable for students in their communities. Further, they also were considering that because their students come from different cultural backgrounds it is important to give different treatments to various children.

T: I have my own teaching problem in my class.

I: May I know what problem it is?

T: I usually arrange my students into heterogenous groups. So, in one group children work with other kids who have different levels of abilities.

I: Why do you do that?

T: Because I think, by doing so, the clever child can help her/his friends in the same group.

I: Does it work on that way?

T: No. That's why I am confused. The clever kid is working while other kids in the same group passively do nothing.

I: Have you ever tried to consider their needs? I mean, you may try to make homogenous groups and provide each group with different levels of problems in accordance with their abilities.

After several meetings with this teacher, she told me her transformative story:

> Before we had our discussion about group arrangements, I was thinking that the best way to arrange students in group is heterogeneous. I wanted my students to be active and help each other. By making heterogenous groups, I thought that clever students would help their fellows. Unfortunately, it did not work in my class. I never dared to try grouping them based on the level of their abilities. Anyway, I've tried it in the last two weeks and miraculously it works in my class. Yes, it's a bit busier because I have to make different levels of mathematics problems for those different levels of groups, but I feel so content because finally all my students are actively participating in their groups, and I could be more focused to help students in the low-level group so that they now can compete with others. Now, I understand that what may work in other classes may not work in my class, because students are different and every class is unique.

Furthermore, this way of knowing made me able to see how outer worlds influence the emergence of this diversity, as my environment influences my perspective, my thinking, and my actions. As a woman who has grown up in a big city, previously I was not concerned about endangered species suffering from forest fires. Now, I began to look at ways of bringing such issues into mathematics lessons. I gained the idea to focus lessons on sustaining our natural environment. When I talked about these matters to my teacher-participants, they also began such contemplation.

I: As a Muslim teacher, you know that the Qur'an guides us to take care of our environment, don't you?

T: Yes, I know it.

I: Have you ever considered it in your mathematics lesson?

T: How? Teaching mathematics whilst caring for the environment? Weuw...I've never thought about it before.

The new national primary curriculum, the *2013 Curriculum* with its integrative approach, has mandated using rich contexts of both diversity and environmental issues. Together, we observed the new primary school textbook, based on the 2013 Curriculum, and were glad to find images of multicultural ethnicity appearing throughout. We could easily find pictures of students with various identities, such as curly hair students, dark skin students, fair skin students, and Muslim female students wearing hijabs. Our co-generative inquiry helped the teachers to more easily bring an awareness of diversity to their teaching. From a macro perspective, this way of knowing brings a discourse as a nation towards dealing with such diversity and brings the message of unity into our mathematics classroom.

The curriculum also requires teachers to be creative, to design learning activities that help to preserve the natural environment. Designing environmental activity may be easier in other subjects such as Yuli Rahmawati's (2012) design of *Green Chemistry*. But putting environmental issues into mathematics lessons is more challenging. However, it is not impossible to do so. The above teacher later confessed:

> After our discussions, I thought about how mathematics lessons in my class can inspire students to preserve the environment. Last week, I designed a 'clean environment project' for my math lesson. Students collected the garbage they found in the school area and each student has a *garbage bank*. At the end of the project, the student who has been able to collect the most garbage is the winner, and all students thought about how to reuse the garbage during a recycle activity.

CRITICAL KNOWING
(POLITICAL ASTUTENESS)

To the past me, being critical was always about pointing at someone else
It is easy to blame power above us
The government, the institution, or the boss
Now I see, my pointing finger to them is only one
While many other fingers are pointing back at me
When I realize that
I begin to criticise myself
There is always space to make a change
If they make a rule to govern
I could look for the space to make improvement

When I reflected on my past actions and decisions as a teacher educator, I realized that most of the time there was a shadow of power hovering above me that influenced my decisions, called *rules and regulations*. This brought me to the third step of consciousness: understanding how power constructs and governs our reality. Interviewing various levels of education stakeholders made me realize that we are always in the middle of two powers. Teachers stand between idealism and policy makers. The school principal and advisors stand between school pride and policy.

Even the curriculum designers, they stand between the dream of the nation and a political and economic agenda. As an example, a teacher confessed to me about his feeling about being a teacher:

> I'm an example since I am administratively correct in their opinion. Since I knew that they do not appreciate my improvisations and creativity in teaching my students, I stopped improving and have done whatever paperwork they need to assess me. That's all. My job is satisfying them and exactly following as they instruct me. While my students...[deep breathe]. Somehow, I want to surrender, but I know I have to keep on and someday I want to be someone who has the power to change these.

Mathematics assessment of the new curriculum brings a dilemma to educational practitioners. On the one hand, most teachers are happy with the curriculum alteration and the holistic approach that opens a space of creativity for their professional development. On the other hand, the paper-based assessment of their work performance inhibits their creativity. Cognitive assessment attracts the most attention and the mandate of the curriculum is still evaluating the accomplishment of each standardised competency. In order to run this mandate, the local government regulations that control mathematics prevent it from being integrated with other subjects, especially in standard assessments which comprise context-free, multiple-choice and short-answer problems. At the end, all teachers' improvisation in designing integrated assessment is formally rejected and seems useless.

Nevertheless, this critical way of knowing helps me and my participants to see a crack in the system. The crack which will bring a way for innovation and improvisation. There is always such a crack in every system which I believe can help desperate teachers or educators who are tired with the bureaucracy and want to be innovative. Instead of cursing the rigid system, I invited my participants to find a way together. We were thinking how to do ideal assessment within our integrated curriculum. In my mind, I imagined separate statements from different people forming the *semi-fictionalised* setting (Taylor, 1997) of the following conversation among local government (LG), curriculum designer (CD), teacher (T) and me:

CD: The most appropriate model of assessment for the new curriculum is portfolio.

LG: But the mandate of the curriculum asks us to assess every standardised competency. Portfolio hardly covers them all. That's why we make this guidance of assessment for teachers. We have to measure competencies one by one, problem by problem.

CD: Then, the soul of this curriculum is at an end [smiles bitterly]

T: So, we cannot make any improvement in assessment. We think that, as teachers, if we teach the subjects in an integrative way then we have to assess students in an integrative way as well. Otherwise, our integrative-thematic approach is useless.

I: Ssst....Come here...closer [I tag the teacher and she comes closer]

I: Are you sure there is no space to do what you think is ideal?

T: I don't know, I'm not sure.

I: Okay, so...the local government will provide the assessment, right?

LG: Yes, but not all.

I: Not all?

LG: Yeah...what we provide is just for mid-semester test and final semester test.

I: Aha!! It means, teachers are free to create daily assessments, aren't they? [I smile and meaningfully glance to the teacher]

Because teachers actually do have freedom to design daily assessments for their students there is a significant opportunity to practice ideal assessment. With this freedom, teachers may design an integrative model of assessment in which several subjects are assessed under the same theme, and students will not see the subjects separately. Also, in their daily practice teachers have the opportunity to embed religious and social values in the contexts of mathematics problems. The problem is solved!

VISIONARY AND ETHICAL KNOWING
(OVER THE HORIZON THINKING)

I love math since I was a child
I love the math of counting candies, receiving more candies
While my teeth were rotten
I don't care
How careless I am now about being healthy
I love the math of thinking about having more money from bank interest,
whereas sharing contexts were barely posed
How I often forget that what I have is what I give and share with others, as the Prophet said
I love the math of shopping, percentages of discounts,
How consumptive I am now
While I always forget to spare 2.5% of my income for zakat and charity

Writing these poetic considerations made me reflect critically on my views about mathematics as a primary school student and how it impacted the way I am now. The visionary and ethical way of knowing helped me reflect on my past, and I could see how the past has affected my current self. This also prompted me to rethink about how better the world could be and, more so, what it should be. In doing so, creative thinking empowered me to make a jump in my thinking process and tried to think *out of the box*.

When I engaged my teacher-participants in this thinking process, I started by posing them reflective questions such as, "How do you usually design mathematics problems for your students?". These are two of their typical answers:

T1: I'm thinking how to make the levels of the problems start from the easiest to the most difficult one. If it doesn't work and few of them need remedial, I redesigned it and made it even easier.

T2: For story problems, I usually use contexts which are [in my opinion] fun for them and they like it, such as candies, lollies, marbles, etc.

These answers made me see myself as one who had experienced similar thoughts, both as a teacher and a child. When my participants felt that this approach was perfect and they were comfortable doing this, my mind was busy with a lot of questions that I needed to discuss with them. We discussed our vision as educators, our idealism, and we looked for the answers together to the following questions.

- Have you ever thought that your approach would be affecting their lifestyle?
- Do you think they would be a mathematician in the future by treating their learning with such increasingly difficult mathematics problems?
- Do you think this approach is valuable for their lives?
- What do you think teaching mathematics to children is for?

Perhaps nobody would come up with one perfect answer because it was not about being totally right or wrong. However, the most important thing was that we had such a strong commitment to ourselves as mathematics educators that we were committed to changing our views. We felt compelled to start considering the values and morals of our future generation.

Recently, the 2013 Curriculum was revised. The revised version instructs teachers to separate mathematics from the themes for Years 4 to 6, whereas other subjects remain thematically integrated until Year 6 primary school (Act, 2016). Moreover, the religious and social aspects no longer need to be embedded into all subjects. However, in Years 1 to 3, mathematics is still to be integrated thematically with other subjects. Themes can focus on inculcating religious and social values. Besides, even in Years 4 to 6, in which mathematics is separated, we still have *a crack* to insert religious and social values into the contexts of mathematics problems. Thus, whatever the curriculum is, for Islamic schools the mission to address ethical and religious values is still necessary and possible.

From a macro-perspective, Indonesia has *Pancasila* as the basis of the nation's educational philosophy. The five principles of Pancasila are: (1) Belief in the one and only God, (2) Fair and civilized humanity, (3) The unity of Indonesia, (4) People led or governed by wise policies arrived at through a process of consultation and consensus, and (5) Social justice for all the Indonesian people. The Pancasila mandates that educational policies and practices should implement these five essential principles which are designed to produce a *fully Indonesian human* who is *religious, nationalist and democrat, knowledgeable, has strong physical and mental personality, and is responsible to society.* Thus, the importance of developing religious and moral values remains for every re-development of the Indonesian curriculum.

KNOWING IN ACTION
(MAKING A DIFFERENCE)

Transformation needs courage
Just like a butterfly which tries to escape from its cocoon
It requires action to move
After reflection in a dormant period, it's time to make a move
In order to see the world, she spreads her wings

Everybody dreams of a better world, but nothing changes without action. Empowering others will have a greater impact if we can become examples of change. I always remember an Islamic saying: "If you want to change the world, start with 3s: start from yourself, start from something simple, and start from now". It is essential to be reflective and critical, but it is also important to start an action. Therefore, the last (but not least) is knowing in action which requires someone who declares him/herself to be an agent of change to develop a movement to action, especially to have a strong commitment to sustainability by thinking globally but acting locally.

As I was engaging in critical self-reflection, I came to realize that my worldview was dominated by my cultural identities as a Muslim, a Javanese and an Indonesian. However, when I put this reflection into my professional practice as a mathematics educator, I found that I was losing these identities in my mathematics lessons. At the same time, I saw Western education culture being hegemonic in our mathematics contexts. At the end of my contemplation, I saw that mathematics lies in three separate worlds: International, Indonesia, and Islam.

During a conversation with a school advisor (SA) he shared his experience of these three worlds. As an international school advisor for many years he had experienced the strengths and the weaknesses of an international curriculum. And as a Muslim he had sound knowledge of Islamic education. When he decided to become an Islamic school advisor he created *The 3Is* model of education for Indonesia (see Figure 13.2).

SA: I believe that the spirit of international learning can be combined nicely with our national curriculum so that the taste and the quality can integrate the three Is of our spirit [in Islamic schools]. The first I is Islam, the second is Indonesia, and the third is International.

Figure 13.2. 3I mathematics

I: If you see there is an intersection amongst those three worlds in education, does it mean that there is something in the international context that is not suitable for us? Can you share your view?

SA: Yes, it does. How perfect it seems, but something is missing in their theory based on our perspectives, which is spiritual values. In order to apply this 3Is concept, all educational elements should be together, returning back and learning about Islam and Indonesia.

IN CLOSING

Within my auto|ethnographic inquiry I had been transforming like a butterfly with a consciousness that my identities as an Indonesian and as a Muslim meant a lot to me and the nation. Now, I can consider the richness of my cultural and spiritual values in my professional practice.

In short, I came to understand that we need to take steps to start learning about our religion and our nation in order to bring proper contexts to our mathematics problems. Our mathematics contexts should be valuable, meaningful and global. Islam can contribute to embedding positive values in shaping the pious characters of our Indonesian Muslim generations. Indonesian contexts could make students appreciate their cultures and give them an understanding of where they belong.

While achieving this, we do not need to get rid of international contexts from our curriculum; rather, they should not continue to dominate our education system. We simply do not want to have a lost generation that does not understand their indigenous knowledge. As long as they do not contradict our beliefs and values, international contexts should continue to exist to encourage students that they are also part of a global society.

To conclude, during my journey I found that engaging in the five dimensions of transformative knowing helped me to become aware of the hegemony in our education system, to find out what is missing regarding our cultural identity, and to better understand myself, our nation's history, and how to undertake transformative research. I recommend that future research explore these powerful ways of knowing with foci such as expanding the pedagogical use of transformative knowing in education as the syntax of a teaching model and a learning approach. Currently, my bachelor degree students are implementing transformative ways of knowing in order to understand the *soul* of transformative research in writing their theses, and they are finding it beneficial and meaningful.

REFERENCES

Act, I. E. (2003). *Act of the republic of Indonesia number 67, year 2013 on primary school curriculum.* Ministry of Education of Republic of Indonesia.

Act, I. E. (2016). *Act of the republic of Indonesia number 24, year 2016 on the main competencies and basic competencies of the 2013 curriculum for primary education and high schools.* Ministry of Education of Republic of Indonesia.

Azra, A., & Afrianty, D. (2005, May 6–7). *Pesantren and madrasa: Modernization of Indonesian Muslim society.* Paper Presented at the workshop on madrasa, modernity and Islamic education, CURA, Boston University, Boston, MA.

D'Ambrosio, U. (2007). Peace, social justice and ethnomathematics. *The Montana Mathematics Enthusiast, Monograph, 1*, 25–34.

Freudenthal, H. (1991). *Revisiting mathematics education: China lectures.* Dordrecht: Kluwer Academic.

Gubrium, J. F., & Holstein, J. A. (2003). *Postmodern interviewing.* London: Sage Publications.

Kitchenham, A. (2008). The evolution of John Mezirow's transformative learning theory. *Journal of Transformative Education, 6*(2), 104–123. doi:10.1177/1541344608322678

Kvale, S., & Brinkmann, S. (2009). *Interviews: Learning the craft of qualitative research interviewing.* Los Angeles, CA: Sage Publications.

Luitel, B. C. (2009). *Culture, worldview and transformative philosophy of mathematics education in Nepal: A cultural-philosophical inquiry* (Unpublished doctoral thesis). Science and Mathematics Education Centre, Curtin University of Technology, Perth, Australia.

Mariana, N. (2017). *Transforming mathematics problems in Indonesian primary schools by embedding Islamic and Indonesian contexts* (Unpublished doctoral thesis). School of Education, Murdoch University, Perth, Australia.

Mezirow, J. (1997). Transformative learning: Theory to practice. *New Directions for Adult and Continuing Education, 74*, 5–12.

Rahmawati, Y. (2012). *Revealing and reconceptualising teaching identity through the landscapes of culture, religion, transformative learning, and sustainability education: A transformation journey of a science educator* (Unpublished doctoral thesis). Science and Mathematics Education Centre, Curtin University, Perth, Australia.

Roth, W. M. (2005). Auto/biography and auto/ethnography: Finding the generalized other in the self. *Auto/biography and auto/ethnography: Praxis of research method* (pp. 3–16). Rotterdam, The Netherlands: Sense Publishers.

Suyatno. (2013). Sekolah Islam terpadu: Filsafat, ideology, dan tren baru pendidikan Islam di Indonesia. *Jurnal Pendidikan Islam, 2*(2), 355–377.

Taylor, P. C. (1997, March). *Tales of the field: Impressions of college teaching.* Paper presented at the annual meeting of the American Educational Research Association (AERA), Chicago, IL.

Taylor, P. C. (2015). Transformative science education. In R. Gunstone (Ed.), *Encyclopedia of science education* (pp. 1079–1082). Dordrecht: Springer. doi:10.1007/978-94-007-6165-0_212-2

Taylor, P. C., Taylor, E., & Luitel, B. C. (2012). Multi-paradigmatic transformative research as/for teacher education: An integral perspective. In B. J. Fraser, K. G. Tobin, & C. J. McRobbie (Eds.), *Second international handbook of science education* (pp. 373–387). Dordrecht: Springer.

Zarkasyi, H. F. (2015). Modern pondok pesantren: Maintaining tradition in modern system. *TSAQAFAH, 11*(2), 223–248.

ABOUT THE AUTHOR

My name is **Neni Mariana**. I was born and grew up in Surabaya, the capital city of East Java Province in Indonesia. I was awarded my PhD in Mathematics Education by Murdoch University, Australia. I am currently Senior Lecturer of Mathematics Education in the Department of Primary School Teacher Education, Faculty of Education, Universitas Negeri Surabaya (UNESA), Indonesia. I am teaching primary-school-mathematics to both undergraduate and postgraduate students. I am coordinator of the bilingual program in my Department, and am coordinating a research team called TLC (Transformative Learning Center) and a STREAM (Science Technology Religion Engineering Arts Mathematics) project at one of UNESA's lab schools. My research interests focus on mathematics education, especially Realistic Mathematics Education (RME) and mathematics for social justice. Currently, I am conducting research with my students and colleagues in 'ethno-pedagogy', especially 'ethno-mathematics'. I am a qualitative researcher and would like to declare myself as a novice transformative researcher.

INDRA MANI SHRESTHA

14. FACILITATING CULTURALLY DE/CONTEXTUALISED MATHEMATICS EDUCATION

An Arts-Based Ethnodrama

This is not my mathematics, Indra! This is only for people having a mathematical mind like you!

It is easy to raise the issue of cultural mathematics but it's very challenging to include it in mainstream mathematics education in Nepal!

As a learner, I had always sought to score better marks in school mathematics. As a teacher, I began my career with the belief that teaching mathematics was about transmitting knowledge to my passive students. This perspective continued until 2007 when I enrolled in a Master of Education (Mathematics) program. As a novice researcher, I was inquisitive to draw on my hidden and untold lived experiences and contradictions (Whitehead, 2008) of school mathematics teaching and learning, so as to unfold them to the world. I came to realise that, as a passive learner, what my teachers, acting as knowledge transmitters, taught me from the mathematics textbook was a package of culturally decontextualised knowledge that excluded (and by implication devalued) my own cultural capital. Now that I have engaged extensively in research that has enabled me to reconceptualise my teaching worldview, I understand my role as fostering meaningful learning of mathematics by encouraging my students to bring their cultural capital into the classroom. Currently, I am a teacher-educator at Kathmandu University School of Education. My role is to facilitate pre-service and in-service school mathematics teachers in designing authentic, inclusive and empowering school mathematics curricula by including students' cultural capital.

The purpose of this chapter is to illustrate my inquiry into the prolonged problem of culturally decontextualised mathematics education encountered by the students of Nepal. Drawing on ethnodramas embedded in my MEd dissertation, I focus on two professional development workshops in which I engaged teachers of mathematics in culturally contextualised mathematics learning and curriculum planning. I hope that this chapter will help my readers to become more critically aware of the need to create *culturally de/contextualised* mathematics education and to develop their critical reflective thinking so as to transform their mathematics curricula and pedagogies.

INDRA MANI SHRESTHA

CULTURALLY DE/CONTEXTUALISED SCHOOL MATHEMATICS

"This is not my mathematics, Indra! This is only for people having a mathematical mind like you!" This is a plea from my former students about their sense of alienation from mainstream (culturally decontextualised) school mathematics; it now echoes in my inner ear. By contrast, when I raise the issue of bringing students' cultural capital into the mathematics classroom, my fellow school teachers and master's students, who are stakeholders in private and public/community schools, typically react: "It is easy to raise the issue of cultural mathematics but very challenging to include it in mainstream mathematics education in Nepal!".

I have cited these narratives to reveal two hotly debatable issues in Nepali mathematics education: culturally decontextualised school mathematics vs culturally contextualised school mathematics. But are they really opposing issues having a dualistic relationship or can they be reconciled so as to co-exist?

As a researcher, I came to realise that school mathematics in Nepal has been designed officially for the purpose of producing future human resources who are meant to enhance scientific and technological innovations (Luitel & Taylor, 2010). In this regard, the mathematics curriculum of Nepal is framed by an ideology that privileges an epistemology of objectivism, the language of universality, and the logic of certainty. This ideology of cultural decontextualisation frames curriculum development, pedagogical innovations and assessment strategies in both school mathematics and mathematics teacher education programs (Luitel, 2013). The result is to neglect students' cultural capital, that is, their community based practical knowledge, values and identities.

In my MPhil research (Shrestha, 2018), I argued that the culturally decontextualised mathematics education of Nepal has given rise to a reductionist pedagogy that directs teachers and students to break down abstract mathematical problems into small parts, thereby studying them in isolation via the assumption that the parts represent the whole (Luitel, 2017). For example, in the past when I taught mathematical problems of the textbook I instructed my students to follow standard algorithmic problem-solving methods in which the solution consists of a sequence of steps, thereby restricting the students from linking the textbook problems with the problems of their cultural lifeworlds. This reductionist pedagogy restricts students' opportunities to engage in authentic mathematical thinking and deprives them of the enjoyment of solving richer, more worthwhile problems, which would forge connections across diverse areas of the subject.

However, I am not in favour of exclusion resulting from naïve dualistic thinking. Rather, despite having bitter experiences of learning and teaching culturally decontextualised school mathematics, I envision the development of a synergistic *culturally de/contextualised* school mathematics education. The dialectical slash ('/') signifies blending culturally decontextualised mathematics education and culturally contextualised mathematics education, meaning that both mathematics educations combine to work together so as to provide students with authentic mathematical thinking. But first, it is necessary to illustrate the potential meaningfulness of culturally contextualised school mathematics. To do this, I use the arts-based method of theatrical ethnodrama.

AUTO/ETHNOGRAPHY AND ETHNODRAMA

During my research, I learned to value and reflect on my own lived experiences and contradictions based on my learning and teaching of school mathematics. In writing narratives of these experiences I interacted critically with self and others, and described and systematically analysed (*graphy*) my personal learning experience (*auto*) in order to understand cultural experience (*ethno*) (Ellis, Adams, & Bochner, 2011). While articulating meaning from my personal experience, I was aware that auto/ethnography challenges canonical ways of doing research and representing others (Spry, 2001), and treats research as a political, socially just and socially conscious act (Adams & Holman Jones, 2008).

Within an arts-based auto/ethnographic research methodology, I employed *ethnodrama* as a specific genre of dramatic literary writing to set a theatrical stage on which both researcher and participants perform together. An ethnodrama – a term joining ethnography and drama – is a written play script consisting of a dramatized selection of narratives collected from various resources, such as personal memories/experiences and journals (Saldana, 2011). Thus, I represented my personal experiences in the form of a stage show designed to invite readers to become involved in my evocative stories. Considering my experience as a student and teacher, this stage show examines critically the following questions: How can Nepali mathematics be contextualised through inclusiveness and ethnomathematics? How can a culturally contextualised mathematics education enable meaningful learning of mathematics?

CULTURALLY CONTEXTUALISED MATHEMATICS

This section comprises a two-act stage play in which I enact the role of an in-service professional developer conducting a workshop with mathematics teachers to sensitise them to the concept of culturally contextualised mathematics.

Act I: Mathematics Is Everywhere

The Director makes an announcement to the audience that Act I is going to start soon, briefly explaining the nature of the drama to be performed.

whistle blows – background music and stage lights on

Story teller-researcher: It could be any Sunday of May some years back. I am in a hall with 12 school teachers and am going to conduct a mathematics workshop on the topic: How to Teach Algebra at a Preliminary Stage. It is mid-day just after lunch. The ceiling fan is on. I can observe the teachers anxiously waiting for the commencement of the workshop. First, I divide the teachers into three groups A, B and C, and distribute three different questions, as follows:

- Group A: Ram had 5 apples in his hand. He gave 2 apples to his friend. How many apples were left with Ram then?
- Group B: Sita had 5 Rupees with her. Her mother gave her 2 Rupees. How much money did Sita have altogether then?
- Group C: Melina collected 5 pebbles and gave them to her father. If her father had 8 pebbles altogether then, how many pebbles did her father have before?

I ask the teachers to find the answer from two perspectives: arithmetically and algebraically. At first, I highlight all the questions and ask them how to teach these questions. Their mixed types of answers compel me to explain how these questions are dealt with while teaching. I then ask them to have a group discussion and prepare their presentations on charts using concrete materials (apples, pebbles, paper money). They start their group discussion. I allow them 30 minutes for discussion and 15 minutes for each group presentation. I wander around, encourage and facilitate them. Finally, it's time for their presentations! I sit at the back and note the points and ask other groups to do the same. The presentation is over. I start my comments on their work.

> Well, all of your presentations were wonderful! I appreciate your confidence in presenting your ideas with the help of materials. If you apply this to your children in your classroom there will be an interactive class, and I am sure every student will understand the preliminary concept of Algebra clearly. Make sure that each and every student is actively participating in group discussion. You have to emphasize why the letters are used in Algebra. What is Algebra all about? In addition, do not forget to tell them that we can find mathematics in and around us, at school, at home, at market, everywhere in our everyday life. By itself, the lecture method and writing on the board are not sufficient to build the conceptual framework in pupils' minds; it should be visualized.

I take a long breath and some water, before continuing.

> I emphasized here the visualization of mathematics. If you go back to your past life and recall, which events do you remember the most and quickly?

One of the teachers immediately tells that he never forgets learning fractions by using apples. He says: "My math teacher taught us fractions by cutting real apples and gave us those apples to eat".

> This is what learning mathematics is all about. Algorithmic problem solving, by itself, does not give the real flavour of mathematics. It may distract the

students from meaningful learning of mathematics. Moreover, you can use concrete objects which are found in our homes, society and cultures.

Immediately, a lady teacher asks how we can find mathematics in our cultures. I first clarify briefly the concept of culture and ask them to find mathematics from their diverse cultures.

Culture refers to a set of values, norms and beliefs that are common to a group of people who belong to the same ethnicity. It also refers to the customs of a particular people. Now, we can find mathematics being practiced in our various cultures. A teacher should be able to convince his/her pupils that all mathematics they are studying originated and developed from people's cultures across the world.

One simple example can be given: we use *dharni* (~2.3 kg) to weigh potatoes, onions, etc.; our previous generations (great-grandfathers) used *mana* (~1 pound) and *pathi* (~8 pounds) to weigh rice, maize, pulses, etc., and they used rice, maize, flour, etc., for the wages of labours. In village farming today we are still using *nanglo* (a winnowing circular tray), *doko* (a frustum-like deep basket), *gundri* (a straw-mat), *piraa* (a small straw-mat), *halo* (a plough), *kodalo* (a spade), and *kuto* (a small spade). In these artefacts we can find different geometrical shapes, such as circle, rectangle, square, polygons, cylinder, frustum.

Another lady teacher raises her hand with a beautiful smile and asks an interesting question: "May I ask my students to collect mathematical shapes from their houses, sir?"

That's it, madam! Before you start your lesson, ask your students to collect geometrical objects that are used in their daily life at home to make them familiar with real objects, rather than photographs, and only then start teaching geometrical shapes. Look! You have contextualised your academic mathematics with your cultures now. If you encourage the students to collect the objects that are found in their own cultures, it will lay an impression that their cultures are valued. In these diverse cultures of our society, we can teach them mathematics in an engaging manner. Students from diverse cultures may bring diverse materials for you in teaching mathematics. Have you noticed the dome on top of Buddhist temples? It is hemispherical. And then there's the pyramid of Egypt on The Discovery Channel! In fact, contextualisation of mathematics not only can increase interest in learning mathematics; it can also enhance their imaginative power and creative skills. You might have heard Einstein say: "Imagination is more important than knowledge".

I again take some water and then continue.

INDRA MANI SHRESTHA

How are you feeling, teachers, bored or...?!

A loud voice roars: "No sir! It's interesting". In the meantime, one of them speaks loudly: "Sir, truly speaking, for the first time I am getting the real flavour of mathematics today".

However, I pause here for I have to conclude their presentations. I draw the conclusions in the following way:

	Solution of Group A Question				
Arithmetically			Algebraically		
Ram had	He gave	Left with Ram	Ram had	He gave	Left with Ram
5 apples	2 apples	? apples	5 apples	2 apples	? apples
5 apples	2 apples	3 apples	5 apples	2 apples	x apples
	5 − 2 = 3			5 − 2 = x	

	Solution of Group B Question				
Arithmetically			Algebraically		
Sita had	Mother gave	Sita had	Sita had	Mother gave	Sita had
Rs. 5	Rs. 2	Rs. ?	Rs. 5	Rs. 2	Rs. ?
Rs. 5	Rs. 2	Rs. 7	Rs. 5	Rs. 2	Rs. x
	5 + 2 = 7			5 + 2 = x	

	Solution of Group C Question				
Arithmetically			Algebraically		
Melina collected	Father had before	Father had altogether	Melina collected	Father had before	Father had altogether
5 pebbles	? pebbles	8 apples	5 pebbles	? pebbles	8 apples
	8 − 5 = 3			5 + x = 8	

After this conclusion we take some snacks and tea. It has already been about two hours. During this tea session the teachers are having lively interactions about today's workshop. One teacher comes to me and asks how to give students the preliminary concept in Algebra of constants and variables. I seize on this topic and draw their attention that after a five-minute break we will be discussing the concept of constants and variables, if they are ready. They agree.

Mr. Jha has just requested me to have an interaction about the constants and variables in Algebra. Therefore, before we conclude today's workshop we are going to have a discussion on the topic. Do you have any idea about the meaning of these terms?

They whisper to each other for a while and one male teacher raises his hand and says: "The constant has its value always the same and the variable has its value changeable".

That's good! Now, tell me, will you connect it with students' daily life situation or will you just tell them the definitions and start your lesson?

I pause for a while expecting a reply from their side; some discussion takes place among them. A while later one of them speaks: "Sir, will you explain from your side, please? I think no one of us has its solution!"

Sure! I will give you an idea. First you need to go straight to the busy highway and stand aside. Then, count the number of vehicles that pass by you every hour and note it down. Spend some hours and come back home. Now, see your recorded data. Are they same or different each hour? If they are the same, it is a constant; if they are different, it is a variable!

"Wow! Sir, you're great!", says one lady teacher. Another male teacher says: "Then, we can also tell students that the number of days in a week is a constant and the number of days in a month is a variable!

Here is another good example. [I am excited] This is how we can teach the conceptual meaning of mathematics! This is how we can contextualise mathematics! One thing more, my friends, for your students you can design projects on the contextualisation of algebra, arithmetic, geometry. Make sure that the projects link mathematics with your pupils' cultures.

I pause for a moment.

For example, I'll tell you one: Collect the geometrical shapes found in your home, community or society related to your culture, list them, write their uses, paste their photographs or bring them to the school if possible. Then, form groups of students from the same locality, so that they are easily accessible to each other for collecting information, and give them this project. Best give sufficient time, maybe two weeks or whatever you feel appropriate. In between, keep on interacting with students to learn about their updates.

I move here and there, to the back and front of the hall, while expressing my views.

When they submit their projects, make an arrangement for their presentations. Reward some of the best ones in the presence of the Principal or Coordinator of the school, because every human being is hungry for appreciation; students wish their hard work to be valued. After their presentations, give your conclusion, highlighting the fact that mathematics is everywhere in and around us, in our homes, community, society and cultures.

I look into their eyes: they are focused and writing notes.

Now when you start your lesson in class, link your teaching with their projects, time and again. This will be a more engaging teaching-learning process. Being teachers, you will never forget to teach mathematics by linking it with cultural contexts. What do you think?

The first session is accomplished. 15 minute break!

> *background music off, curtain falls slowly*

Act II: Ethnomathematics: A Means for the Contextualisation of Mathematics

The Director makes an announcement that Act II is going to start soon, briefly explaining to the audience about the nature of the drama to be performed.

> *whistle blows – background music and stage lights on*

Story teller-researcher: After the break, I arrange readings for the teachers and wait for their arrival in the hall. Now it is time and they come in one by one, taking the papers from me and resuming their seats. In this second session, I am going to conduct a workshop on the topic: Contextualisation of Mathematics: An Ethnomathematics Perspective. My objective is to introduce the term to the teachers. When I write the topic on the whiteboard everyone seems surprised at the new term – ethnomathematics – which they have not previously encountered. Before I begin the workshop I read their faces for a moment and give a charming smile. I observe that they are eagerly waiting to know the meaning of ethnomathematics. Moreover, I want to explore the possibility of inclusion of ethnomathematics in Nepali mathematics curricula. For this purpose I want to collect the views of these school teachers. That's why I have designed this workshop.

> A warm welcome again! Today, we are going to deal with this new stuff 'ethnomathematics'. I hope you will cooperate.

As soon as I pronounce the word, they call out curiously in one voice: "What is this ethnomathematics, sir?"

> Ethnomathematics refers to the study of mathematics in relation to culture. Its credit goes to a Brazilian mathematics educator, called Ubiratan D'Ambrosio. In the case of Nepal, Dr. Bal Chandra Luitel, one of the prominent educationists of Nepal serving in Kathmandu University School of Education, has done his PhD research on ethnomathematics. I have provided you papers in which information about ethnomathematics is given. Today, I just want to introduce it to you and expect your views about its possible inclusion in Nepali mathematics curricula though it is completely a new concept in Nepal.

Mr. Jha [inquisitively]: "It means the mathematics being practiced in different cultures!"

> Very good, sir. That is what we also discussed in the last session. It is very complex to understand but for now we just think that it is a mathematics practiced or being practiced by different groups of people, such as carpenters,

potters, farmers, vendors, in their daily cultural lives. Today, we are going to have an open discussion about this type of mathematics. Whatever we know and whatever experiences we have, we will share here and try to explore its possible inclusion in our Nepali curriculum.

Mrs. Shrestha [humorously]: "Oh, yes, sir! How could you come up with this idea in this 21st century? It is very hard to find ethnomathematics unless we visit various places".

Yes, Madam! We need to do deep research, visiting person to person from place to place to study their cultures and find the types of mathematics they are practicing. You can collect the information from your *Newari* community, Jha Sir, you can collect from your *Maithili* community, Madan Rai Sir from your *Kirat* community, and so on. I think you all are getting my point!

Mr. Santosh [smiles]: "What information shall I collect from my community?" [Mr. Santosh is from a culturally marginalised community, called *Biswakarma (ironsmith)*. In this community is practiced metalwork, such as making home appliances, for example, *karai* (cooking pot).]

Mr. Santosh, there are many mathematics practiced in your community. People make metal pots of different shapes such as knives and pots.

Mr. Santosh: "Oh! I got it. Thank you, sir".

Madam Shrestha, you can also inquire with your grandparents how they practice counting numbers. I know that our grand-grandparents used to exchange different things for food before the tradition of money was introduced. For example, they exchanged cattle for food. These were the history of mathematics.

Mr. Mohan [excitedly]: "I think ethnomathematics is all about contextualisation of mathematics in relation to cultures of our diverse society.

Why not! You are right, Mohan Sir. Here today I just want to let you know about this new term, but my purpose is to make you aware of our cultural mathematics. That's why I suggested that you link our academic mathematics to the cultures of our society and encourage students by designing projects! [I take a long breath] My intention is to pave a path towards cultural mathematics that we call now ethnomathematics. No matter how successful we might be, it will be a valuable support for students to recognise their own cultural mathematics.

Mr. Jha [long breath]: "I think it is huge, sir! It needs maximum exercise before it is included in the curricula of our current academic mathematics. Our nation is culturally diverse and the political situation is also unstable. Whose practices should be included in the curriculum is problematic for us. I mean, if we include the practices of mathematics from the cultures of a particular community, then others may raise their voice against it, sir!".

> Here comes the critical idea from Mr. Jha. That's why I have brought it for open discussion with you. Whatever you said is genuine! It is an issue. If we raise it as an issue all over the country there are many educationists in Nepal who can solve this genuine issue. For now, we only seek its possibility in our accessible cultures. Am I right, sir?

Mr. Jha nods his head. Other teachers are perhaps in a dilemma. They remain quiet. Mr. Jha again comes up with more ideas.

Mr. Jha [excited]: "I think first we need to study what it is exactly and then only we can decide what to collect as information".

> I agree with you Mr. Jha! I am also a learner. I have got this idea from Kathmandu University during my MEd and MPhil studies. There I learned that due to decontextualised mathematics education our pupils are unable to get meaningful, empowering and authentic learning of mathematics and hence some are distracted from mathematics.

Mrs. Shrestha [interrupting]: "That's fine, sir. As Jha Sir said, we first study about it and decide about it. But the overall impression is that it is related to our culture and we teach our students the academic mathematics in the context of their cultures. Certainly, it will be helpful for the study of ethnomathematics".

> This is true, Madam! You should teach mathematics in a way that students will be aware of valuing their cultures. They are the future; they can do something about ethnomathematics in future. But it is our duty to pave their paths for the future.

All the teachers are listening to the conversation. They whisper and nod their heads, change their facial expressions, and most keep quiet. I notice that this has been enough for today. Before they think that ethnomathematics is a boring subject I make up my mind to conclude the workshop.

> Ok, this is enough for today! In conclusion, I say that today we learned how to contextualise our academically decontextualised mathematics and learned some ideas about the new term ethnomathematics. Ethnomathematics can be a means for contextualisation of academic mathematics. I hope you will apply it in your classroom before you jump straight to the algorithms and calculations of problem solving. Also I hope you will keep inquiring about ethnomathematics directly or indirectly. Thank you very much for your patience!

The workshop concludes.

---

background music off, curtain falls slowly

FACILITATING CULTURALLY DE/CONTEXTUALISED MATHEMATICS EDUCATION

REFLECTIONS

I have argued that culturally decontextualised mathematics education has been preventing students from learning an authentic and empowering cultural mathematics in the schools of Nepal. Based on my experience, I have also attempted to portray how culturally contextualised mathematics can be valuable for students' meaningful learning in the classroom by introducing the perspective of ethnomathematics.

I have given emphasis to the reform of Nepali mathematics curricula directly/ indirectly with the help of an ethnodrama by creating situations and awareness in students and teachers. In the USA, the reform movement in mathematics education carried out in the mid-1980s was a response to the failure of traditional teaching methods. Battista (1990) states that in a contemporary mathematics education, students must learn to read, write and discuss mathematics, use demonstrations, drawings and real-world objects, and participate in formal mathematical and logical arguments. However, in Nepal, we have a practice of following the traditional algorithmic problem solving methods without connecting the textbook problems to the cultural lifeworlds of students. Though reforms have been taking place in Nepal, mathematics education has yet not been able to integrate the cultural capital of students. If the USA can reform its curricula in a way that fits their students' culture, then why doesn't our nation seek to reform mathematics curricula in a way that *fits our soil*?

My mind is usually distracted by the education system of Nepal. I think that the school mathematics curricula of Nepal are inclined towards *upgrading* students rather than *updating* curriculum knowledge for students. Students are taught in a closed monotonous environment for many years, much like animals are trained in a circus. Our curriculum does not fit our many cultures. Foreigners discover or invent new things; we unquestioningly include them in our curricula. Some questions always come to my mind: "Why do we follow foreigners' footsteps blindly? Do they do the same as we do or do they collect knowledge from all over the world and mould them into their own shape? Can't we mould foreign knowledge into our shape?"

In this regard, it is worthwhile turning to the history of mathematics. Historically, mathematics was linked with culture. Mathematical ideas and concepts were developed simultaneously across the world, and different cultures had different features in their mathematics. The foundations of mathematics emerged from the need to trade in ancient times. For example, in Nepal a traditional *apple-to-pig* exchange consisted of a variable number of apples for one pig (Hammond, 2000, p. 16). Babylonians invented a place-value number system, different methods of solving quadratic equations, and a formula for the relationship between the sides of a right-angled triangle, which later came to be known as the *Pythagorean theorem* (Joseph, 1997 as cited in Hammond, 2000, p. 18). Egyptians pursued geometry to aid in the creation of complicated architectural structures. India developed the number system and pursued more theoretical aspects of mathematics. Greeks have been credited with the development of a more sophisticated form of mathematics that serves as the basis of what we use today. Hence, we can examine how mathematics was linked with cultures and how mathematics differs from culture to culture. However, culturally decontextualised mathematics is being taught in Nepal as a pure and rigid mathematics without contextualising it culturally.

But, my intention is not to urge that culturally decontextualised mathematics is to be excluded. Rather, my expectation is that mathematics teachers, including me, can link to students' local cultures and design projects on culturally contextualised mathematics. I think that this noble attempt will certainly lay some positive impressions on students that mathematics is not only brought from foreign countries, but also derives from historical practices in our local communities (Luitel, 2009).

Overall, what have I learned from my research? I have learned to express my views based on my personal experiences using arts-based inquiry. Before my master's studies, as a mathematics teacher I simply followed Freire's (1993) *banking* concept of education: teachers actively deposit information into students as passive recipients. Since completing my MEd and MPhil research, I have become conscious about and practiced Freire's *conscientization* – learning to perceive social, political and economic contradictions – by developing critical awareness and taking action against oppressive elements of social reality (Freire, 1993).

Now I feel capable of continuing to grow as a learner, a teacher, an educator and a researcher with a transformative sensibility. This process involves constantly reviewing (and perhaps changing) my ways of knowing (epistemology), ways of being/becoming (ontology), ways of valuing (axiology) and ways of sensing (aesthetics). To Mezirow (1997), transformation means change in a person's worldview by integrating different worldviews. Therefore, at this time I believe that I can make a shift beyond existing structures and formations by means of a radical change in my cultural self.

Another valuable learning is that I have become playful in writing my own stories and connecting them to others' life stories. My stories may act as metaphors to supply a bundle of messages (new knowledge) to my readers (students, teachers, educators, educationists, parents, etc.) who wish to rid themselves of the coercion and deceit of culturally decontextualised mathematics curricula in Nepal that gives rise to (reductionist) linear teaching and learning, and who are eager to transform themselves into critical thinkers for the sake of meaningful teaching and learning of mathematics in schools through culturally contextualised mathematics education.

Finally, I have experienced how students are victimized by teachers (among whom I was one) and schools. Rote-memorization and practice methods have produced students as mechanistic learners deprived of conceptual and meaningful learning due in no small way to culturally decontextualised mathematics curricula. In this regard, before closing the chapter, I want to present a piece of text that illustrates how decontextualised education can compel a student to drop out from school and how practical knowledge transformed his life.

...Imprisoned every day in the one-room classroom, he felt utterly lost...Al was frightened of the cane, but he still couldn't learn the great lists of facts the teacher told him to. His habit of asking questions just made the teacher even more angry...Then he heard the schoolmaster talking about him; there was something wrong with young Edison, the man said. He was "addled"...In a rage he rushed out of the schoolroom and refused to go back. (Sproule, 1995, pp. 12–13)

This is the story of one of the great inventors of all time, Thomas Alva Edison, who harnessed electricity for domestic use. I agree with Sproule (1995) that the one-way-traffic teaching method in a tightly controlled and managed environment does not create (new) knowledge, rather it most often suppresses children's creativity. The curriculum is also responsible for creating such a monotonous environment in the classroom. Sproule (1995, pp. 13–14) wrote further:

At home, his mother, Nancy, took his side in battle...One day when he was nine, she gave him his first book on science, the "School of Natural Philosophy", it gave readers simple experiments they could carry out at home. From that time Al's life was transformed.

REFERENCES

Adams, T. E., & Holman Jones, S. (2008). Autoethnography is queer. In N. K. Denzin, Y. S. Lincoln, & L. T. Smith (Eds.), *Handbook of critical and indigenous methodologies* (pp. 373–390). Thousand Oaks, CA: Sage Publications.
Battista, M. (1999). The mathematical miseducation of America's youth. *Phi Delta Kappan, 80*(6), 424–433.
D'Ambrosio, U. (1985). *Ethnomathematics: Link between traditions and modernity*. Sao Paulo: Editora Atica.
D'Ambrosio, U. (1990). *Etnomatemática* [Ethnomathematics]. São Paulo: Editora Ática.
Fraser, S. P., & Bosanquet, A. M. (2006). The curriculum? That's just a unit outline, isn't it? *Studies in Higher Education, 31*(3), 269–284.
Freire, P. (1993). *Pedagogy of the oppressed*. New York, NY: Continuum.
Hammond, T. (2000). *Ethnomathematics: Concept, definition and research perspectives* (Unpublished master's thesis). New York, NY: Columbia University.
Luitel, B. C. (2009). *Culture, worldview and transformative philosophy of mathematics education in Nepal: A cultural-philosophical inquiry* (Unpublished doctoral thesis). Curtin University, Bentley, Australia.
Luitel, B. C. (2013). Mathematics as an im/pure knowledge system: Symbiosis, (w)holism and synergy in mathematics education. *International Journal of Science and Mathematics Education, 11*(1), 65–87.
Luitel, B. C. (2017). A mindful inquiry into reductionism in mathematics education. In M. Powietrzynska & K. Tobin (Eds.), *Weaving complementary knowledge systems and mindfulness to educate a literate citizenry for sustainable and healthy lives* (pp. 1–26). Rotterdam, The Netherlands: Sense Publishers.
Luitel, B. C., & Taylor, P. C. (2010). 'What is ours and what is not ours?' Inclusive imaginings of contextualised mathematics teacher education. In D. J. Tippins, M. P. Mueller, M. van Eijck, & J. Adams (Eds.), *Cultural studies and environmentalism: The confluence of eco-justice, place based (science) education, and indigenous knowledge systems* (pp. 385–408). Dordrecht: Springer.
Mezirow, J. (1997). Transformative learning: Theory to practice. *New Directions for Adult and Continuing Education, 74*, 5–12.

INDRA MANI SHRESTHA

Saldana, J. (2011). Ethnotheatre: Research from page to page. In N. K. Denzin & Y. S. Lincoln (Eds.), *Qualitative inquiry and social justice.* Walnut Creek, CA: Left Coast Press.
Shrestha, I. M. (2011). *My journey of learning and teaching: A trans/formation from culturally decontextualised to contextualised mathematics education* (Unpublished master's thesis). Kathmandu University, Nepal.
Shrestha, I. M. (2018). *My pedagogical sensitisation towards holistic mathematics education: A practitioner's inquiry* (Unpublished MPhil thesis). Kathmandu University, Nepal.
Sproule, A. (1995). *Scientists who have changed the world: Thomas A. Edison.* Hyderabad: Orient Longman.
Spry, T. (2001). Performing autoethnography: An embodied methodological praxis. *Qualitative Inquiry, 7*(6), 706–732.
Whitehead, J. (2008). Using a living theory methodology in improving practice and generating educational knowledge in living theories. *Educational Journal of Living Theories, 1*(1), 103–126.

ABOUT THE AUTHOR

I am **Indra Mani Shrestha.** I am working as a Kathmandu University lecturer and a mathematics teacher in a secondary school in Kathmandu. I have been teaching master's courses and working with school mathematics teachers and teacher educators in Nepal, advocating culturally de/contextualised curricula, critical pedagogical practices, and holistic assessment practices under critical mathematics education. I am a practitioner of transformative educational research and critical reflective practices in teaching and learning processes.

INDRA MANI RAI (YAMPHU)

15. UNSHACKLING FROM CULTURAL HEGEMONY VIA THIRD SPACING PEDAGOGY

Learning to Think Indigenously

Chawa is our root. Without Chawa, there is no way to talk about social life: what and how to speak? Chawa is vital while introducing one to other. Chawa is inevitable to make a link with ancestors and to communicate with them. The ancestors cannot hear and recognize you until you recite your Chawa. Without Chawa, we will not be human, but we become like animals. Imagine what will happen if there is no kinship and social relations in the society? How do you communicate with each other? How do you identify yourself? Who is who? Therefore, Chawa is recited in every lifecycle rituals. For us, life is not possible without Chawa. It is with reference to the Chawa of each person and each clan/ group, Yamphu establishes relations between the individuals and groups.

This piece of mythology, or *Mindhum*, is part of the oral tradition of the Yamphu community which, for centuries, has been inhabiting the villages of East Nepal (Yamphu, 2014, p. 12). I grew up in this community. Although I am unaware of much of the detail of Yamphu mythology, I know that this mythology represents the origin and dispersal of our ancestors in the territory. We believe, for example, that the particular source of spring water – *Chawa* – is where the ancestors of a particular clan group drank water for the first time, and hence we assume Chawa to be the soul of our ancestors. Hom Prasad Yamphu (2014, p. 12) interprets Chawa as signifying:

> ...Yamphu way of life, [it] provides a set of values through which every Yamphu sees world and acts, offers a source of Yamphu thought and ideology symbolizing Yamphu spiritual attachment to the ancestral lands, stands for ancestral order and authority in the present, and legitimizes kinship, marriage and other social relationships among Yamphu.

Thus, Chawa is an example of a body of indigenous knowledge, beliefs and worldview of the Yamphu community. This holistic body of indigenous knowledge, passed down from generation to generation, guides the whole of living and life of the Yamphu. However, it was not valued in my schooling. I was not allowed to learn about or reflect on these indigenous beliefs, knowledge and worldview. In other words, the indigenous knowledge that I already had was unrelated in the process of learning at school. Teaching and learning activities were guided and directed by structural forces such as centralized curriculum, textbook, teacher management and governance, making the entire system rigid. The education system emphasized transmitting values drawn from a privileged external worldview as depicted in the standardized and set curriculum and textbooks. The transmissionist pedagogical approaches made the teaching and learning activities decontextualized and detached from the everyday context of we learners. Further, these approaches kept me as a passive listener who accepted everything the teachers said. I was not encouraged to engage in my indigenous real-life social contexts to promote my indigenous knowledge. The approach of educational development ignored contextual knowledge and knowing practices. This was a kind of systematic educational neglect. Arguably, this approach works to reproduce present power relations in the education system (Bourdieu & Wacquant, 1992).

In this context, the purpose of this chapter, partly based on my doctoral thesis (Rai, 2018), is to consider why *hybridization* (Bhabha, 2006) of pedagogical practices in modern schools could serve justifiable and inclusive teaching and learning approaches. I argue that transformative ways of educating learners can facilitate integration of indigenous knowledge, thereby promoting meaningful learning. In so doing, I portray my inner world of lived experiences based on my interaction with the phenomena of teaching and learning activities across multiple contexts and times. I use my retrospective gaze of an inquiring self in order to explore my own worldviews and practices (Spry, 2001) that were shaped by the modernization of learning and teaching. I engage in writing self-reflexively about past and present epiphanies as a learner, teacher, and teacher educator, excavating experiences connected with my cultural context and sociality (Freeman, 2007; Ellis & Bochner, 2000). More so, I articulate my vulnerability while learning and teaching in schools and universities.

I unpack my experiences of forming and constructing transformative notions and practices that resist the process of standardization of pedagogies. In this sense, this is an advocacy for more equitable and fair pedagogical practices (Taylor & Medina, 2011). I put forward confessions about my *false consciousness* that directed me to reproduce suppressive pedagogical practices in the process of materializing a Western modern worldview. I begin by articulating a subjugated indigenous worldview and knowledge as an example of my own community. I then unpack my confessions about how I learnt in structured settings and reproduced similar strategies in my professional milieu, as a hegemony. In subsequent sections I deal with how I became a transformative learner through critically reflecting on indigenous knowledge. Finally, I argue that in Nepali schools third spacing pedagogy, as a dialectical space, would engage indigenous students in transformative learning, enabling them to reflect on their own beliefs, knowledge and worldviews.

SUBJUGATED INDIGENOUS WORLDVIEWS AND KNOWLEDGE

Paruhang (Shiva) created humankind under the ground, *iei* we came over here by following River path, *i ei poppo* on this *pitta sambok* (*cynodon dactylon – a sacred grass*), mankind was created; after creating mankind, death was also created; he also created knowledgeable and stupid humans as well. (Yamphu, 2014, p. 40)

This piece of *Mindhum* is an example of a garland of mythology that talks about the origin, migratory routes (river paths), formation of culture and civilizations, rites and rituals, or in a broader sense the way of life of Yamphus. This explains my cultural roots embedded in the land. This represents a philosophy of Yamphu that guides the whole living and life patterns of Yamphus. My early ways of thinking and seeing the world were guided by the beliefs created by this indigenous mythology. Mindhum is an oral tradition that represents a comprehensive worldview in my community which shaped my cultural life in the context of living. I had particular cosmologies constructed based on the beliefs transmitted down from generation to generation. These indigenous cosmologies shaped my life activities and sense of seeing self and others. Thus, Yamphu worldview and culture is rooted in and emerged through the intactness of ancestors with the land and the water resources – *Chawa* – they used for the first time. The oral traditions also represent spiritual and cultural attachment with nature and worshipping ancestral souls as spiritual beings. However, modern schools in Nepal have disregarded indigenous worldviews, emotions, social norms and values, ethics, activities, cultural behavior and beliefs.

The bodies of wisdom that have been handed down by generations and experiences gained through interaction with the cultural world remain under represented in the process of learning in modern schools. Moreover, indigenous knowledge embedded in local stories, songs, poetic chanting and local proverbs/sayings are deemed to be not useful in modern classroom practices. *Arti-Upadesh,* that is, telling others about what is good and what is not, is the way through which elders or wise persons would informally educate young ones in their lives (Chemjong, 2003). The elders were the main source of knowledge. I remember the Arti-Upadesh given by my father, mother and grandfather, either directly or metaphorically, through songs, stories, riddles, proverbs. This was the way that indigenous knowledge was passing to me from my father, mother and forefathers. They did not only pass on wisdom but also their own experiences. These included all sorts of knowledge, from moral education to health education, from agriculture to forestry. However, this body of knowledge and skills remains unrecognized in the process of teaching and learning in modern schools.

Shamanism is another form of oral knowledge system that helps to overcome the trouble and healing from diseases. Shamanic performers – *Yadangba* or *Mangba* – are mediators for building connection and harmony between the spiritual world and the human world (Maskarinec, 1995). They are traditional healers. Shamans use multiple acts and ways – dreaming, meditation, shamanic dance, recitation of mantra, and magical acts – for healing people's troubles. This practice is lively among many communities of Nepal. They recite mantra with particular beliefs for healing and in the process of worshipping ancestors. Moreover, it is believed that shamans and priests have the capacity to communicate with the spirits of ancestors. The beliefs of the ancestors (as supernatural beings) are transferred to community members and children. Shamanic practices help to shape their social activities, actions and behavior in the community. However, in the process of learning in school, I had no opportunity to reflect on beliefs associated with Shamanic acts; a body of wisdom that is subjugated and devalued in modernized schooling.

SCHOOL AS A LION'S DEN

My schooling began in a small village in east Nepal in the 1980s. Many of the students, including me, were from the Yamphu indigenous community. The school in such a distinct community with a different language (i.e., Nepali), culture, traditions, lifestyles and way of living was not so friendly to me. I was from a tribal family and did not like to go to school as I felt the teachers were strangers. I could not speak about my feelings, even with friends. This might have been due to my fear of others' negative or undermining responses. Thus, the back seats in the class kept waiting for me most of the time. I wanted to be ignored by the teachers. I felt inferior among others. This might also have been due to my torn clothes and inadequate learning materials. I was one of the weakest students in the class in terms of achievement as measured by paper-and-pencil based examinations. I could not conceptualize the ideas of mathematics and science taught in class based on text-books. It was difficult for me to pronounce and sense the meaning of the words and sentences in Nepali and English. I felt like a stranger in the class.

A public school in a rural indigenous context with a tin roof and rows and columns of wooden desks and benches on a dusty earthen floor was not conducive to my learning. Memorizing the alphabet of the Nepali language and numerals was our work most of the time. The teachers instructed us to read and recall by heart tables of maths and poems. I copied the contents of the text-books as my assignments. Sometimes the teachers read aloud the text-books and translated the contents. They were transmitting knowledge to us. This traditional approach of depositing text-book codified knowledge felt oppressive (Freire, 1993). Moreover, the teachers often entered the classroom holding sticks in their hands, making us mute with our heads bowed down. Because I was not be able to satisfactorily perform learning tasks I often came home with slapped cheeks, twisted ears and painful knuckles and palms. School, for me, was fearful.

Looking back, I now understand that my sense of alienation was due largely to the spread of modern schooling promoted by the democratic government after the end of the autocratic Rana rule in the 1950s. The new democracy promoted a permeable membrane of leaking in the ideas and practices of modernization. The universalization and uniformity of the education system was promoted by the Nepal National Education Planning Commission (1956). The policies promoted universal (Western) values and restricted the diversity of students in terms of culture (Awasthi, 2004). Clearly, this educational expansion was not in favor of indigenous ways of learning. Due to the efforts of non-governmental structures education was one of the key development themes and aid began to flourish in international discourse in the decade of the 1950s (Rist, 2014). In embracing the interests of external power structures, modernization of Nepali education might have been accepted as an act of benevolent kindness.

As a result, the modern education system was heavily influenced by the ideals of teacher-centered activities, strict disciplinary engagement of students, structured paper-pencil based assessment, and so on. My later research raised my critical awareness that educational policy is a "political process in which certain interests and agendas were always pursued at the expense of others, in which curriculum inevitably promoted some content as an exercise of the power" (Taylor, Cranton, & Associates, 2012, p. 135). Thus, it seems that the schools of Nepal were serving the interests of Western power structures that aimed to homogenize the schooling of students from culturally and linguistically diverse backgrounds. For me, these practices were suppressive as my learning was not based on my interests and expectations.

During the later days of my village schooling I started to achieve better marks as a result of studying by heart the limited ideas and concepts of the text-books. But I continued to have no opportunity to share my indigenous knowledge and skills. The centrally designed curricula focused on imported knowledge and skills which were largely irrelevant to my day-to-day life (Koirala, 2003; Semali, 1999). My indigenous worldview, shaped by oral traditions, did not serve as a prerequisite for further learning. I agree with critical scholars that in Nepal, due to prevailing power structures, a *Westo-centric* curriculum enforced *epistemic oppression* against local ways of knowing (Semali & Kincheloe, 1999). Later, as a school teacher, I replicated this modern curriculum approach as I had no ideas other than those that I had experienced as a student. On reflection, I realise that school as a modern social structure shaped my agency which compelled me to reproduce similar teaching and learning activities.

REPRODUCING THE STATUS QUO

In the early 1990s, higher education in Kathmandu took me out of my rural indigenous world after completing my School Leaving Certificate (i.e., standardized exam after 10th grade). Initially, living in the city was miserable for me. I started to hunt for a job after I completed my Intermediate level (i.e., 12th grade) of education from Tribhuvan University. I might not have been adequately equipped by modern education as it was difficult for me to be placed in an appropriate job. After several attempts I was recruited by a private school as a science cum math teacher. I felt that teaching mathematics and science at primary level was a very difficult task. I needed to prepare problem-solving techniques in mathematics to arrive at the exact answer before entering class. I used similar strategies of teaching to those of my own teachers, which have been critiqued as "disempowering pedagogical models of listen-repeat-remember-recall and do-what-teacher-says" (Luitel, 2009, p. 7). On reflection, my one-size-fits-all curriculum approach compelled students to be passive recipients of imported knowledge. At that time, however, I thought that structured and teacher-dominant practices were the best way to promote the learning of students.

My students had a different culture and everyday life to the one that I taught in school. Looking back on that time, it seems to me that "the students learned social truths in the society through their everyday living but they learned universal truth through textual learning" (Koirala, 2003, p. 152). The structured pedagogical practices set by the school authority marginalized local cultural values, beliefs and non-verbal background knowledge. These imported pedagogical practices put the emphasis on transmissible knowledge from the textbooks while ignoring students' tacit knowledge of their real-world experiences. I agree with Larry Ray (2007) who attributed this approach to "modern societies that had undergone a 'crisis of meaning' as it undermined common-sense 'knowledge' and personal identity" (p. 13). Disregarding the knowledge of the life-world of learners in the process of learning has the effect of denying the legitimacy of their indigenous knowledge and ways of knowing.

My teaching ensured that the students from indigenous groups were subordinated and marginalized (like I had been) as they were required to put aside their cultural ways of learning. This act of falsifying a sense of identity (Dourish, 2008) goes against creating solidarity and strengthening of presence in the learning context. Ignoring indigenous students' prior knowledge and ways of knowing serves to construct a homogenized and externally imposed identity. On reflection, I realised that, as a teacher, I had accepted and adopted the practices and ideas of the powerful Western modern worldview in a taken-for-granted manner without challenging or questioning it. I had tacitly rationalised that the hegemony of existing pedagogical practices was serving the public good. My later research led me to understand that the Nepali education system in which I had taught could be seen as a *colonial tool* that ensured indigenous students adopted Western ways of knowing the world with decontextualised knowledge and skills. Coming to this realization during my doctoral research was due to my transformative learning in a process of self-inquiry as an auto/ethnographer.

BECOMING A TRANSFORMATIVE LEARNER

It was in the context of my postgraduate studies at Kathmandu University's School of Education (KUSOED) in 2011, and onward, that I engaged in transformative learning which allowed me to *think indigenously*. The ideals of transformative learning, rooted in the work Jack Mezirow which surfaced in the 1990s, enabled me to unshackle from Western modern hegemonic ideas and learning practices. Transformative learning theory puts forward the notion of change in *meaning perspective* through *critical self-reflection* (Mezirow, 2012). It focuses on meaning construction from experience and modification of presuppositions or prior thinking. "At its heart, transformative learning theory is about the nature of change, and about the processes through which we produce a shift in the way we see and make meaning of the world" (Jones, 2015, p. 268). Thus learning through critical thinking is at the core of transformative learning theory. Critical reflection liberates us from existing ideas shaped by our experiences and improves our awareness (Taylor, 2015). Thus, transformative learning focuses on reassessing our own ideas and practices, making us critical thinkers who contest taken-for-granted ideas and practices. At the time, I was unaware of these ideas but, on reflection, I realised that I had engaged in a process of shifting my viewpoints through critical self-reflection.

When I first started my postgraduate coursework studies at KUSEOD I expected the classes to run the same way as during my earlier university days: the traditional lecture method. But the pedagogical practices at KUSOED were very different, with more caring of individual students and flexible learning. I engaged in activity-based learning and sharing of ideas with group members. Initially, I had little idea about academic debates and discourses. I accepted the ideas as taken for granted and did not raise questions or challenge them. I often panicked about my own contributions because previously I had not received positive comments from my professors, and so I imagined that my current work would be dreadful. Initially, I had little idea about reviewing academic documents, critiquing, arguing, contesting, challenging, doubting, reflecting, synthesizing, assessing, analyzing and interpreting and reporting. However, the way that my professors shared ideas in class, their feedback on my assignments, and my regular interaction with them helped me to develop myself by visualizing things differently.

As an example, consider a day when I first presented a review paper in class. In reviewing the paper my thoughts had been shaped by my indigenous knowledge and worldview. In presenting my review of the article to the class I critiqued the author's emphasis on modern education. Surprisingly, my professor appreciated my way of thinking indigenously and my challenge to the ideas in the paper. He praised my argumentation and my disagreement with the author's ideas. I was stunned. I had thought that I was a good student, but not that good! I felt that this signaled a transformation in my academic work. I shifted my way of thinking and working academically. I was terrified and exhilarated at the same time. Perhaps, I was becoming able to work successfully in academia. I realized that I had developed my critical thinking ability for assessing literature. I felt that I could engage in academic discourses and debates in a more meaningful way. Thus, engaging in critical thinking and reflecting on my indigenous knowledge and worldview was a transformative learning experience.

I altered my vision through interactive and discussion-based learning with professors and colleagues in Kathmandu University. The shared learning enabled me to think about my prior indigenous knowledge. I engaged more in thinking about the weaknesses I had and how others argued with different ideas about my work. Perhaps, I engaged in *reflective discourse* for assessing critically my earlier assumptions, interpretations and beliefs (Mezirow, 2012, p. 78). Learning through interaction and reflection on indigenous knowledge helped me to develop a critical perspective. I started to question existing ideas and practices based on my prior knowledge. My learning to challenge the status quo constituted my self-transformation (Mackeracher, 2012). Moreover, I started to think about my own indigenous experiences and assess my *false consciousness* (Luitel, 2009). My critical self-reflective practice helped me to reassess my orientation and promoted further my critical thinking and learning. Possibly, I was reinterpreting the predispositions and presuppositions (Freire, 1993) of my taken-for-granted ideas. This distinctive way of reinterpreting my experiences enabled me to understand the world differently.

I developed a sense of visualizing issues from alternative perspectives, which enabled me to understand social realities differently. Possibly, I had changed my *structure of assumptions* or *frame of reference* (Mezirow, 2012, p. 82). This helped me to reassess my indigenous knowledge, beliefs, and worldviews. Development of this sensibility enabled me to revise my prior interpretation of the meaning of my experiences. I shifted my schema which helped me, to some extent, to build my academic competency. In other words, development of critical thinking and practices provided me with the opportunity to engage critically with academic premises through academic discourses and debates.

For example, in conducting my PhD thesis I explored the *identity paradoxes* of Kirat migrants in an urban context and I critiqued urbanism, modernization and globalization, positioning myself at the vantage point of indigeneity-indigenous beliefs and worldviews (Rai, 2018). Moreover, as an auto/ethnographer, I assessed my own false consciousness and practices of engaging in the urban world. Thus, critical self-reflection enabled me to gain close access to the plausible and realistic articulation of both the self and other Kirat migrants. This was how I engaged in transformative learning: reflecting on indigenous worldviews and global/modern perspectives. Transformative learning allowed me to create a space for respecting both indigenous and modern knowledge and ways of knowing.

THIRD SPACING PEDAGOGY

I believe that my own engagement in transformative learning is transferable to Nepali school contexts by means of *third spacing pedagogy*. Homi Bhabha's (2006) notion of the *third space*, created by *cross-breeding* two seemingly opposing worldviews and practices, can include both modern and indigenous knowledge, ways of knowing, and ways of educating Nepali students. Third spacing pedagogy would engage indigenous students in transformative learning by enabling them to reflect on their indigenous beliefs and worldviews. I do not mean to deny the teaching and learning practices guided by the Western modern worldview. Rather, I am in favor of building synergy between global practices and indigenous practices that arise from collective cultural practices (Luitel, 2009). A hybrid form of pedagogy can promote cultural inclusiveness and social justice. Arguably, hybridization of knowledge and ways of knowing can facilitate respectful and meaningful learning. For me, this is the notion of an *ambivalent* pedagogical practice consisting of two opposing dimensions. I believe that combining local indigenous knowledge and imported Western knowledge is a way to promote cultural inclusiveness and social justice. In such a curriculum third space students would respectfully and meaningfully compare and contrast their indigenous knowledge and newly imported knowledge. The space would provide students with opportunities to reflect on their experiential knowledge acquired in their living cultural contexts and the beliefs and worldviews passed down from generation to generation.

Thus, I argue that the education systems of Nepal need to recognize hybrid curriculum spaces that identify the cultural differences of students. This is how schools can respect cultural diversity and adopt pedagogical practices in a culturally sensitive manner. Developing synergistic pedagogical practices would facilitate transformative learning in classrooms. Students bring a broad range of ideas, beliefs, values, and experiences to the classroom which forms a spectrum of viewpoints. This indigenous knowledge influences students' conceptual development (Snively & Corsiglia, 2001) and would support their comprehension of modern or global abstract ideas and concepts. A hybrid curriculum space would promote a coherent view of knowledge that recognizes the metaphysical orientation in which Western ideas are embedded.

Border Crossing

This is understandable inasmuch as students, like me, from indigenous communities are *border-crossers* from their home-cultural worlds to the modern school-cultural world. I am not talking about a physical border; rather, cultural borders that have been historically constructed and socially organized and that serve to either limit or enable their particular identities for learning (Giroux, 1991). Participating in the modern school-cultural world involves crossing over into a new domain of meaning, maps of knowledge, social relations and values. Students have to engage in a new (alien) context of remapping, reterritorializing and decentering their knowledge (Giroux, 1991). I argue that it is in the third space – a hybrid of home and school cultures – that students from indigenous groups would have the opportunity to speak, to locate themselves, and to become subjects in the construction of their identities. The third space would not only provide opportunity to speak but also to engage in transformative learning, thereby promoting critical thinking on ideology and other forms of cultural (re)production.

Dialectical Thinking

For me, schooling in Nepal should be re-engineered by linking it with the everyday needs of local indigenous students and their worldviews. In so doing, third spacing pedagogy would serve as an empowering critical cultural construct for resolving historic dualisms associated with the seemingly incompatible contradictions that separate Western modern and indigenous worldviews. The idea of the third space is about thinking and acting inclusively via *dialectical thinking* to generate synergies from prevailing antagonisms, thereby developing inclusive and interdependent perspectives and practices (Luitel, 2009; Wong, 2006). Dialectical thinking arises from critical reflective thinking.

Cultural Self Knowing and Relational Knowing

As a key transformative learning practice, critical self-reflection enables us to realize our own indigenous knowledge, beliefs and worldviews. This *cultural self-knowing* helps us understand our culturally situated selves and worldviews that shape our behaviors, especially how and why we make (habituated) sense of our socio-cultural worlds (Taylor, 2015). More so, *relational knowing*, another transformative learning practice, enables learners to reconnect with their local community and the natural world (Taylor, 2015). These are crucial learning practices for Nepali schools that can empower students to bring their indigenous knowledge inside the classroom and link it with modern or global knowledge perspectives. Like me, students from indigenous communities would be taught to reflect on their own worldviews and experiences gained through their day-to-day engagement in their socio-cultural worlds. They would connect the shared ideas of their families and communities with classroom learning. Arguably, third spacing pedagogy in Nepali schools would engage indigenous students in transformative learning with the ability to engage in *two-way cultural border crossings* between their indigenous and global communities.

FINAL REMARKS

During my doctoral research I came to the insight that, in Nepal, pedagogical practices guided by the Western modern worldview of universalization and homogenization of education systems is suppressive of indigenous knowledge, beliefs and worldviews, and ways knowing. Our centrally designed curricula and controlling pedagogies promote imported knowledge and knowing while marginalizing contextual knowledge. Modern schooling in Nepal maintains the corpus of indigenous knowledge and ways of knowing in a subjugated, devalued, unused and restricted position. To resolve this problem, I believe that hybridization of imported and indigenous knowledge and ways of knowing can help to promote cultural inclusiveness and social justice through meaningful and respectful learning.

In this context, Homi Bhabha's third space concept offers the exciting prospect of creating a synergy of modern and indigenous pedagogical ideas and practices, and may serve as an empowering force for promoting democratic practices in classroom teaching and learning in the Nepali context. Third spacing pedagogy would engage indigenous students in transformative learning with critical reflection on their indigenous knowledge, beliefs and worldviews, and modern or global perspectives. Thus, third spacing pedagogy could help to unshackle us from the controlled and structured pedagogical practices currently framed by the Western modern worldview of universalism and homogenization.

Of course, we need to be mindful that the discourse of transformative education might also be a hegemonic ideal and practice constructed elsewhere in the world. Nevertheless, it does allow thinking and acting more autonomously and indigenously for promoting locally contextualised learning processes.

REFERENCES

Awasthi, L. D. (2004). *Exploring monolingual education practices in multilingual Nepal* (Unpublished doctoral dissertation). Danish University of Education, Copenhagen, Denmark.

Bhabha, H. K. (2006). Cultural diversity and cultural differences. In B. Ashcroft, G. Griffiths, & H. Tiffin (Eds.), *The post-colonial studies reader* (pp. 155–157). London & New York, NY: Routledge.

Bourdieu, P., & Wacquant, L. J. D. (1992). *An invitation to reflexive sociology.* Cambridge: Polity Press.

Chemjong, I. S. (2003). *Kirat Mundhum khahun (education).* Lalitpur, Nepal: Kirat Yakthung Chumlung, Central Office.

Dourish, P. (2008). *Points of persuasion: Strategic essentialism and environmental sustainability.* Irvine, CA: University of California.

Ellis, C., & Bochner, A. P. (2000). Autoethnography, personal narrative, and personal reflexivity. In N. K. Denzin & Y. S. Lincoln (Eds.), *Handbook of qualitative research* (2nd ed., pp. 733–768). Thousand Oaks, CA: Sage Publications.

Freeman, M. (2007). Autobiographical understanding and narrative inquiry. In J. Clandinin (Ed.), *Handbook of narrative inquiry: Mapping a methodology* (pp. 3–33). Thousand Oaks, CA: Sage Publications.

Freire, P. (1993). *Pedagogy of the oppressed.* Oxford: Penguin Books.

Giroux, H. A. (1991). Border pedagogy as postmodern resistance. In H. A. Giroux (Ed.), *Postmodernism, feminism, and cultural politics: Redrawing educational boundaries* (pp. 358–363). New York, NY: State University of New York Press.

Jones, P. (2015). Transformative learning theory: Addressing new challenges in social work education. In M. Li & Y. Zhao (Eds.), *Exploring learning and teaching in higher education* (pp. 267–286). Verlag Berlin Heidelberg: Springer.

Koirala, B. N. (2003). Managing paradoxes: Education for the sustained future. In B. B. Bhandari & O. Abe (Eds.), *Education for sustainable development in Nepal: Views and visions* (pp. 151–158). Tokyo: Institute for Global Environmental Strategies (IGES) and School of Environmental Management and Sustainable Development (SchEMS)/Nepal.

Luitel, B. C. (2009). *Culture, worldview and transformative philosophy of mathematics education in Nepal: A cultural philosophical inquiry* (Unpublished doctoral dissertation). Curtin University, Australia.

Mackeracher, D. (2012). The role of experience in transformative learning. In E. W. Taylor, P. Cranton, & Associates (Eds.), *The handbook of transformative learning: Theory, research, and practice* (pp. 342–354). San Francisco, CA: Jossey-Bass.

Maskarinec, G. G. (1995). *The rulings of the night: An ethnography of Nepalese shaman oral texts.* Kathmandu: Mandala Book Point.

Mezirow, J. (2012). Learning to think like an adult: Core concepts of transformative theory. In E. W. Taylor, P. Craton, & Associates (Eds.), *The handbook of transformative learning: Theory, research and practice* (pp. 73–95). San Francisco, CA: Jossey-Bass.

Rai, I. M. (2018). *Identity paradoxes of Kirat migrants in urban context. An auto/ethnographic inquiry* (Unpublished doctoral dissertation). Kathmandu University, Nepal.

Ray, L. (2007). *Globalization and everyday life.* New York, NY: Routledge.

Rist, G. (2014). *The history of development: From Western origins to global faith* (4th ed.). London: Zed Books.

Semali, L. M. (1999). Community as classroom: (Re)valuing indigenous literacy. In L. M. Semali & J. L. Kincheloe (Eds.), *What is indigenous knowledge? Voices from the academy* (pp. 95–118). New York, NY: Falmer Press.

Semali, L. M., & Kincheloe, J. L. (1999). Introduction: What is indigenous knowledge and why should we study it? In L. M. Semali & J. L. Kincheloe (Eds.), *What is indigenous knowledge? Voices from the academy* (pp. 3–58). New York, NY: Falmer Press.

Snively, G., & Corsiglia, J. (2001). Discovering indigenous science: Implications for science education. *Science Education, 85*(1), 6–34.

Spry, T. (2001). Performing autoethnography: An embedded methodological praxis. *Qualitative Inquiry, 7*(6), 706–732.

Taylor, E. W., Cranton, P., & Associates. (2012). *The handnook of transformative learning: Theory, research, and practice.* San Francisco, CA: Jossey-Bass.

Taylor, P. C. (2015). Transformative science education. In R. Gunstone (Ed.), *Encyclopedia of science education* (pp. 1079–1082). Dordrecht: Springer.

Taylor, P. C., & Medina, M. (2011). Educational research paradigms: From positivism to pluralism. *College Research Journal, 1*(1), 1–16.

The Nepal National Education Planning Commission (NNEPC). (1956). *Education in Nepal: Report of the Nepal national educational planning commission.* Kathmandu: Bureau of Publications, College of Education.

Wong, W. (2006). Understanding dialectical thinking from a cultural-historical perspective. *Philosophical Psychology, 19*(2), 239–260.

Yamphu, H. P. (2014). *Mindhum: Account of Yamphu origin and indigeneity* (Unpublished M.Phil. dissertation). Tribhuvan University, Nepal.

ABOUT THE AUTHOR

My name is **Indra Mani Rai** (Yamphu). I am a teacher educator, researcher and trainer. I am working as a lecturer at Tribhuvan University, Central Department of Education, Kirtipur, Kathmandu, Nepal. My area of research interests are identity, transformative learning, urbanism, ethnicity, and indigenous knowledge.

SITI SHAMSIAH SANI

16. ENVISIONING CREATIVE LEARNING IN SCIENCE TEACHER EDUCATION

Currere, Emancipation and Creativity

Unconnected Holes

I am sitting on a chair in a cosy classroom
Waiting for the others to come
My eyes observing the whole class
Everything seems familiar to me
I keep on looking at what is around me
I see something strange
As I glance up at the ceiling
I see many holes above me
Every hole seems close to the others
But the holes do not join together
They are, like me, unable to see the connection with the knowledge that I have

"I simply do not see the connection!", Aiman said to his group members. He expressed his frustration during one of the "Teaching Strategies" workshops that I was conducting in my university. His comment still echoes in my mind.

The workshops are part of a course for preparing pre-service science teachers with a range of teaching strategies before they embark on their careers as science teachers in secondary schools throughout Malaysia. The course aims to produce science teachers who can inspire young learners to be competitive, dynamic, robust, and resilient citizens. The teachers are responsible for educating young learners to be scientifically literate citizens, able to make informed decisions on socio-scientific issues. In the workshops, the pre-service science teachers carry out prescribed activities to enable them to experience different teaching and learning strategies in science. At the time I began to teach this course I felt that that it did not provide these pre-service science teachers with the opportunity to experience teaching and learning activities that embrace the diversity of local knowledge, cultures and communities.

The university is located in one of the States of Malaysia. The local communities are unique and form a multi-ethnic and multi-cultural landscape. Malays, Chinese, Indians and Orang Asli/indigenous people live together and share unique cultural identities in terms of languages, education, economy and food. The university is surrounded by tropical rainforest and is home to a diverse flora and fauna.

However, I felt that not enough attention was being paid to this rich diversity as a means of enhancing the pre-service science teachers' creative teaching skills. The workshops and the course were using activities and examples that embraced Western cultures and values. It seemed to me that limited exposure to local cultural knowledge was hindering the pre-service science teachers' ability to teach creatively. As teachers, they might not be able to connect the knowledge they gained from the workshops with their own cultural traditions and local environment.

Later, during my master's degree, I conducted a critical autoethnographic inquiry to address this concern (Sani, 2008). In this inquiry I explored my experiences as a student, a pre-service science teacher, and a science teacher educator. Critical reflection on my experiences, coupled with consideration of contemporary theories of curriculum and creativity, enabled me to envision a learning environment for emancipating pre-service science teachers, enabling them to be creative in generating meaningful learning experiences for our young learners.

In this chapter, I refer to my experience of learning science from childhood until I embarked on a teacher education program, share my dilemma of teaching the Teaching Strategies workshops, and present my vision of transformed workshops for producing creative science teachers.

MY TRANFORMATIVE RESEARCH JOURNEY

As I embarked on my master's degree I perceived science education research through other than the positivist and post-positivist paradigms. Neither fitted well with my inquiry. I intended to develop a vision of a transformed learning environment in which to conduct the Teaching Strategies workshops. Thus, I based my inquiry on the paradigms of postmodernism and criticalism.

The critical paradigm enabled me to deconstruct the disempowering learning environment of the Teaching Strategies workshop and promote a learning environment that aims to develop scientific knowledge without neglecting the local culture and values through creative teaching. The postmodernist paradigm added a creative, literary, playful dimension to my inquiry (Taylor, 2008). Multiple logics were applied to the writing, as I used metaphorical thinking (Luitel & Taylor, 2007) to describe the learning culture in the workshop. Composing poems strengthened my feelings towards the learning experiences, and it was appropriate to use a prosaic writing style in presenting my inquiry (Taylor, 2008).

The combination of critical and postmodernist paradigms created an interesting hybrid research methodology for an autoethnographic inquiry to imagine and enact a creative learning praxis for the Teaching Strategies workshop. Autoethnography provided opportunities for me to explore and represent my own life stories as a pre-service teacher and teacher educator in different ways – poetry, narrative, imagery and dialogues. This enabled me to present my ideas in various forms, such as propositional, metaphoric, perspectival, dialectical and nondual (Luitel & Taylor, 2008).

I examined curriculum and learning theories for redesigning the instructions for the Teaching Strategies workshops. These theories helped me to reconceptualise how knowledge is delivered, processed and retained during learning, and thus to reimagine the roles of the pre-service science teachers and the lecturer during the workshops. I came to understand how cognitive, emotional, environmental and prior knowledge shape, change or maintain the worldviews of students. This insight enabled me to envision a transformed learning environment for the Teaching Strategies workshops.

AN UNCHANGEABLE SCIENCE LEARNING JOURNEY

When I was required to think about possible topics for my master's research project, I started to think about the learning culture that I had experienced over 11 years in the late 1980s and 1990s. I started to revisit my past experience as a student who was very optimistic about what school could offer. But, the learning environment that I actually experienced changed my perceptions about the roles of schools, teachers and education.

Based on my learning experiences at primary and secondary school, I perceived science lessons merely as a subject. Each concept stood alone without a connection to local culture and knowledge. Teachers' aims in teaching science were to complete the syllabus, equip students with scientific knowledge and skills, and prepare students for the end-of-year national examination. My views about my science learning journey of 25 years ago are expressed in the poem that opens this chapter.

As I continued my studies in a teacher education programme at a local university in Malaysia, I experienced a similar learning cycle, with only a little improvement in the performance and presentation of lessons. I no longer needed to copy lengthy notes from the board as the lecturers provided PowerPoint presentations that could be downloaded from DVDs. The lecturers explained each point from the PowerPoint presentation with limited opportunity for students to contribute ideas or their understanding. Teaching was one-way communication with limited interaction with students. Not a great deal had changed in terms of my previous learning experiences.

The learning cycle that I experienced is the typical process experienced by students from the late 1980s until the early years of the twenty-first century. The teaching approach used by the teachers or lecturers was like one-way traffic; they controlled the flow of communication in the classroom. Students were passive listeners with limited involvement in classroom discourse. The government had put great effort into improving the teaching and learning of science by supplying high quality teaching materials such as computers, projectors and teaching software. The Ministry also suggested different teaching strategies and conducted continuous professional development programs, but transmission teaching approaches continued to govern science classrooms.

SITI SHAMSIAH SANI

AN UNMOTIVATING LEARNING MODULE

I was appointed as a lecturer at one of local universities in Malaysia that offers various education programmes. One such programme for undergraduate students focuses on the disciplines of science and mathematics. Students enrol in courses such as Environmental Science, Biotechnology, Biodiversity, Analytical Chemistry, Applied Statistics, Natural Compounds and Material Physics. In addition, they also enrol in educational courses that specialise in science education and mathematics education. These courses cover theories of learning, teaching strategies, technology and curriculum. The courses aim to prepare pre-service teachers with scientific content knowledge and scientific skills, teaching skills, and the ability to inspire the younger generation.

As a new lecturer, I was given the task of teaching the fortnightly workshops for the Teaching Strategies course. The workshops aim to give pre-service science teachers the opportunity to experience a variety of teaching strategies. In order to ensure the workshops run smoothly a prescribed module has been prepared. The following vignette describes my dilemma about conducting the workshops.

> Once I reach my office, I flip through the module in my hand and read each activity in detail. There are six activities embedded in the prescribed activities in the module. All the activities are aimed at covering the topics that have been discussed during the lecture. The pre-service secondary science teachers can engage with different teaching approaches: scientific investigations, teaching by using analogies, cooperative learning, multiple intelligences. Before I continue reading the prescribed activities I go to the pantry to make a hot drink, but my mind dwells on the workshop activities.

> "Why am I so worried about the workshop activities? Don't be so idealistic as to change the whole workshop. Just follow the existing module. It will make your life easier. There must be a good explanation for why the activities were designed as such". I have a serious conflict within myself.

> But the other voice inside me whispers the opposite, "You are an educator. If you don't change it, your students won't get any benefit. Just think carefully about it. The choice is in your hands". The voice fades slowly.

> I slowly sip my hot chocolate while my hand busily turns over the prescribed module, page by page. It is a ten-page booklet. The first page contains only instructions about the details that the students should write for the report for each of the workshops. It is a typical framework for a scientific investigation report, requiring the students to include an introduction, instruments and materials, procedure, results, discussions, and conclusions, all written in the passive voice. Then, the students have to answer the questions enclosed with each of the activities.

> As I turn to page 3, the title for the first activity catches my eye: "What is Inside the Bag?". It seems interesting. Then I glance at the materials and the instructions. It is only a black bag, an eraser, paper clips, marbles and a stone.

All the materials have been inserted into the black bag and the students are to use their senses to figure out what is inside. I understand that the activity is to introduce the students to the basic science process skills of observation. This activity aims to provide an experience about the observation skills that they will learn about during the lectures.

"This observation skill is suitable to teach science to year one students. How can I make it appropriate for pre-service science teachers who are going to teach science in secondary schools?", I wonder.

At first glance, the prescribed module appears to help the instructors to handle the workshop with relative ease. The materials, precautions and instructions are well written and the module gives guidance to pre-service science teachers about completing the activities and obtaining the desired results. The structure of the module is similar to what Brian Woolnough (1991) described as a "cookbook activity". The instructor prepares all the materials, instructions, and procedures in detail prior to the workshop to assist student learning.

I run the first workshop by conducting the first activity of the module: "What is Inside the Bag?" After briefing the pre-service science teachers about the activity, I go from one group to another. As I approach Aiman's group I hear his opinion about the activity.

We have followed the instructions. Well, we already know what's inside the bag. What is the point of asking us to do the observation? I don't get it. But what is the connection with science in secondary schools? Is this activity sufficient as we are going to teach science in secondary schools? I simply do not see the connection.

On the one hand, the activity ensured that the pre-service science teachers completed the task within the allocated time and produced the desired outcomes. On the other hand, their actions were also closely guided – they were instructed what to do, how to do it, what to observe, and how to explain. Their actions could only answer the questions of "What?" and "How?", proposed by Parker Palmer (1998). It seems that the prescribed module neglected to address other important questions, which are "Who?" and "Why?". As I reflect on my own educational practice, I contemplate the questions: "What am I going to teach?" and "How am I going to teach?" It appears to me to be selfish to complete the tasks without also considering, "Who are the students?" and "Why am I teaching this way?".

I compare the activities in the module with the "Curriculum Specification for Science in Secondary School: Form 4" (MOE, 2005). Unfortunately, none of the activities seem to be suitable for any of the themes proposed by the Ministry of Education.

- Scientific Investigation
- Maintenance and Continuity of Life

- Matter in Nature
- Energy in Life
- Technological and Industrial Development in Society

I wonder how the activities in the workshops could inspire pre-service science teachers to plan teaching and learning strategies that develop students' scientific knowledge and skills without neglecting their local culture and knowledge. I ask myself how those activities can help pre-service science teachers to understand the teaching strategies used to teach science: "Why have the activities been designed as such?" and "Who are the activities designed for?".

This course is important as it is intended to provide a platform for pre-service science teachers to develop their teaching skills, experience different teaching strategies, and become creative teachers who can inspire the younger generation. They bear a great responsibility for educating the younger generation to become "individuals who are competitive, dynamic, robust, and resilient..." (MOE, 2005, p. ix). However, if the pre-service science teachers are exposed to activities that have limited connection with their cultural contexts, it is unsurprising that the learning cycles that I experienced 25 years ago will continue to be inherited by future generations.

THEORIES UNDERPINNING MY ENVISIONED WORKSHOP

Three Curriculum Images

In envisioning my ideal Teaching Strategies workshop I strongly embraced three contemporary curriculum images introduced by William Schubert (1986): "curriculum as experience", "curriculum as currere", and "curriculum as an agenda for social reconstruction". These curriculum images helped me to redesign the workshops.

"Curriculum as currere" provided the opportunity for me to explore my own life experiences, to understand myself as a student teacher and teacher-educator, and to develop a platform that leads to reconstructing the social hierarchy that disempowers both myself and the pre-service secondary teachers from being reflective, creative, and critical learners (Pinar, 2004). To gain depth of understanding about myself, I followed the four steps of the currere method proposed by Pinar (2004): "regressive", "progressive", "analytical", and "synthetic". In the regressive stage, I generated a data source regarding my past experiences as a pre-service science teacher and teacher educator through my personal journal writing. For the next step, I examined any possible action that I may take in the future that be effective in the present time. Then, in the analytical stage, I analysed both the past and the present. Lastly, I synthesised the possible actions to represent the present.

Then, I adopted the image of "curriculum as experience". Curriculum as a set of activities or predetermined objectives received strong criticism from John Dewey, as cited in Shubert (1986), who promoted a "means-ends" continuum. In that sense, the process and product of teaching and learning cannot be separated if we wish to provide meaningful learning experiences for students. Thus, I endeavoured to counter-balance my role as a teacher-educator who controls the pre-service science teachers' actions during the course with my role as a facilitator who promotes their professional growth as creative, reflective and critical science teachers.

The image of "curriculum as an agenda for social reconstruction" emerged from the assumption that no culture or society is perfect (Shubert, 1986). The concept of culture is not necessarily related to belief or religion, but can be related to everyday activities that occur in the classroom setting. This curriculum image focussed me on developing positive characteristics in my pre-service science teachers, especially their creative thinking for manipulating the government's mandated science themes. The content of the workshops would no longer focus simply on how to teach science as a "body of knowledge", but would emphasise integrating science with social issues, social needs, current ideals and future aspirations. The learning environment would endeavour to educate pre-service science teachers to become agents of future social reconstruction by fostering their creative learning.

Emancipatory Interest

The social philosopher, Jurgen Habermas, proposed three fundamental human cognitive interests – "technical", "practical" and "emancipatory" – that lead to the development of distinctive types of human knowledge. I focused on the emancipatory interest which has the goal of empowerment, that is, the ability of individuals and groups to take control of their own lives in an autonomous and responsible way (Grundy, 1987).

The emancipatory interest is implemented in the proposed Teaching Strategies workshops to empower the pre-service science teachers to be creative learners. The emancipatory interest is embedded in a socially reconstructive curriculum designed to empower both the teachers and the students to form a new culture within the classroom setting. Practicing the emancipatory interest involves contesting the hegemony of the prescribed activities and teacher-centred teaching approach that have cast a shadow over the pre-service science teachers' actions, judgements and values during existing workshops. This interest is also important in developing critical self-reflection among the pre-service science teachers to identify their own strengths and weaknesses.

Furthermore, the emancipatory interest aims to provide enhanced autonomy for the pre-service science teachers to take control of their own learning. They will learn for themselves, and not simply to complete the task for me as the teacher. In this sense they will be able to maximize their creativity by manipulating the science themes in the curriculum specification to teach science in secondary schools.

Creative Learning

In a book on teaching creative learning I found several interesting ideas (Craft, Cremin, Burnard, & Chappell, 2007). First, creative teaching develops students' capacity for imaginative activity (Spendlove, Wyse, Craft, & Hallgarten, 2005). Second, creative teaching and learning has four characteristics: relevance, ownership of the knowledge, control of the learning process, and innovation (Jeffrey & Craft, 2004). From this perspective for the Teaching Strategies workshop activities to be perceived by the students as relevant to them the activities should be designed according to the themes specified by the Ministry of Education (MOE, 2005). The element of ownership of the knowledge refers to the combination of new ideas and adaption of others' ideas to produce new teaching and learning approaches. With the third element the students and I would share control of conducting the workshops. The final element is innovation which refers to the novel instructional materials that I would produce for the workshops. It seems to me that creativity will bring significant change to the workshops and emancipate my students and me from a dull teaching and learning experience.

MY ENVISIONED WORKSHOP FOR THE TEACHING STRATEGIES COURSE

In order to transform the workshop activities I have blended three major theories: emancipatory interest, creative learning and three curriculum images. This is intended to enable the pre-service teachers to become creative learners and to greatly enhance their social interactions during the workshops. The integration of these theories is represented in Figure 16.1.

Transformed Objectives

In the transformed workshops the objectives and learning activities provide extensive opportunities for the pre-service science teachers to engage in creative learning experiences. The objectives, which frame the learning activities, are designed to foster positive attitudes and produce science teachers with the capability to design a range of contemporary teaching strategies. The activities provide opportunities

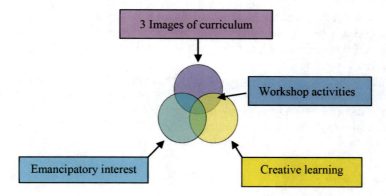

Figure 16.1. Integration of curriculum as agenda for social reconstruction, emancipatory interest, and creative learning

for the pre-service science teachers to explore science concepts and design teaching approaches that have direct connections with communities, the environment and local knowledge. The objectives of the transformed workshops are to develop pre-service science teachers who can:

- make appropriate judgements in selecting teaching strategies to create learning experiences and environments that support creative learning,
- explain various scientific concepts and make meaningful connections with communities, the environment and local knowledge,
- interpret the main features of the science themes in the Government's mandated curriculum specification, and
- demonstrate creative thinking through the activities they perform.

Transformed Activities

Figure 16.2 is an example of an activity for the theme of Scientific Investigations.

During the first half of the 3-hour workshop the pre-service science teachers discuss with their group members the scientific concept they want to address. They are directed to use a wide range of resources, including the library, computer laboratory and interviews with the local community. The activities are open-ended as there are no rigid instructions that govern their actions. In each of the fortnightly workshops a new scientific theme is introduced. The students choose any scientific concept within the theme and think of appropriate teaching strategies to address the concept and create connections with local knowledge, the environment and communities (Brickhouse & Kittleson, 2006). The pre-service science teachers have the freedom to use their imagination to design teaching approaches suitable to address the scientific concepts. Original ideas are highly valued.

During the second half of the workshop, the pre-service science teachers perform "mock teaching" activities to teach the other students about a scientific concept using the teaching strategy they have developed. Mock teaching is an artificial teaching and learning session whereby students are required to teach their peers who pretend to be students (Remesh, 2013). Finally, the pre-service science teachers provide written reports on their teaching strategies. They need to justify why they chose the teaching strategy and in what ways it can help to nurture local knowledge, the environment and communities. The report should contain reflections on their learning experience in designing the teaching strategy, identifying strengths and weaknesses and any problems they encountered. The report can take the form of an oral presentation, cartoon characters, dialogues, or poems.

Transformed Assessment

Workshop assessment is divided into two parts. The first part takes place during the workshop and the second part covers the report on each workshop. The pre-service

> **Activity 1**
>
> Theme: Scientific Investigation
>
> Instructions:
> Science is referred to as a way of knowing how to seek an understanding of the world around us (Bentley et al., 2000). Imagine that you want to introduce the concept of investigation in science to high school students for the first time.
> - Discuss in your group, what will you do to address the most important component in science?
> - What are other approaches that you can think of to understand and provide an explanation about the nature processes that occur in the world rather than scientific investigation?
> - Remember investigation in science does not always occur in a laboratory. Then, develop one example of investigation processes that are used in the world of scientific endeavours.
> - Prepare a 15-minute presentation to share your ideas about the concept of investigation in science.
>
> Remember, these are only examples of issues or topics that you can discuss. You are encouraged to explore other ways to do the investigation.
>
> Write a report about the concept of investigation that you have chosen. In your report please include:
> - Justification of why you chose this teaching strategy.
> - In what ways does this teaching strategy help to nurture local knowledge (e.g., local language, culture, beliefs), the environment, and communities?
> - Write individual reflections about the learning process that you have experienced in constructing the teaching strategy to address this scientific concept, the weaknesses, the strengths, and the problems that you encountered about this teaching approach (cartoon characters, dialogues, poems).

Figure 16.2. Outline of the activity for the scientific investigation theme

science teachers are assessed by themselves, their peers, and by co-assessment during mock teaching.

Self-assessment refers to the pre-service science teachers being involved in making judgements about their own work, especially about their achievement in relation to the workshop objectives (Dochy, Segers, & Sluijsmans, 1999). Self-assessment can help the pre-service science teachers to reflect on their learning process during the workshop (Boud, 1995 as cited in Dochy, Seegers, & Sluijsmans, 1999).

Peer assessment is a process that involves students evaluating other students' learning (Falchikov, 1995 as cited in Prins, Sluijsmans, Kirschner, & Strijbos, 2005). The process involves use of rubrics that I design. The rubrics are an introductory commentary that exposes the pre-service science teachers to the criteria against which their work will be evaluated (Hubar & Freed, 2000). The criteria align with the learning outcomes of the workshops:

- presentation
- engagement
- organisation
- content knowledge
- confidence
- team work

All six criteria are graded according to three levels of achievement: low, intermediate, high. The attributes that represent each level of achievement are stated clearly to help the students work toward the standard. Peer assessment is intended to have a positive impact on the pre-service science teachers' learning because they gain both praise and critique from their peers. Importantly, this provides first-hand experience of the assessment process, which is a valuable experience as they embark on their careers as secondary science teachers (Prins, Kirschner, & Strijbos, 2005).

Co-assessment is a collaborative process between myself, as the tutor, and the pre-service science teachers (Hall, 1995 as cited in Dochy et al., 1999). The main goal of this type of assessment is to provide the opportunity for the pre-service science teachers to change their role from students to teachers, thereby developing the skill of self-assessment.

A WAY FORWARD

Once I had finished reflecting on my learning and teaching experiences and envisioning my utopian workshop for the Teaching Strategies course, I wondered whether my inquiry about producing creative science teachers was complete? Or, was this only a starting point in my journey of searching for alternative approaches to produce creative science teachers. I asked myself, "What should I do with the module that I have envisioned for transforming the Teaching Strategies course workshops, should I keep it to myself, or should I share my ideas with my colleagues?".

Finally, in my mind I have a clear mission: transforming the Teaching Strategies course so that it not only fosters creative learning but also creative teaching. In this course the pre-service science teachers will experience creative teaching strategies that not only teach scientific concepts but also teach science that has strong connections with local knowledge, the environment and communities.

REFERENCES

Alberts, R. V. J., Beuzekom. P. J. V., & Roo, I. D. (1986). The assessment of practical work: A choice of options. *International Journal of Science Education, 8*(4), 37–41.

Bentley, M., Ebert, C., & Ebert, E. S. (2000). *The natural investigaton: A constructivst approach to teach elementary and middle school science*. Belmont, CA: Wadsworth.

Brickhouse, N. W., & Kittleson, J. M. (2005). Visions of curriculum, community, and science. *Educational Theory, 56*(2), 191–204.

Bryman, A. (2007). *Social research methods*. Oxford: Oxford University Press.

Cohen, L., Manion, L., & Morrison, K. (2007). *Research methods in education* (6th ed.). London & New York, NY: Routledge and Taylor & Francis.

Craft, A., Cremin, T., Burnard, P., & Chappell, K. (2007). Teacher stance in creative learning: A study of progression. *Thinking Skills and Creativity, 2*, 136–147.

Dochy, F., Segers, M., & Sluijsmans, D. (1999). The use of self-, peer, co-assessment in higher education: A review. *Studies in Higher Education, 24*(3), 331–351.

Ellis, C., & Bochner, A. P. (2000). Autoethnography, personal narrative, reflexivity: Researcher as subject. In N. K. Denzin & Y. S. Lincoln (Eds.), *Handbook of qualitative research* (pp. 733–761). Thousand Oaks, CA: Sage Publications.

Grundy, S. (1987). *Curriculum: Product or praxis?* New York, NY: The Falmer Press.

Guba, E. G., & Lincoln, Y. S. (1989). *Fourth generation evaluation.* Newbury Park, CA: Sage Publications.

Hubar, M., & Freed, J. (2000). *Using rubrics to provide feedback to students.* Boston, MA: Allyn & Bacon.

Luitel, B. C., & Taylor, P. C. (2007). The Shanai, the pseudosphere and other imaginings: Envisioning culturally contextualised mathematics education. *Cultural Studies of Science Education, 2*(3), 621–655.

Mayer, R. E. (1989). Cognitive views of creativity: Creative teaching for creative learning. *Comtemporary Educational Psychology, 14*, 203–211.

Palmer, P. J. (1998). *The courage to teach.* San Francisco, CA: Jossey-Bass.

Pinar, W. F. (2004). *What is curriculum theory?* Mahwah, NJ: Lawrence Erlbaum.

Prins, F. J., Kirschner, D. A., & Strijbos, P. A. (2005). Formative peer assessment in a CSCL environment: A case study. *Assessment & Evaluation in Higher Education, 30*(4), 417–444.

Remesh, A. (2013). Microteaching, an efficient technique for learning effective teaching. *Journal of Research in Medical Sciences: The Official Journal of Isfahan University of Medical Sciences, 18*(2), 158–163.

Richardson, L. (2000). Writing – A method of inquiry. In N. K. Denzin & Y. S. Lincoln (Eds.), *Handbook of qualitative research* (pp. 923–935). Thousand Oaks, CA: Sage Publications.

Sani, S. S. (2008). *Envisioning the implementation of creative learning in the teaching strategies Workshops: A critical autoethnographic inquiry* (Unpublished master's dissertation). Curtin University of Technology, Perth, Australia.

Schubert, W. H. (1986). *Curriculum: Perspective, paradigm, and possibilities.* New York, NY: Macmillan.

Schwandt, T. A. (2007). *The Sage dictionary of qualitative inquiry* (3rd ed.). United States of America: Sage Publications.

Taylor, P. C. (2008). Multi-paradigmatic research design spaces for cultural studies researchers embodying postcolonial theorising [Editorial]. *Cultural Studies of Science Education, 3*(4), 881–890.

Taylor, P. C. S., & Campbell-Williams, M. (1992, August 17–23). *Discourse towards balanced rationality in the high school mathematics classroom: Ideas from Habermas' critical theory.* Paper presented at the 'Sociological and Anthropological Perspectives' Working Subgroup of the Seventh Internasional Congress of Mathematics Educators (ICME-7), Quebec.

Tytler, R. (2002). Teaching for understanding: Constructivist/conceptual change teaching approach. *Australian Science Teachers' Journal, 48*(4), 30–35.

Woolnough, B. E. (1991). Setting the scene. In B. E. Woolnough (Ed.), *Practical science* (pp. 1–10). Milton Keynes: Open University Press.

ABOUT THE AUTHOR

I am **Siti Shamsiah Sani**. I was born in Melaka, Malaysia. I hold a PhD in Education from Victoria University of Wellington, New Zealand. Currently I am working as a senior lecturer in the Biology Department, Faculty of Sciences and Mathematics, Universiti Pendidikan Sultan Idris. My research interests are in areas of Biology Education, curriculum and instruction.

PART 5

SUSTAINING TRANSFORMATIVE PEDAGOGIES

YULI RAHMAWATI

17. RETURNING HOME

Key Challenges Facing a Transformative Educator

Where Am I: Following Or Leading?
Looking back on the journey
Black, white, and grey
Looking at different faces and roles
Reflect, reconceptualise, and envision

In the different pathways, I stand
In different voice, I fight
Empowering and disempowering
Following or leading

Shaping my mind and thinking
Open up closed mind and heart
Playing language games
Differences and similarities

Exploring my identity
A transformative educator
One truth and multiple truths
Objectivity and subjectivity
Playing dialectical thinking

Where am I?
In the middle of different roles
Teacher educator, researcher, and supervisor
In the wave of the rainbow of research paradigms
In the pathway of shaping my identity
I keep staying for being empowered
In the landscape of transformative education
In the line of colourful pathways

In my doctoral research I adopted the role of *researcher as transformative learner* In this role I reflected critically on my teaching, my research practice and my teaching identity, and I revisioned my future pedagogical practice as a transformative teacher educator (Rahmawati, 2013). I am now continuing this commitment with a passion for educating my students (pre-service chemistry teachers) as holistic individuals who understand deeply and reflect on their lives. I endeavour to empower my students as social agents to participate in creating a better world. I believe that every student is "an active initiator and reactor" for his or her environment (Marsh, 2000, p. 215). I believe this kind of journey will inspire them to continuously empower themselves and envision their future roles as teachers. I expect that my student teachers will eventually inspire their own students to achieve a better future for the nation and the world.

Previously I have portrayed several aspects of my transformative learning journey: first, as a pre-service teacher who didn't have any passion for becoming a teacher, and as a chemistry teacher who had to deal with the misbehaviour of my students (Rahmawati & Taylor, 2015); and second, the role of my cultural beliefs in shaping my identity and practice as a chemistry teacher educator (Rahmawati & Taylor, 2017). The above poem portrays my mixed feelings on return to my home university in Indonesia after completing doctoral studies. Although I wanted to be accepted in my university, I realised that several values and beliefs were contradicted within myself. Furthermore, I faced the considerable challenge of remaining empowered as a transformative educator within the hegemony of the prevailing paradigm of positivism. The challenge I faced was not only connecting with my colleagues' different values and beliefs while striving to empower my student teachers, but also to understand myself within my different roles.

In this chapter I revisit the transformative learning perspective that I developed during my masters and doctoral studies that continues to drive my ongoing teaching values, beliefs and practices. I portray some of the key challenges that I addressed soon after returning to my home university as I struggled to introduce my transformative learning perspective in my various roles. As a chemistry teacher educator I struggled to empower my student teachers. As a research supervisor, I drew on my transformative learning values to adapt and create changes in students' research projects. And I reconceptualised my research identity to empower myself and others in engaging in research as a transformative process.

I hope that this portrayal of my experience of struggling to introduce and sustain a transformative practice will be valuable for beginning educators and researchers returning to their home universities and facing an entrenched worldview.

A TRANSFORMATIVE TEACHER EDUCATOR

My transformative learning experience, which began in Peter's master's research project class and continued throughout my doctoral research, motivated me to think critically and reflectively about myself (professionally and personally) and caused me to revision my future life, especially my pedagogical practice. As Jack Mezirow (1997) pointed out, transformative learning affects our frames of reference, changes how we understand our experiences and redefines our world. In this learning I had opportunities to negotiate and think critically about my own experiences, values, meaning and purposes in my journey as a student, teacher, and teacher educator

(Garbove, 1997). My transformative learning involved critical incidents, metaphor analysis, concept mapping, consciousness raising, writing stories, repertory grid analysis, and participation in social action (Mezirow, Taylor, & Associates, 2009).

I continue to experience transformative learning as a lifelong journey of revealing my identity by understanding my unfolding self through reflection on my psychological structures of ego and shadow self, and personal and collective unconscious (Taylor, 2008). As an ongoing transformative learner, I continue to reflect on and reconceptualise my own identity within the different roles of my life.

On return to my home university I passionately wanted to empower my students (pre-service chemistry teachers) as transformative learners. I realised that to be successful my teaching practice would need to (i) model transformative ethics and dialectical thinking, (ii) enrich their scientific worldviews, and (iii) help them construct identities as transformative teachers.

Challenge: Ethics of Emancipation and Care

Ever since I became a teacher I have believed that the teaching profession has a great moral responsibility for the betterment of my society and the empowerment of its people. In striving to empower my student teachers, I am committed to practicing emancipatory ethics and an ethics of care.

An ethic of care, which is concerned with the educative relationship between a teacher and student, helps me to avoid the hegemony of the *technical interest* that shapes the teacher's role purely as deliverer of curriculum content and students' role as passive receivers. I engage my students by "creating mutual trust, respect, good will, qualities that involves disclosure of personally significant meaning-perspectives" (Taylor, 1996, p. 18) as it is important to understand students as human beings rather than as *empty vessels* in which to replicate scientific knowledge. I start to practice an ethic of care in the very first class by respecting and getting to know my students (Rice, 2001; Solis & Turner, 2017) as I believe caring is a fundamental ethical value required for helping students to grow and achieve their potential (Sumsion, 2000).

I practice an emancipatory ethic by establishing a communicative classroom environment with *critical discourse* opportunities. I encourage my students to challenge my ideas and assumptions, as I challenge theirs. Importantly, both my students and I are aware that critical discourse can also be a *two-edged sword*, a challenge that we discuss in class. Although teachers may try to enhance their students' learning in this way, such an approach might negatively affect the learning of those who find comfort in the realm of an objectivist epistemology.

Challenge: Dialectical Thinking

Dealing with the power of contradictory ideas requires me to employ dialectical thinking through the processes of inquiry (Basseches, 2005) and creativity (Paletz, Bogue, Miron-Spektor, & Spencer-Rodgers, 2018). Dialectical thinking is "a kind of higher psychological process in the Vygotskian sense" (Wong, 2006, p. 250). Dialectical thinking involves reflecting critically and creatively on how to reconcile the co-existence of two competing ideologies – thesis and antithesis. For example, reflecting critically and creatively on the competition between the metaphors of objectivism (thesis) and constructivism (antithesis) in science teaching (Willison & Taylor, 2006) enables me to understand and reconcile how this (psychological and emotional) tension influences my pedagogical practice.

Dialectical thinking is powerful in order for me to understand that my colleagues have different views (ideologies), my students have their own entrenched ideas, and my system also creates cultural borders. In order to survive in my classroom, in my university and in my country, I apply the method of dialectical thinking to these competing social realities. I also teach my students to adopt dialectical thinking in order to understand and reconcile competing perspectives in chemistry education. On the one hand, there is the standard curriculum perspective (thesis) of covering chemistry concepts and misconceptions, objectivity, observables and measurables. On the other hand, there is the transformative perspective (antithesis) of student empowerment and personal experiences that involves understanding how to resolve the dilemmas they will face as they cross the cultural border between transformative learning and established classroom teaching practices.

Given their prior learning experiences, my student teachers tend to focus on the traditional learning theory of *behaviourism*, even though they may be aware of constructivist theory that emphasises the active role of the mind in making sense of experience. I have found that the metaphor of *constructivism as a referent* (Tobin & Tippins, 1993), which focuses their thinking on how students are making sense of their learning experiences, helps them to reconcile the dilemma of promoting meaningful learning in large teacher-centred classes. Although learning science knowledge is largely based on social construction, individuals also generate their own science knowledge through reflecting on their experiences (Fox, 2001; Valera, Thomson, & Rosch, 2016). In class, I give my students opportunities to understand the teaching dilemma of focusing on students' achievement (knowledge as a social product) versus focusing on their meaningful learning experiences (knowing as an intersubjective process). To enable them to adopt the latter focus, I direct them to create learning designs that focus on their students' experiences, characteristics and competences.

Challenge: Enriching Scientific Worldview

When I was a student and a beginning chemistry teacher I simply thought science was the way to understand the world through systematic methods, namely the *scientific method*. The scientific method was one of the main chapters in our school textbook. I remember my teacher asking me to memorise the steps of the scientific method, which I recognised as science *per se*. I had never thought about the philosophy of science, the truth, or the scientific community. I believed that science is developed in the belief of one truth; in science there is only right answer, there is no opportunity for other beliefs. Later, I came to understand that scientific knowledge is not only recognised because of its symbolic nature but is constructed and validated through social interaction – a dialogic process – within the scientific community.

On returning home I found it challenging to help my student teachers to make sense of scientific knowledge as a socio-cultural process. In chemistry education the constructivist teaching strategy of *conceptual change* is very popular, however, it tends to serve the primary goal of achieving the *single absolute truth* of chemistry knowledge. This hegemonic perspective is reinforced by standardized assessments that require only correct answers. For student teachers, the goal of achieving good marks in the discipline of chemistry as the main indicator of a high standard of teaching tends to cause them to focus on passing the chemistry exam and achieving the minimum score (KKM-Kriteria Ketuntasan Minimal).

To counter this hegemonic perspective, Glen Aikenhead's (2000) idea of *conceptual pluralism* in learning science inspired me to integrate *ethnochemistry* into my chemistry classes. My students face a range of cultural experiences: the cultures of their daily lives and the *multiscience* cultures of science itself. I believe, therefore, that my teaching should help students learn to recognise the implicit *border crossings* of their multicultural experiences. In the role of a *cultural broker* I introduce the concept of *cultural borders* and guide students back and forth across the borders, a process that is reminiscent of *the equilibrium concept* in chemistry. I help them to make sense of these different cultures and motivate them to consider the contributions of *Western science* to their everyday lives.

Challenge: Constructing Teacher Identity

Do You Want to Be a Teacher?

I walk slowly into the classroom, I am excited as it is the first day of my teaching after returning from my study in Australia. I open the door and look at my students have been sitting quietly. I believe they are probably curious who their lecturer is. I am also excited as they are third-year student teachers, which means they already have the comprehensive competences of being a teacher. I start the lesson with an introduction.

Me: Assalamu'alaikum everyone

Students: Wa'alaikumussalam Bu Yuli

Me: How are you all?

Students: We are fine, Alhamdulillah

Me: Great, as the first meeting, I think it is important for us to know each other, so we can start our lesson by introducing ourselves.

I start to introduce myself. I only give information of my educational background, including that I am an alumni of this university who probably had similar experiences to them. I do not want to tell them that I struggled being a teacher who didn't have any passion for being a teacher. However, when I look at their faces, I become curious and recall my experiences in the first meeting in Peter's class when he asked me to reflect on being a teacher.

Me: I have a question: Do you want to be a teacher?

Student: [silence]

Me: Could you please raise your hand? Does any one of you want to become a teacher?

Student: [4 of them raise their hand]

Me: How about the others?

Student: [silence]

I am shocked! Only 4 out of 34 raised their hand. Suddenly, I reflect on myself who didn't want to be a teacher, even when I had completed my degree. I felt miserable to start teaching. So what should I do now? Should I change their view? Should they follow my way? How can I empower them, if they are losing their identity as a teacher?

This vignette recounts my first experience with my student teachers when I suddenly realised that I was facing the challenge of their lost identity. Only 4 out of 34 wanted to be teachers, the rest preferred other jobs or didn't have any plan for their future. It shocked me until I reflected on my own journey in which I also didn't have any passion to be a teacher until my graduation day. I realised that it was not only them, but it was also me. So, I decided to put more emphasis on the importance of internalising the values of being a teacher.

Based on my own experience as a student teacher, I understand the importance of enabling my students to develop their teaching identities, not only as student teachers, but importantly also during the transition to becoming practicing teachers. During transition there are likely to be "some feelings of isolation, mismatch between idealistic expectations and classroom reality and lack of support and guidance" (Flores & Day, 2006, p. 219). Therefore, I need to enable them to explore their identities as emerging teachers (Witt, 2011). To do this I employ transformative learning strategies such as writing a reflective log (Graham & Phelps, 2003), metacognition and reflection (Cattley, 2007), and praxis and socialisation (Hoffman-Kipp, 2008).

I am confident that transformative learning is the way to engage my students in understanding their developing identities as teachers. My students are facing the challenge of shifting their comfort zones to explore themselves as well as their understanding about *what is learning?*. In the basic chemistry and chemistry education courses that I teach I ask my students to write their reflections on questions such as: Why would I like to be a teacher? Who am I as a teacher? What is my vision as a teacher? At first, they feel these questions are weird. They ask me why they have to do these reflections, and what is the relationship of the questions with the course being taught?

The journey is not easy; reflections are not a common practice in their classes. However, critical reflection on their experiences enables them to develop awareness of their agency to transform society and their own lives (Taylor, 2008). I try to empower my student teachers not to be passive learners who wish to receive *the transferring file* from my mind while ignoring their experiences and social processes. I have learnt to be a mediator of their critical thinking as they need to learn how to express their critical voices in the classroom.

In addition to shifting their standard paradigm of passive learning, I also stimulate them to become aware of their agency to change society and to empower their own students to do the same. I often remind them of this teaching role, even though they state that the overloaded school curriculum is a challenge to students' empowerment. I am not surprised as I have observed my student teachers during their school teaching experiences. They conduct the lecture teaching method more often than group work because of the challenge of time management and the heavy load of subject matter they need to cover.

A TRANSFORMATIVE RESEARCH SUPERVISOR

As a chemistry teacher educator, I am required to supervise my students' research projects in which they implement and evaluate innovative teaching approaches in local schools. A transformative teaching approach that I introduced to them is *ethical dilemma story teaching*. Ethical dilemma stories are used to stimulate students to engage in reflecting critically on their (implicit) social values and beliefs (Settlemaier, 2009). Ethical dilemma stories relate to everyday life and current social issues, and involve students in making well-informed decisions on how to resolve the conflict between the beneficial and harmful impact of science and technology on the natural environment and people's lives (e.g., Taylor & Taylor, 2018). My student teachers are researching their implementation of ethical dilemma story teaching in chemistry classrooms. In this practitioner-research, they are investigating students' development of critical thinking, problem solving skills, decision making, and working collaboratively, which are important *transdisciplinary* skills for 21st century citizens (Taylor, 2018). This student research is not without its challenges for both the student teachers and me.

Challenge: Mentoring

Should We Learn Story in the Chemistry Classroom?

Today, I have a regular meeting with my student teachers who are conducting research on their implementation of ethical dilemma story teaching in local schools. After the challenging journey of being introduced to ethical dilemma story teaching, including their research proposal examination, my students are motivated to implement new ways of conducting research. This is a conversation with one of the student teachers.

Me: So, how is the research going?

Student: It is going well, although the students feel that their learning experiences are unusual.

Me: What is unusual?

Student: They are used to being asked to remember chemistry facts and complete chemistry tests.

Me: How are they feeling about it?

Student: Most of them are excited, but two students are not engaged. They asked me whether we should be learning stories in the chemistry classroom? Will it be in the chemistry exam? Is this a chemistry subject or a social science subject?

I just smile and look at their faces. I knew this would happen.

Student: Is it ok to use this qualitative data?

Me: Yes, it is the process of empowerment, students are used to learning by rote learning, recalling facts. The new learning experience has forced them to move from their comfort zone. They need to shift their paradigm of what is learning.

Student: Yes, actually it is relevant to the current curricula, however, it is really challenging.

Me: Yes, we also can see that this negative perspective will enrich our data by giving the different perspective of other voices, it is naturally happening in our classroom.

This vignette illustrates my first experience of supervising student teachers in conducting research on ethical dilemma teaching. In this research, school students are engaged in dilemma stories to help them understand chemistry concepts and social issues. My student teachers need continuous mentoring as they develop new knowledge about qualitative research and chemistry learning. I have had similar experiences with my students over the past four years. In mentoring them, I practice ethics of care and emancipation to support their development as agents of social change.

I continue to collaborate with my students after their graduation, and am deeply gratified that as new chemistry teachers they have become agents of change in their schools, especially by engaging their students in transformative learning. Their stories and experiences have empowered me to maintain my own transformative supervision practice.

Currently, my students and I are working on a range of transformative research topics: new ethical dilemma stories, socio-critical problems, socio-emotional learning, green chemistry, culturally responsive teaching, STEAM education, conceptual understanding and mental modelling. My students collaborate in groups which helps them to empower each other in understanding transformative research approaches.

I also face the challenge of students understanding quantitative research, including the value of objectivity and generalisation. As a former quantitative researcher, I believe that a good academic environment should provide a range of research approaches, including those framed by the paradigm of positivism.

Challenge: Final Examination

Qualitative Research Is Impossible

It is the final examination of one of my Bachelor's degree students whose research focussed on her implementation of ethical dilemma story pedagogy in a school chemistry classroom. I walk slowly to the room; it's my first time as a research supervisor to join the final research examination since returning home from my doctoral research in Australia. Its 10am and two examiners, who are my colleagues in the Chemistry Education Department, are in the room with my Head of Department. I take a seat and the Head of Department asks if we are ready to start the final examination of my students' research. My student looks nervous, even though I know that she is good at conducting the research and has a well-prepared slide presentation. She presents her research for 15 minutes. Even though she looks nervous, she gives an excellent presentation. Then the questions by the examiners start. The student answers the questions of the first examiner about what is a dilemma story, how it was implemented in the chemistry classroom, and how it impacted students' learning. The next questions come from the second examiner.

Examiner: Is it qualitative research?

Student: Yes it is.

Examiner: How can you conduct qualitative research in one semester?

Student: I have been engaged with the students since last semester when I conducted field teaching in this classroom. This semester for my final research project, I conducted the research by implementing dilemma stories in the chemistry classroom. I consider that I have engaged with and known the students well as part of the quality standard of prolonged engagement.

Examiner:	It's impossible, qualitative research has to be conducted for more than 1 year since you have to engage with the participants. You have to work closely with the participants. Qualitative research is impossible for students' research projects.
Student:	I have worked closely with the students. I have been doing practical teaching in their class. I understand their learning.
Examiner:	No, it's not valid. How are you measuring their engagement?
Student:	It's qualitative. We didn't use numbers. I conducted interviews, classroom observations, and reflective journals. I analysed by data coding and categorising.
Examiner:	I don't think that is sufficient to show that your research is valid. Qualitative research is questionable to be conducted here.
Student:	[Silence...]

On return to my university I began introducing transformative research in my teaching of Bachelor's degree students. But I realised that I needed to tread carefully as most of my colleagues undertake research shaped by the positivist paradigm. I needed to be accepted in the academic forum of my university. I also needed to think about my students as their research would be assessed in the final examination by my colleagues. What language should I use? What research methods are acceptable? And the fundamental question: What are the truths that are held by the academic community?

I chose to use the established terminology of qualitative research that was likely to be familiar to my colleagues, rather than unfamiliar terminology of transformative research – *multi-paradigmatic research, auto/ethnography* – that I had used in my doctoral research.

This vignette illustrates a challenging event that happened to one of my first research students who had undertaken qualitative research on her implementation of an ethical dilemma story in a local school. I had mixed feelings about the reluctance of my colleagues to accept my approach to qualitative research. Epistemologically naive questions about measurement, research time, and validity were commonly asked. Even though I continue to work with critical auto/ethnography as my chosen research methodology, it is not yet well accepted as a methodology for supervising my student teachers' projects, mainly because it is perceived as being *too subjective*.

However, there was a light at the end of the dark tunnel. It has been four years since I introduced transformative educational research into my university. Now, the university provides an opportunity to deliver qualitative research courses from undergraduate to doctoral study. During this time, I have supervised many students conducting qualitative research across a range of research topics and have received supportive grants from the Higher Education Department. Several universities have invited me as a speaker at seminars on qualitative research and transformative education.

A TRANSFORMATIVE RESEARCHER

I often participate in science and mathematics education conferences at the national level in my country, where I present transformative (qualitative) research on classroom teaching. I believe that teacher education programs, especially in science and mathematics education, should provide a range of research approaches that can help to empower student teachers in their future roles as classroom teachers. I also encourage my student teachers to present their research in these conferences. However, I often experience the challenge of not having my proposals accepted on their epistemic merits.

Challenge: Getting Published

The Methodology Must Be Scientific

> I open the online conference platform to look at the review of my two papers that I submitted for an international conference in my country. Today is the decision of acceptance to present papers at the conference. I click on the reviewer's comments on my first paper, and expect that the revisions will be minor as I prepared it well in order to fulfilled conference requirements. I read carefully the comments and am shocked. It states that the methodology must be scientific, it is major revisions! I look at the reviewer's comment on my second paper, and it states minor revisions. In this paper I had employed a questionnaire with numbers in it. I look back and read through the qualitative methodology of my first paper. Is it not scientific because of no numbers in my paper? I keep questioning.

This vignette illustrates my experience of submitting papers for an international conference in my country. It was not my first experience of being neglected and rejected. I continue to struggle to introduce transformative ways of knowing in conducting research. The strong positivism paradigm should not be a problem if academics open up their minds to an acceptance of differences. As lecturers we need to be aware of different ways of knowing, different values, and different beliefs. Borderless information should encourage us to continue as learners.

In terms of research publications, I have published in different areas of research with different research foci and methodologies. The experience of having my manuscripts on qualitative research rejected by journals and being asked to add numbers in my research presentations has been part of my journey. However, the feeling of being alien has been countered by my understanding that I am being consistent with my views on the value of transformative research and by opportunities to share my views in conferences and seminars at the national level.

CODA

The journey of returning home was challenging. It required me to reconceptualise my transformative teaching and research identity. I have found that it is very important to understand ourselves in relation to others in order to create the changes we believe are important. As a chemistry teacher educator I am focusing on empowering my students to become inspiring chemistry teachers. In empowering my students I start with reflections on self-understanding. As a researcher and research supervisor I need to adjust the value of transformative learning for it to be accepted in creating change in my university. I believe that understanding different worldviews has helped me *to dance with differences*. I have come to realise how a *rainbow* of worldviews has shaped my perspective on conducting research.

When I Have to Choose

When I have to choose…
different ways of worldviews
different ways of thinking
different ways of understanding

When I have to choose…
I am questioning what the truth is
I am questioning what the values are
I am questioning what the hegemony is

When I have to choose…
I choose to embrace the differences
I choose to be transformed, struggling to be empowered
I choose to stay in the rainbow of different worldviews

Practicing the values of transformative learning that I constructed during my doctoral study are helping me to continue to negotiate cultural border crossings. These perspectives have helped me to develop the habit of fostering critical self-reflection throughout the ongoing journey of empowering myself and my student teachers. My reflections in this chapter have helped me to continue constructing my identity, and I hope they will be valuable for beginning educators and researchers in dealing with differences when they return home. The journey is not easy, however the experience of being neglected and rejected has enriched my empowerment to stay on the pathway as a transformative teacher educator.

I am a teacher who started a journey without any passion for being a teacher and any understanding of her teaching identity.
I am a teacher who started to understand the real challenges to remain empowered and to understand different forces that constitute the life journey within her professional practice.
Within this storm of challenges I choose to stay.

REFERENCES

Aikenhead, G. S. (2000). Renegotiating the culture of school science. In R. Millar, J. Leach, & J. Oxtoby (Eds.), *Improving science education* (pp. 245–265). Philadelphia, PA: University Press.

Basseches, M. (2005). The development of dialectical thinking as an approach to integration. *Integral Review, 1*, 47–63.

Cattley, G. (2007). Emergence of professional identity for the pre-service teacher. *International Education Journal, 8*(2), 337–347.

Flores, M. A., & Day, C. (2006). Contexts which shape and reshape teachers' identities: A multi-perspective study. *Teaching and Teacher Education, 22*, 219–232.

Fox, R. (2001). Constructivism examined. *Oxford Review of Education, 27*(1), 23–35.

Grabove, V. (1997). The many facets of transformative learning theory and practices. In P. Cranton (Ed.), *New directions for adult and continuing education* (pp. 89–96). New York, NY: John Wiley & Sons.

Graham, A., & Phelps, R. (2003). Being a teacher: Developing teacher identity and enhancing practice through community, metacognitive and reflective learning processes. *Australian Journal of Teacher Education, 27*(2), 1–14.

Hoffman-Kipp, P. (2008). Actualizing democracy: The praxis of teacher identity construction. *Teacher Education Quarterly, 35*(3), 151–164.

Marsh, C. (1996). *Handbook for beginning teachers*. New South Wales: Longman.

Mezirow, J. (1997). Transformative learning: Theory to practice. In P. Cranton (Ed.), *New directions for adult and continuing education: No. 74. transformative learning in action: Insights from practice* (pp. 5–12). San Francisco, CA: Jossey-Bass.

Mezirow, J., Taylor, E. D., & Associates. (Eds.). (2009). *Transformative learning in practice: Insights from community, workplace, and higher education*. San Fransisco, CA: Jossey-Bass.

Paletz, S. B. F., Bogue, K., Miron-Spektor, E., & Spencer-Rodgers, J. (2018). Dialectical thinking and creativity from many perspectives: Contradiction and tension. In J. Spencer-Rodgers & K. Peng (Eds.), *The psychological and cultural foundations of dialectical thinking* (pp. 267–308). New York, NY: Oxford University Press.

Rahmawati, Y. (2013). *Revealing and reconceptualising teaching identity through the landscapes of culture, religion, transformative learning, and sustainability education: A transformation journey of a science educator* (Unpublished doctoral thesis). Curtin University, Perth, Australia.

Rahmawati, Y., & Taylor, P. C. (2015). Moments of critical realisation and appreciation: A transformative chemistry teacher reflects. *Reflective Practice, 16*, 31–42.

Rahmawati, Y., & Taylor, P. C. (2017). The fish becomes aware of the water in which it swims: Revealing the power of culture in shaping teaching identity. *Cultural Studies of Science Education, 13*(2), 525–537. doi:10.1007/s11422-016-9801-1

Rice, C. J. (2001). Teacher's level of care. *Education Technology, 122*(1), 102–105.

Settelmaier, E. (2009). *Adding zest to science education: Transforming the culture of science classrooms through ethical dilemma pedagogy*. Saarbrucken: VDM.

Solis, O. J., & Turner, W. D. (2017). Building positive student-instructor interactions: Engaging students through caring leadership in the classroom. *Journal on Empowering Teaching Excellence, 1*(1), Article 4.

Sumsion, J. (2000). Caring and empowerment: A teacher educator's reflection on an ethical dilemma. *Teaching in Higher Education, 5*(2), 167–179.

Valera, F. J., Thomson, E., & Rosch, E. (2016). *The embodied mind: Cognitive science and human experience*. London: MIT Press.

Taylor, P. C. (2008). Multi-paradigmatic research design spaces for cultural studies researchers embodying postcolonial theorising. *Culture Studies of Science Education, 3*(4), 881–890.

Taylor, P. C. (2018). Enriching STEM with the arts to better prepare 21st century citizens. In *Proceedings of the 5th International Conference for Science Educators and Teachers (ISET) 2017* (pp. 020002-1–020002-5), Phuket & Melville, NY.

Taylor, E., & Taylor, P. C. (2018). *Socially responsible science: A living resource*. Retrieved from http://sociallyresponsiblescience.com.au

YULI RAHMAWATI

Taylor, P. C., & Wallace, J. (Eds.). (1996). *Contemporary qualitative research: Exemplars for science and mathematic educators.* Rotterdam, The Netherlands: Sense Publishers.
Tobin, K., & Tippins, D. (1993). Constructivism as a referent for teaching and learning. In K. Tobin (Ed.) *The practice of constructivism in science education* (pp. 3–21). Washington, WA: AAAS Press.
Willison, J. W., & Taylor, P. C. (2006). Complementary epistemologies of science teaching: Towards an integral perspective. In P. J. Aubusson, A. G. Harrison, & S. M. Ritchie (Eds.), *Analogy and metaphor in science education* (pp. 25–36). Dordrecht: Springer.
Witt, S. C. (2010). *Becoming a teacher: An interpretive inquiry into the construction of pre-service teachers' teaching identity* (Unpublished doctoral dissertation). Curtin University, Perth, Australia.
Wong, W. C. (2006). Understanding dialectical thinking from a cultural-historical perspective. *Philosophical Psychology, 19*(2), 239–260.

ABOUT THE AUTHOR

Yuli Rahmawati. I am a chemistry teacher educator at Universitas Negeri Jakarta, Indonesia. As a university educator, I engage in transformative learning and research practices. My interests are the impact of transformative education on teaching and cultural identity, new ethical dilemma stories, socio-critical problems, socio-emotional learning, green chemistry, culturally responsive teaching, STEAM education, conceptual understanding and mental modelling. My passion is engaging my student teachers in transformative research approaches in different research areas. Reflecting on my pedagogical experiences, I have a passion for developing transformative science education in Indonesia.

NALINI CHITANAND

18. TRANSCENDING BOUNDARIES

Enacting a Transformative Philosophy of Professional Practice

An Epiphany

One morning I had an epiphany
For years I wondered
Where do I fit?
Chemistry graduate in Education field!
For years I wondered
How do I fit?
Two worlds apart

One morning I had an epiphany
Chemistry field I had to be
Same as dad, brothers and sister
But never as a chemist did I practice
A teacher, I was destined to be

One morning I had an epiphany
And the puzzle suddenly fit
This is where I'm meant to be
This is where I ought to be
This is where I love to be

One morning I had an epiphany
That this was my gateway
To transformative educational research
And practice, My home

One morning I had an epiphany
But this does not mean
That I have arrived
For we can never truly 'arrive'
To arrive, is the end of a journey
Rather we are in-becoming
Constantly learning, constantly changing

We often go through our lives questioning why we do what we do. Or the purpose(s) of the many roles we assume in our personal and professional contexts. As a science graduate with a chemistry major, working in the field of academic development (a sub field of higher education) for almost two decades, I often wondered why I needed to have studied a science field and yet never really practiced in it. Should I have perhaps studied something else, not science? For the first five years of my university teaching career I taught and tutored science subjects to chemistry and chemical engineering students. Later I joined an academic development unit and did not teach science subjects again. My role in academic development initially involved teaching generic academic literacy courses to students across disciplines, from science and engineering to arts and humanities. Later I moved on to academic staff professional development, also working with academic staff across disciplines engaged in conversations on how to improve learning and teaching in university contexts.

And so, I often wondered about the purpose of my academic science qualification. One morning, as I reflected on this chapter that I was about to write, I suddenly realised that my science qualification was my entry (and the road) into the Science and Mathematics Education Centre (SMEC) at Curtin University, Australia, where I completed a master degree in science education. And so began my journey into transformative educational practice and research.

In this chapter, I reflect thoughtfully on my master's study and how it subsequently shaped my *knowing, acting* and *being* (Barnett & Coate, 2005) in higher education. Specifically, it was the research project that made a profound impact on my development as an educational researcher. As I engaged in the deeply reflective and reflexive process of writing this chapter I realised the extent to which my master's study as well as my sustained collaboration with Peter Taylor (my research supervisor) and the growing International Transformative Education and Research Network (or family), were instrumental in shaping my professional practice and philosophy.

I have chosen to use a journey metaphor to illustrate the stories of my lived experience. At this time, the metaphor of a butterfly best describes my journey of more than a decade which has seen me undergo many stages of metamorphosis[1].

In the first part of this journey, I reflect on my master's research experience, which sowed the seeds for my transformative educational practice and research. I draw on key moments that revealed my *ontological* positioning and that have seen me transcend *epistemological* and *methodological* boundaries as an educational researcher. In the next part of this journey I describe my evolving professional practice as an academic development practitioner and scholar in a South African university. Embracing *theoretical pluralism* I draw on and share a number of theoretical perspectives that have underpinned my practice and research in academic development. The final section, bwy no means the end of the journey, illustrates my continuing professional learning as a researcher, journeying toward an *integral perspective*. Here, I touch on my research and ongoing doctoral study which, as I now reflect, seems to have spiralled off from where my master's study ended.

BEING AND BECOMING AN EDUCATIONAL RESEARCHER

In 1993 I joined the chemistry department at the university where I am currently employed, but later I was transferred to the Academic Development Unit. The latter was not by choice but provided greater options for permanency at the university. It was also not my choice to enter the field of higher education in the first place. I did not know how to teach, let alone how to research in higher education. My entry into academic development, or higher education for that matter, may best be described as *happenstance* (Baume & Popovic, 2016). Following academic developers' diverse pathways into the field (McDonald & Stockley, 2008), I too began the journey as a *disciplinary migrant* (Green & Little, 2013; Manathunga, 2007) after having spent a short time as a lecturer in chemistry.

As I experienced over the years, these were two completely diverse fields of practice, each with particular norms, language, ways of being and acting, writing and researching. So, I found myself crossing boundaries, from the science field to humanities (i.e., education), which is where the field of academic development is located. I struggled. I have written elsewhere (Chitanand, 2005) about the challenges I experienced, especially in researching and writing as a researcher in academic development. As I reflected on this part of my journey, I learned that this was due to the hegemony of positivism that was firmly rooted by my science professional identity.

Just over a decade later, I enrolled for a master's degree at Curtin University in Australia. In my research project I employed an *arts based critical autoethnography* to explore the dilemmas of learning and teaching physics through the lens of a second language. This experience took me on a journey of self-discovery and offered me fresh new perspectives for researching (my) educational practice. Engaging in this study enabled me to transcend epistemological and methodological boundaries. I will illustrate how this research experience contributed to my growth and subsequently shaped my professional practice and philosophy. However, this was not an easy process at first. I was beginning to take on a new identity which, in part, rested on my own agency as a developing researcher as well as the conditions of the master's study programme at Curtin University. As Peter Taylor explains in Chapter 3, he carefully and skilfully scaffolded the approach and inducted his students into this way of knowing, acting and being as emergent researchers. For me, this journey was about *being and becoming* (Dall'Alba, 2009) an educational researcher, which was facilitated through *enculturation* and *border crossings* (Aikenhead, 1996).

Border Crossing I: Research Can Be Creative, Fun, Stimulating...Transformative?

My first encounter of border crossing was during the first research project class. Peter asked us to write down some words associated with research. My responses were:

> inquiry, method, reflection, reasoning, quantitative, qualitative, nervousness, practice, sharing, teacher, classroom.

Peter's subsequent responses were:

> self-study, professional development, personal growth, have fun, creative, enjoy, useful, stimulating, enabling, empowering, transformative.

> Why didn't I think about them, I wondered. And so I asked: "Why is it that you have those words and I have these?". Peter's response was: "It's a process of enculturation", "of moving from one border to the next". With these words, I began taking my first steps into the creative, fun, stimulating, enabling, empowering, transformative aspects of research. (Chitanand, 2005, p. 86)

In the above excerpt from my master's research report, I narrated my first experience of border crossing. I experienced a certain amount of naivety, not uncommon for science students new to educational research. As I began taking my first steps into the *creative, fun, stimulating, enabling, empowering* and *transformative* aspects of research, I experienced nervousness. This was brought about by my own positivistic standpoint and objectivist writing style. But as I began to craft the story of my life, my autobiographical tale, this formed the basis of my research.

Border Crossing II: Autobiographical Inquiry and Narrative Representation

Does the old adage *we teach the way we were taught* really govern our practice as teachers? How important is understanding our own experiences as students and teachers for improving/transforming our educational practices? What can it reveal about our own situatedness in our professional practices and the assumptions we make about our students, about learning and teaching, and about researching educational practice? And how do we represent these critical learning experiences in our research reports? Should we?

In the next key moment of my master's study experience I share an extract of the creative, fun, stimulating, enabling, empowering and transformative aspects of research.

Inspired by Ducks

When I started the master's course at SMEC I had a project in mind that I thought I would investigate. I had been exploring the use of writing-to-learn strategies. So, in my first meeting with Peter (my supervisor) I already had an idea in mind. Peter mentioned something about autobiographical writing and I told him that I did not make use of autobiography in any of my writings. Nevertheless, I relayed a short story to him about one of my teaching experiences and why I began using writing-to-learn strategies…Peter then told me, "There, you've given me a part of your autobiography".

Motivated by my discussion with Peter, I decided to find out more about myself as a learner. Was it any different to what my learners were experiencing in their classrooms, or were there similarities? So, a few days later, armed with a pen in one hand and a notebook under the other arm, I made my way to a pond/small lake just across my home and sat on a bench beneath a tree.

It was a warm Saturday afternoon in March. The climate in Perth was a lot like in my home city, Durban, except in Perth the temperatures soared up to a blistering 42°C. Though, this day was not too hot. It was a peaceful day. Kids were playing in a park adjoining the pond and I wondered what my own kids were up to back home in South Africa.

I have always enjoyed nature. I could spend hours watching the sunset, or drifting clouds or bare trees on an open field. And thus I found sitting on the bench under a tree, near the pond on a warm Saturday afternoon a most relaxing experience. It was the most relaxed I had felt in the last few weeks. Leaving my family at home to travel 9000kms to pursue my studies was no easy task. Nevertheless, it was what I had wanted to do and I was excited about the new things I was learning. New place, new cultures and new learning experiences. It gave me a chance to get to know myself too. I realized then it was the first time that I had sat and watched ducks.

Have you ever watched ducks search for their food? They would dip their heads below the surface of the water. As they did this, the rear of their bodies and feet would pick up. They would continue in this rhythmic fashion till they found some food. I was enjoying the peace and tranquillity of watching the ducks search for their food. But as I watched them dig deep below the surface of the water, I too began to dig deeper into my mind in search of some 'truth' about my past learning experiences.

At first I found this to be a very difficult exercise. Why could I not easily remember anything from my primary and secondary school life? Was it because it was too long ago? Or was it that it was too boring and did not make much impact on my life to remember it? Or perhaps if I knew then that 15 or 20 years later I would have to remember it I probably would have paid more attention to what I was learning and how I was learning it. As I continued to watch the action of the ducks searching for food, I began to ponder deeper and deeper into my life. Slowly the images began forming and it was as if I was re-living the whole experience.

…

In one hour of watching ducks, eighteen years of my life just replayed itself as if I was watching snippets of a movie. (Chitanand, 2005, pp. 4–5)

Narrative representation. As I journeyed through my master's study I was attentive to which stories were being represented in my research report and how I represented them. As I crafted the narratives of my lived experiences and those of my participants, I was drawn to Carolyn Ellis who suggests that "perhaps telling our stories might encourage others to speak their silences as well" (Ellis, 1997, p. 134). So how could my stories promote *pedagogical thoughtfulness* (van Manen, 1990) and evoke critical reflexivity in my readers? I was inspired by John van Maanen's (1988) book on writing ethnography, Tales of the Field, that introduced me to *realist*, *confessional* and *impressionistic* tales. On the back cover of the book he states:

> Once upon a time ethnographers returning from the field simply sat down, shuffled their note cards, and wrote down their descriptions of the exotic and quaint customs they had observed. Today scholars in all disciplines are realizing that how their research is presented is at least as important as what is presented. Questions of voice, style, and audience – the classic issues of rhetoric – have come to the forefront in academic circles. (van Maanen, 1988)

Following Laurel Richardson (2005), I used *writing as a method of inquiry* to excavate my life history (Samuel, 2015) of being a student and teacher of science. These deeply moving revelations spurred further scholarly critical inquiries confronting our South African higher education context, especially with respect to teaching in multilingual classrooms. These autobiographical inquiries offered a glimpse of my evolving teacher identities, but not "without ever problematizing previously held assumptions" (Guillory, 2012, p. 15). As will be seen in the next section, these reflexive inquiries brought to the fore deeply held assumptions which, if not interrogated, would serve to maintain the status quo. These autobiographical inquiries provided spaces for disrupting my current conceptions about learning and teaching, and created possibilities for social justice pedagogies (James, 2007).

Border Crossing III: Transformative Educational Research – Embracing Epistemological and Methodological Pluralism

It was the "process of self-examination and discovery that helped me to ground my own evolving research and teaching agendas in the context of my past that pushed me to ask new and difficult questions about my assumptions" (James, 2007, p 161). I found Jack Mezirow's (2000) transformative learning theory to be a useful theoretical construct to effect changes in my existing frames of reference and ways of thinking about educational research. The writing-to-learn strategy that I was interested in exploring at the beginning of my masters study, I realised, would not address some of the pressing problems confronting post-apartheid South African higher education science classrooms, as expressed in the following excerpts that illustrate my early practice as a science lecturer in a multilingual class.

PROLOGUE

[Musi thinks to himself:] "Maybe Nalini will ask Jabu to solve the problem she wrote on the board. Oh no, she's walking in my direction. Please don't ask me. I won't know where to start. As it is, physics is a difficult subject. Doesn't she realise that it is more difficult learning this subject in English. I guess she won't. She does not speak *isiZulu* or understand it. Although science was difficult at school, at least Miss Mabaso explained it to us in Zulu when we did not understand. How will I tell her that I don't understand the question? What will others in the class say? They will probably laugh at me. She turns away and walks towards the board. Phew! Thank goodness."

Nalini makes a correction to the physics question she wrote on the board. She turns around.

This time she's looking at me. Maybe if I look away she won't ask me. Please don't…please, please, please.

Musi!

No, did she call me?

Musi, would you please solve this problem on the board for us? … (Chitanand, 2005, p. 2)

AUTUMN, 2003

I was satisfied with the progress I was making in my teaching practice, until:

Please ma'am can we have some more?

We were discussing a problem, which I had written on the board. I asked Musi, who always sat diligently in the front of the class, to try and solve the problem. Musi tried but could not. Having taught them previously how to deconstruct a problem, I told Musi that it was easy and that he should be able to do it. He replied,

It's not that we don't understand physics, but we sometimes have a problem understanding English as well.

Musi, like at least 90% of the learners in the class, did not have English as their first language. South Africa is a multicultural country with 11 official languages. Any one class in the institution could have learners from a variety of ethnic backgrounds. My particular class had learners speaking Zulu, Xhosa, Sepedi, Tswana, and others as their first language.

I felt pedagogically challenged. I spoke English. I could not speak any of the above languages. Here I was, an English-first language speaker teaching a subject that was traditionally labelled as being 'difficult' in a language that was almost equally 'foreign' to many of the learners. What was I to do? What would you do? (Chitanand, 2005, p. 11)

Thus, in my study under the broad umbrella of an *arts-based critical auto/ethnography*, I drew on multiple epistemologies of the interpretive, critical and postmodern research paradigms, and justified it by means of the quality standards of legitimation, praxis and representation. The research methods that I used included critical reflective inquiry, autobiographical inquiry, narrative inquiry, researcher as transformative learner, and fictive writing. One perspective on autoethnography views the researcher as "both the 'subject' and the 'object' of research" (Badenhorst, 2016, p. 8). In designing my autoethnographic study for my masters research project I was more inclined to align my research with Neni Mariana's explication of autoethnography (see Chapter 13):

> The slash ('|') in auto|ethnography signifies that the study was *coloured* at the same time by auto-ethnography and ethnography. Thus the slash indicates my *dialectical experience* (Roth, 2005) of considering my culturally situated personal experiences as well as those of my participants.

I adopted the stance of the *researcher as bricholeur* and attempted to produce a *bricholage* (Denzin & Lincoln, 2000) drawn from the multiple experiences of my own practices and those of my participants. Besides myself, my other participants included a teacher, *Robert* (a composite character, drawn from my own experience, the experiences of other science teachers, and the teacher that I observed for a few months) and students; and my analysis drew on interview and observational data. Rather than examining how learning and teaching could be improved with alternative teaching methods – a *reformist* approach – I sought to first understand from a critical perspective the experiences of teachers and students learning science in multilingual classrooms in post-apartheid South Africa, as depicted in the following vignettes.

In Conversation with Robert, a Teacher

Nalini: Do you know who your students are?

Robert: Well, I do have a chat with them now and again.

Nalini: Do you consider the learners' language issues to be an obstacle?

Robert: To tell you honestly, I have not given it much thought. I focussed more on getting the concepts right.

Robert ponders for a while then adds:

Robert: But perhaps there is a language problem or perhaps there isn't – I can't be sure. But come to think of it, I notice that when concepts are explained in the mother tongue, not by me, but by other students it makes it easier for them to understand. I know that if I would have to learn physics in say Afrikaans, I know it would be difficult. So yes, language could be a problem, but then again I would not know to what degree. But if this is the case, I don't think that language is the only problem. I think it's a conceptual problem, their poor maths skills and even their attitude. You know what I would really like to do? I would like to learn Zulu?

Nalini: Why?

Robert: So I could help those students that have a problem with English.

Nalini: And what about other learners who speak the other languages?

Robert: Well, once you start somewhere then I'm sure it will get easy. (Chitanand, 2005, p. 61)

I drew on Patti Lather's notion of *catalytic validity* which "refers to the degree to which the research process re-orients, focusses, and energizes participants in what Freire (1973) terms 'conscientization', knowing reality in order to better transform it" (Lather, 1986, p. 67). I did not want to just understand the experiences that my participants and I brought to the research. I was also interested in how the research could move participants to teach them something profound as teachers and learners in South African higher education. I was also mindful about how I was representing the stories from these experiences. In this sense I was traversing the intepretivist, critical and postmodern paradigms.

Embracing Pluralism

In the process of *becoming* a researcher I drew on multiple epistemologies and methodologies in my master's study which took me on a journey crossing multiple borders into new terrains for conducting educational research.

Along this journey, I realised that my pluralistic worldview and epistemologies connected to my Hindu self. Hinduism is known for embracing different views and supports the process of spiritual growth and awareness through multiple ways of *coming to know*. There is often a misunderstanding that Hinduism draws on many deities (Gods and Goddesses). This comes from an individualistic understanding of each of the deities as a singular. However, each form is actually different manifestations of divinity. For example, the Trinity[2] Brahma, Vishnu and Shiva are not three Gods but one manifesting in three forms for particular purposes. Brahma is considered the creator, Vishnu is the preserver, and Shiva is the protector. Likewise, the Tridevi[3] (trinity of Goddesses) Lakshmi denotes light (in various forms, wealth, health, happiness, wisdom), Saraswathi (learning and knowledge) and Durga (courage and strength). There are many other manifestations in Hinduism. And we would draw on each manifestation depending on where we are on our journey in life and the growth, guidance, knowledge and empowerment we seek.

Engaging in the master's study introduced me to the *creative, fun, stimulating, enabling, empowering and transformative* aspects of research. I realised that research was more than finding immediate solutions to fix pedagogical challenges. Engaging in transformative educational research (Taylor, Settelmaier, & Luitel, 2010), which involves excavating and critically examining our own personal and professional experiences, values and beliefs, offered me opportunities to disrupt my own thinking about education with bold new possibilities. Having completed my master's study in 2005, I was excited about enacting my new learnings in my academic development programmes.

MY EVOLVING PROFESSIONAL PRACTICE

Toward the end of 2005, I was invited to share my learnings at a departmental strategic planning workshop. I titled my presentation "Using Autobiographical Narratives as a Reflective Tool". The session was well received by my peers and I had new-found confidence in my ideas around transformative educational practice. It was the same year that my journey in academic staff development began, and I became passionately interested in *transformative and sustainable* academic development.

Over the years, shifting pedagogical roles from teaching mainstream science courses to facilitating *academic staff development* I soon learned that curriculum and pedagogic reform merely perpetuate the status quo and that to move beyond these crossroads and transform the higher education landscape a critical epistemological framework is required. Transformative learning (Mezirow, 2000) which is at the heart of transformative research provided an appropriate framework for this much needed paradigm shift, and thus was foregrounded in my academic development programmes through fostering critical reflexivity (Ryan, 2009) and a transformative intention. Education for sustainability became an important consideration in my educational endeavours. This was especially important in light of the current global crises and the demands on higher education institutions to prepare students who will be socially responsible citizens capable of contributing favourably to the well-being of the country and society at large. I began questioning the purposes of higher education and the extent to which our practices are c*onforming, reforming* or *transformative*.

> In the South African context academic development includes a "range of development and research practices aimed at the professionalization of teaching and learning in higher education, most commonly associated with various forms of student, staff, curriculum and policy development" (Shay, 2012, p. 311).
> Academic staff development (ASD) is a subset of academic development and is concerned with the professional development of academic staff for their teaching role in higher education. This includes research on learning, teaching and assessment in higher education.

Reimagining Education

In the words of Nelson Mandela, the first president of the democratic South Africa (1994),[4] "Education is the most powerful weapon we can use to change the world"

(Mandela, 2003). How can higher education contribute to personal, professional and societal well-being? How do we move beyond the status quo to a greater social justice praxis in line with the democratic principles of our institutions, our country and our world? And within an uncertain future, one that we cannot predict (Barnett, 2004). This poem captures some of my thoughts as I grappled with these dilemmas as a facilitator of academic staff development.

>A Sustainable Future
>
>Reimagining education
>Thinking again, thinking about
>Reflexivity! A deep inward gaze
>Bending backwards, on ourselves
>
>Thinking again, thinking about
>For a sustainable future
>Bending backwards, on ourselves
>We learn anew
>
>For a sustainable future
>Reflexivity! A deep inward gaze
>We learn anew
>Reimagining education
>
>(Chitanand, 2016)

This poem reflects some of my current thoughts about education. It was written for the 2016 South African Education Research Association (SAERA) Conference Special Interest Group meeting with the focus on *Reimagining Education Through Poetic Inquiry*. At the time of writing the poem I felt strongly that education can play a major role in efforts of sustainability, especially as it affects our planet and also our daily lives. I represented my thoughts about the poem in the following narrative which accompanied the poem.

> Each day our planet is being depleted before our very eyes; human induced climate changes and cultural degradation due to loss of our indigenous knowledge systems are threatening the very fabric of our lives. How can (higher) education contribute to a sustainable future? Do we need a radical rethink of our current educational practices? Reimagining education, perhaps? Reimagining, according to Southwood (2012) is "not necessarily suggestive of new thinking, but of thinking again and thinking about" (p. 89). However, the kinds of thinking that happens in education spaces is crucial for the kinds of changes we want to see happen, for a sustainable future. This calls for, not just reflection but reflexivity, a *deep inward gaze* (Ryan, 2009, p. 2) or bending backwards on ourselves (as depicted in the hammer bending backwards on itself). This process of bending backwards on ourselves enables us to question

'why we do what we do' (Hugo, 2015), that is, question our taken for granted assumptions and re-examine our preconceptions, values and beliefs that (un) consciously drive our behaviours. Engaging in this process as universities may lead us to ask, what are we educating for? What kinds of society do we want to produce and how might education contribute to it? (Chitanand, 2016)

While my vision for transformative and sustainable academic development focussed on a transformative higher education has been my passion for the last decade, enacting this vision has not been without challenges. I discuss this in the next section and share some of the theoretical perspectives I drew on in my staff development programmes.

Challenges

Globally, higher education is impacted by a number of forces – massification, globalisation, the *fourth industrial revolution*, and the changing role of the university, to name a few – that push and pull in multiple directions to drive and direct higher education. Within this evolving landscape, *neoliberalism* and *performativity* prevail, resulting in competing demands and purposes of higher education.

In addition, tensions between teaching and research and the hegemony of disciplinary research over researching learning and teaching feature prominently in national and international literature. This is exacerbated by the "perceived status accorded to universities by large numbers of publications, [and which] have often consumed an inordinate amount of the time and resources needed to develop and sustain quality university teaching" (CHE, 2015, p. 15). Increased workload and the need to focus on improving qualifications and engage in research are further factors that prevent academic staff from participating in professional development activities.

Within this context, academic staff developers are expected to contribute to improving learning and teaching in a somewhat piecemeal fashion and to show immediate impact (Di Napoli, 2014), most often in contrast to their own values of transformative educational practice. I felt that while I/we espoused transformative ideals and philosophies our practices did not yield the transformed practices we aspired to. For example, much of the staff development programmes resulted in minor tinkering of curricula or pedagogy. Feeling like a living contradiction (Whitehead, 1989), I questioned what we did and why as academic staff developers.

Over the years of facilitating academic development programmes my practice has undergone a number of iterations, each time based on the needs of the participants, institutional and national (and global) imperatives, and my own evolving professional identity and learnings from the field of academic staff development and higher education studies (including philosophy and sociology of education). In fostering a scholarly approach to learning and teaching, staff development activities/ programmes are conceptualised to strengthen the nexus between teaching and research at the university. Scholarly interrogation of theory, practice and research underpins the design of these programmes.

Embracing Theoretical Pluralism

I drew on a number of theoretical perspectives and lenses in my staff development programmes and research to evoke critical reflexivity and pedagogical thoughtfulness (van Manen, 1990) and inspire change. For the purposes of this chapter I focus on an academic staff development programme that I coordinate and facilitate, the Academic Staff Induction Programme for newly appointed staff. The front cover of the induction booklet states that:

> The Academic Induction Programme provides a safe space for fostering transformative educational practice and exploring student centred learning, teaching and assessment (LTA) strategies that empower students to become active, responsible and critical students and citizens.

Since taking over the coordination and design of the programme, it has undergone a number of changes from a discreet list of topics (tips for improving learning and teaching) to attempts to foster scholarly teaching and the scholarship of teaching and learning. In its current form the programme is a short programme (of six month duration, meeting in a 4-day block session and 5 monthly workshops) and is repeated twice a year.

The key theme that is embedded within this programme is the critical reflection on practice and asking questions of the kind *how do I improve what I do?* (Whitehead, 1989). In line with my vision for the programme, I draw inspiration from Parker Palmer who postulates that *we teach who we are* and contends that "good teaching comes from the identity and integrity of the teacher" (Palmer, 2007, p. 10). In the early sessions of the programme I use a metaphor drawing activity (van Laren et al., 2016) to enable participants to visually represent who they are as academics in higher education, what has shaped their professional practices, and what their aspirations are for learning and teaching.

A recent participant, Mary[5] is a coffee lover, of "real coffee", she would say. It was no surprise that she based her reflection on the metaphor of coffee.

Mary indicates that she would be attentive to each stage that will lead to the perfectly brewed coffee. This includes how she would grow and nurture the seeds. The coffee beans represents her students and she says that she needs to understand the conditions from where they came. Mary sees herself as the barista that brews the beans to get the perfect cup of coffee. She understands that each bean has its own unique taste – and she would have to know this for each of her students. She adds further that sometimes she would need to put them under some heat to get that "perfect shot of espresso". She feels that just as a barista would continually grind the beans and redo if needed for the best taste, she too would have to constantly evaluate how she deals with each student, "how she brews and develops them".

The metaphor drawing activities enable participants to excavate their embodied lived experiences of being in the world, build a philosophy for teaching and learning in higher education, and contribute to the development of their professional identity of being and becoming an academic (Chitanand & Rambharos, 2016).

Part of this personal self-knowledge is a critical understanding of our assumptions and preconceptions that are usually unconscious and which drive and shape our actions and behaviours.

As depicted in Figure 18.1, I draw on ideas around reflexivity (Ryan, 2005; Bolton, 2010; Brand, 2015), double loop learning (Argyris, 1976, Cartwright, 2002) and transformative learning (Mezirow, 1997, 2000) to enable participants to uncover their taken-for-granted assumptions about learning and teaching.

Gillie Bolton (2010) claims that reflexivity involves "finding strategies to question our own attitudes, thought processes, values, assumptions, prejudices and habitual actions, to strive to understand our complex roles in relation to others…to examine, for example, how we – seemingly unwittingly – are involved in creating social or professional structures counter to our own values" (p. 13). This process is often an uncomfortable experience that forces us to gaze inward (Ryan, 2010) to reveal values, beliefs and assumptions which often remain dormant and hidden (Brand, 2015). Through this process of bending backwards we engage in *double loop* learning (Argyris, 1976, Cartwright, 2002) that enables us to question our assumptions governing *why we do what we do*, providing knowledge for action (Argyris, 1993). This links to transformative learning theory (Mezirow, 1997), a process of effecting change to our existing frames of reference (our belief systems) and enabling *perspective transformation.*

Through the process of firstly uncovering and then questioning our taken-for-granted assumptions and re-examining our preconceptions, values and beliefs that (un)consciously drive our behaviours we are in a more informed position to critique our existing ideologies and challenge the status quo. Staff development thus becomes *spaces for disruption* (Quinn, 2012) of our current thinking and enables re-envisioning of transformative educational practices for a sustainable future; for ourselves, our students, our institutions, professions and society.

In promoting scholarly teaching I draw on the principles of a number of research methods to foster critical reflection on practice. These include action research, self-study, autobiographical inquiry, Living Educational Theory. I have found Jack Whitehead's (2010) framework and rationale for researching teaching and learning with probing questions has been beneficial to encourage critical reflection:

- What really matters to me? What do I care passionately about? What kind of difference do I want to make in the world?
- What are my values and why?
- What is my concern?
- Why am I concerned?
- What kinds of experiences can I describe to show the reasons for my concerns?
- What can I do about it?
- What will I do about it?
- How do I evaluate the educational influences of my actions?

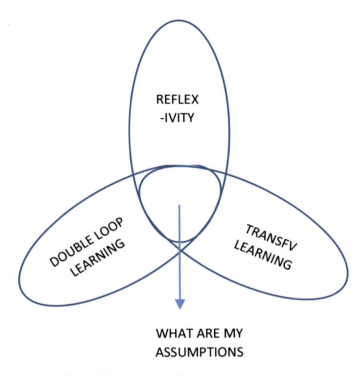

Figure 18.1. Strategies for uncovering assumptions

- How do I demonstrate the validity of the account of my educational influence in learning?
- How do I modify my concerns, ideas and actions in the light of my evaluation?

In facilitating the Academic Induction Programme I have had to caution against being over ambitious to expect grand transformations of participants' practices, especially given that the programme is of a short duration. Having said that, during the last session of the programme, participants share their reflections for improving their practice. These presentations reflect deep introspection and critical reflection, which suggests that the programme provides opportunities to *sow the seeds* for transformative educational practice.

Toward a Scholarship of Teaching and Learning

Donald Harward (2016) argues that the connection between higher education and well-being matter for students, teachers, our institutions and a democratic civic society. How can higher education contribute to a sustainable and just society?

And what is/are the role(s) of academic staff developers? These were some of the questions that I grappled with as I confronted the challenge of facilitating (transformative and sustainable) academic staff development, which within the South African context, remained on the periphery, was considered atheoretical and unscholarly (Shay, 2012)

However, the *decolonial turn* in South African higher education history, marked by mass student protests (in 2015–2016) disrupted current conceptions of higher education, pulling academic staff development from the margins to more centralised positions. Widening debates of relevance and access of the curricula of higher education, in the context of calls for decolonising higher education, the curriculum and pedagogy, suggested that it cannot be business as usual in higher education.

In light of the numerous challenges facing higher education, researching learning and teaching is an imperative. With this in mind, the Scholarship of Teaching and Learning (SoTL) Fellows Programme was initiated in 2018. An extract from the programme states:

> This project is underpinned by the principles of transformative educational practices that seek to develop ongoing critical, systematic inquiry into student learning that is beyond reformist approaches and remediation. The project seeks to engage academics in researching challenging problems associated with student learning in light of the complexities and challenges currently confronting higher education in South Africa. (Chitanand, 2018)

In designing the SoTL Fellows Programme I was attentive to transformative and democratic pedagogy. I concur with Yusef Waghid (2017) who argues that "democratic pedagogy should always represent a responsible commitment to the future, and it remains the task of academics to ensure that the future points the way to a socially more just world" (p. 5). The current programme is thus premised on a social justice framework. While it is not a panacea for solving the problems of teaching and learning, the programme seeks to create safe critical spaces to foster scholarly inquiries and develop the scholarship of teaching and learning. The current cohort of participants, forming a multidisciplinary group have coined the phrase *SoTL for Inspirational learning* as a theme for the group's research activities.

MY EVOLVING RESEARCH JOURNEY: TOWARD INTEGRALISM

My master's study experience introduced me to the creative, fun and transformative aspects of research which I have included in my pedagogical and research practice.

As an academic developer for more than two decades I have become increasingly concerned about how to ensure that our practices as staff developers are beyond reformist approaches that merely perpetuate the status quo, but rather engender a transformative praxis addressing some of the pressing concerns of higher education and society at large. This provided the impetus for my ongoing doctoral inquiry.

My doctoral research adopts a qualitative approach that attempts to decolonise the process of inquiry and traditional research design through engaging in a multi-paradigmatic research design (Taylor, 2014) that embeds aspects of critical theory, interpretivism and postmodernism. This *integral perspective* seeks to examine critically the biography of the field of academic staff development, to understand the shifts in the overall higher education system, its challenges and systems, not operationally, but philosophically. I seek to theorise what was and is academic staff development and to envision future possibilities.

Making Connections and Other Research

I was fortunate on returning home from my master's study at Curtin University, to have an existing family of practitioner-researchers at my university under the leadership of my colleague Joan Conolly (now retired) to provide support and a space to further transformative educational practices. Joan had led the Self Study for Transformative Higher Education (SeStuTHE) group which later collaborated with two other participating universities in South Africa, forming the Transformative Education/al Studies (TES) inter-institutional project (Harrison, 2012), which was nationally funded and provided a national forum for engaging in transformative education.

Since completing my master's study, ongoing sustained collaboration with Peter Taylor, Director of the International Transformative Education and Research Network (ITERN), has spurred a network of collaborative relationships. Through Peter's participation in workshops, seminars and keynote presentations at my university, further connections with my colleagues and those from neighbouring universities developed, including participants from SeStuTHE and TES.

Through my participation in ITERN, I have collaborated with other members. Emilia Afonso, Alberto Cupane (both from Mocambique, a neighbouring country to South Africa) and Bal Chandra Luitel (Nepal), have been presenters at workshops and conferences at my university. More recently, Bal Chandra Luitel has served as keynote speaker to a large national conference (HELTASA, http://www.dut.ac.za/heltasa2017/) in South Africa in 2017, generating further interests and future collaborations. I further participate in the Transformative Educational Research Group which is a sub group of ITERN with ten members from seven countries across a geographic spread from South Africa and Sydney Australia over a time zone of eight hours.

KNOWING, ACTING, BEING

Learning to become a professional involves not only what we know and can do, but also who we are (becoming). It involves integration of knowing, acting, and being in the form of professional ways of being that unfold over time. (Dall'Alba, 2009, p. 34)

Throughout this chapter I have reflected on how my master's research study shaped my professional ways of being in higher education. At the beginning of this chapter I used the metaphor of a butterfly to depict this metamorphosis-like development that unfolded over a period of just over a decade.

Along this journey I crossed a number of borders. My new learnings in the process of crossing borders took me to elevated levels of consciousness and offered me new ways of seeing (and being in) the world as a higher education practitioner-researcher. In effect I was not just crossing borders, but transcending boundaries, ontologically, epistemologically, axiologically and methodologically in my professional practice (and research). In this regard, I find the metaphor of the butterfly somewhat limiting (if considered as just a closed loop cycle). Rather, I am now more inclined to relate to the metaphor of a spiral that suggests continuously learning, continuously changing, and continuously learning. Within this super complex world (Barnett, 2009) in which we find ourselves we never really *arrive*. Rather, we are constantly in the process of questioning, learning, evolving and *becoming*.

So, on reflection, in 2004 I enrolled in a master's study that led me to…Wait!… Hold on! Perhaps it was an earlier road I had taken, that led me here. Perhaps things may have turned out differently had I selected another path, another road. I don't know!

I don't know how many others have walked a similar path, or if our paths could be similar at all. I do know that the journey of my lived experience of engaging in the master's study (specificlly the masters research project) has had a profound impact on my evolving professional practice and philosophy.

The Road Not Taken

Two roads diverged in a wood, and I –
I took the one less traveled by,
And that has made all the difference.
(Frost, 1916)

NOTES

[1] Source: https://www.tes.com/lessons/OylZCXXOuhTQdg/metamorphosis
[2] Source: http://www.bbc.co.uk/religion/religions/hinduism/beliefs/intro_1.shtml
[3] Source: https://www.hindufaqs.com/tridevi-the-three-supreme-goddess-in-hinduism/
[4] Prior to 1994, the era in South African history was marked by Apartheid. The Policy of Apartheid was instituted in 1948 and separated the people of the country politically, economically, geographically and socially, along racial lines. During this period, education too was divided along racial/ethnic lines privileging only the smaller minority group. In 1994 South Africa became a democratic country.
[5] A pseudonym.

REFERENCES

Aikenhead, G. S. (1996). Science education: Border crossing into the subculture of science. *Studies in Science Education, 27*, 1–52.

Argyris, C. (1976). Single-loop and double-loop models in research on decision making. *Administrative Science Quarterly, 21*(3), 363–375.
Argyris, C. (1993). *A guide to overcoming barriers to organizational change.* San Francisco, CA: Jossey-Bass.
Barnett, R. (2004). Learning for an unknown future. *Higher Education Research and Development, 23*(3), 247–260.
Barnett, R. (2009). Knowing and becoming in the higher education curriculum. *Studies in Higher Education, 34*(4), 429–440.
Barnett, R., & Coate, K. (2005). *Engaging the curriculum in higher education.* Berkshire: McGraw-Hill Education.
Baume, D., & Popovic, C. (2016). *Advancing practice in academic development.* New York, NY: Routledge.
Bolton, G. (2010). *Reflective practice: Writing and professional development* (3rd ed.). Thousand Oaks, CA: Sage Publications.
Brand, G. (2015). Through the looking glass space to new ways of knowing: A personal research narrative. *The Qualitative Report, 20*(4), 516–525.
Cartwright, S. (2002). Double-loop learning: A concept and process for leadership educators. *Journal of Leadership Education, 1*(1), 68–71.
Chitanand, N. (2005). *A window through their eyes: On the dilemmas of teachers and learners in a multilingual physics classroom* (MSc master's project). Curtin University of Technology, Perth.
Chitanand, N. (2018). *Scholarship of teaching and learning fellows programme: Information handout.* Durban: Durban University of Technology.
Chitanand, N., & Rambharos, S. (2016). Using metaphor drawings to creatively imagine new possibilities for practice. *Journal for New Generation Sciences, 14*(1), 1–20.
Council on Higher Education. (2015). *Content analysis of the baseline institutional submissions for phase 1 of the quality enhancement project.*
Cranton, P. (1996). *Professional development as transformative learning: New perspectives for teachers of adults.* San Francisco, CA: Jossey-Bass.
Dall'Alba, G. (2009). Learning professional ways of being: Ambiguities of becoming. *Educational Philosophy and Theory, 41*(1), 34–45.
Di Napoli, R. (2014). Value gaming and political ontology: Between resistance and compliance in academic development. *International Journal for Academic Development, 19*(1), 4–11.
Ellis, C. (1997). Evocative autoethnography: Writing emotionally about our lives. In W. G. Tierney & Y. S. Lincoln (Eds.), *Representation and the text: Re-framing the narrative voice* (pp. 115–139). Albany, NY: State University of New York.
Frost, R. (1916). *The road not taken* [Online]. Poetry Foundation. Retrieved from https://www.poetryfoundation.org/poems/44272/the-road-not-taken
Green, D. A., & Little, D. (2013). Academic development on the margins. *Studies in Higher Education, 38*(4), 523–537.
Guillory, N. A. (2012). Moving toward a community of resistance through autobiographical inquiry: Creating disruptive spaces in a multicultural education course. *Multicultural Education, 19*(3), 11–16.
Harrison, L. (2012). Learning from the first year of the transformative education/al studies project, *Alternation, 19*(2), 12–37.
Harward, D. W. (2016). Well-being essays and provocations: Significance and implications for higher education. In D. W. Harward (Ed.), *Well-being and higher education: A strategy for change and the realization of education's greater purposes* (pp. 3–17). Washington, DC: Association of American Colleges and Universities.
Hugo, W. (2015, May 5). *Institutional change and assessment workshop.* Durban: Durban University of Technology.
James, J. H. (2007). Autobiographical inquiry, teacher education, and the possibility of social justice. *Journal of Curriculum and Pedagogy, 4*(2), 161–175.

Lather, P. (1986). Issues of validity in openly ideological research: Between a rock and a soft place. *Interchange, 17*(4), 63–84.

Leibowitz, B., & Bozalek, V. (2015). The scholarship of teaching and learning from a social justice perspective. *Teaching in Higher Education, 21*(2), 109–122.

Manathunga, C. (2007). "Unhomely" academic developer identities: More post-colonial explorations. *International Journal for Academic Development, 12*(1), 25–34.

Mandela, N. (2003, July 16). *Lighting your way to a better future.* Address at launch of Mindset Network, Johannesburg, South Africa.

Marguet, P. (2014). *Managing new complexity, part 3: Potential of Reflexivity in the understanding of socio-technical systems* [online]. Retrieved from http://labs.sogeti.com/managing-new-complexity-part-3-potential-reflexivity-understanding-socio-technical-systems/

McDonald, J., & Stockley, D. (2008). Pathways to the profession of educational development: An international perspective. *International Journal for Academic Development, 13*(3), 213–218.

Mezirow, J. (1997). Transformative learning: Theory to practice. In P. Cranton (Ed.), *Transformative learning in action: Insights from practice. New directions for adult and continuing education* (pp. 5–12). San Francisco, CA: Jossey-Bass.

Mezirow, J. (2000). Learning to think like an adult: Core concepts of transformation theory. In J. Mezirow (Ed.), *Learning as transformation: Critical perspectives on a theory in progress* (pp. 3–34). San Francisco, CA: Jossey-Bass.

Palmer, P. J. (2007). *The courage to teach: Exploring the inner landscape of a teacher's life* (10th anniversary ed.). San Francisco, CA: Joey-Bass.

Quinn, L. (2012). Introduction. In L. Quinn (Ed.), *Re-imagining academic staff development: Spaces for disruption* (pp. 1–14). Stellenbosch: Sun Media.

Richardson, L. (2000). Writing: A method of inquiry. In N. K. Denzin & Y. S. Lincoln (Eds.), *Handbook of qualitative research* (2nd ed., pp. 923–946). Thousand Oaks, CA: Sage Publications.

Ryan, T. G. (2005). When you reflect are you also being reflexive? *The Ontario Action Researcher.* Retrieved from http://oar.nipissingu.ca/pdfs/v812e.pdf

Samuel, M. (2015). Beyond narcissism and hero-worshipping: Life history research and narrative inquiry. *Alternation, 22*(2), 8–28.

Shay, S. (2012). Educational development as a field: Are we there yet? *Higher Education Research & Development, 31*(3), 311–323.

Southwood, S. (2012). Spaces of development: A dialogical re-imagination. In L. Quinn (Ed.), *Re-imagining academic staff development: Spaces for disruption* (pp. 89100). Stellenbosch: Sun Media.

Taylor, P. C. (2014). Contemporary qualitative research: Toward an integral research perspective. In N. Lederman & S. Abell (Eds.), *Handbook of research on science education* (pp. 113–169). New York, NY: Routledge.

Taylor, P. C., Taylor, E., & Luitel, B. C. (2012). Multi-paradigmatic transformative research as/for teacher education: An integral perspective. In B. Fraser, K.Tobin, & C. McRobbie (Eds.), *International handbook of science education* (pp. 373–387). Dordrecht: Springer.

Van Laren, L., Pithouse-Morgan, K., Muthukrishna N., Naicker, I., Singh, L., Chisanga, T., Harrison, L., & Meyiwa, T. (2016). 'Walking our talk': Exploring supervision of postgraduate self-study research through metaphor drawing. *South African Journal of Higher Education, 28*(2), 639–659.

Van Manen, M. (1990). *Researching lived experience: Human science for an action sensitive pedagogy.* Albany, NY: State University of New York Press.

Van Maanen, J. (1998). *Tales of the field: On writing ethnography.* Chicago, IL: University of Chicago Press.

Waghid, Y. (2017). A university without ruins: Some reflections on possibilities and particularities of an African university. *South African Journal of Higher Education, 31*(3), 1–5.

Whitehead, J. (1989). Creating a living educational theory from questions of the kind, 'how do I improve my practice?' *Cambridge Journal of Education, 19*(1), 41–52. Retrieved from http://www.actionresearch.net/writings/livtheory.html

Whitehead, J. (2010, October 28). *Action research and living theories methodologies.* Paper presented at the Self-Study for Transformative Higher Education and Social Action (SeStuTHESA) Workshop, Durban University of Technology, Durban.

ABOUT THE AUTHOR

Nalini Chitanand: I am an Academic Development Practitioner/Scholar at the Durban University of Technology (DUT) and have been working in the field of academic development for almost two decades. My current role is Coordinator: Academic Staff Development. As a practitioner-researcher I am interested in transformative educational practice and research, research informed learning and teaching and developing scholarship around academic staff development. I am also interested in multi paradigmatic research design and exploring the use of innovative research methodologies, including auto|ethnography, narrative inquiry, action research, poetic inquiry.

EMILIA AFONSO NHALEVILO

19. VIEWING CURRICULUM AS POSSIBILITIES FOR FREEDOM

An Ndo'nkodo of My Research Path

PERFORMING NDO'NKODO

Ndo'nkodo is a Mozambican dance practiced mainly in the central provinces. It is based on improvisation; to perform this dance we make a circle and clap our hands which are the main instrument for producing riffs. Once the circle is formed and we start to clap our hands one of the participants starts to sing and the rest of the group makes an improvised chorus. The chorus is continuous and the clapping of our hands can be accompanied by any instrument that comes to hand, for example, an old pot or two pieces of bamboo or perhaps an old can of condensed milk. Loss, joy, pain, complaints are usually the themes and each may have a turn around the circle as the leading singer. Because Ndo'nkodo is based on improvisation when one person leads the singing we do not know beforehand what she/he will be saying. And as the themes in Ndo'nkodo can be of sadness or of happiness the tone of the voices may vary, and from time to time the voices may be interspersed with hushed weeping or laughter. Usually there are no answers for concerns raised and no judgements. When dancing Ndo'nkodo we all listen, and our responses, if we wish to give them, are comments or questions on the issues raised rather than statements. (Afonso, 2007, p. 126)

I have chosen to write this chapter as if I was performing in Ndo'nkodo. Drawing on arts-based research, I use Ndo'nkodo as a metaphor for my writing, which entails both joy and discomfort in my practice as a teacher educator in an African university as I endeavor to cultivate transformative paradigms in research. As a participant in Ndo'nkodo, I make use of different voices to convey my story: mine and my students' writings (similar to different instruments in Ndo'nkodo). I use italics to signify my historic voice drawn from my doctoral thesis and master's dissertation. I see Ndo'nkodo as "oral autoethnography" in which one's experiences are exposed to a larger group. Autoethnography is a mode of writing that connects the self with the broader cultural context (Ellis & Bochner, 2000) in ways that it becomes both a method and data in research. Here, I narrate my experiences in embracing and mentoring research based on new paradigms with a transformative agenda and making use of arts-based methods.

EMILIA AFONSO NHALEVILO

SINGING/WRITING MY STORY

Susan Chase (2005) states that narratives can be of three types: a short topical story about a particular event, an extended story about a significant aspect of one's life, or a narrative of one's whole life. In Ndo'nkodo the performer will often tell a story about a particular event or even an extended story featuring significant aspects or events that shapes one's life. However, in Ndo'nkodo there is always a sense of a continuous narrative. A narrative does not necessarily end at a certain point. It may continue on other occasions when the group meets again. Joana Nyala, for example, was well known in her village for her compelling talent in telling her multiple life stories in a continual way. She had grown up in that rural village and had never attended school. When she was born her parents thought that as a girl she did not need to be schooled. When she sang in Ndo'nkodo she would tell of her anguish for being the only illiterate in her family, her disillusionment with the first husband who abandoned her when she was pregnant with their second child, her second marriage (arranged by her parents) to someone strange to her who died a few years after their marriage. People participating in the Ndo'nkodo most of the time silently shed tears. But she could also narrate happy chapters of her life, as for example her journey in becoming one of the best-known painters in the village. It is a cultural habit in that village that houses be artfully painted featuring diverse themes. She could paint flowers, animals, pots, etc. Each painting had a story behind it and she would tell the story singing Ndo'nkodo, and so people would know about the meanings of her many paintings around the village. She would then claim that she is one of the best doctorates in painting and agriculture (she had huge farms). When I heard her sing I wondered about the interesting curriculum that made her so skilled.

In adopting Ndo'nkodo as a metaphor for this chapter I am emphasizing the narrative power of Ndo'nkodo for transforming, healing and resisting. Narration in Ndo'nkodo is accompanied and preceded by reflection in terms of how to represent the story, and why one should share that certain episode of life. It is also highly self-transformative because the narrator is not expecting an answer from the audience or straightforward advice. It is instead a moment for self-reflexivity and it transforms the singer through "self-explication", a term Peter McIlveen (2008) uses in relation to autoethnography. Although the topics in Ndo'nkodo, as in autoethnographic writing, are primarily of the personal sphere, telling one's experiences can be transformative for others too because stories of our experiences are not wholly our own; they implicate relational others in our lives (Ellis, 2004). They can also be transformative for others because hearing is important. By listening to others' experiences readers are moved to learn from stories similar to those they may have experienced or from stories they have never heard before.

As in autoethnography, in Ndo'nkodo by exposing self-narratives to the public without the protection of anonymity the teller risks the stigma of "negative judgments by university colleagues, and undesired career consequences" (Lapadat, 2017, p. 594). Vulnerability is a fact as there is also a risk of being misinterpreted but, as Christine Davis and Carolyn Ellis (2008) reflect, "This is what I've learned about autoethnography: it is in the sharing that we heal, in vulnerability that we become strong" (p. 300).

A PRIVILEGED STANDPOINT TO WRITE FROM

> The brick wall in this context is a metaphor. It is not that really that there is a wall. But that the wall isn't an actual wall makes the wall even harder…if there was an actual wall we would be able to see it and touch it. I could say, "Look at that wall". (Ahmed, 2014)

Sarah Ahmed (2014) is a lecturer who uses *brick walls* as a metaphor to tell about barriers faced by people who do not fit into the taken for grant as the norm. These barriers are not physical but they become physical as they exist "often because of what we are not. Not male, not straight, not white" (Ahmed, 2014). They exist because of our physical appearance. As she says, a wall can be how one is stopped from doing something or being in a certain place, or a wall can be the additional effort one has to make in order to be accepted, heard or respected. She gives examples of how, as a female non-White professor, she has experienced many of these walls as she enters the university professorial space dominated by male White professors. The atmosphere can become a wall. As a female, non-White native of Mozambique I have come up against many walls. I have indeed learned that gender, skin color and even language and geographical origin also are brick walls.

Mozambique is one of the few countries in Africa where Portuguese is the official language, even though the majority of the population do not have Portuguese as a mother tongue. Instead, they have diverse local languages. Portuguese was adopted as the official language after the country got its independence from Portuguese colonization. There are many issues that can be discussed in regard to having a foreigner language governing the country, but it is not the focus of this chapter. Instead, my reference to the language issue is to situate my standpoint because I see how a language can be turned into a barrier, a brick wall.

I am lecturing in the Faculty of Natural Sciences and Mathematics in a university devoted mainly to teacher training. It is the biggest university in the country and is composed of eleven branches, including the one in the capital city considered as the main branch. In my department in the capital city branch, I am the only female professor. There is only one other female professor in all the branches in the provinces. No doubt it is a male-dominated department. In my department I perceive some gendered brick walls that I have to face.

About 30 years ago when the university was created all the senior lecturers in my department were males from Europe, mainly from the now extinct Democratic Republic of Germany and the Soviet Union. These professors were in the country under bilateral agreements to prepare local lecturers to become professors. Most of the senior professors in my department today were supervised both in undergraduate and postgraduate studies (in those countries) by these Eastern European professors. We inherited a lot from them, such as books and lab materials and philosophies. In philosophical terms, for example, the emphasis in my department has been more on didactics and less on curriculum theory.

From a Deweyan perspective, Zongyi Deng (2016, p. 77) argues that "curriculum theory, largely associated with America and English-speaking countries, refers to a body of concepts, models and discourses concerning the relationship between school and society, the nature of schooling, curriculum planning", while "didactics, largely associated with German and German-speaking countries, refers to a theory of teaching and learning. Deng (2016, p. 81) argues that curriculum theory is concerned with a broader view of educational practices and asks questions such as:

- What educational purposes should the school seek to attain?
- What educational experiences can be provided that are likely to attain these purposes?
- How can these educational experiences be effectively organized?
- How can we determine whether these purposes are being attained?

A transformative perspective on curriculum theory will have a critical dimension and will ask the broader question of whose *interests* are (not) being served by a certain curriculum. According to Edmund O'Sullivan (2002), criticism can be in the form of *reform criticism* or *transformative criticism*. Reform criticism occurs when a culture is assumed to be formatively appropriate but the current practices do not seem to address the original purpose or original qualities, and thus criticism is in order to get *back on track*. A transformative criticism, by contrast, assumes that the culture is not formatively appropriate. A transformative perspective will question structures and taken for granted norms. For Deng (2016), didactics is concerned with three essential aspects – goals, content and methods – not allowing much space to question the actual curriculum's vision and practices. Didactics may have a critical dimension but only in the form of reform criticism. With the emphasis on didactics that we inherited I have experienced the existence of brick walls in my attempts to introduce a transformative curriculum agenda with my students. Trying to accommodate a transformative agenda has, at times, made me feel that perhaps if I was a White male I would be more easily heard. I have thought that maybe there would not be walls stopping me from doing certain things, that my views on innovative research paradigms, for example, would be more easily accepted. The American professor and critical scholar, bell hooks (1996, p. 31), writing about herself in the third person, lamented:

> She has learned to fear white folks without understanding what it is she fears (…) They learn without understanding that the world is more a home for white than it is for anyone else.

Here in my country, far away from bell hooks' America, the fear turns into unquestionable submission. It is my experience that new ideas brought by White men can be more easily accepted than if they come from a Black female. By saying this I am not *pointing a finger* at Whites, but am acknowledging that racism is a hegemonic force that needs the efforts of all to be uncovered and pointed out as a brick wall. As Steve Biko (2004) said, Blacks have to come to a realization of this unjust reproduction of conferred advantage and privileged White space. Thus, his call for *Black consciousness* which means, in short, to gain awareness of our values as Blacks. According to Sarah Ahmed (2014), for Black female African scholars there are uncountable walls that we have to come up against, but only a practical effort to bring about transformation will allow these walls to become apparent.

It is from this perspective that I speak from a privileged standpoint, because I not only experience but am able to *see* these walls. I know about the extra work I have to do in order to be heard. The effort that I have to make when I come up against the barriers of language supremacy (English), skin-color supremacy (White), gender supremacy (male), geography supremacy (non-African). I have come to see from a privileged standpoint that there are many who cannot *see* these walls, either because they belong to the taken for granted norm or because they are accustomed to living within these walls so that they see them as natural.

TEACHING: WHAT CONCEPT, WHICH PRACTICE/PRAXIS?

After I finished high school in 1984 and due to the political, social and economic situation in my country at that time, I was directed to an education course. All of us had to wait for official government lists, which informed us what course we should take in order to help our own country face the problem of lack of trained people in many areas. Education was one area that few wanted to take voluntarily. The Education list was regarded as the sad list; the worst of the lists especially compared with medicine, agriculture and engineering. I was no exception, so I hated the education list as well. I couldn't guess that my name would be on such a list. I had done well in high school, I thought.

Nevertheless, I took up my studies to become a teacher…I was a number, like others, to fill the course of chemistry and biology teachers for high school. I was a number, just a number, to address the necessity for preparing professional teachers. There were hundreds, thousands of children at schools without teachers…

In 1986, I completed my course in the Faculty of Education. And I was a chemistry teacher. One of those many people who had responded to the need for professional teachers in Mozambique post-independence. One of those many people who had obeyed the needs of the country according to the government program and perspectives. I was not a hero. I was a number, only, within ten, a hundred or maybe a million other numbers recorded in the programs of the government. Yes, a number!

> I took some time to realize that I was dealing with people, that I was there not only to teach, but also to help students learn the content. (Afonso, 2002, p. 8)

Curriculum is one of the words that bear varied definitions and understandings in the field of education. Philip Jackson (1992), for example, refers to the traditional definition of the 19th century and illustrates how the concept has gone through many re-definitions. He says that "the boundaries of the field are diffuse, so much so that one may wonder sometimes whether it has any boundaries at all" (p. 37). From an ontological perspective, Linda Behar-Hornstein, Ellen Amatea, and Peter Sherrard (1992) state that different world views generate different knowledge about schools and what counts as knowledge. Shirley Grundy (1987) describes well that the concept of curriculum is not the same as if we are dealing with the concept of hydrogen, which has a series of distinct properties that identify it as hydrogen. Acknowledging the complexity of giving an objective concept to curriculum, Orhan Aknoglu (2017, p. 264) says that "views about curriculum can be better explained using metaphorical images". In the same vein, William Schubert (1986) refers to *curriculum images* as a way to categorize major conceptions of curriculum. Although the concept of curriculum varies widely, when operationalized it determines the style, pedagogy and agenda of teaching. Thus, its conceptualization is an important issue in our profession as educators. No-one can teach without a curriculum and each curriculum concept leads to a distinct set of practices or praxes.

The journey of writing/singing made me reflect on the idea of curriculum I held in my first years as a teacher at a high school. Curriculum was for me the content and the numbers (pupils!) that filled the rows of chairs in my classroom. Words were only about the content, not about the people. Words were, for example, in the summary I had to write in the book of summaries at the end of each class. People were numbers and I would write in the book those numbers who were absent. I would also call the students by their numbers.

> "No 1? Present. 2? Absent. 3?...3?! Alexandre, will not you answer the call?", asked the teacher. "Only when you call me by name," answered the boy. The teacher in her ninth class of the day retorted: "Stop messing up. We call by numbers to make it easier". He's never been convinced that the easiest is the right one. And he made the decision: from that moment he would call them all by numbers: "No. 8, why do we have to learn the 2nd degree equation? No 5, can I go to the bathroom?" At home, he continued. His father wanted to start bossing: "I'll be No 1, after all I'm the head of the family. The mother complained: "I work as hard as you and I still do things from home. (…) The pastor was No 2, the priest No 3. (…) Confusing! The school principal called everyone involved. Alexandre was objective: "No. 14, I just want to be called by name." After much discussion, his request was accepted. And are all the students no longer mere numbers? Not really. Only the way to make the call changed. (Pagliosa, 2017, p. 53)

Curriculum represented a prison encapsulating my students and myself. It took me years to come to construct the idea of *curriculum as possibility of freedom*. And that was the transformation I endeavored from embracing transformative research in my master's and doctoral voyages (Afonso, 2002, 2007).

> I wrote an autoethnographic research thesis in which I narrated and interrogated many of the research practices that were taken for granted in the environment in which I worked back in Mozambique, including my experiences as a primary school pupil during the colonial era, my experiences as a high school student during the first post-independence era, my experiences as a student teacher in a faculty of education, as a teacher, and lately as a science teacher educator. I felt as though I was going through a metamorphosis in which the caterpillar became a butterfly (…). (Nhalevilo, 2011, p. 754)

During my ongoing transformative journey, I have come to think of curriculum as encompassing life in a broader sense. Yes, curriculum is still about the content but it is also about me, my students, the buildings, and the culture of the institution. It is about the gardens and the trees that we plant and those we do not plant, the neighborhood and the country. It is about the books that we read and those books we do not read. It is also about the bounds of possibilities we dare to challenge. Yes, curriculum can be the boundaries of prison or possibilities of freedom!

In my reconceptualization of curriculum, I started to interrogate *Didactics of Chemistry*, a subject I teach to undergraduate students. I had the feeling of it as a colonized subject. It held us tied to the orthodox content when we talked about the art of teaching. It is my experience that the content and the concept of this subject constrains my students and myself to a narrow view of curriculum. Although methodologically Didactics prescribes sound learning principles, ontologically it tends to minimize people and contexts in favor of the course content. It is concerned with goals, content and methods. I barely *see people*. The unfamiliar overrides local realities and local people. Countless times I have wondered when looking at the syllabus: where are the *people*? They are obscure figures, faded like enslaved zombies idolatrizing the eternal principles from the distant past. The people were, in my eyes, imprisoned still by the doctrinal principles of the art of teaching, trapped as I had also been in the narrow view of curriculum, locked in by the only one paradigm setting.

As in many subjects, every topic in Didactics of Chemistry starts with theories or concepts. Seldom ever do we start with the *people*. Knowing each other is just a quick ritual so that we have names of those attending the class. As Parker Palmer (1998) says, we usually ask the *what?*, the *how?* and occasionally the *why?* questions but rarely, if ever, do we ask the *who?* question – *who is the self that teaches*? (and *the selves who learn?*). From the first class, we perpetuate the inherited culture: first and foremost, it's about the content to be taught. Every teacher carries his/her own sentence: the syllabus. This is what we show to the students, to the department, and to all the gatekeepers when we move from one to another class or semester. No-one is willing to bring in the people, not even in the form of their lived stories, their poems or their different lenses, or even their dreams, as the prime condition to begin the semester.

DIDACTICS

Etymologically, *didactics* means the art of teaching. However, this art of teaching chemistry was studied and explored from a standpoint very different from a Mozambican society, and was imported ready made into Mozambique. Chemistry itself is a sub product of a foreign culture to Mozambique. Within this scenario, how and where could I locate my students, the subject chemistry, the art of teaching chemistry, and myself? The teaching of Didactics of Chemistry constitutes a dilemma for me and, with a desire to inquire into my own epistemological position in my professional practice, I embarked on the journey of this research in which I was willing to pass through the complexity of a metamorphosis that could enable me and my students from caterpillars to become butterflies, but not just any kind of butterfly, not butterflies humiliated, colonized, diminished and shaped by exaggerated positivism. I wanted to allow and to contribute so that the native caterpillars, like me, could proudly become native butterflies. (Afonso, 2007, p. 9)

I wondered whether within the limits of Didactics of Chemistry, in fact within the limits of reform criticism, I could fit the native butterflies with their own ontologies and axiologies, their own different colors.

INTRODUCING TRANSFORMATIVE RESEARCH TO MY STUDENTS

Writing is an exercise through which we heal, make sense of and strategize social change. (Shahjahan, 2014, p. 233)

In 2008 a master's degree program in science education was introduced in my university. With my failure to come up with a *transformed* didactics for my undergraduate teaching, I moved my interest to introducing transformative research to my master's students. After all, I had complained that to the detriment of students we put curriculum content up front. In my experience transformative research puts primary emphasis on the self. Jack Mezirow (1991) argues that transformation theory is based on retroactive reflection. So, transformative research challenges us to critically reflect on the lenses we are using. Discovering our voices and those of our students is part of transformative research. Paulo Freire (2004) was right: "To deny the importance of subjectivity in the process of transforming the world is naive and simplistic. It is to admit the impossible: a world without people" (p. 50). So, I decided that before asking my students to nominate their research topics, I would ask about their life stories, their values and their dreams. I would ask about the *words* they have in relation to their profession, be it in narratives, poems or the lyrics of songs. I would invite them to be creative and imagine images that illustrate their visions and contexts. I embarked on a journey across what I thought to be unstable but rewarding territory which had as its main purpose bringing my students into the foreground of their research, and only after them the topics to be researched.

It was unstable territory because of the emphasis on didactics, as opposed to curriculum, that reigned in my department. It was unstable also because we had no history of previous transformative research at the institution to refer to. It was unstable because I felt my gender (and ethnicity) would play a role in making people disbelieve the seriousness of my work and that of the students whose dissertations I was supervising. The *White male* reference is still taken as a standard for many judgements. From my privileged standpoint, I could see a number of brick walls that I would have to come up against. There was a lot that we (my students and I) would have to endure because moving from a didactic view of research to a curriculum view of research implied moving from a positivist paradigm to new paradigms such as Interpretivism, Criticalism and Postmodernism. I felt that shifting paradigms was more easily achieved individually than institutionally.

In the following paragraphs, I present extracts from four of my students' writings to illustrate the path of transformation they have taken while writing their masters' research dissertations or while writing in our research methods classes. I have used pseudonyms to mask identities.

Abel

In 2010, Abel was ready for his master's examination. He is a lecturer at another branch of my university teaching Didactics of Chemistry, a subject I am also teaching in the capital city. He attended in 2008 the first group of candidates for a master's degree in science education at my university. He had been a science teacher for about 20 years. That included teaching in a secondary school and lately at the university.

Often student-teachers choose topics to research that already exist in the program. They will ask questions such as, "How can I teach the concept x and theory y?" or "What can I recommend as didactic materials for topic z?" With a transformative agenda, I had set up the challenge of involving my students (the *people*) in reflections about themselves and their students, and to subordinate the theories, didactic principles, and even the content, under these reflections. In that respect, the topic for Abel's dissertation arose from conversations in class and outside class as we talked about how pupils in high school, especially in rural areas, have many difficulties in learning science concepts. We talked about ourselves and teachers in general. We talked about how in chemistry we have so many concepts which students never get to see and so there is a need to use analogies. This is how Abel identified the topic for his research: "How do teachers select analogies they use in chemistry classes?".

This was the first dissertation in science education at the department clearly mentioning and locating the paradigm from which he was doing research as a non-positivist approach. We embraced the challenge, though I had fears as I mentioned. It was a risk in that context that we could not be understood, and that Abel's dissertation would be condemned to failure. A big loss for him! And for me as well! We also had against us the fact that Abel did not speak English while most of the literature I had or could recommend was in English. The official language being Portuguese, only very few people speak English. I could clearly see language and these other issues as hard walls to come up against. The terrain felt very tricky. Nevertheless, we embarked on the challenge.

We had chosen the perspective of *people first*. So, Abel applied an interpretivist approach, referring to interviews and conversations as a way of generating data and enlightening his own views and analysis of the data. Steine Kvale (1996) refers to two metaphors for the interviewer: *miner* and *traveler*. He explains that "in the miner metaphor knowledge is understood to be buried metal and the interviewer is a miner who unearths the valuable metal" (p. 3). From this perspective, the data the interviewer is collecting is not *contaminated* by the interviewer and "the precious facts and meanings are purified by transcribing them from the oral to the written mode" (p. 3). In the travel metaphor, by contrast, the researcher is a traveler who experiences the landscape and asks questions of the people s/he encounters. On return home s/he has a tale to tell which may be shared with the people interviewed and those who wandered along with him/her (Kvale, 1996).

Abel took the perspective of *interviewer as a traveler* and engaged in the experience of *inter/viewing*, that is, exchanging views with teachers working in rural schools. On his return home (to his university department) he had a lot to tell and share with colleagues, and this stimulated further conversations. I saw Abel overwhelmed with new views arising from conversations with colleagues. Thus, we see conversation being an integral part of his research with others impacting Abel's interpretations and his own growth in understanding self and others. During this journey, I could see a transformation of Abel, and the topic he had chosen soon became part of his life. In my mind, he had embraced the idea of *curriculum as freedom*. He was no longer a prisoner of the topic but an accomplice with the teachers and students. He had embarked on the idea of freeing people – teachers and students – making them aware of the narrow image of curriculum that imprisoned them in decontextualized teaching and learning through their use of analogies. That is what we saw as most relevant in his research, as Abel wrote in his dissertation:

> The relevance of this research can be viewed from two perspectives. First, for the researcher the study can be viewed as an opportunity for professional development. By engaging in reflecting about the analogies in use by teachers and in textbooks at the selected schools the researcher critically reflected on his own practice as a chemistry teacher educator. Secondly for the teachers who participated in the study, the research contributed to raise their awareness about the use of analogies. It is further expected that other readers may also gain some inputs in reference to their practice in similar or different contexts. (p. 17)

In terms of his research findings, he added:

The findings showed that most of the teachers use analogies in their lessons, without taking into account the context of the students. They normally use the analogies out of context of their students. Analogy of the pudding for atoms, for example, showed to be one mostly used even in rural areas where it was likely that students have never seen a real pudding. The study also revealed that the textbooks in use at secondary schools present some analogies although most of them do not reflect the reality in Mozambique.

One of the recommendations from the study is that analogies should be included as a topic to be studied in the context of Didactic of Chemistry classes at Universidade Pedagogica. (p. 110)

Like me, Abel teaches Didactics of Chemistry. We did not want to prescribe a list of analogies that teachers should use. Rather, we wanted to support teachers in their own reflections on the issue, something that would make them critical about the analogies used in the textbooks and that they would think about analogies that work better in their local contexts. At the same time, we also entered the path of reflections about our own teaching practices in Didactics of Chemistry, a path that I see as a way to decolonize the curriculum. And this involved Abel's colleagues, as well. With his excitement about his own growth, he shared with his colleagues who found themselves reflecting on the analogies they were using in class with their students.

At the end of Abel's dissertation, there was no recommended list of analogies to be used; *only* the account of the journey that was of great value for his professional growth. On the examination day, the main criticism from the group of examiners was that there was "no list of analogies to be used". So, they did not see the value of the research. Could our attempts to refer to different criteria for determining the value of research make sense? Could Abel's explanations of his enlightening learning journey which *contaminated* his department colleagues justify the validity of his research? Posing this question makes me recall a poem I composed during my doctoral research (Afonso, 2007, p. 42):

Validity

I read Tierney, Ellis, Bochner, Richardson and others
While reading, I enjoy their words
My heart echoes things they speak about
My mind sees light on the texts
And my soul...invites my courage to learn
And I feel capable to write!
Write from the profession of my heart
About the practice of my profession

Ah...but my heart complains
It complains about my insistent thoughts about validity
I have to write the criteria to validate my research

> Still somewhere in between epistemology and methodology
> The dilemma catches me and…
> And time gives space to this dilemma
> Tic toc, tic toc, time is going indeed!
>
> How can my research validate the validity?
> How will one of these criteria standing in these books
> Choose my way of knowing about my practice?
>
> This is the threat:
> Do I construct a story to validate?
> Or do I validate a story to construct?
> Do the events shape validity by themselves?
> Or does validity shape the events?
> Does my writing colonize validity?
> Or does validity colonize my writing?
>
> Silly questions…!
> I swear
> These words printed in my research, write my story
> This text reads my journey of my practice
> And within this hermeneutics of writing and reading
> And then, reading and writing,
> I am learning

I was greatly relieved that the objective aspects of Abel's research saved him from failure. He had accomplished all the technical requirements of dissertation writing, so there were no concerns about, for example, spelling and grammar or referencing!

Arts-Based Research

Norman Denzin and Yvonna Lincoln (2005) refer to the *triple crises* that impact qualitative research: the crises of *legitimation, representation* and *praxis*. The transformative agenda my students and I embarked on were grandly illuminated by the crisis of representation and the crisis of praxis. In terms of representation, which raises questions about how we represent people and events, we embraced diverse genres to illuminate our texts – poems and pictures – and multiple genres to represent our data, thoughts and feelings. We broke away from the exclusive use of *realistic* writing, which dominates the texts of our Science department, and we made use of *impressionistic* and *confessional* tales (Maanen, 1988).

In terms of praxis, we challenged what constitutes validity in our research, a move that invited us to revisit our agenda. We questioned from the start not only *what?* and *how?* questions but also *why?* questions. Why would we take a particular topic and a specific methodology? We questioned the (political) interests behind our research. Whose interests were being well served and whose were not? In this environment, arts-based research emerged not only as a way to represent but also a way to criticize the taken-for-granted standards of educational research validity and representation.

> We started writing poems and narratives of our practice, and we took them to critically adorn the curriculum, both the written and the perceived. With poems, we made the curriculum look like crystal buildings and with narratives we made it taste like our culture. And that resuscitated the green smell of the environment. (Nhalevilo, 2011)

In our research methods classes arts-based research is one of the approaches to choose, as when we do singing of Ndo'nkodo. It is not reserved just for the final dissertation. We write narratives and poems as a normal practice. Usually students are reticent, even a bit ashamed, of using arts-based tools in our classes but after a few examples I see their satisfaction grow. I remember when one of my students said loudly: "I am a man of numbers. I appreciate, but I don't like to write poetically. That is not my paradigm". All the other students laughed because of his use of the word *paradigm*. It was a new word for most of them and I was happy to see that they could now locate their agendas or method in a paradigm. I did say that as long as they are aware of the existence of different possibilities (paradigms) I am happy with what at the end they will choose. I would, however, call their attention to the fact that as science educators we should not be blinded by the epistemology of objectivism. As Bal Chandra Luitel (2013, p. 71) says, "An objectivist epistemology promotes the view that any mathematical [or science] knowledge is constitutive of 'pure forms' unaffected by cultural, personal and political influences". By contrast, I invite my research students to discover their authentic voices, "to be alert to the voices inside us that are not our own, the voices that have been deliberately implanted by outside interests" (Brookfield, p. 45), especially in our case as an ex-colony and a so-called "least developed" country, because our voices have been historically and systematically silenced.

Quembo

As I write this chapter Quembo is still attending some classes, and I will not be his supervisor. He is a primary school teacher in one of the central provinces of the country. He was one of the students who immediately fell in love with the idea of writing poetically within the context of his research. The following extract is how he represented the rationale of his study in his project proposal, entitled: *Medicinal Plants as Local Knowledge in Primary School Education*.

> I am a son of flat lands,
> flat lands where plants develop freely like birds in the air, fish in water;
> lover of medicinal plants as friends of life;
> These plants that men enjoy, enjoy and enjoy to brighten life;
> I am from the lands where man learns to live as the plants themselves live;

Lands where man produces nectar as plants produce;
I am a son that his parents used plants to heal any illness of their creatures
at the time;
Do all plants cure diseases?
Do the current communities restore medicinal plants as they used to?
Do the communities see medicinal plants as friends?

Capece

Capece teaches Biology in a high school located in Chimoi, the central province of Mozambique. As with Quembo, I will not be Capece's master's research supervisor but the seed is sown, as can be seen with the following poem written by Capece during our research class.

Who Am I?

In the past, I could just say: I am an innocent child, you can understand me.
My father is a teacher,
But when I grow up to be a teacher, I will reject
My mother is a seamstress and she likes gardening.
This last profession, yes, I can accept.
Oh! Who am I?
From the steep lands of Manica, where I was born and raised
Where I started ABC in 1st grade, and never gave up
But who am I?
Long years spent in this life
I compare to a long road with climbs and descents
I spent three years in the training as an agro-livestock farming technician
I learnt the techniques of plant and animal production
Then another four years attending the university to become a Biology teacher
Drinking from the theories of learning of Jean Piaget and Vygostky
And from every repertoire of biological sciences
Today, I am a truly unfinished product in constant learning and discoveries
Teacher and son of a retired teacher,
With various subjectivities but with only one identity
Influenced by traditional indigenous education of my parents
By the critical thinking of José Saramango
By the incisive socio-cultural approach of Paulina Chiziane
By the quite abstract fiction of the texts of José Craverinha
And by the paradigms of simplicity that I was taught by my Professor
I want always to be
Someone who cares about the current problems of education in Chimoio
Concerned with Biotechnology and its integration in the curriculum for high school
There is a gap

I am looking to respond to this gap
This is who I am!

We know the impossibility of a world without people (Freire, 2004) and have learned the utility of dialectically being both objective and subjective, and we have learned the transformative road by embracing a multi-paradigmatic approach to research (e.g., Taylor & Medina, 2013). In bringing our voices to our research and profession, we reflect on who we are and why we are doing things the way we do. Writing poetically allows us to reflect, but also to be ethically and aesthetically authentic to our own existence.

Bela

Bela was one of the recent group of master's students. She works as an academic in a northern branch of our university. She has light in her eyes because of her constant enthusiastic expression, especially when learning new paradigms. She was hesitant at the beginning to experiment with innovative ways of doing research. She was used to the traditional data collection techniques, such as questionnaires, observations and interviews; interviews in the sense of Kvale's *miner* metaphor. Perhaps as a Black female, like me, she wondered if her research would ever gain any credit if she was to embrace alternative paradigms. How could she dare to do things in a different way! Perhaps she even wondered if I would be capable of convincing my colleagues of the validity of her research. Perhaps she even wondered if I was able to mentor her on that journey. I wondered how many brick walls did she feel at the beginning of the journey. However, once she engaged with readings and started to generate data I could see how the light in her eyes became visionary and I could see her developing an agenda for her research. There were times, however, when she would fall again into a doubtful mood as, for example, on the day when she came to see me and asked: "Do you think the colleagues in the department will accept these things that my students produced from their portfolio as data? Maybe I have to add another technique so that I have *real data* to show when they will ask me about it". I assured her this was the reason that she should explain how her assessment practice was part of her data generation and was based on the literature supporting the paradigm standpoint she had taken. The other day she asked me if the colleagues at the department had access to literature on paradigms in research. She added: "This is very new for me, not sure if others know about this". With these moments of hesitation, doubts and *ahaa* stances, she walked the path of her transformation. She tells me how transformed she felt by doing this research.

On the day of her master's dissertation examination she could *see* the brick walls she would have to face, and thus she was in a privileged standpoint. She had lived each chapter of her dissertation, and thus she was strong and happy. In September 2017, she was successfully examined and assessed as *Passed with Distinction*. In my eyes, she is a promising female academic at my university. In my eyes, *Distinction* denotes her transformation and willingness to help others to transform. She has presented in international conferences, making an extra effort by rehearsing her presentations and slides in English. Dismantling many walls! The following is part of her dissertation.

> I lived moments of prohibition and arguments without foundation, which led me to the feeling of a loser and sometimes to postpone my dreams because of not knowing how to express myself, to defend my interests within family and people around me. I remember that I feared my parents so much. They would tell me what to do and what not to do, anything they said was an order for me even if I did not agree. My fear swallowed my words to express my point of view…I am the victim of a discouraging education, in which there was no voice to say anything, or discuss my ideas with a classmate. I could not express my opinion about something that the teacher said. During the entire primary education, I felt guarded and controlled, repeating the domestic repression of my parents…I do not remember my teachers being interested to listen, to know of our dreams and personal stories.
>
> At secondary school, sometimes we could be invited to express our opinion around one and another point, but reflecting on my pronouncement today I see my limitations to make critical analysis and to produce a logical foundation on the situation.
>
> And this has made me an unhappy person, no doubt!
>
> Now, all this has already happened in my life, I cannot change anymore, it's part of my story. But today I reflect on how to avoid this situation to happen to others. (p. 14)

Referring to a traditional classroom, Peter Taylor (1996) says how it "is framed by powerful culturally-determined networks of beliefs and values, or *cultural* myths, that serve to reproduce a unitary and unproblematic social reality" (p. 2). He points to the myth of *cold reason* that imprisons students' creativity and the myth of *hard control* which is "a repressive myth that renders as natural the teacher's classroom role of a *teacher as controller* and that locks teachers and students into grossly asymmetrical power relationships designed to reproduce (rather than challenge) the established culture" (p. 11). Although Taylor was writing in relation to a mathematics classroom, the myths of cold reason and hard control can also be seen in many science classrooms. Writing was for Bela a platform to free herself from the dogmatic myths that had suppressed her self and her humanity. Writing was for her a possibility to bring her self more fully into existence and to cultivate an agenda of transformation for more fully developing the personhood of other colleagues. Research writing was for her walking the path of curriculum as a possibility of freedom.

Bela's final reflections on her research emphasize her personal growth which she understood as a key issue to being a better teacher.

This study left me motivated; from this I learned beautiful lessons of personal and professional life. I became another person. This work allowed me to reflect on my life story, how I relate to people, and especially how I have managed knowledge I learn on a daily basis to solve problems in the community. (p. 74)

Bela's research on her own practice allowed her to uncover and set strategies for how to challenge the myths of hard control and cold reason. Her research journey can be seen as a path of transformation, especially a *journey of resistance* against the taken for granted myths that prevent students and teachers from discovering curriculum as a possibility of freedom.

From this resistance framework, oppression takes place through the colonization of the mind and cultural imperialism. Resistance, then, is about opposing and rewriting dominant cultural values, codes, narratives and behaviors. (Shahjahan, 2014, p. 222)

Bela opposed and rewrote dominant cultural values she had held from her earlier years. Values that had made her silence her own voice and postpone her dreams. She overcame the feeling of being a loser and she broke the bricks of a discouraging education that had held her a victim for so many years. She discovered that curriculum can be a possibility of freedom.

BECOMING NATIVE BUTTERFLIES?

I have narrated in this Ndo'nkodo of mine stories that compose my path of personal and professional transformation. I view it as a path, uttering the sense of a continuous narrative. Each day there are more episodes to be sung, and I may find new instruments that come to my hand. By writing this chapter as Ndo'nkodo I had moments of self-reflexivity, of self-explication. Writing this chapter helped to heal the wounds from encounters with many brick walls that I face daily as a Black female from an African country. Singing this Ndo'nkodo made me vulnerable but also strengthened me to continue my journey as a lecturer in a university department that still struggles to accommodate multi-paradigmatic research. A department that is predominantly male. Writing this chapter helped me to resist the colonization of the mind and cultural imperialism – see how I insist on calling this writing an Ndo'nkodo! It made me revisit my agenda for cultivating curriculum as a possibility of freedom, and thus with that freedom I see many butterflies gaining their authentic colors and becoming proud native butterflies.

REFERENCES

Afonso, E. Z. (2002). *Rethinking science teacher education in Mozambique: An autoethnographic inquiry* (Unpublished master's dissertation). Curtin University of Technology, Perth, Australia.
Afonso, E. Z. (2007). *Developing a culturally inclusive philosophy of science teacher education in Mozambique* (Unpublished doctoral thesis). Curtin University of Technology, Perth, Australia.

Ahmed, S. (2014). *"Brick walls: Racism & other hard histories"*: Unsettling conversations, unmaking racisms & colonialisms. Retrieved from https://vimeo.com/110952481
Akınoğlu, O. (2017). Pre-service teachers metaphorical perceptions regarding the concept of curriculum. *International Journal of Instruction, 10*(2), 263–278.
Arao, J. (2010). *Uso de analogias no ensino de química nas escolas da provincia de Manica* (Unpublished master's dissertation). Universidade Pedagógica. Maputo, Mozambique.
Behar-Horenstein, L. S., Amatea, E. S., & Sherrard, P. (1999). From theory to practice: Contemporary curriculum issues. In A. Ornstein & L. B. Horenstein (Eds.), *Contemporary issues in curriculum* (2nd ed., pp. 3–12). Boston, MA: Allyn & Bacon.
Biko, S. (1978). *I write what I like.* London: The Bowerdean Press.
Brookfield, S. D. (1995). *Becoming a critically reflective teacher* (1st ed.). San Francisco, CA: Jossey-Bass.
Chase, S. E. (2005). Narrative inquiry. In N. Denzin & Y. Lincoln (Eds.), *The Sage handbook of qualitative research* (3rd ed., pp. 651–679). Thousand Oaks, CA: Sage Publications.
Davis, C., & Ellis, C. (2008). Emergent methods in autoethnographic research: Autoethnographic narrative and the multiethnographic turn. In S. N. Hesse-Biber & P. Leavy (Eds.), *Handbook of emergent methods* (pp. 283–302). New York, NY: The Guilford Press.
Deng, Z. (2016). Bringing curriculum theory and didactics together: A Deweyan perspective. *Pedagogy Culture and Society, 24*(1), 75–99.
Denzin, N. K. ., & Lincoln, Y. S. (Eds.). (2005). *The Sage handbook of qualitative research* (3rd ed.). Thousand Oaks, CA: Sage Publications.
Ellis, C. (2004). *The ethnographic I: A methodological novel about autoethnography.* Walnut Creek, CA: Altamira Press.
Ellis, C., & Bochner, A. (2000). Autoethnography, personal narrative, reflexivity. In N. K. Denzin & Y. S. Lincoln (Eds.), *Handbook of qualitative research* (2nd ed., pp. 733–762). Thousand Oaks, CA: Sage Publications.
Freire, P. (2004). *Pedagogy of the oppressed* (30th anniversary ed.). New York, NY: Continuum.
Grundy, S. (1987). *Curriculum: Product or praxis?* London: The Falmer Press.
hooks, b. (1996). *Bone Black.* New York, NY: Holt Paperbacks.
Jackson, P. (1992). Conceptions of curriculum and curriculum specialists. In P. Jackson (Ed.), *Handbook of research on curriculum* (pp. 3–40). New York, NY: Macmillan.
Kvale, S. (1996). *Inter/views.* Thousand Oaks, CA: Sage Publications.
Lapadat, J. (2017). Ethics in autoethnography and collaborative autoethnography. *Qualitative Inquiry, 23*(8), 589–603.
Luitel, B. C. (2013). Mathematics as an im/pure knowledge system: Symbiosis, w(h)olism and synergy in mathematics education. *International Journal of Science & Mathematics Education, 11*(1), 65–87.
Maanen, J. V. (1988). *Tales of the field.* Chicago, IL: University of Chicago Press.
Macie, B. (2017). *Estudo da capacidade de argumentação dos estudantes no ensino de química* (Unpublished master's dissertation). Universidade Pedagogica, Maputo, Mozambique.
McIlveen, P. (2008). Autoethnography as a method for reflexive research and practice in vocational psychology. *Australian Journal of Career Development, 17*(2), 13–20.
Nhalevilo, E. A. (2011). Telling a tale: Pieces of SMEC in my wind of memories. *Cultural Studies in Science Education, 6*(3), 747–756.
O'Sullivan, E. V. (2002). The project and vision of transformation education. In E. V. O'Sullivan, A. Morrell, & M. A. O'Connor (Eds.), *Expanding the boundaries of transformative learning* (pp. 1–12). New York, NY: Palgrave.
Pagliosa, M. (2016). *Contos para insónia.* Rio de Janeiro: 7 Letras.
Palmer, P. J. (1998). *The courage to teach.* San Francisco, CA: Jossey-Bass.
Schubert, W. H. (1986). *Curriculum: Perspectives, paradigms and possibility.* New York, NY: Macmillan.
Shahjahan, R. A. (2014). From 'no' to 'yes': Postcolonial perspectives on resistance to neoliberal higher education. *Discourse: Studies in the Cultural Politics of Education, 35*(2), 219–232.
Taylor, P. C. (1996). Mythmaking and mythbreaking in the mathematics classroom. *Educational Studies in Mathematics, 31*(1–2), 151–173.

Taylor, P. C., & Medina, M. N. D. (2013). Educational research paradigms: From positivism to multiparadigmatic. *Journal for MeaningCentered Education, 1*. Retrieved from http://www.meaningcentered.org/journal/volume-01/educational-research-paradigms-from-positivism-tomultiparadigmatic/

Taylor, P. C., Nhalevilo, E. A., & Rahmawati, Y. (2015). Transformative educational research: Meeting global challenges of the 21st century. *The Newsletter of the East Asian Science Education (EASE), 8*(4), 8–10. Retrieved from http://new.theease.org/list.php?bdid=2

Taylor, P. C., Taylor, E., & Luitel, B. C. (2012). Multi-paradigmatic transformative research as/for teacher education: An integral perspective. In B. J. Fraser, K. G. Tobin, & C. J. McRobbie (Eds.), Second international handbook of science education (pp. 373–387). Dordrecht: Springer.

ABOUT THE AUTHOR

Emilia Afonso Nhalevilo is my name. I was born in the northern province of Nampula in Mozambique. I hold a PhD in Science Education from Curtin University of Technology, Australia and I am currently teaching at Universidade Pedagogica where I am also the Director of the Center for Mozambican Studies and Ethnoscience. My main research interests lay in two fields: Science Education and Indigenous Knowledge Systems.

NAME INDEX

A
Abrams, E., 16
ACARA, 4
Acharya, S., 24
Act, I. E., 208, 219
Adams, J., 193
Adams, T. E., 80, 197, 227
Adorno, T. W., 64
Afonso, E. Z., 42, 77, 193, 197, 295, 301, 306–308, 311
Afrianty, D., 213
Ahmed, S., 303, 305
Aikenhead, G. S., 2, 5, 39, 269, 281
Allen-Collinson, J., 121, 122
Alsop, C. K., 48, 49
Alsulami, N. M., 89, 103
Amatea, E. S., 306
Ameyaw, A. A., 195, 197
Amorado, R. V., 54
Anderson, L., 33
Arcus, T., 4
Argyris, C., 292
Ashcroft, B., 132, 137, 140, 141, 190
Atweh, B., 174
Ausubel, D. P., 193
Awasthi, L. D., 242
Awuah, P., 52
Azra, A., 213

B
Bagley, C., 67
Bajracharya, H., 24
Baldwin, A., 2
Banda, K. N., 188
Barad, K., 66
Barleet, B. L., 117
Barnett, R., 280, 289, 296
Barone, T., 7, 40

Baroudi, J. J., 98
Basseches, M., 267
Battista, M., 235
Baume, D., 281
Becker, C. U., 5
Beg, M. A., 6
Behar-Hornstein, L. S., 306
Belbase, S., 77, 109, 112, 116, 119
Bendix, E., 183
Benolt, B. A., 117
Bentley, M., 260
Bentz, V. M., 7
Berlin, D. F., 197
Bhabha, H. K., 240
Bhattacharya, K., 30
Biko, S., 305
Bilton, T., 132, 138, 141
Birch, K., 63
Birmingham, S., 4
Blake, W., 55
Bochner, A. P., 33, 71, 91, 96, 103, 104, 120, 122, 123, 197, 227, 240, 301, 311
Bodner, G. M., 193, 195
Bogue, K., 267
Bolton, G., 292
Bonnett, K., 132, 138, 141
Boson, K., 4
Bourdieu, P., 240
Boyd, R. D., 153
Brady, K., 174
Brand, G., 292
Brickhouse, N. W., 259
Brinkmann, S., 208, 214
Britzman, D. P., 65, 197
Brookfield, S. D., 313
Brouwer, W., 24
Brown, B., 85

NAME INDEX

Browne, J., 183
Bryman, A., 96, 97, 100, 104
Buchholtz, N., 77
Bulletin of the Atomic Scientists, 2
Bunnin, N., 175
Burke, P. J., 116
Burnard, P., 257
Butler-Kisber, L., 11

C

Cabras, A. A., 52
Cahnmann, M., 23
Capra, F., 112–114, 120
Carroll, J., 4
Carspecken, P. F., 182
Carter, C., 182
Cartwright, S., 292
Cary, L., 197
Cassam, Q., 115
Cattley, G., 270
Chakrabati, P., 5
Chappell, K., 257
Chase, S. E., 302
Chemjong, I. S., 241
Cheon, Y.-C., 5
Chinmayananda, S., 27
Chisanga, T., 291
Chitanand, N., 281–283, 285, 287, 289–291, 294
Chow, M. L., 3, 6
Christians, C. G., 4
Clandinin, D. J., 78, 183
Clough, P., 23
Coate, K., 280, 289, 296
Cobb, P., 190
Code, L., 70, 71
Coffey, P., 121
Cohen, L., 68, 96–98, 104
Comte, A., 62–71
Connelly, F. M., 78, 183
Corsiglia, J., 247
Craft, A., 257, 258
Cranton, P., 6, 243

Cremin, T., 257
Creswell, J. W., 104
Crutzen, P. J., 39
Cupane, A. F., 77, 130, 190, 295
Custer, D., 85

D

D'Ambrosio, U., 208, 232
Dall'Alba, G., 281, 295
Daly, C., 175
Damanhuri, M. I. M., 42
Das, K., 80
Davies, B., 183
Davis, C., 303
Day, C., 270
Dei, G. J. S., 195, 197
Deng, Z., 304
Denshire, S., 120, 121
Denzin, N. K., 5, 22, 68, 77, 80, 100, 111, 112, 286, 312
Derrida, J., 122
Désautels, J., 22
Desmond, K. K., 98–100
Deussen, P., 26
Devine, M., 155
Di Napoli, R., 290
Dirkx, J. M., 68, 155
Dochy, F., 260, 261
Dourish, P., 244
Duit, R., 191

E

Earth Charter Commission, 3, 39
ECOSOC, 3
Edwards, G., 10
Edwards, L. D., 26
Egxea-Kuehne, D., 174
Eichstaedt, J. C., 32
Eisner, E. W., 7, 40
Ellis, C., 7, 33, 45, 71, 80, 91, 96, 103, 104, 119, 120, 174, 197, 227, 240, 283, 284, 301–303, 311

F
Fanon, F., 12, 141
Faulkner, S. L., 11
Ferreira, F., 3
Fien, J., 3
Filipe Matos, J., 26
Fleener, M. J., 198, 199
Flick, U., 31
Flores, M. A., 270
Foster, V., 63
Fox, R., 268
Freed, J., 260
Freeman, M., 240
Freire, A. M. A., 7
Freire, P., 3, 7, 75, 89, 197, 210, 236, 242, 246, 287, 308, 315
Freudenthal, H., 208
Frost, R., 296
Fumerton, R., 23

G
Gannon, S., 183
Gautam, S., 30–32, 61, 70
Gergen, K. J., 68
Gidley, J. M., 25, 84
Golmohamad, M., 139
Gonski, D., 4
Goodman, D. J., 69
Gould, V., 4
Graham, A., 270
Green, D. A., 281
Greene, M., 7
Greenwood, D. J., 165
Griffiths, G., 132, 137, 141, 190
Grundy, S., 50, 83, 193, 194, 257, 306
Guba, E. G., 50, 79, 95–98, 177, 188
Guillory, N. A., 284
Gunstone, R. F., 191
Guo, C. J., 4

H
Habermas, J., 5, 75, 81–83, 157, 193, 210, 257

Hammond, T., 235
Hanh, T. N., 175
Harmon, D., 2
Harrison, L., 295
Harward, D. W., 293
Hashweh, M., 194
Haverkamp, B. E., 68
Hayler, M., 119
Hayne, H., 111
Hoffman-Kipp, P., 270
Holman Jones, S., 277
Honan, E., 183
hooks, b., 304
Hornby, A. S., 135
Hubar, M., 260
Hugo, W., 290
Humphreys, M., 67
Hunkins, F. P., 164

I
Infosys, 1
Iqbal, A. M., 154

J
Jack, F., 111
Jackson, P., 306
Jackson, T., 2
James, J. H., 284
Joanna, W., 10
Johnson, C., 27
Johnson, M., 78, 175
Johnston, E. H., 30
Jones, P., 132, 138, 141, 245
Jost, M., 67

K
Kauffman, S. A., 84
Kearney, R., 23
Kelle, U., 77
Kern, M. L., 32
Key, E., 164–166
Kincheloe, J. L., 6, 7, 12, 31, 39, 50, 97, 132, 135, 136, 243

NAME INDEX

Kirschner, D. A., 261
Kittleson, J. M., 259
Koestler, A., 45
Koirala, B. N., 24, 243, 244
Krauss, S. E., 90
Krauze, A., 131
Kuhn, T., 7, 210
Kunst, A., 30
Kvale, S., 145, 208, 214, 310, 315

L

Ladson-Billings, G., 5
Lakoff, G., 78, 177
Lapadat, J., 302
Lapum, J. L., 182
Laszlo, E., 3, 39
Lather, P., 69, 287
Lavallee, L. F., 182
Laws, C., 183
Lawson, T., 132, 138, 141
Le Nguyen, K. D., 32
Leggo, C., 44
Lerman, S., 75
Levin, M., 165
Levi-Strauss, C., 65
Lincoln, Y. S., 5, 22, 50, 68, 79, 80, 95–98, 100–112, 188, 286, 312
Literat, I., 9
Little, D., 281
Loh, J., 2
Long, L., 121
Loomba, A., 2
Loy, D., 26
Luitel, B. C., 5, 8–10, 19–22, 26–33, 42, 63, 71, 75–78, 81, 98, 100, 110–112, 119, 147, 151, 161, 164, 174, 178, 193, 209, 226, 232, 236, 243, 246, 248, 252, 253, 288, 295, 313

M

Macedo, D. P., 7
Mackeracher, D., 246
Maffi, L., 2
Maglana, W. P., 52
Maharshi, R., 32
Mahony, W. K., 33
Manathunga, C., 281
Mandela, N., 289
Manion, L., 68, 96–98, 104
Mariana, N., 207, 208, 286
Marsh, C., 266
Martin, L. S., 182
Maskarinec, G. G., 241
Maslow, A. H., 40
Matthew, 40
Matthews, E., 198
McDonald, J., 281
McIlveen, P., 302
McLaren, P., 6, 7
McNiff, J., 82
McNiff, S., 100
Medina, M. N. D., 8, 45, 46, 52, 67, 77, 78, 91, 177, 240, 315
Mendez, M., 117–119
Mertova, P., 182
Meyiwa, T., 291
Meynell, H. A., 99
Mezirow, J., 5, 6, 14, 40, 81, 82, 149, 152, 153, 156, 176, 209, 210, 236, 244–246, 266, 267, 284, 288, 292, 308
Michell, H., 39
Michell, M., 2, 5
Miron-Spektor, E., 267
Mission, N. R., 24
Molz, M., 84
Morrell, A., 6, 40, 82
Morrison, K., 68, 96–98, 104
Mtemang'ombe, D. P., 188
Mueller-Rockstroh, B., 183
Muller, F. M., 27
Mullick, P. D., 80
Muthukrishna, N., 291
Mutua, K., 2

N

Nabayra, E. S., 52
Nadarajah, M., 2, 5
Nagarjuna, A., 30
Naicker, I., 117
Newberg, A. B., 32
Nhalevilo, E. A., 307, 313
Nikhilananda, S., 28
Nkrumah, K., 1
Núñez, R. E., 26

O

O'Brien, L., 4
O'Connor, M. A., 6, 40, 82
O'Sullivan, E. V., 304
O'Sullivan, S., 63
OECD, 2013
Omnès, R., 8
Orlikowski, W. J., 98
Ornstein, A., 164
Otsuji, H., 162, 163

P

Pagliosa, M., 306
Paletz, S. B. F., 267
Palmer, P. J., 7, 55, 129, 255, 291, 307
Pangeni, S. K., 31
Panikkar, R., 33
Pant, B. P., 30–32, 78
Patai, D., 183
Perry, L.-A., 4
Phelps, R., 270
Pillay, D., 117
Pinar, W. F., 7, 147, 198, 256
Pinney, C., 70
Pithouse-Morgan, K., 117, 291
Polanyi, M., 24
Polkinghorne, D. E., 100
Popovic, C., 281
Poudel, A. B., 32
Pradhan, R., 24
Prawat, R. S., 194
Prendergast, M., 44

Presmeg, N., 83
Prins, F. J., 261
Prusak, A., 139

Q

Quinn, L., 292
Qutoshi, S. B., 30, 31, 80, 112, 147, 150, 153, 154, 156

R

Rae, A. I. M., 8
Raheem, K., 195, 197
Rahmawati, Y., 42, 216, 265, 266
Rai, I. M., 30, 69, 240, 246
Raju, P. T., 26
Rambharos, S., 291
Ray, L., 244
Reed-Danahay, D. E., 80, 103, 104, 117, 118
Reese, R., 111
Remesh, A., 259
Ricard, M., 8
Rice, C. J., 267
Richards, R., 117, 119
Richardson, L., 22, 105, 197, 284, 311
Rist, G., 243
Ritzer, G., 69
Roberts, J. M., 62
Roberts, M., 4
Robertson, R., 5
Robinson, K., 53
Rohmann, C., 162
Rorty, R., 27
Rosch, E., 268
Roth, W. M., 22, 100, 119, 120, 122, 207, 286
Roy, K., 30
Rumi, J., 147, 154
Ryan, T. G., 289, 292

S

Saldana, J., 70, 227
Sameshima, P., 44

NAME INDEX

Samuel, M., 284
Sani, S. S., 252
Savasci, F., 197
Schiralli, M., 99
Schubert, W. H., 256, 306
Schwartz, H. A., 32
Segers, M., 260, 261
Semali, L. M., 39, 132, 135, 136, 243
Settelmaier, E., 3, 169, 288
Sfard, A., 139
Shahjahan, R. A., 308, 317
Shapiro, J. J., 7
Shay, S., 288, 294
Shea, C. M., 28
Sheldon, E. A., 168
Sherrard, P., 306
Shivanand, A., 6
Shrestha, A., 24
Shrestha, I. M., 30, 112, 226
Simanjorang, M., 174
Singh, A., 155
Singh, L., 291
Skinner, D., 132, 138, 141
Skutnabb-Kanga, T., 2
Sluijsmans, D., 260, 261
Smith, L. T., 39
Snively, G., 247
Snow, C. P., 85
Solis, O. J., 267
Song, J., 42
Southwood, S., 289
Spady, W., 199
Spencer, L., 131
Spencer-Rodgers, J., 267
Sproule, A., 237
Spry, T., 22, 111, 227, 240
Sri Aurobindo, 25, 32
St Pierre, E., 22, 99
Stanworth, M., 132, 138, 141
Stockley, D., 281
Stoermer, E., 39
Strijbos, P. A., 261
Sumsion, J., 267

Suyatno, 213
Swadener, B. B., 2

T
Taylor, E., 3, 8, 9, 28, 42, 63, 71, 75, 78, 98, 100, 119, 151, 161, 164, 174, 178, 209, 271
Taylor, E. W., 6, 152, 243
Taylor, P. C., 3–12, 22, 26–28, 39–45, 63, 67, 71, 75–79, 95, 98, 100–105, 111, 112, 119, 151, 152, 161–164, 169, 174–178, 190, 193, 199, 209, 210, 217, 226, 240, 243, 245, 248, 252, 253, 266–268, 271, 281, 288, 295, 315, 316
Thakur, R., 31
Thapa, A., 32
Thompson, R. L., 117
Thomson, E., 268
Thuan, T. X., 8
Tiffin, H., 132, 137, 141, 190
Timm, D. N., 117
Tippins, D., 81, 268
Tobin, K., 12, 22, 31, 50, 81, 97, 175, 268
Treagust, D. F., 191
Turner, J. H., 65
Turner, W. D., 267

U
UNESCO, 1–3, 5
UNICEF, 189, 190, 195

V
Valera, F. J., 268
Van Laren, L., 291
Van Maanen, J., 284
Van Manen, M., 79, 112, 152, 156, 284, 291
Vinden, P. G., 98
Von Glasersfeld, E., 116
Vygotsky, L., 43, 165

W

Wacquant, L. J. D., 240
Waghid, Y., 294
Wagle, S. K., 31, 32
Warrier, A. G. K., 34
Watson, T. J., 67
Webster, A., 132, 138, 141
Webster, L., 182
Welch, C., 75
Werlen, B., 8
Westad, O. A., 62
Whitehead, J., 81, 82, 152, 154, 225, 290–292
Wilber, K., 8, 25, 71, 102, 103
Williams, B., 192, 201
Willis, J. W., 10, 44, 67, 77, 95, 96, 117, 177
Willison, J. W., 268
Wintering, N. A., 32
Witt, S. C., 270
Wong, W. C., 24, 268
Wood, M., 75
Woolnough, B. E., 255

Y

Yaden, D. B., 32
Yamphu, H. P., 239, 241
Yan, C., 111
Young, R. A., 68
Yu, J., 175
Yusuf, L., 42

Z

Ziman, J. M., 164

SUBJECT INDEX

A

Aesthetic, 4, 5, 42, 43, 100, 117, 236, 315
Anthropocene, 2, 39
Autoethnography, 7, 19, 20, 22, 23, 26, 27, 33, 49, 55, 76, 78, 80, 81, 85, 89, 90, 97, 100, 103–106, 109, 110, 112, 116–123, 150, 161, 169, 174, 208, 209, 227, 252, 274, 281, 285, 286, 301–303

C

Colonialism, 132, 134, 135, 144, 145, 213
   European colonialism, 4
   linguistic colonialism, 70
   neo-colonialism, 1, 2, 4, 138
   Portuguese colonialism, 132, 133
Comprador intelligenstia, 12, 30, 137
Consciousness, 1, 3, 6, 8, 9, 23, 24, 26, 32, 40, 68, 71, 96, 98, 149, 151, 154, 207, 208
   black consciousness, 305
   critical consciousness, 79
   cultural consciousness, 195
   ecological consciousness, 154
   false consciousness, 83, 240, 246
   meta-consciousness, 112, 117, 120
   planetary consciousness, 39
   positivistic consciousness, 69
   relational consciousness, 117
   self-consciousness, 45, 115
   shift in consciousness, 153
   transformative consciousness, 151, 156, 176, 183, 210, 216, 221, 267, 296
Critical knowing, 43, 208, 210, 216

Culture
   biocultural diversity, 2, 16, 57, 164
   cultural capital, 2, 4, 5, 7, 16, 84, 225, 226, 235
   cultural diversity, 1–3, 247
   cultural self-knowing, 43, 150, 152, 154, 210, 248

D

Dialectics
   dialectical co-existence, 141, 315
   dialectical experience, 208, 286
   dialectical logic, 10, 25, 70, 78, 100
   dialectical method, 150, 253
   dialectical philosophy, 69, 131
   dialectical relationship, 22, 100, 140, 174
   dialectical slash '/', 226
   dialectical space, 240
   dialectical thinking, 28, 44, 71, 131, 132, 136, 140, 142, 143, 247, 248, 265–268
   eastern dialectics (see eastern below)
   self-culture dialectics, 22
Dualism, 4, 10, 25, 26, 28–30, 33, 69, 76, 99, 148, 226, 247

E

Eastern
   Advaitin neti-neti dialectic, 28, 29
   Atma, 22
   Bodhisattva, 169
   Buddhist traditions, 7, 8, 24, 26–28, 32, 162, 229
   Eastern-Western nexus, 24
   Eastern wisdom traditions, 5

SUBJECT INDEX

Eastern and Western wisdom traditions, 24, 71
Hindu-Buddhist values, 28, 34
Lila-Rita dialectics, 20, 32, 33
Madhyamika Buddhist co-arising dialectic, 20, 28, 30
Mahayana Buddhism, 161, 162, 169, 170
Mukti, 20, 32–34
Tandav, 112, 114, 115, 120
Tathagata, 169
Vedic/Vedantic, 8, 22, 24–26, 28, 30, 32, 33
Zen Buddhism, 162
Ecology, 2
ecological sensibilities/thinking, 24, 70, 71
ecological turn/consciousness, 71, 154
ecological wellbeing, 10
epistemic ecology, 62, 70, 71
transformative researcher as ecologist, 63, 70
Essentialism, 4, 10, 132–136, 139–142
nonessentialism, 30, 130, 136, 138–142
non/essentialism, 140–143
strategic essentialism, 140, 141
Ethics, 4, 6, 26, 52, 53, 100, 123, 138, 174, 183
ethical challenge/dilemmas/issues, 3, 6, 39, 67, 122, 123
ethical dilemma story teaching, 271–274
ethical knowing/understanding/ astuteness, 4, 5, 40, 43, 71, 175, 208, 210, 218
ethical living/being, 174, 175, 315
ethical perspective/lens/view, 26, 109, 117, 118, 179, 181
ethical standards/judgement, 52, 82
ethical standpoint, 8, 26, 41

ethical values (see values below)
ethics of care/responsibility/privacy/ emancipation/ 34, 121, 173, 174, 177, 181, 267, 272
indigenous ethics, 241
integrative ethics, 179, 180, 181, 183
sustainability ethics, 5
transformative ethics, 267

G
Glocal, 5

H
Hegemony, 5, 7, 9, 10, 24, 42, 43, 49, 51, 62, 63, 77, 81, 83, 89, 92, 95, 97, 98, 100, 102, 129, 137, 161, 190, 195, 201, 210– 213, 220, 222, 239, 240, 244, 249, 257, 266, 267, 269, 276, 281, 290, 305
counter-hegemony, 42, 63, 83, 257, 276

I
Identity, 7, 49, 69, 85, 111, 116–118, 120–123, 129, 130–136, 139–148, 151, 152, 156, 159, 161, 163, 170, 210, 212, 244, 250, 265–267, 270, 276, 281, 291, 314
cultural/spiritual identity, 2, 39, 129–135, 152, 163, 170, 210, 222, 278
teacher/professional identity, 269, 276, 281, 290
Indigenous, 1, 69
indigenous culture/identity, 135, 141
indigenous education, 314
indigenous worldviews/knowledge systems/science, 2, 5, 40, 130–144, 202, 208, 222, 239–251
Islam/Islamic, 89, 90, 92, 104, 207–209, 212, 213, 219–221
the Holy Qur'an, 90–92, 99, 103–105, 213, 215

SUBJECT INDEX

K
Knowing in action, 43, 208, 210, 220

M
Metaphor, 5, 20–23, 27, 28, 32, 34, 44, 70, 83, 90, 95, 103, 109, 115, 117, 148–150, 154, 176, 198, 236, 241, 253, 267, 268, 280, 291, 296, 302, 303, 306, 310, 315
   epistemic metaphor, 19, 22, 34, 267
   metaphorical logic/thinking/writing, 10, 28, 44, 78, 100, 252, 301
   transgressive metaphor, 22
Multi-paradigm research, 8, 19, 25, 30–32, 34, 45, 75, 78, 80, 81, 85, 102, 151, 174, 178, 179, 183, 209, 274, 295, 315, 317

N
Narrative, 4, 11, 20, 22, 24, 25, 27, 28, 30, 45, 61, 71, 76, 78–82, 84, 85, 105, 106, 110–112, 115, 116, 118, 119, 121, 123, 148, 226, 227, 252, 302, 308, 317
   grand/meta/counter narratives, 62, 65, 81, 99, 136, 140
   narrative inquiry, 7, 24, 32, 66, 70, 85, 104, 150, 152, 162, 169, 182, 183, 286, 288
   narrative logics/genres, 11, 28, 70, 78
   narrative writing/portrayal/voice/stories/vignettes/representation, 10, 40, 41, 43–45, 93, 100, 109, 112, 120, 123, 156, 183, 207, 282, 283, 289, 313
Nondualism, 5, 33, 102, 253
Non-Western, 2, 5, 24, 30, 82

P
Poetry, 32, 43, 44, 46, 53, 90, 100, 252
   mythopoetic, 23, 25
   poet philosopher, 154

poetic agency/self, 111, 116
poetic logic/genre/truth/narrative, 11, 23, 25, 28, 40, 41, 54, 70, 100, 104, 106, 109–112, 116–118, 123, 218
poetic research/inquiry/writing/chanting, 71, 241, 289, 313, 315

R
Relational knowing, 43, 208, 210, 214, 248
Research Paradigms
   integralism, 8, 44, 71, 102, 151, 294, 295
   interpretivism, 8, 10, 11, 23, 27, 44, 79, 95–98, 101, 102, 150, 295, 309
   criticalism, 8, 10, 11, 22, 24, 26, 44, 79, 97, 98, 101, 102, 150, 164, 167, 309, 252
   positivism, 9, 24, 31, 42–44, 49, 51, 61–71, 101, 102, 150, 157, 161, 162, 165, 167, 168, 266, 273, 275, 281, 308
   postmodernism, 8, 10, 11, 23, 27, 28, 42, 44, 79, 85, 98–103, 150, 178, 252, 295, 309
   post-positivism, 177

S
Spiritual/spirituality, 1, 2, 4–6, 10, 24, 39, 40, 70, 71, 115, 121, 141, 153, 176, 207–210, 212, 213, 221, 239, 241, 287
Soul/soulful inquiry, 62, 66, 68, 153, 174, 176, 177, 217, 222, 239, 241, 311
Sustainability
   cultural/societal sustainability, 84, 293, 143
   education for sustainable development, 2, 3, 12, 55

SUBJECT INDEX

sustainable academic development, 288, 290, 294
sustainable development, 2, 3, 5, 6, 8, 12, 40, 55, 85
sustainable eco-systems, 164
sustainable futures, 1, 154, 155, 158, 289, 292
sustainable research practices, 62, 71

T

Transdisciplinary
transdisciplinary capabilities/skills, 4, 5, 271
transdisciplinary paradigm shift, 8
Transformative
research as transformative learning, 1, 40, 42, 45, 55
teaching/learning transformative research, 40, 45
Transformative Education Research Group, 31, 51
transformative learning/theory, 5–7, 9, 12, 31, 40, 41, 43, 45, 54, 81, 82, 90, 93, 105, 106, 149–151, 154, 156, 158, 207–210, 240, 244–248, 266–268, 270, 272, 276, 284, 288, 292
transformative perspective, 1, 268, 304
transformative research/er, 7–9, 11–13, 19, 51–53, 63, 70, 71, 78, 80, 90, 92, 147, 176, 197, 209, 210, 222, 271, 273–275, 288, 307–309

V

Values, 4, 22, 39, 48–50, 53, 82, 92, 119, 121, 176, 179, 182, 196, 210

Christian values, 134
colonial values, 137, 143
cultural/identity values, 3, 10, 69, 97, 100, 129, 139, 152, 153, 155, 208, 209, 212, 226, 229, 239, 241, 244, 247, 252, 305, 316, 317
epistemic values, 43, 275
ethical/moral values, 5, 8, 34, 52, 53, 103, 134, 183, 219, 220, 267
Hindu-Buddhist values, 28, 34
humanistic values, 62
Islamic values, 92, 154, 207, 208, 212, 213, 218–222
numerical values, 66
professional values, 7, 93, 266, 270, 276, 288
social values, 79, 179, 219, 271, 308
spiritual values, 207–209, 221
transformative learning values, 42, 266, 276, 290, 292
universal/western values, 64, 138, 242, 252
values education, 3, 194, 202, 240, 247, 257, 266
values seeking, 179
visionary and ethical knowing, 43, 208, 210, 218

W

Western, 1, 24
Western education, 2, 3, 7, 8, 62, 84, 130, 135–137, 140, 143, 144, 162, 189, 220, 247, 269
Western modern worldview, 4–7, 12, 41, 70, 133, 142, 145, 156, 191, 220, 240, 242, 244, 246–249
Western power structures, 243